# 实用英汉翻译教程
## （修订版）

A Practical Course in English-Chinese Translation
(Revised Edition)

何三宁 主编

何三宁 唐国跃 范 勇 编写

东南大学出版社
·南京·

## 内容提要

本书为高等院校英语专业英汉翻译教材,内容包括翻译的基本知识、词法翻译、结构翻译、文化翻译、文学翻译、科学文本与应用文本的翻译、常用翻译术语的讲解以及实用的附录,同时各章节配有不同要求的练习。本书特色之一是全部讲解用英语写成,翻译方法、技巧、知识点及其例句后都作了分析性极强的点评。特色之二是突出了英汉语言的对比,引导学生掌握翻译技巧的实战运用和英汉语言的行文差异。本书适用于高校英语专业高年级学生,也适用于具有一定英语水平的自学者。

## 图书在版编目(CIP)数据

实用英汉翻译教程/何三宁主编. —2版(修订本). —南京:东南大学出版社,2009.9(2022.7重印)

ISBN 978-7-5641-1843-3

Ⅰ.实… Ⅱ.何… Ⅲ.英语—翻译—高等学校—教材 Ⅳ.H315.9

中国版本图书馆 CIP 数据核字(2009)第 161026 号

### 实用英汉翻译教程(修订版)

| | |
|---|---|
| 出版发行 | 东南大学出版社 |
| 出 版 人 | 江建中 |
| 社　　址 | 南京市四牌楼 2 号 |
| 邮　　编 | 210096 |
| 网　　址 | http://press.seu.edu.cn |
| 电子邮件 | press@seu.edu.cn |
| 经　　销 | 全国各地新华书店 |
| 印　　刷 | 南通印刷总厂有限公司 |
| 开　　本 | 700mm×1000mm　1/16 |
| 字　　数 | 436 千字 |
| 印　　张 | 19.5 |
| 版　　次 | 2022 年 7 月第 2 版第 5 次印刷 |
| 书　　号 | ISBN 978-7-5641-1843-3 |
| 印　　数 | 8001~9000 册 |
| 定　　价 | 29.80 元 |

东大版图书若有印装质量问题,请直接向读者服务部调换,电话:(025)83792328。

# 再版前言

翻译是一门快速发展的学科,及时修订教科书是非常必要的一项工作。为了使教材内容更科学、更实用、更适应于时代的需求,我们决定进行合理的修订、整合和增补。具体做法如下:补充和完善了原第1章"翻译简述";把原第2、3、5章(Lexical Translation, Semantic Translation, How to Translate Numbers)整合在了一起,设置为第2章"词法翻译",显得更为合理科学;把原第4、6、7章(How to Translate the Negative, How to Translate the Passive, How to Translate Long Sentences)整合在一起,更名为现在的第3章"句法翻译";把原第9章(Cultural Translation)前移为现在的第4章"文化翻译",以突出文化在翻译中的重要性;增设补充第5章"文学翻译"和第6章"科学翻译";分解和修订原第8章,单设为现在的第7章"应用翻译",其中包括"行业翻译"、"实用翻译"和"媒体翻译",以体现其实用性;原有的第10章(Some Terms in Translation and Their Understanding)自然成为现在的第8章,并补充了部分常用的概念,以满足英语专业学生考研的需求。"附录"部分保持不变,只是做了少量的修订。

本教材此次修订幅度比较大,主要是出于几种考虑:第一,该教材自2005年8月第一版以来,受到了广泛肯定,屡次重印。部分高校还把此教材列入2008年、2009年的硕士研究生招生参考书目中。我们深感有责任去完善教材,使其能够与时俱进,适应时代的需求。其次,原教材主张的教学模式和"讲授→分析→总结→对比→实践→讲评→阅读"的理念适合我国学生翻译课的学习和实践,在我校英语专业使用的效果很好。学生普遍反映此教材实用性强、知识点易于掌握。由此2006年原教材获得了校级教学成果一等奖。更为重要的是,本次修订对讲授内容及其划分做了更加科学化的调整。

我们认为,文本及其分类对翻译的影响是巨大的,较为科学地划分讲授内容对学生深层了解翻译起着潜移默化的作用。分类学(taxonomy)是人类认识世界的一种最基本的方法,它帮助人们运用哲学方法对事物进行分类,以利于对该事物的分析与研究。广义讲,分类学就是分门别类的科学;狭义而言,分类学是研究某一事物分类的科学,即研究该事物的鉴定、命名和描述,把该学科科学地划分到一种等级系统,以此反映其系统发展的情况。其实,人们对翻译活动早已有了分类的尝试,比如,按表达形式分为口译、笔译和机器翻译;按语言自身分为母语到外语的翻译和外语到母语的翻译;从文体分类有文学翻译、科技翻译、文献翻译、应用翻译;从语言的处理方式划分有全文翻译、节选翻译和改译,等等。这些足以说明人们已经意识到了翻译类型的多样性,并在不断探索和总结其中的规律和各种功能。翻译学所涉及的领域越来越宽,翻译研究的内容越来越细,说明翻译的分工更具体、更专业、更精细,需要尝试创建翻译分类学,以利于探索不同类型的翻译策略与方法,也有助于翻译理论的系统化研究。

根据最新国内外文本类型学在翻译中的理论,我们大致把文本划分为4类:第一类为文学翻译,包括小说、诗歌、戏剧、典籍等的翻译。这些"是文学类型上的基本文类,也即一般美学上认可的分类"。文学翻译还有派生的杂交类型如"史诗"、"传记"、"散文诗"、"歌词"、"诗剧"等(王宏印,2006:147-148)。文学翻译体现的是文本的各种功能,侧重的是文本的形式。第二类是科学翻译,包括科技、社科、科普等翻译(黄忠廉、李亚舒,2004:181-184)。这里的科学翻译是真正意义上的科学翻译,不含应用类翻译。科学翻译体现的是文本的所指功能,侧重文本的内容。第三类是应用翻译,其中包括:(1) 行业翻译,如新闻、外交、党政文献、商务、经贸、金融、法律、体育、医学、旅游等翻译;(2) 实用翻译,如公文、公示语、广告、商标等翻译;(3) 多媒体翻译,如广播影视翻译、互联网翻译等;(4) 其他翻译,如非通用语种翻译(民族语言翻译)等。应用翻译主要体现的是文本的操作或呼唤功能,侧重文本的感染作用。第四类是口译,包括会议口译、视译、联络口译等。口译体现了语言的各种功能。

作为一本英语专业使用的翻译教材,不可能涵盖所有翻译形式和类型。我们只是选择常见且较为实际的内容,以期对学生掌握笔译技能起到指导作用。

在此谨向对本教材再版修订工作给予支持的各位老师表示感谢。同时恳请教材的使用院系及师生在教与学中不吝赐教,以便今后修正、完善本书。

何三宁
于南京百合果园
**2009 年 8 月 1 日**

# 前　言

　　我们给本书取名为《实用英汉翻译教程》(A Practical Course in English-Chinese Translation)，主要是考虑到"实用"二字。为此，我们在各章节列举大量实例，给学生讲授翻译的技巧和方法。所选例句力求典型，具有代表性。我们在列举句子的同时，引导学生了解英语与汉语的行文差异。我们信奉的原则是：翻译家不是在课堂上教出来的，优美的译文也不是用翻译技巧套出来的。古人云："授之以鱼，不如授之以渔。"翻译技巧是通过大量练习和理论的掌握获得的，我们在编著过程中力求让学生通过练习、对比、阅读等手段，有效地培养和形成自己的语感。第1章为翻译简述部分，我们简要介绍了翻译的概念，讲述了国内外代表性的翻译理论、翻译原则及程序，译者应具备的素质以及如何提高翻译水平等。第2章是词法翻译，讲述了常用词法翻译的技巧与方法。第3章为语义翻译，主要解决学生在选词方面遇到的问题。第4章、第6章、第7章涉及句法翻译，我们没有把它们合在一起讲解，主要考虑到我们坚持"以句为主，望眼语篇"的翻译单位，分开来讲会较为详细一些。第5章中我们把数字的翻译单列出来，目的是突出本教材的应用性。随着科技的发展和不同文化间交流的加强，数字的翻译越来越受到人们的重视。第8章是应用文体的翻译，主要讲述了科技英语、法律文献和英文广告的翻译。第9章讲述了文化翻译，以解决学生在翻译实践中遇到的有关双语间的一些文化障碍和文化差异问题。第10章中我们提及部分翻译理论，其中有些是编著者个人的研究成果，有些是自己的理解，掌握这些概念对指导翻译实践不无益处。

　　各章节前有叙述性文字，讲述将讨论的理论或技巧的意义、作用。各章中涉及的理论或技巧都结合例句进行评述，充分说明翻译理论与技巧的运用，真正做到理论联系实际。

每一章或节后附有对比分析。这些译文或者是精心挑选的,或者是编著者结合技巧精雕细刻的,这一部分是本书的特点之一。我们所强调的对比分析研究,旨在让学生进行双语比较研究,以达到了解双语的表述差异以及翻译鉴赏的目的,培养学生的实战意识。

各章练习包括单句练习与篇章翻译。练习部分不附参考答案。单句练习可在课堂操练。短文翻译作为学生课外练习,也是老师课堂的讲评内容。书中共有20余篇短文练习,教师布置作业时可以自己取舍。

附录中,我们挑选了10篇短文。这些文章涉及不同的体裁、文体,根据其难易、长短等穿插安排。每篇短文后适当增加注释,主要解释一些文化背景知识和翻译技巧的运用。我们认为,掌握翻译技巧和提高翻译水平不外乎三种途径:多练、多比、多读。大量练习是我们必须做到的,翻译是实践性很强的学科,没有量的保证,就无法保证翻译水平的提高。其二,进行对比分析和研究。我们在各阶段的学习之后都设有"比较与分析"(Compare and Analyze)一节,目的就是要让学生在老师的引导下,学习他人的经验,弥补自己的不足,增强实战意识。其三,应该给学生灌输这样一个观念,那就是多读。阅读是学习提高英语水平的有效途径,同样也是提高翻译水平行之有效的方法。学生在课后去阅读研究,或者在老师的辅导下对比分析这10篇文章,必定会有很好的效果,这就是我们的目的。

我们的讲授过程是:简述所要讲授的内容→分析例句→总结要点→对比研究→实践练习→讲评作业→阅读。这样的安排大大增强了课堂教学的可操作性,学生可以在老师的引导下进行学习。当然,授课教师可以根据具体情况去调整链条间的顺序,也可增加新的内容。

用英语编著英语专业翻译教材还不多见,是一种尝试,也算是该教材的一个特点吧。目的是让学生能够用英语思考翻译的方法与理论,更好地打好英语语言基础;同时有助于学生掌握一些专业术语,在写论文时能够正确使用这些词语。附录中的"论文参考题目"和"阅读书目"配合此目的帮助学生进行选题及阅读。

《实用英汉翻译教程》是以何三宁老师多年来积累的翻译课教案为蓝本,由三位作者分工协作完成。其中,第1章、第2章、第3章、第9章、第10章以及附录部分由何三宁老师完成;第4章、第5章由唐国跃老师完成;第6章、第7章、第8章由范勇老师完成。最后,全书由何三宁老师统稿、修改、总纂。

该教材侧重翻译的基本方法技巧、对比研究以及文化差异,侧重翻译的实用性,涉及面并不是很宽。由于我们水平有限,所谈到的内容势必出现挂一漏万的问题,敬请同仁和学习者批评指正,以便今后修改完善。

# Contents

## Chapter 1: A Brief Introduction to Translation  翻译简述

1.1 What Is Translation 什么是翻译 ·········································· 1
1.2 The Makings of a Translator 译者的素质 ································ 4
   1.2.1 A Translator Should Be Well Acquainted with the Source Language
       译者应熟练掌握原语 ················································ 5
   1.2.2 A Translator Should Be Well Acquainted with the Target Language
       译者应熟练掌握目的语 ·············································· 5
   1.2.3 A Translator Should Be Armed with Professional Knowledge Needed
       译者应有丰富的专业知识 ············································ 6
1.3 Why We Study the Skills of Translating 翻译技巧的重要性 ············· 6
1.4 Criteria in Translating 翻译原则 ············································ 7
   1.4.1 Faithfulness to the Original 忠实 ···································· 10
   1.4.2 Smoothness and Expressiveness 通顺 ······························ 11
1.5 Procedures in Translating 翻译的过程 ···································· 12
   1.5.1 The Procedure of Understanding 理解 ····························· 12
   1.5.2 The Procedure of Expressing 表达 ·································· 14
   1.5.3 The Procedure of Proofreading 审校 ······························· 16
1.6 Six Major Trends of Translation 翻译工作的六大趋势 ················· 16
1.7 Ways to Success in Translation 提高翻译水平之道 ····················· 18
   1.7.1 Practice More 多练 ·················································· 18
   1.7.2 Compare More 多比 ················································· 19
   1.7.3 Read More 多读 ····················································· 19
1.8 A Test in Class for Evaluation 课堂评估测试 ····························· 23

## Chapter 2: Lexical Translation  词法翻译

2.1 Conversion of Word Classes 词类转译 ···································· 24

2.1.1 Convert English Nouns into Chinese Verbs, Adjectives, or Adverbs
英语名词转换成汉语动词、形容词或副词 …………………………………… 24
2.1.2 Compare and Analyze 比较与分析 …………………………………… 26
2.1.3 Exercises 练习 …………………………………………………………… 27
2.1.4 Convert English Adjectives into Chinese Adverbs, Verbs or Nouns
英语形容词转换成汉语副词、动词或名词 …………………………………… 28
2.1.5 Compare and Analyze 比较与分析 …………………………………… 30
2.1.6 Exercises 练习 …………………………………………………………… 30
2.1.7 Convert English Adverbs into Chinese Nouns, Verbs or Adjectives
英语副词转换成汉语名词、动词或形容词 …………………………………… 31
2.1.8 Convert English Verbs into Chinese Nouns
英语动词转换成汉语名词 ……………………………………………………… 33
2.1.9 Convert English Prepositions into Chinese Verbs
英语介词转换成汉语动词 ……………………………………………………… 34
2.1.10 Compare and Analyze 比较与分析 ………………………………… 35
2.1.11 Exercises 练习 ………………………………………………………… 36
2.2 Omission and Amplification 省词与增词翻译 ………………………………… 37
2.2.1 Omission 省词翻译 …………………………………………………… 37
2.2.2 Compare and Analyze 比较与分析 …………………………………… 42
2.2.3 Exercises 练习 …………………………………………………………… 43
2.2.4 Amplification 增词翻译 ……………………………………………… 44
2.2.5 Compare and Analyze 比较与分析 …………………………………… 50
2.2.6 Exercises 练习 …………………………………………………………… 51
2.3 Semantic Translation 语义翻译 ………………………………………………… 52
2.3.1 Diction 遣词用字 ……………………………………………………… 52
2.3.2 Principles in Diction 选词的原则 …………………………………… 57
2.3.3 Commendatory and Derogatory 词义的褒贬 ………………………… 59
2.3.4 Compare and Analyze 比较与分析 …………………………………… 61
2.3.5 Exercises 练习 …………………………………………………………… 62
2.4 Number Translation 数字的翻译 ………………………………………………… 63
2.4.1 Some English Numbers 一些英语数字的翻译 ……………………… 64
2.4.2 Translation of Approximate Numbers 约数的翻译 ………………… 65

2.4.3 Compare and Analyze 比较与分析 ………………………………… 68
2.4.4 Exercises 练习 ……………………………………………………… 69
2.4.5 Translation of English Multiple 英语倍数的翻译 ……………… 70
2.4.6 Compare and Analyze 比较与分析 ………………………………… 74
2.4.7 Exercises 练习 ……………………………………………………… 75

## Chapter 3: Syntactic Translation 结构翻译

3.1 Translation of Negative Sentences 否定句的翻译 ………………… 76
   3.1.1 Complete Negation 完全否定 ……………………………………… 76
   3.1.2 Partial Negation 部分否定 ………………………………………… 76
   3.1.3 Compare and Analyze 比较与分析 ………………………………… 81
   3.1.4 Exercises 练习 ……………………………………………………… 81
   3.1.5 Double Negation 双重否定的翻译 ………………………………… 83
   3.1.6 Connotative Negation 内涵否定的翻译 …………………………… 84
   3.1.7 Compare and Analyze 比较与分析 ………………………………… 87
   3.1.8 Exercises 练习 ……………………………………………………… 88
   3.1.9 Transferred Negation 否定转移 …………………………………… 89
   3.1.10 Affirmative in Meaning 含有否定词的肯定翻译 ……………… 91
   3.1.11 Compare and Analyze 比较与分析 ……………………………… 92
   3.1.12 Exercises 练习 …………………………………………………… 92
3.2 Translation of Passive Sentences 被动句的翻译 ……………………… 94
   3.2.1 Common Methods of Translating the Passive-Voice
       被动句的翻译方法 ………………………………………………… 95
   3.2.2 Compare and Analyze 比较与分析 ……………………………… 101
   3.2.3 Exercises 练习 …………………………………………………… 102
3.3 Translation of Long Sentences 长句的翻译 …………………………… 103
   3.3.1 General Procedures of Translating Long English Sentences
       长句翻译的总体原则 ……………………………………………… 104
   3.3.2 Some Techniques of Translating Long English Sentences
       长句翻译的方法 …………………………………………………… 105
   3.3.3 Compare and Analyze 比较与分析 ……………………………… 113

3.3.4 Exercises 练习 ·················································· 114

## Chapter 4: Cultural Translation 文化翻译

4.1 Differences between "Culture" in English and 文化 in Chinese
　　汉英文化的差异 ················································· 115
4.2 Relationship between Culture and Language 文化与语言的关系 ········ 116
4.3 Translation and Culture 翻译与文化 ································· 117
4.4 Lexical Translation in Culture 文化中的词义翻译 ····················· 119
　　4.4.1 Words and Conceptual Meaning 单词与概念意义 ············· 120
　　4.4.2 Words and Associative Meaning 单词与联想意义 ············· 123
　　4.4.3 Compare and Analyze 比较与分析 ···························· 133
　　4.4.4 Exercises 练习 ············································· 134
4.5 Cultural Connotations of the Idiomatic Phrases and Their Translation
　　习语的文化内涵与翻译 ············································ 134
　　4.5.1 Set Phrases and Their Translation 成语的翻译 ················ 135
　　4.5.2 Proverbs and Their Translation 谚语的翻译 ·················· 138
　　4.5.3 Allusions and Their Translation 典故的翻译 ·················· 146
4.6 Cultural Connotations of Euphemisms and Their Translation
　　委婉语的文化内涵与翻译 ·········································· 149
　　4.6.1 General View to Euphemisms 委婉语概述 ···················· 149
　　4.6.2 Methods of Translating Euphemisms 委婉语的翻译方法 ······· 150
4.7 Compare and Analyze 比较与分析 ··································· 152
4.8 Exercises 练习 ······················································ 154

## Chapter 5: Literary Translation 文学翻译

5.1 Definition of Literary Translation 文学翻译的定义 ···················· 156
5.2 The Domain of Literary Translation 文学翻译的范畴 ················· 157
5.3 The Criteria of Literary Translation 文学翻译的标准 ················· 158
5.4 The Procedures of Literary Translation 文学翻译的过程 ·············· 159
5.5 Attentions for Literary Translation 文学翻译需要注意的方面 ········· 160

5.5.1　Character Depiction 人物刻画 ………………………………… 160
　　5.5.2　Scene Description 景色描写 …………………………………… 161
　　5.5.3　Linguistic Art 语言艺术 …………………………………………… 162
　　5.5.4　Narrative Movements 情节发展的层次 ……………………… 163
　5.6　Exercises 练习 ……………………………………………………………… 164

## Chapter 6: Translation of Scientific Texts　科学文本翻译

　6.1　Text Types and Domain of Scientific Translation
　　　科学翻译的文本类型和范畴 ………………………………………… 165
　6.2　Characteristics of Scientific Texts 科学文本的特点 ……………… 166
　　6.2.1　Lexical Characteristics 词法特点 …………………………… 166
　　6.2.2　Syntactical Characteristics 句法特点 ……………………… 168
　　6.2.3　Organizational and Rhetorical Characteristics 结构与修辞特点 …… 171
　　6.2.4　Scientific Translation Techniques 科学翻译的方法 ………… 173
　6.3　Compare and Analyze 比较与分析 …………………………………… 182
　6.4　Exercises 练习 ……………………………………………………………… 184

## Chapter 7: Translation of Applied Texts　应用文本翻译

　7.1　Professional Translation 行业翻译 …………………………………… 186
　　7.1.1　Legal Translation 法律翻译 …………………………………… 186
　　7.1.2　Compare and Analyze 比较与分析 …………………………… 195
　　7.1.3　Exercises 练习 …………………………………………………… 197
　　7.1.4　Tourist Translation 旅游翻译 ………………………………… 198
　　7.1.5　Compare and Analyze 比较与分析 …………………………… 212
　　7.1.6　Exercises 练习 …………………………………………………… 213
　7.2　Practical Translation 实用翻译 ………………………………………… 213
　　7.2.1　Translation of Signs 公示语翻译 ……………………………… 214
　　7.2.2　Exercises 练习 …………………………………………………… 216
　　7.2.3　Advertising Translation 广告翻译 …………………………… 217
　　7.2.4　Compare and Analyze 比较与分析 …………………………… 229

7.2.5 Exercises 练习 ·················· 230
## 7.3 Multimedia Translation 多媒体翻译 ················ 231
7.3.1 A Brief Introduction 简要介绍 ················ 231
7.3.2 Subtitling 字幕翻译 ················ 231
7.3.3 Dubbing 配音翻译 ················ 235
7.3.4 Film Translation in Brief 电影翻译简介 ················ 238
7.3.5 Exercises 练习 ················ 240

# Chapter 8: Some Terms in Translation Studies and Their Understanding 一些翻译术语及其理解

## 8.1 Literal Translation and Free Translation 直译与意译 ················ 241
## 8.2 Domesticating Translation and Foreignizing Translation 归化与异化 ········ 245
## 8.3 Exercises 练习 ················ 250
## 8.4 Semantic Translation and Communicative Translation 语义翻译和交际翻译 ················ 250
## 8.5 Formal Equivalence and Dynamic Equivalence 形式对等和动态对等 ········ 251
## 8.6 Flexibility and Accuracy 灵活与准确 ················ 252
## 8.7 Fuzziness and Accuracy 模糊与精确 ················ 254
## 8.8 Exercises 练习 ················ 256
## 8.9 Rhythm and Flavor 节奏与韵味 ················ 256
8.9.1 Thought-Rhythm 意义节奏 ················ 257
8.9.2 Sound-Rhythm 声音节奏 ················ 259
## 8.10 Sentence and Text 句子与语篇 ················ 260
## 8.11 Exercises 练习 ················ 262

Appendix 1　Bilingual Reading 对比阅读 ················ 263
Appendix 2　Common Titles 常用头衔 ················ 280
Appendix 3　Common Expressions for Signs 常用公示语 ················ 284
Appendix 4　Topics for Consideration in Theses on Translation 论文参考题目 ················ 292
Appendix 5　Recommended Reading List 阅读书目 ················ 294
Bibliography 参考文献 ················ 296

# Chapter 1: A Brief Introduction to Translation
# 翻译简述

## 1.1 What Is Translation 什么是翻译

Translation, generally speaking, implies rendering from one language into another of something written or spoken. It is essentially the faithful representation in one language of what is written or spoken in another. It is the replacement of the information of the source language by its counterpart of the target language. Also it can be roughly defined as a reproduction or recreation in one language of what is written or said in another language.

However, translation, in a narrow sense, is the practice of finding the equivalent both in form and essence between two cultures. The two terms translation and translating should be distinguished for a translator. Translation just refers to the act that the translator translates from one language into another, and translating is the process in which the translator does his best to convey the message of the source language. Furthermore, translating is not a word-for-word conversion, but a process of bilingual and intercultural communication. It expresses the message of the source language from the receptor language message, and the relationship between receptor and message should be substantially the same as that between the original receptor and the message.

Translating means communicating, and this process depends on what is received by persons hearing or reading a translation. Judging the validity of a translation cannot stop with comparison of corresponding lexical meanings, grammatical classes, or rhetorical devices. As a means of communication, translation plays an important role in human civilization. In the West, literary translation can be traced back to 300 B. C., while in China, recorded translation activities were even earlier, dating from the Zhou Dynasty (1100 B. C.). However, not until recent centuries, especially by the end of the 19th century did systematic study of translation get under way. In the past decades translation theories and activities have developed fast both at home and abroad.

World-famous British writer and dictionary compiler, Sammel Johnson, once said, "To translate is to change into another language, retaining as much of the sense as one can." This definition for translation has two key points. One is "to change into", which tells us that translation is an act of putting one language in place of another language. The other is "retaining much of the sense", which implies avoiding losing the sense or meaning of the original. It seems to be simple because translation cannot simply reproduce, or be the original. "A translator is always trying to extend his knowledge and improve his means of expression; he is always pursuing facts and words. He works on four levels: translation is first a science, which entails the knowledge and verification of the facts and the language that describe them—here, what is wrong, mistakes of truth, can be identified; secondly, it is a skill, which calls for appropriate language and acceptable usage; thirdly, an art, which distinguishes good from undistinguished writing and is the creative, the intuitive, sometimes the inspired, level of the translation; lastly, a matter of taste, where argument ceases, preferences are expressed, and the variety of meritorious translation is the reflection of individual differences." (Peter Newmark, 1988)

What is important is the extent to which receptors correctly understand and appreciate the translated text. Accordingly, it is essential that functional equivalence be stated primarily in terms of a comparison between the way in which the original receptors understand and appreciate the text with the way in which receptors of the translated text understand and appreciate the text. Being a very complicated human activity, its whole picture is never easy to describe. Scholars with different academic backgrounds have attempted to define it from various perspectives.

In the linguistic views, translation theorists from the linguistic school conceive of translation as a linguistic activity, and some believe that translation theory is a branch of linguistics, approaching the issues of translating primarily from the viewpoint of the linguistic differences between source and target texts.

Catford (1965:20) thinks that translation may be defined as the replacement of textual material in one language or the source language by equivalent textual material in another language or the target language.

Nida & Taber (1969:12) suppose that translating consists in reproducing in the receptor language the closest natural equivalent of the source-language message, first in terms of meaning and secondly in terms of style.

Newmark (1982; 1988:5) believes that translation theory derives from comparative linguistics, and within linguistics, it is mainly an aspect of semantics; all questions of semantics relate to translation theory.

In the cultural views, some scholars think that translation, is regarded not only as a transfer of linguistic signs, but also as a communication of cultures, i.e. translation is an "intercultural communication"; hence the terms of "intercultural cooperation", "acculturation", and "transculturation" are usually used in translation studies.

Shuttleworth & Cowie (1997:35-82) think that translation is a process which occurs between cultures rather than simply between languages. A translator who uses a cultural approach is simply recognizing that each language contains elements which are derived from its Culture (such as greetings and fixed expressions, that every text is anchored in a specific culture, and that conventions of text production and reception vary from culture to culture.

Nida (2001:82) believes that biculturalism, for truly successful translating, is even more important than bilingualism, since words only have meanings in terms of the cultures in which they function.

In fact, Chinese scholars are also conscious of the importance of culture in translation. Wang Zuoliang (王佐良, 1989) thinks that translation is not only involved in linguistic issues, but also involved in cultural ones. The translator needs to be acquainted himself or herself with foreign cultures and self-ethical ones. In addition, he or she compares the two cultures constantly because the translation should be equivalent in meanings, function, scopes, emotion, effects and others.

In the literary views, translators who hold this view believe that translation is an artistic recreation or a recreated art. Some modern Western scholars from the literary school take literary translation to be "the manipulation or rewriting of the source texts". The task of literary translation is to show the intact social life of the works from one language to another, to aspire after its language artistry and value. As Mao Dun(茅盾) puts, literary translation needs to get hold of the same elicitation, inspiration and esthetical reception of the original as what the reader reads the source text when he or she is reading the target text.

In a sense, all the above-mentioned are correct because language is a kind of tool to mold the literary image, and therefore the quality of the literary visualization is certainly put up in language. The features of literary language like image, lifelikeness, trenchancy, connotation, coagulation, fidelity, humor, jocularity, ethnical qualities, local touches, jargons, idioms and proverbs, etc, are all the necessities to mold the image. Translation needs to keep the characteristics and style of the original.

In the semantic views on translation, the translator attempts, within the bare syntactic and semantic constraints of the target language, to reproduce the precise contextual meaning of the author (Newmark 1982:22). Translation is rendering the meaning of a text into another language in the way that the author intended the text (Newmark 1988:5). This view focuses on the semantic equivalence between the two languages, as well expressed by Eugene Nida (1986): "Translating means translating meaning". In semantic translation, greater attention is paid to rendering the author's original thought-processes in target language than to attempting to re-interpret source text in a way which the translator considers more appropriate for the target setting (Shuttleworth & Cowie 1997:151).

In the functional views, translation is a specific form of human action with a certain purpose, a kind of linguistic service provided to the society. Translators should take into account the needs of the client, the reader as well as the purpose or use of the translation. It is not the source text, or its effects on the source-text recipient, or the function assigned to it by the author, that determines the translation process, but the prospective function or purpose of the target text as determined by the initiator's, i.e. client's needs (Baker 2001:236)

In the communicative views on translation, the translator attempts to produce the same effect on the target language readers as was produced by the original on the source language readers (Newmark 1982: 22). This approach views translation as a communicative process which takes place within a social context. Communicative translation is generally oriented towards the needs of the target language reader or recipient. A translator who is translating communicatively will treat source text as a message rather than a mere string of linguistic units, and will be concerned to preserve source text's original function and to reproduce its effect on the new audience (Shuttleworth & Cowie 1997:21).

In all, we conclude that translation is a kind of social and communicative act, with reference to the text and with the specific purposes, of cross-cultural and inter-lingual, which investigation objects and processes vary from the different desires and social demands of the translator.

In addition, translation covers a very broad range. As far as the form of expression is concerned, translation is classified as oral interpretation, written translation and machine translation. In terms of language, it can be divided into two categories, native language to foreign language and vice versa. In terms of the categorical coverage, it is classified as translation of social science and that of physical science, namely, the translation of scientific materials; translation of literary works such as novels, stories, prose, poetry, drama, etc.; translation of political essays such as treatises on social problems, reports, speeches, etc.; translation of practical writing such as official documents, contracts and agreements, notices, receipts, etc. As far as the disposal, it is classified into full text translation, abridged translation or adapted translation.

## 1.2 The Makings of a Translator 译者的素质

No matter what sort of translation it may be, it surely serves as an intermedium between two different languages and cultures, between the peoples of two countries, just like the matchmaker between a boy and a girl. To be a successful matchmaker one must be very familiar with the boy and the girl. In addition, one should learn some good methods and work flexibly. To do an adequate translation is very like to act as a successful matchmaker. The translator had to be well acquainted with languages, the source language and the target language. Besides, one should learn the methods used in translating and the theory guiding translation. The modern theory is closely related to practices, stylistics, comparative linguistics, sociolinguistics, semantics, psychology, semiotics, comparative literature and logic, and others, among which, comparative linguistics, stylistics and transformational generative grammar are most influential to translation. Therefore, a qualified translator must be also good at linguistics, stylistics and semantics, and he had better be a versatile scholar. The well-known American translator and translation theorist Eugene A. Nida puts forth the following indispensable qualifications, which translators must have if they are to produce satisfactory translations.

### 1.2.1 A Translator Should Be Well Acquainted with the Source Language 译者应熟练掌握原语

To begin with, a translator has to possess overall knowledge of English grammar and plenty of English vocabulary. Only thus can one understand the original accurately and render it faithfully. Meanwhile he may speed up his translation. Every beginner has such experience that he is inclined to feel too confident of his comprehension when he reads foreign literary works. He thinks he knows it wholly, yet when he starts translating it he finds it difficult and there are many points misunderstood by him. Therefore, translation serves as the best possible approach to the study of a foreign language.

### 1.2.2 A Translator Should Be Well Acquainted with the Target Language 译者应熟练掌握目的语

Some students usually take no notice of this aspect while rendering something from English into Chinese. They think that Chinese is their mother tongue and they can completely cope with the problems appearing in translating. Actually, we cannot even find a satisfactory or ideal version for a word, a phrase, or a pattern. We all hear of the story about Lu Xun(鲁迅), who spent days in pondering over one better translation of one word. In translating, we frequently misunderstand some places of the original, which results in inaccuracy of translation; even we don't misunderstand, sometimes we cannot hunt for proper Chinese expressions for our understanding of the source language, which more or less influences the quality of our translation. Therefore, it is very indispensable for a translator to possess down-to-earth Chinese level in translating. To achieve this, one translator, for one thing, should master Chinese grammar through textbooks; for another, he should browse a lot of classics and fine literary works so as to acquire standard expressions of Chinese.

Only by acquainting oneself with both the source language and the target language, can one produce a satisfactory translation. An awkward translation is caused either by the poor source language or by the poor target language. In addition, there are still some other causes. The main cause among them is the diversities between the two languages. So far as English-Chinese translation is concerned, there are great diversities between English and Chinese which are classified into two different families, the former, Indo-European Family, the latter, Sino-Tibetan Family. Great diversities lie in history, geography, politics, economy, culture, customs and so on. These diversities cause great difficulties or sometimes even impossibility in translation.

### 1.2.3 A Translator Should Be Armed with Professional Knowledge Needed 译者应有丰富的专业知识

Besides the source and the target languages, one must familiarize himself with a wide range of knowledge. To well achieve this one should read plenty of materials ranging from social science to physical science. Otherwise one would often find himself at his wit's end in translation and the translation would be an awkward one. For example, if one, even though he has high English level, does not know anything about American history, he cannot translate the materials correctly concerning certain events in American history. If one doesn't well know the customs and cultural background in the Qing Dynasty, he can not translate Chinese classic work *The Dream of Red Chamber*(《红楼梦》).

## 1.3 Why We Study the Skills of Translating 翻译技巧的重要性

As an English learner, everybody should know the five skills in learning English, which are listening, speaking, reading, writing and translating. Translating is one of them. With the development of science and technology, and more exchanges between countries, translating becomes more and more important. In this course, we chiefly talk about written translation, which can also be divided into two parts, English-Chinese translation and Chinese-English translation. English-Chinese translation is the major topic in this book.

To well master English language, learners should possess the integrated skills. They are not merely good at listening and speaking, but also at writing and translating. At the same time, the skills of translation still need comprehensive abilities because a translator has to be familiar with the different cultures and backgrounds underlying the two languages, and have concrete English knowledge.

Translation is not merely a transmitter of culture, but also of the truth—a force for progress. It has the special purpose of demonstrating the learner's knowledge of the foreign language, either as a form of control or to exercise his intelligence in order to develop his competence. This is its strong point in foreign language classes, which has to be sharply distinguished from its normal use in transferring meanings and conveying messages. Therefore, translating skills should be well known in learning English.

## 1.4 Criteria in Translating 翻译原则

The so-called criteria of translation are actually the two sides of the same thing. The former lays emphasis on the translator, who should follow them while translating; while the latter on the reader or critic, who may use the criteria to evaluate translation versions. In fact, the criteria of translation practically concern three fundamental aspects: firstly the nature of translation as linking together content and form; secondly, the principles for adequate and acceptable translation; and lastly the problems one translator ought to be able to recognize and resolve in order to produce a satisfactory translation. Some well-known translators or translation theorists at home and abroad have put forward criteria to judge the quality of a translation.

In Chinese history, we have got a few influential criteria during the different ages. Early in the Tang Dynasty (ca 620 A.D.), the learned monk Xuan Zang (玄奘, 602—664 A.D.) contributed his life to translation and put forth the criteria of translation "既须求真,又须喻俗", which placed emphasis on accuracy and general knowledge, and it is still acceptable and useful in translation today. In the Qing Dynasty (ca 1898 A.D.), Yan Fu (严复, 1853—1921 A.D.), a famous translator, put forth the famous criteria of translation "信、达、雅"(faithfulness, communicability and elegance) when he finished translating *Evolution and Ethics and Other Essays*(《天演论》). He once said, "译事三难:信、达、雅。求其信,已大难矣! 顾信矣,不达,虽译,犹不译也,则达尚焉。" (There are three difficulties in translation: faithfulness, communicability and elegance. The consideration of faithfulness to the original is so difficult; when it is got, communicability is unavailable, and if one gives a version that is faithful without being communicative at the same time, the translated work is almost tantamount to nonexistence. Hence communicability should be required too.) His criteria of translation have been generally considered as the plumb line for measuring the professional level of translation and the goal for translation to strive after in the past decades. However, people have argued about his criteria of translation because they think that there are some limitations in the application of them.

On the basis of Yan Fu's criteria of translation, some scholars put forward various criteria of translation. Lu Xun(鲁迅) proposed faithfulness "信" and smoothness "顺" as the criteria of translation, and talked about the relationship between them.

Qu Qiubai(瞿秋白) pointed out the principle of equivalent in *A Letter to Mr Lu Xun* (《给鲁迅的信》)in 1931. He said,"我的意见是,翻译应当把原文的本意,完全正确的介绍给中国读者,使中国读者所得到的概念等同于英俄日德法读者从原文得到的概念。"(《鲁迅全集·二心集》,人民文学出版社,1981). He thought that a translation should introduce the original meaning to Chinese readers in a completely adequate way, and enable them to get concepts equivalent to those readers of Great Britain, Russia, Japan, Germany and France extract from the original. His principle of equivalent firstly, in Chinese translation history, concentrated on the conversion of the readers of the original from the writer of the original. That is, he had already noticed that the information sender should be converted to the information receiver, and that communication or translation is always considered as the matter of both sides.

Fu Lei(傅雷) had his criteria of translation, spiritual conformity "神似", which emphasized the reproduction of the spirit or the flavor of the original. He once said,"以效果而论,翻译应当像临画一样,所求的不在形似而在神似。"(转引自刘季春《实用翻译教程》,中山大学出版社,1996) In other words, it is called "meaning conformity" if the translation can be conformed with the contents of the original; it is called "spiritual conformity" if the translation can be conformed with the form and spirit or flavor of the original.

Qian Zhongshu(钱钟书)advocated the criteria, sublimed adaptation "入化/化境", which focuses on the translator's smooth and idiomatic Chinese version for the sake of Chinese readers. He thought that:文学翻译的最高标准是"化"。把作品从一国文字转变成另一国文字,既能不因语文习惯的差异而露出生硬牵强的痕迹,又能完全保存原有的风味,那就算得入于"化境"。(《林纾的翻译》,上海古籍出版社,1979)That is to say, the so-called sublimed adaptation means that though the literal form of the original is converted into another, the thought, feeling, style and flavor of the original are formerly conveyed in the translation version so that the reader reads the translation version as reads the original.

Professor Xu Yuanchong(许渊冲) raised his own principle of translation in his book *The Art of Translation*(《翻译的艺术》,中国对外翻译出版公司,1985). He thinks that a literary translator should exploit the advantage of the target language. Now let us study his words:忠实于原文内容,通顺的译文形式,发扬译文的优势,可以当作文学翻译的

标准。翻译可以不发挥译文语言的优势,但发挥了译文语言的优势的是更好的翻译。是否符合必要条件是个对错问题,是否符合充分条件却是个好坏问题。(Those that are faithful to the original, smooth in form of the version, enhancing the advantages of the version, can be treated as criteria in literary works. Translation had better develop the advantages of the target language, though it may not do. Whether it conforms with indispensable conditions is a matter of something right or wrong, whereas whether it conforms with adequate conditions is a matter of something good or bad.)

Here it is worth mentioning another Chinese scholar Si Guo(思果). He supposed that the translation principle might be changed into faithfulness, expressiveness and appropriateness"信、达、贴"on the basis of Yan Fu's principle. The so-called faithfulness refers to the responsibility to the writer. A translator should express the original meaning faithfully. Expressiveness means that a translator should stand beside the reader's side after faithfully translating the original. The reader should understand the translation. As for the third character, it wants to say that the translation should be proper or appropriate to the original style, manner, flavor, strength etc.

In the West, translation principles are also discussed in different times. In 1789, British translator and scholar George Campbell firstly put forward his translation principle. He stressed that a translator should do three things. The first thing is to give a just representation of the sense of the original. The second thing is, to convey his version, as much as possible, in a consistency with the genius of the language which he writes, the author's spirit and manner.... The third and last thing is, to take care, the version have at least. So far the quality of an original performance, as to appear natural and easy....

The year after the creation of the above-mentioned principles, another British translator Alexander Fraser Tytler (1747—1814), professor of history at Edinburgh University, published his milestone book *Essay on the Principles of Translation* (1790). His theory is very similar to Campbell's. He wrote, "1. The translation should give a complete transcript of the ideas of the original work. 2. The style and manner of writing should be of the same character with that of the original. 3. The translation should have all the ease of original composition."

The other famous American translator who established influential criteria of translation is Dr. Eugene A. Nida who took part in translating *The Bible* and devoted himself to studies of linguistics, semantics, anthropology, etc. In his book *Towards a Science of Translating*, which is regarded as one of his representative works, he laid down the following fundamentals:

1. True to the original(忠实原文)

2. Vivid(传神)
3. Smooth and natural(语言顺畅自然)
4. Equivalence of response(同等效应)

Of these fundamentals, the last one is the key point. The so-called equivalence of response means that a good translation can call forth the response of its readers equivalent to that of the readers of the original work. The influence of his theory was so great in China that almost every translator thought of it as true and heatedly discussed it. But after a long time discussion, they began to doubt its feasibility and to criticize it. This is because it overestimates translators, abilities in understanding cultures between both languages, neglects readers, differences in recognizing things, negates the effect of transplanting in translation, confuses direct (face-to-face) communication with indirect (written) communication, and denies the features of different styles in writing.

Eugene A. Nida puts forward his recent interpretation of functional equivalence in his *Language and Culture*: *Context in Translating* (2001:87): (1) A minimal, realistic definition of functional equivalence: The readers of a translated text should be able to comprehend it to the point that they can conceive of how the original readers of the text must have understood and appreciated it. (最低限度而又切合实际的功能对等定义:译文读者对译文的理解应当达到能够想象出原文读者是怎样理解和领会原文的程度) (2) A maximal, ideal definition of functional equivalence: The readers of a translated text should be able to understand and appreciate it in essentially the same manner as the original readers did. (最高限度合乎理想的功能对等定义:译文读者应当能够基本上按照原文读者理解和领会原文的方式来理解和领会译文)

Peter Newmark puts forward his concepts of communicative and semantic translation in his *Approaches to Translation* (1982/1998: 39): Communicative translation attempts to produce on its readers an effect as close as possible to that obtained on the readers of the original. (交际翻译力图对译作读者产生尽可能接近原作读者所获得的效果) Semantic translation attempts to render, as closely as the semantic and syntactic structures of the second language allow, the exact contextual meaning of the original. (语义翻译力图在译作语言的语义结构和句法结构允许的情况下,译出原作在上下文中的准确意义) Details about Nida and Newmark's translation principles will be seen in Chapter 8.

Despite the variety of opinions, the following criteria are almost unanimously accepted and followed, namely, the criteria of faithfulness, smoothness and expressiveness.

### 1.4.1 Faithfulness to the Original 忠实

This criterion is the most important one because translation tries to match the receptor language message with the source language message, and the relationship between receptor and message should be substantially the same as that between the original receptor and the message. Otherwise, it will bring about mistakes in translating. Simply speaking, by faithfulness, we mean to be faithful not only to the original contents, to the original meaning and views, but also to the original form and style. For example, the general meaning of the word "theater" is a place for the performance of plays. Its specific meaning is an operating room. The general meaning of "master" refers to a man who is the head of a house and family. Its specific meaning refers to a skilled worker. The general meaning of "gay" is cheerful or happy. Its specific meaning is homosexual. Now let us look at the following sentences and analyze the underlined words.

- ❖ The development of an *economical* artificial heart is only a few transient *failures* away.
  只消再经过几次**实验**,价格**低廉**的人工心脏不久可望研制成功。
- ❖ The commuter *dies* with *tremendous* mileage to his *credit*...(E. B. White: *The Three New Yorks*)
  上班族一生有着惊人的行程。

In the two English sentences, beginners would believe that they know every word and translate them without thinking it over carefully, and they usually make mistakes. The problem is that they do not understand the original. So we can say that faithfulness is the key point in translating, and understanding is the premise of faithfulness.

### 1.4.2 Smoothness and Expressiveness 通顺

It is the necessary requirement in translating. On the premise of faithfulness, we should come along with the language naturally, and try to avoid translationese. By smoothness and expressiveness, we mean not only easy and readable rendering, but also idiomatic expression in the target language, free from stiff formula and mechanical copying from dictionaries.

- ❖ This season saw an ominous dawning of the tenth of November.
  在这个季节,11月10日黎明时分的景象,是个不祥之兆。
- ❖ Size doesn't matter, chopping wood...(M. K. Rawlings: *Integrity*)
  个头没啥关系,劈柴嘛……

The versions of the two sentences are smooth in expression and intelligible in meaning. We Chinese can easily understand it and feel it fluent, genuine and authentic. Suppose that you read the version like this"这个季节遇到了11月10日一个不祥的黎明""说到劈柴,个头并不重要", how do you feel?

Whatever we translate, whether they are documents or fiction, the target language should be expressive.

❖ Rubber is not hard; it gives way to pressure.
   Version 1:橡胶不硬,屈服于压力。(not expressive)
   Version 2:橡胶性软,受压会变形。(expressive)

## 1.5 Procedures in Translating 翻译的过程

Translation is a very complex task, which is not merely the job that renders the original into the smooth target language, but also the job that reveals and shows its beauty and culture. Although various and different proposals are suggested about the stages in translating, some procedures can be followed. Translating may be roughly classified into three procedures, namely the procedure of understanding, the procedure of expressing and the procedure of proofreading.

### 1.5.1 The Procedure of Understanding 理解

Understanding the original is the first thing to do in translating. In this procedure, we should clearly know what we ought to do. In general, the more we understand the original, the better version we will have. This requires us to understand the original thoroughly and fully as possible as we can. At the same time, it will be done through the context, and the original will be read at least three times or more. The first time roughly read the original to understand the general meaning and mark some places new or difficult to us. The second time carefully read the original to solve the difficult points, and if necessary, read it paragraph by paragraph, sentence by sentence, and even word by word. The third time thoroughly read the entire passage to completely understand it. Now let us look at the procedure of understanding in detail.

#### 1) Understanding the language focus points

For the first time reading, a translator has to systematically understand word meanings, sentence structures and idioms of the original, etc., by means of dictionaries or reference books. In other words, he should understand the general idea of the original and solve the lexical and grammatical problems.

#### 2) Understanding the logical relationship

For the second time reading, a translator had better understand the logical relationship between words, phrases and sentences in order to accurately find right or correct translation. That is to say, he will be required to carry on language analysis and solve the problems between the lines. We can say that it is true that language analysis does not continue without logical and contextual analysis. Only thus can we thoroughly understand the text and have a smooth, faithful, reasonable and reliable translation version.

- It is good for him to do that.

  Version 1:这样做对他有好处。

  Version 2:他这样做是件好事。

This sentence may have two translations. It will have different meanings when it is placed in different contexts or texts. A translator has to find the correct answer from the context.

- "And you are my uncle, then!" she cried, reaching up to salute him. "There—damn it! If you have any kisses to spare, give them to Linton: they are thrown away on me." (E. Bronte: *Wuthering Heights*)

  "这么说,你是我的姑父啦,"她嚷道,走到他跟前,行了个礼。

  "去——该死! 你要是有多余的吻,就送给林顿吧,给我是白费。"

The Chinese version appears reasonable and correct because the word "*salute*" does have the meaning 行了个礼. But after we read the context and his answer, we may find that we have made a mistake because he answered then "There—damn it! If you have any kisses to spare, give them to Linton: they are thrown away on me." Therefore we should consider the word "salute" once again in order to make sure whether we completely understand it. When we consult our dictionaries, we find that the word really has the meaning "kiss". Obviously the Chinese version is wrong. The corrected version should be:"这么说,你是我的姑父啦,"她嚷道,走到他跟前,吻了他一下。

- In his *classic* novel, *The Pioneers*, James Fenimore Cooper has his hero, a land developer, take his cousin on a tour of the city he is building. He describes the broad streets, rows of houses, *a teeming metropolis*. But his cousin looks around bewildered. All she sees is a forest. "Where are the beauties and *improvements* which you were to show me?" she asks. He's astonished she can't *see* them. "Where! Why everywhere," he replies. For though they are not yet built on earth, he has built them in his mind, and they are as concrete to him as if they were already constructed and finished.

  Cooper was illustrating a distinctly American trait, future-mindedness: the ability to see the present from the vantage point of the future; the freedom to feel unencumbered by the past and more emotionally attached to things to come. As Albert Einstein once said, "Life for the American is always becoming, never being." (It is taken from TEM8, 2003)

  詹姆斯·费尼莫尔·库柏在其**著名**小说《拓荒者》中,记述了主人公——一位土地开发商——带着表妹游览一座他将要建造的城市的情景。他向表妹描绘了宽阔的街道,成排的房屋,**俨然一座繁华的大都市**。然而,表妹环顾四周,却一脸迷茫,她所看到的只是一片森林而已。于是她问:"你要给我看的美景与**繁荣**在哪儿啊?"他很惊讶,她居然还不能**心领神会**。他回答说:"还问哪里?这不到处都是嘛。"因为尽管他还没有把它真正建成,他却早已在心中构想好了。它们对他来说是如此具体真实,仿佛它们早已建成。

库柏在这里刻画了一种美国人独有的特征,即未来意识:他们能够站在未来的高度来看现在的一切;他们更加亲和未来而不受过去的羁绊。正如埃尔伯特·爱因斯坦曾言:"对美国人来说,生活永远意味着将来,决不是现在。"

In this short passage, the meanings of the underlined words can be decided by the contextual and logical analysis. The word "classic", according to the context, should be translated into 著名的 or 经典的 because it is an adjective meaning having the highest quality, of the first or highest class or rank, or well known in the stated way. The phrase "a teeming metropolis" can be translated into 一座繁华的大都市 instead of 一座热闹的大都市. This is because 繁华 can often modify a big place like a town, a city or a country; on the contrary, Chinese term 热闹 may be seldom collocated with a big place. The meanings of the words "improvements" and "see" can not directly decided by the dictionary entries. This still requires contextual and logical analysis. According to the context, "the beauties and improvements" really refers to the broad streets, rows of houses, a teeming metropolis that the hero describes. And "see" does not mean that his cousin can see the "beauties and improvements", instead it implies the distinctly American trait, namely, future mindedness that Cooper was illustrating.

### 3) Understanding the culture relating to the original

As a translator, he has to understand the different cultures underlying two languages. As everyone knows, some customs and practices may exist in one country, but not in another. We may feel puzzled when we read the sentence "He is your half-brother." It is hard for us Chinese to know whether half-brother is 同父异母兄弟 or 同母异父兄弟. Cultural factors usually condition our understanding of the original and affect the translation quality as well. In a sense, translation is the process that the original culture is revealed. Therefore our suggestion is that, in this stage, beginners read the original carefully and make penetrating analysis before rendering. "White wine", for example, can not be translated into 白酒. "Lover" does not mean 爱人 in Chinese. "Afterlife" can not be simply understood as 来世.

## 1.5.2 The Procedure of Expressing 表达

The task in this stage is to convey the well understood contents to the reader faithfully and smoothly. This is a very complex process because a translator has to think about manifold factors and relations, and deal with a lot of contradictions and difficulties, such as the relationships between "faithfulness" and "smoothness", "readers" and "writers", "cultures" and "languages", etc., among which faithful and smooth conveyance is the key point. For this point, we should well cope with the following.

First, correctly handle the relation between faithfulness and expressiveness. The two points are contradictory but dialectically identical. Both exist and develop with each other, and make your version perfect. Expressiveness is a kind of property of a language and objective reality. Faithfulness or accuracy is the translators' aim. We cannot neglect both points or show partiality to either side.

Second, correctly handle the relation between content and form. Actually, translation consists in a reunification of the content and form of a work on a new linguistic basis. The so-called "form" is generally made up of types of works, structures, characters, rhetoric devices, etc., which should be shown in translating, apart from the content of a work. Therefore we should keep our translation faithful in content and form. That is to say, if possible, we try to not only convey "what the work says", but also express "how it expresses". Meanwhile, we should notice the factor that "This process is one in which content and form are mutually transferred. Some elements of content are to be elevated into form; some elements of form put into content. Of course, there are also some elements of form which are nowhere to be seen, nor are they put into content. That is sacrifice. Why is it possible for content and form to be mutually transferred on a new foundation of language? It is because, judging from the perspective of aesthetics, elements of form are always no more than the externalization of elements of content whereas the latter are often the internalization of the former. The linguistic forms that are originally accurate, distinct, vivid and natural in the original language may not go to the same extent when copied into the target language. In such a case, therefore, it is necessary to read just the relation between content and form on the new basis of language." (张今:1987,转引自《汉英双向翻译学语林》,山东大学出版社,2001)

Third, correctly handle the relation between faithfulness and creation. In translating, we should be firstly faithful to the original. In other words, our version has to be faithful on the basis of the original work, and respect the author and the language he uses, not follow our inclination in translation. On the other hand, we should notice that there are a lot of differences between English and Chinese, which exist in both languages and cultures. This brings many difficulties to us translators, and needs creation in translating. Creation in translating, in fact, exists in language. We have to create the parts that do not exist in either language. Strictly speaking, it is a secondary creation. "Translation is also a secondary creation, so of course, also an art. It is even truer of the case in which

Chinese is used to translate a foreign language that is so different in nature. It is definite, first of all, that to translate is not to 'copy'. Neither is it a report. It is, instead, a kind of creation after he converts the thoughts and feelings in the original into those of his own. What makes this different from the creation by the original author is that the restriction of the original work is imposed upon the translator, but he has to employ his creative power, under such conditions, to give the original creation a new life."（焦菊隐：1951，转引自《汉英双向翻译学语林》，山东大学出版社，2001）

### 1.5.3 The Procedure of Proofreading 审校

After finishing translating, a translator has to proofread his translation. We can say that proofreading actually is a procedure deepening stages of understanding and expressing. Following points should be considered in this stage.

1) Examine whether some paragraphs, sentences, clauses, and words, etc. are left out. Scrutinize whether some names, places, dates, directions, numbers, etc. are neglected. Check out whether some errors in grammar, spelling or punctuations remain.

2) Polishing is needed. The effective and useful way is to read the version several times to see whether it is expressive, fluent, harmonious, and wordy or not.

3) Proofreading twice is necessary. We suggest that we proofread the version again after the first time proofreading if time permits. Sometimes we have such a feeling that when the version is put on the desk, we can still find some mistaken places after a while. If we proofread it once again, the version will have a chance to be more satisfactory.

4) We should, if possible, ask someone else to proofread our translation. This is the best way to find errors in our translation. If it is a version from Chinese to English, you may ask one English speaker to proofread it.

## 1.6 Six Major Trends of Translation 翻译工作的六大趋势

Translation is a complex work, which no longer is a kind of one that anyone can do easily. It changes in many aspects with the development of science and technology. We now excerpt some paragraphs from *Verbal Forest of Translation*（《汉英双向翻译学语林》）by Sun Yingchun(孙迎春).

Since the 1980s the work of translation in all corners of the world has been undergoing changes in several aspects, of which the following are included in the most conspicuous trends—The work of translation has become

1) Specialized: Having received the regular kind of training recognized by society or one's own profession and obtained a qualified seniority, the employees will behave according to the regulations and spirit stipulated by their profession. Translation is no

longer a kind of work that anyone can casually do who knows some foreign language and depends simply upon a dictionary.

2) Academic: Translation theory and translation teaching, carried out by employing rational, positive methods, have gradually become an academic object of research. The work of translation and of training interpreters no longer simply depends upon genius, intuition, personal experience and traditions, since translators and translation educators have all commanded ways of academic research, by which professional problems that crop up will be solved.

3) Service: The work of translation has once again been restored to a status in which the customer becomes the center; the users (government, private companies and readers ignorant of foreign languages) are helped to overcome their language barrier so as to serve their purpose of obtaining data and information or any other purpose. Translation thus gradually leaves its ivory tower and enters the marketplace.

4) Multipurpose: As regards the readers in the past who used the literary or religious translations, they were relatively uniform in purpose and pure in background and fairly identical in attitude (they all aimed to appreciate, worship, seek after enlightenment, etc.). The users and customers of translations today and future are much more complicated. Advertisements, international conventions, legal instances, scientific and technical essays, dispatches and speeches are quite different from one another in "use" and essence, so the specific ways adopted in translation need much adjustment.

5) Practical: Translation is no longer for "translation's sake", i. e. the purpose is not necessarily to produce another discourse equivalent to the original, but to reach the predetermined effect (usually the effect wanted by the customer, or what the translator judges to be the best effect to be received by the user). The translator has to be clear about the target of every job so as to choose the most appropriate ways in fulfilling his task.

6) Scientific and technological: With the development of communication science and technology and artificial intelligence, translation combines more and more with advanced scientific and technological products, e. g. such equipments as discourse treatment, document retrieval from the data bank, electronic dictionary and desk publication have already been in common use for a long time in all kinds of translations in European and American societies, thus greatly heightening productivity, reliability, uniformity and printing quality. The times in which the translator consults his own dictionary and rock his own pen will soon become history, and the translators illiterate in computer will feel it difficult to find a place to live in.

Just as many other occupations, translation is stepping into automation. All kinds of simple, repetitious translations (these constitute a fairly large part of documents awaiting translation in the world) can be handled to the machine for treatment and the translator's task is to supervise and revise. In the near future many translators' routine work will become program design, sorting out words, pre-editing, translation management, etc., with the man-machine cooperation becoming even closer. （周兆祥:1998,《译学大词典》,转引自《汉英双向翻译学语林》,山东大学出版社,2001）

## 1.7 Ways to Success in Translation 提高翻译水平之道

Just like the above-mentioned words, translation is no longer a simple work to do. Meanwhile a translator has to possess different qualifications and abilities if he or she wants to be successful in this field. But it does not mean that we cannot become a qualified and experienced translator for ever. In fact, every person has his own way to success in translation field. Here we suggest a couple of ways how a beginner improves his translation skills and level quickly.

### 1.7.1 Practice More 多练

Actually the task of translation is a kind of practical activity, that is, in a sense, a kind of skill. You can handle it throughout practice. Practice makes perfect. A language, everyone knows, is learned through both practice and skills. Both practice and skills are necessary. But practice is most important. Unlike children, adults in English learning will be much affected by instances of mother tongue inference. For them learning a foreign language actually is a conscious process of accumulating knowledge of a second language obtained in school settings. Most of English learners in China, however, after clear of school settings, suddenly lose their teachers, classrooms, language labs and so on. They hardly study it and quickly lose the practice of English learning. As a result, their English level gradually goes down. Translation is one of the five skills. It still needs more practicing.

The work of translation is just like a piece of music. If you are well acquainted with its rhythm and melody, you may give an instrumental performance perfectly and wonderfully, exactly and accurately. Also the work of translation is just like a piece of painting. If you are well acquainted with its skills and techniques, you can excellently convey the spirit and exquisitely portray the image of a figure. The more you practice, the more skills and techniques you have; the more skills you have, the better you can convey the formal and spiritual similarities of the original. Therefore, the beginner can gain complete mastery of the methods and experience that other scholars have already accumulated after practice, and make progress little by little.

## 1.7.2 Compare More 多比

A person is not born a great translator. On the one hand, he or she has to practice constantly and learn by themselves. On the other hand, he or she needs consistently learning from others. Comparison is a very good way for a beginner to follow. Here are two aspects for us to pay attention to. The first aspect is that the beginner, by comparison, may compare and contrast between the source language and target language so carefully that he or she can find the shortcomings and flaws in their own translation versions. Our purpose is to improve the quality of our translation and raise our translation level. This way to success in translation also requires us to compare the original with a piece of good translation first and then find the way and style the translator uses. We should clearly find out why the good translator translates a word, a phrase, a sentence or a paragraph this way or that way. The purpose is to study and learn the excellent translator's word choices and construction of the translated text.

Firstly, when he or she compares their own translation, the beginner should pay attention to two points. One is to compare both languages that we have to deal with, and find the different writing styles and language features. The other is to compare the cultural factors appearing in the original with the version, and see whether the cultural factors are intended to be translated in the way we Chinese prefer reading, or the way English speaking people originally have.

Secondly when he or she compare the good translator's version, the beginner should understand how the translator organizes his version by means of comparing the original, and why the translator organizes and develops his translation in the same way or in the different way.

As far as comparison between the source language and the good version is concerned, it is not the only way to follow. Another way is worth mentioning to compare. That is, we can compare the original with more than two versions so that we can find different styles that different translators show in translation.

In short, nowadays some scholars and theorists are already aware of the importance of improving our translation level by means of comparison. Therefore you may intentionally pick up different versions of the original you are interested in if possible.

## 1.7.3 Read More 多读

It is last but not least. Some Chinese students of English, especially junior students, feel that their translation standards stagnate or develop very slowly. Although they have learned grammar, memorized thousands of words and phrases, and also spoken everyday

English, they, after that, still have difficulty making further improvement in translation. And then they are wondering why the pace in this field comes to a standstill and how they make further progress and take a longer step. Even some of them give it up. This is a really common phenomenon and also an awkward situation for translation teachers because they cannot find the solutions that students are eager to know. The conditions that restrict the further and faster development are many-sided. They are possibly for lack of the knowledge between two cultures, of the grammatical rules, of English vocabulary, or of diligence; probably because of one's experience, age, sex, interest, motivation, etc. Such a lot of factors, which influence its improvement, could make many learners withdraw. It is unnecessary, we think, for Chinese learners of English to think much about these factors in order not to form a big barrier to their goal.

What, you may ask, is the way to better advance translation progress? Though it is hard to give a satisfactory answer to this question, let us elbow our way through the difficulties.

As soon as they are talking about translation, Chinese students of English always think over the language's focal points, words and phrases firstly. They then make efforts to translate them. But as some of them have grasped thousands of vocabulary and understood basic grammatical rules, they begin to realize that they can still not render it well. Just then they would complain that their teachers taught them little. Some of them could not translate the original well into the target language because they misunderstood some of the words and phrases, or context. Why? The root cause is nothing but lack of reading and, therefore lack of sensitivity to the language, lack of intellectual and cultural aspects.

Reading, that is, is one of the best ways to improve translation quality. The four major reasons are as follows.

Firstly, through reading a reader can be familiar with the types of writing, which refer to the way in which language is expressed. Generally speaking, there are 4 types of writing such as narration, description, exposition and argumentation, which are the most useful ones. The style, that is to say, is the linguistic characteristic of a specific text. Each type has its own style. Narration, which simply means storytelling, is a basic pattern of organizing our thoughts that we use almost daily. Description, different from the method of narration, emphasizes our sensory impressions instead. Exposition deals with processes and relationships and answers questions of how something works, how something happens, what the outcome of a certain event may be, or why a certain situation exists. Argumentation is to persuade the listener or the reader to embrace a viewpoint. If a reader wants to know more detailed information about the features of each type, reading is still an effective way. English fictional prose, for example, has the following features:

Lexis is plentiful, esp. adjectives and adverbs are more frequent, and at some time visual and auditory words are adequate; sentence structures are more involved and longer; metaphor, simile, personification, irony, parallelism, hyperbole, etc. are much rhetorically used.

Let us see a couple of sentences from *Odour of Chrysanthemums* by D. H. Lawrence.

"A woman, walking up the railway line to Unerwood, drew back into the hedge, held her basket aside, and watched the footplate of the engine advancing. The trucks thumped heavily past, one by one, with slow inevitable movement, as she stood insignificantly trapped between the jolting black wagons hedge; then they curved away towards the coppice where the withered oak leaves dropped noiselessly, while the birds, pulling at the scarlet hips beside the track, made off into dusk that had already crept into the spinney."

The excerpt only has two sentences. But we can notice that the sentences are much longer and the structure is complex. Adjectives and adverbs are frequently used to bring visual imagery and emphasize movement and activity. As English prose has the traits above, an English reader can learn the way that the writer shows and the style of writing, through reading, therefore, the writing methods. Acquainted with the types of writing and writing methods, he or she can better comprehend reading materials, and increase his or her speed in reading. Simultaneously he or she, through more reading, can learn and get a lot. This is because reading a large number of materials, which cover such wide ranges as literature, art, history, popular science, biographical sketches, etc., could broaden one's knowledge and horizons, increase one's interest in learning English. And then a reader will step by step improve his or her translation capacity and heighten his or her confidence in translation.

Secondly, a reader, through reading, can master all such aspects as idioms, expressions, grammatical rules and structures because all of them are involved in reading materials. If a reader reads much enough, and focuses his or her attention on them whenever necessary, he or she will automatically know what pronouns, adjectives, articles etc. are, how structures and forms are built up, and why tenses are used in this or that way. He or she does not need to make every effort to recite every word and phrase. Though he or she does it, this word or phrase is only an isolated one, and he or she can't use it naturally and flexibly because English learning needs practice. The more one reads, the better he or she comprehends English language.

Vocabulary is a headache for any English learner because English is a kind of language with a large vocabulary. Some learners try to find manifold ways to enlarge (enrich) their vocabulary, but most of them fail. The reason is that they simply learn words or phrases by rote, or even recite dictionaries. Gradually they lose interest in learning English because reciting from memory is a really dull and drab task. Reading, however, can solve the problem. The reader, on basis of his or her English level, should select reading materials which contain a certain number of new words that he or she can fully understand, memorize and know how to use. In this way, the reader can make much progress gradually.

Thirdly, a good reader, through reading, can not only pick up the useful idioms and expressions from the materials, but also learn and understand the different cultures between two languages, the knowledge a passage concerns and the background that relates to. The cultural differences between China and the West are frequently talked about in reading materials of the original. As you know, misunderstandings often occur between Chinese and Westerners not simply because of grammatical inaccuracy or incorrect usage of vocabulary items, but also because of differences in both customs and cultures. As a result, some of the common errors that Chinese make and the problems that may arise often occur in translation. In a sense, understanding customs and cultures of a country is the biggest barrier in translating. We should acquire a language while learning knowledge. Reading a lot is about to solve the problem. As a matter of fact, some Chinese students of English don't realize the importance of reading. As a learner reads enough English books, magazines and others, the language of English will be naturally acquired.

Fourthly, in our country although there are thousands of learners of English, few can just further study English abroad. Only those lucky birds have the good circumstance to practice English. Most of the learners of English in China can only stay at home, neither communicating with English-speaking people nor watching something good for listening practice. How can they improve their English? We are certain that reading is the best way because, through reading, each learner can touch upon the very real language, real foreign culture and real structures and forms, and create a moderate circumstance which he or she is suitable for. As a result, he or she may enlarge his or her vocabulary, widen his or her field of vision, and gradually improve his or her translation ability. After a translator, through reading, obtains a number of useful language expressions, helpful idioms and beautiful sentences, he or she can translate a passage with facility. The Tang Dynasty poet Du Fu(杜甫)said,"读书破万卷,下笔如有神。"(After you have read over ten thousands books, you find yourself writing like magic.) In short, reading plays an important role in translation. Reading ability is one of the important symbols to measure whether English level is high or low.

In short, a translator's sensitiveness to the languages is one who is sensitive to the subtleties and nuances of words and expressions, and the elegance and strength of the syntactic structures. Newmark explains it this way, "The translator's craft lies in his command of an exceptionally large vocabulary as well as all syntactic resources—his ability to use them elegantly, flexibly, succinctly." (Newmark: 1988, *Approaches to Translation*) Either to develop a sensibility to the language, or to be able to appreciate the aesthetic value of the literary works, one thing the translator cannot do without is reading. As a rule, a good translator is a good writer, and a good writer is a good reader. Therefore, to be a good translator, he or she has to read more.

## 1.8 A Test in Class for Evaluation 课堂评估测试

Translate the following passage into Chinese.

### The Story of My Life

The most important day I remember in all my life is the one on which my teacher, Anne Mansfield Sullivan, came to me. I am filled with wonder when I consider the immeasurable contrast between the two lives which it connects. It was the third of March 1887, three months before I was seven years old.

On the afternoon of that eventful day, I stood on the porch, dumb, expectant. I guessed vaguely from my mother's signs and from the hurrying to and fro in the house that something unusual was about to happen, so I went to the door and waited on the steps. The afternoon sun penetrated the mass of honeysuckle that covered the porch, and fell on my upturned face. My fingers lingered almost unconsciously on the familiar leaves and blossoms which had just come forth to greet the sweet southern spring. I did not know what the future held of marvel or surprise for me. Anger and bitterness had preyed upon me continually for weeks and a deep languor had succeeded this passionate struggle.

Have you ever been at sea in a dense fog, when it seemed as if a tangible white darkness shut you in, and the great ship, tense and anxious, groped her way toward the shore with plummet and sounding-line and you waited with beating heart for something to happen? I was like that ship before my education began, only I was without compass or sounding-line, and had no way of knowing how near the harbor was. "Light! Give me light!" was the wordless cry of my soul, and the light of love shone on me in that very hour.

(By Helen Keller)

# Chapter 2: Lexical Translation
# 词法翻译

## 2.1 Conversion of Word Classes 词类转译

First of all, we should know what word classes are. In English, word classes are sometimes called parts of speech traditionally. There are 2 major kinds of word classes: open classes and closed classes. Nouns, verbs, adjectives and adverbs are known as open classes because their membership is fairly open-ended, in the sense that we can readily coin new words to add to them. The closed classes, however, have a fairly fixed membership. They are pronouns, prepositions, conjunctions, auxiliaries. Numerals and interjections are marginal classes. Conversion, one of the commonly adopted translation techniques, means the change of word classes in translation. Owing to the syntactical differences between English and Chinese, it is usually impossible for the translator to keep to the original word class in the process of translation. As a matter of fact, a word belonging to a certain word class in English language sometimes has to be converted into a different word class, so as to bring forth a readable and coherent sentence. In conversion from English into Chinese, there are following cases for us to consider while translating.

### 2.1.1 Convert English Nouns into Chinese Verbs, Adjectives, or Adverbs
英语名词转换成汉语动词、形容词或副词

#### 2.1.1.1 Convert nouns into verbs 英语名词转换成汉语动词

In translation, it is necessary for us to convert some English nouns into Chinese verbs because they usually indicate sorts of actions, are derivatives of English verbs, or can be used both as nouns and verbs. Now compare and analyze the following sentences, paying attention to the conversion of English nouns into Chinese verbs.

❖ International trade is the *exchange* of goods and services produced in one country for goods and services produced in another.
国际贸易就是将一个国家生产的商品和提供的服务与另一个国家生产的商品和提供的服务进行**交换**。

❖ The *application* of electronic computers makes a tremendous *rise* in labour productivity.
**使用**电子计算机可以大大**提高**劳动生产率。

- I am afraid I can't teach you swimming. I think my little brother is a better *teacher* than I.

  我未必会教你游泳。我想我的小弟弟比我**教**得好。

- They took a final *look* at the tower, still intact in the darkness.

  他们最后**看了**那座塔一眼——它依旧安然无恙地耸立在黑暗中。

- The government called for the *establishment* of more technical schools.

  政府号召**建立**更多的技术学校。

- My *suggestion* is that he should quit smoking at once.

  我**建议**他立刻戒烟。

**Comments** In the 6 sentences above, we've probably found the ways that some nouns are employed in the original. When we translate them, we use Chinese verbs, not nouns. That is, we may convert these nouns into Chinese verbs. At the same time, we notice that these nouns remain the way that we can follow:

1) The nouns containing action may be converted into Chinese verbs.

2) The nouns derived from verbs can be converted into Chinese verbs.

3) The nouns with the suffix -er or -or can be converted into Chinese verbs. Here are two more examples to examine: *I am no drinker, nor smoker.* 我既不喝酒,也不抽烟。*He is both a bibliomaniac and a lover of calligraphy.* 他不仅热衷藏书,而且爱好书法。

4) The nouns contained in such English idioms as "*to have a look*, *have a look at*", etc. are often converted into Chinese verbs.

Look at the last sentence carefully. This conversion from English noun to Chinese verb is a very typical case for us to follow. The modifier "*my*" is converted into the subject in Chinese version, in a sense that the noun "*suggestion*" should be converted into a verb, which really suits the Chinese expression.

### 2.1.1.2 Convert nouns into adjectives 英语名词转换成汉语形容词

Now let us compare and analyze the versions of following sentences and find the way in which the underlined words are converted.

- This experiment was a *success*.

  这次实验是**成功的**。

- Independent thinking is an absolute *necessity* in study.

  独立思考对学习是绝对**必要的**。

- We found *difficulty* in solving this complicated problem.

  我们感到,解决这个复杂的问题是**困难的**。

- The spokesman admitted the *feasibility* of the American proposals.

  发言人承认,美国的建议是**可取的**。

**Comments** 1) Some English nouns with indefinite articles as a subject complement can be converted into Chinese adjectives. The first two sentences are the examples.

2) In other cases, nouns may be changed into adjectives if necessary so as to agree with Chinese grammatical features just like sentences 3~4.

### 2.1.1.3 Convert nouns into adverbs 英语名词转换成汉语副词

Now compare and study the following sentences and find the way in which some nouns or phrases are converted into Chinese adverbs.

❖ The new mayor earned some appreciation by the *courtesy* of coming to visit the city poor.

新市长**有礼貌地**来看望城市贫民,获得了人们的一些好感。

❖ When he catches a glimpse of a potential antagonist, his *instinct* is to win him over with charm and humor.

只要一发现有可能反对他的人,他就**本能地**要用他的魅力和风趣将这个人争取过来。

❖ I had the *fortune* to meet him.

我**幸运地**遇到了他。

❖ I have the *honour* to inform you that your request is granted.

我**荣幸地**通知您,您的请求已得到批准。

**Comments** On the one hand, some English nouns or phrases with abstract conceptions can be converted into Chinese adverbs in translating when they are systematically related to the other parts of sentences. On the other hand, we can follow the regulation that the nouns with abstract conceptions, followed by the infinitive "*to*", may be converted into Chinese adverbs. The last two examples belong to the case.

### 2.1.2 Compare and Analyze 比较与分析

Speech of Farewell

My friends: No one not in my situation can appreciate my feeling of sadness at this ① parting (*n.* →*adj.*). To this place, and the ② kindness (*n.* →*adj.*) of these people, I owe everything. Here I have lived a quarter of a century, and have passed from a young to an old man. Here my children have been born, and one is buried. I now leave, not knowing when or whether ever I may return, with a task before me greater than that which rested upon Washington. Without the ③ assistance (*n.* →*v.*) of that Divine Being who ever attended him, I cannot succeed. With that

告别演说

亚伯拉罕·林肯

朋友们,不处在我的位置,就不会体会到①**离愁别绪的**伤感。我所拥有的一切归功于这里的土地和这些②**善良的**人们。我在这里已度过了25个春秋,从青年步入了暮年。我的几个孩子就诞生在这片土地上,其中一个已撒手人寰。我现在就要走了,不知道何时或者能否重返故里。我所面临的任务要比华盛顿将军肩负的使命更为艰巨。

assistance, I cannot fail. Trusting in Him who can go with me, and remain with you and be everywhere for ④good (n. →adv.), let us confidently hope that all will yet be well. To His care commending you, as I hope in your ⑤ prayers (n. →v.) you will commend me, I bid you an affectionate farewell.　　(By Abraham Lincoln)

如果没有上帝曾像庇佑过华盛顿将军那样③**保佑**我,我是不会成功的。正是有这样的庇佑,我决不会失败。愿上帝与我同行,与你们同在,④**永远地**和我们在一起。让我们坚信一切都会随顺人愿。愿上帝保佑你们,也希望你们为我⑤**祈祷**,为我祝福。我在此充满深情地向你们告别。

(何三宁　译)

**Notes**:①②The underlined are nouns, which are converted into adjectives in Chinese because nouns may be changed into adjectives if necessary so as to agree with Chinese grammatical features.

③⑤The nouns derived from verbs can be converted into Chinese verbs.

④Some English nouns or phrases with abstract conceptions can be converted into Chinese adverbs. This one is the case.

### 2.1.3 Exercises 练习

Ⅰ. Sentence translation.

1. *An acquaintance* of world history is helpful to the study of current.
2. *The operation* of a machine needs some knowledge of its performance.
3. We found *difficulty* in solving this complicated problem.
4. *The rehabilitation* of the cabin became a necessity.
5. He had *the kindness* to show me the way.
6. I had *the fortune* to become a teacher.
7. This little present is a *token* of our friendship.
8. While no one questioned his word, he was never a financial *success*.
9. The railway bridge is still under *construction*.
10. His *suggestion* is that we should set out before 8 o'clock.

Ⅱ. Passage translation.

**A Day in My Life**

I get up at about 6:15 each morning since I've got a husband and four cats to feed, and a long way to drive; I like to do a quarter-hour of yoga, too. I'm usually at the zoo by 8:15.

Whenever possible, I use the first hour to go around the zoo. I walk or drive, and talk to the keepers and gardeners to see what's born, what's hatched, what's in bloom, what's been moved to somewhere else, because I have to write a news sheet about what's new at the zoo each month.

Already this morning I've had a call from a TV channel to do some hot weather shots because of the predicted 40 degrees today; you know, elephants are hosing themselves down, seals swimming, penguins flapping in their pool. Animals are more sensible than we are. In the hot weather they don't rush around in ever-decreasing circles—they just swim or lie down in the shade.

By nine, the phone starts ringing constantly; I have countless calls each day, and every call is different. We get a lot of media requests from people wanting to borrow animals to appear on shows. Then there's the travel industry wanting zoo posters, people asking where to get feral pigs or dingoes for documentaries, overseas photographers asking for special permission to take pictures; they're very keen on our koalas and kangaroos.

I walk around a lot. Often one of the keepers is wanted instantly and can't be reached by phone—then I go and look for him. Taronga Zoo is quite hilly and in the first six months, I've lost some weight.

### 2.1.4 Convert English Adjectives into Chinese Adverbs, Verbs or Nouns 英语形容词转换成汉语副词、动词或名词

#### 2.1.4.1 Convert adjectives into adverbs 英语形容词转换成汉语副词

Compare and study the following sentences and find the way in which the underlined English words are converted into Chinese adverbs.

- This is *sheer* nonsense.

  这<u>完全</u>是胡说。

- Below 4℃, water is in *continuous* expansion instead of *continuous* contraction.

  水在4℃以下,是在<u>不断地</u>膨胀,而不是<u>不断地</u>收缩。

- Every time you meet someone in a social situation, give him your *undivided* attention for four minutes.

  每当你在社交场合遇到某人,<u>专注地</u>看他四分钟。

- There is a *big* increase in demand for all kinds of consumer goods in every part of our country.

  目前,我国各地对各种消费品的需求量已<u>大大</u>增加。

- I am so grateful to my father for his *continuous* encouragement during my childhood.

  我非常感谢父亲,因为他在我小时候总是<u>不断地</u>鼓励我。

**Comments** In translation, if an English noun is changed into a verb, then the adjective that modifies the noun is generally converted into a Chinese adverb. Let us examine the last sentence in particular. The preposition "*for*" introduces a prepositional phrase, which serves as an adverbial of reason in Chinese version. In this sense, "*for*" means 因为, and the version of "*his*" is 他 in Chinese. So the adjective "continuous" should be converted into Chinese adverb 不断地. The noun "*encouragement*" is translated into a verb 鼓励. And also the prepositional phrase "*during my childhood*" can be translated into a Chinese adverbial.

#### 2.1.4.2 Convert adjectives into verbs 英语形容词转换成汉语动词

Many English adjectives after a link verb indicating one's consciousness, feelings, emotions, desires, etc. are always converted into Chinese verbs. These words include: *confident*, *certain*, *careful*, *cautious*, *angry*, *sure*, *ignorant*, *afraid*, *doubtful*, *aware*, *concerned*, *glad*, *delighted*, *sorry*, *ashamed*, *thankful*, *anxious*, *grateful*, *able*,

*informative* and so on. Look at the following examples.
- ❖ Scientists are *confident* that all matter is indestructible.
  科学家们**深信**物质是不灭的。
- ❖ Doctors have said that they are not *sure* they can save his life.
  医生说他们不敢**肯定**能否救他的命。
- ❖ He said the meeting was *informative*.
  他说这个会议使人**了解**了许多事情。
- ❖ The noon sun clarified the air. I became *aware of* two surfers well out from the shore, patiently paddling their boards while they waited for a perfect wave.
  正午时分天空晴朗,我**瞥见**两个冲浪者离岸很远,耐心地踏着滑板,等待一个最理想的浪头。
- ❖ The fact that she was *able* to send a message was a hint. But I had to be *cautious*.
  她**能够**给我带个信儿这件事就是个暗示。但是我必须**小心谨慎**。

**Comments** Some adjectives can often be converted into Chinese verbs after verb "*be*" as subject complements (predicatives 表语). Another case is when an adjective used as a predicative introduces a (that) clause, it can be converted into a verb in Chinese version. The first two sentences are good examples for this point.

### 2.1.4.3 Convert adjectives into nouns 英语形容词转换成汉语名词

Compare and study the following sentences and find the way in which English adjectives are converted into Chinese nouns.
- ❖ The *rich* are not always happy.
  **富人**未必总是幸福的。
- ❖ Everyday experience shows us that heavy objects are more *stable* than light ones.
  日常生活经验告诉我们,重东西比轻东西的**稳定性**要好些。
- ❖ Nylon is nearly twice as *strong* as natural silk.
  尼龙的**强度**几乎是天然丝的两倍。
- ❖ The new treaty would be *good* for 10 years.
  这个新条约的**有效期**为十年。
- ❖ *Official* Moscow is going to object the proposal.
  莫斯科**官方**反对此项提议。

**Comments** As English adjectives are converted into nouns, we should pay attention to 3 points.

1) Some adjectives with definite articles, which indicate specific groups of persons or things, are usually converted into nouns. The first sentence is a good example.

2) Some adjectives, which are used as predicatives to indicate the nature of things, or with Chinese characters 期、性、度、体 remaining in context in translating, can be converted into nouns. Sentences 2~4 typically show us this skill.

3) We should pay attention to the differences between English and Chinese in lexical arrangement. In English, the relationship between the modifier and recipient is flexible because English language highlights form or structure whereas Chinese language lays stress on meaning. This distinction calls for our adjudgement in translation.

## 2.1.5 Compare and Analyze 比较与分析

Voltaire

A hundred years' today a man died. He died ① immortal. He departed ② laden with years, laden with works, laden with the most illustrious and the most fearful responsibilities, the responsibility of the human conscience ③ informed and rectified. He went ④ cursed and blessed, ⑤ cursed by the past, blessed by the future, and these are the two superb forms of glory. On the death-bed he had, on the one hand, the acclaim of contemporaries and of the posterity; on the other hand, that triumph of hooting and of hate which the implacable past bestows upon those who have combated it. He was more than a man; he was an age. He had exercised a function and fulfilled a mission. He had been evidently chosen for the work which he had done by the Supreme Will, which manifests itself as visibly in the laws of destiny as in the laws of nature.

伏尔泰

一百年前的今天,一个伟人与世长辞了。他已离我们而去,可他的业绩却①流芳百世(永垂不朽)。他去世时年事②已高,著述颇丰,肩负着极为光荣、极为艰巨的职责,即③培养良知、教化人类的职责。他既受到人们的④诅咒,又受到人们的赞誉,过去的人⑤诅咒他,未来的人赞美他,这些都是至高无上的荣誉。一方面,在生命弥留之际,他听到的是同时代的人们以及子孙后代的喝彩声;而另一方面,他则听到无情的过去对与之抗争的人们充满憎恨和呵斥的呼喊声。他不仅仅代表他个人,而是整整一个时代。他已完成了一项使命。显而易见是上帝选择他去完成这项业已完成的使命。上帝的意志同样体现在自然法则与命运法则之中。

(何三宁　译)

Notes: ①③The adjectives "immortal", "informed" and "rectified" are respectively converted into V + N structure 流芳百世, 培养良知, 教化人类 in Chinese.

②In the original, the word "laden" with the same construction has different conversions. The first two are respectively put into 已高 and 颇丰, but the last one is translated into a Chinese verb.

④⑤Both of words "cursed" and "blessed" are converted with different parts of speech. Firstly they are put into Chinese nouns, and then verbs.

## 2.1.6 Exercises 练习

Ⅰ. Sentence translation.

1. *Warm* discussions arose on every corner as to his achievements.
2. "Yes," he said with a *slow* nod or two.
3. We are quite *sure* that the socialist system will replace the capitalist system in the end.

4. They were not *content* with their present achievements.
5. They did their best to help *the sick and the wounded*.
6. Air, for instance, is perfectly *elastic*.
7. The woman teacher is very *strict* with us.
8. Kerosene is not so *volatile* as gasoline.
9. Jackson was *eloquent* and *elegant*, but *soft*.
10. It was a *stormy* morning, with rain and mist.
11. We have made a *careful* study of the soil properties in that region.
12. Our country places the *highest* value on good relations with developing countries.

II. Passage translation.

### The Quest

Taking the train, the two friends arrived in Berlin in late October 1922, and went directly to the address of Chou En-lai. Would this man receive them as fellow countrymen, or would he treat them with cold suspicion and question them cautiously about their past career as militarists? Chu Teh remembered his age. He was thirty-six; his youth had like a screaming eagle, leaving him old and disillusioned.

When Chou En-lai's door opened they saw a slender man of more than average height with gleaming eyes and a face so striking that it bordered on the beautiful. Yet it was a manly face, serious and intelligent, and Chu judged him to be in his middle twenties.

Chou was a quiet and thoughtful man, even a little shy as he welcomed his visitors, urged them to be seated and to tell how he could help them.

Ignoring the chair offered to him, Chu Teh stood squarely before this youth more than ten years his junior and in a level voice told him who he was, what he had done in the past, how he fled from Yunnan, talked with Sun Yat-sen, been repulsed by Chen Tu-hsiu in Shanghai, and had come to Europe to find a new way of life for himself and a new revolutionary road for China. He wanted to join the Chinese Communist Party group in Berlin, he would study and work hard, he would do anything he was asked to do but return to his old life, which had turned to ashes beneath his feet.

As he talked Chou En-lai stood facing him, his head a little to one side as was his habit, listening intently until the story was told, and then questioning him.

When both visitors had their stories, Chou smiled a little, said he would help them find rooms, and arranged for them to join the Berlin Communist group as candidates until their application had been sent to China and an answer received. When the reply came a few months later they were enrolled as full members, but Chu's membership was kept a secret from outsiders.

(Agnes Smedley: *The Great Road*)

## 2.1.7 Convert English Adverbs into Chinese Nouns, Verbs or Adjectives
英语副词转换成汉语名词、动词或形容词

### 2.1.7.1 Convert adverbs into nouns 英语副词转换成汉语名词

Compare and study the following sentences and find how English adverbs are converted into Chinese nouns.

- It was *officially* announced that they agreed on a reply to the USA.

  <u>官方</u>宣布,他们就给美国复函(答复)一事取得了一致意见。
- The image must be *dimensionally* correct.

  图形的<u>尺寸</u>必须正确。
- The paper said *editorially* that Mcmillan had stolen the Western leadership during Dulles' absence.

  这家报纸的<u>社论</u>说,麦克米伦在杜勒斯卧病期间窃走了西方领导权。

**Comments** Some English adverbs can be converted into Chinese nouns as circumstances require. This, different from the expressing form in English, is also the need of expressing in Chinese language. If we convert these adverbs directly into 官方地,尺寸地,以社论形式, the versions will appear wordy and awkward.

### 2.1.7.2 Convert adverbs into verbs 英语副词转换成汉语动词

This is the same case as the conversion of English adjectives into Chinese verbs mentioned in the preceding section. We can say that it is one of the most remarkable differences between English and Chinese syntax. It is taken for granted that an English sentence contains no more than one predicate verb, while in Chinese it is not unusual to have clusters of verbs in a simple sentence. Let us look at the following examples.

- I must be *off* now.

  我现在得<u>走</u>了。
- The oil in the tank is *up*.

  油箱里的油已经<u>用完</u>。
- That day he was *up* before five o'clock.

  那天,他5点前就<u>起床</u>了。
- Why should we let *in* foreign goods when Americans walk the streets because they can't sell their own goods?

  在美国人由于推销不出自己的产品而失业之际,为什么我们还要让外国货<u>进口</u>呢?
- When the switch is off, the circuit is open and electricity doesn't go *through*.

  开关断开时,电路就形成开路,电流不能<u>通过</u>。

**Comments** English adverbs like "on, off, over, up, out", etc., used as subject complements (predicatives), can be converted into Chinese verbs. In English, some adverbs and prepositions are usually used to describe a series of actions. We Chinese have to translate them into Chinese verbs.

### 2.1.7.3 Convert adverbs into adjectives 英语副词转换成汉语形容词

English adverbs are more extensively used than Chinese adverbs, and many of them can be converted into Chinese adjectives. Now compare and study the following sentences and find how some English adverbs are converted into Chinese adjectives.

- Everything in China has *greatly* changed since liberation.

解放以来,中国的一切都发生了**巨大的**变化。

❖ This college impressed us *deeply*.
这所学院给我们留下了**深刻的**印象。

❖ The President had prepared *meticulously* for his journey.
总统为这次出访作了**十分周密的**准备。

❖ It is demonstrated that gases are *perfectly* elastic.
已经证明,气体具有**理想的**弹性。

❖ *Traditionally*, there had always been good relations between them.
他们之间一直有着**传统的**友好关系。

**Comments** In translating, as an English adjective or verb is changed into a Chinese noun in one sentence, the adverb that originally modifies the adjective or verb is mostly converted into Chinese adjectives. In the first 3 sentences, the verbs "*changed*", "*impressed*" and "*prepared*" are converted into Chinese nouns; the adverbs, in this case, can be translated into Chinese adjectives, modifying these nouns converted. An adverb can be converted into a Chinese adjective when the adjective modified by the adverb is translated into a noun. The fourth sentence is the case. By comparison, English adverbs are more extensively employed than Chinese adverbs, and many of them can be converted into Chinese adjectives. But we probably need to add some necessary words for smoothness and fluency in Chinese. We take "*generally*" and "*physically*" for example, and they may be translated into 总体而言,就体力来说。

### 2.1.8 Convert English Verbs into Chinese Nouns 英语动词转换成汉语名词

Compare and study the following sentences, and find how the underlined English words are converted into Chinese nouns.

❖ The man I saw at the party *looked* and *talked* like an American.
我在聚会上见到的那个人,**外表**和**谈吐**都像美国人。

❖ He was *motivated* by a desire to reach a compromise.
他的**动机**是希望达成某种妥协。

❖ Most U.S. spy satellites are *designed* to burn up in the earth's atmosphere after completing their missions.
美国绝大多数间谍卫星,按其**设计**是在完成使命后在大气层中焚毁。

❖ As the war progressed, he would *symbolize* their frustrations, the embodiment of all evils.
随着战争的进行,他成了他们受挫的**象征**,成了一切坏事的化身。

**Comments** In English, many verbs derived from nouns like "*symbolize*" in the last sentence can be usually converted into Chinese nouns because they hardly can be translated literally. And some verbs transformed from nouns can be converted Chinese nouns like "*motivate*", "*design*", "*look*" and "*talk*" in the first three sentences.

## 2.1.9 Convert English Prepositions into Chinese Verbs 英语介词转换成汉语动词

Compare and study the following sentences, and understand how the underlined English words below are converted into Chinese verbs.

- Are you *for* or *against* the plan?
  你**赞成**还是**反对**这项计划?

- I paid 50 yuan *for* an old bicycle.
  我花50元钱**买**了一辆旧自行车。

- Break the circuit first *in case of* fire.
  如**遇**火灾,首先切断电源。

- Some longtime associates and friends wanted to protect him *from* the White House; some, protect him *from* the public; and others, to protect him *from* himself.
  有些老同事和老朋友想保护他,使他**免受**白宫的连累;一些人是想保护他,使他**不受到**公众的攻击;还有一些人则想保护他,使他本人不要**说**错话或**做**错事。

- Downstairs, then, they went, Joseph very red and blushing, Rebecca very modest, and holding her green eyes *downwards*. She was dressed in white, *with* bare shoulders as white as snow—the picture of youth, unprotected innocence, and humble virgin simplicity.
  他们一路下楼,约瑟夫涨红了脸,丽贝卡举止端庄,一双绿眼**望着**地下,她穿了一件白衣服,**露出**雪白的肩膀,年纪轻轻,越发显得天真烂漫,活是一个娴静又纯洁的小姑娘。

- "Coming!" Away she skimmed *over* the lawn, *up* the path, *up* the steps, *across* the veranda, and *into* the porch.
  "来了!"她转身蹦蹦跳着跑了,**越过**草地,**跑上**小径,**跨上**台阶,**穿过**凉台,**进了**门廊。

**Comments** English prepositions imply the relationship between words. When we come across them in translation, we should cope with them in accordance with their relations and context. From the conversion of word classes, we may find the differences in forms between English and Chinese. That is to say, we Chinese prefer using verbs, while English-speakers more frequently use other parts of speech.

Generally speaking, we may not translate prepositions in some fixed phrases literally into Chinese, several phrases for instance, "*arrive at/in*", "*put up with*", "*take care of*", etc. However, the prepositions or prepositional phrases with action are often converted into Chinese verbs.

- Go *by* car.
  **乘**汽车去。

- This is a present *for* Susan.

  这是**给**苏珊的礼物。

- I have a letter written *in* English.

  我有一封**用**英语写的信。

Although there are some laws or methods for us to follow in translation, the conversion of word classes is frequently and flexibly used. Whether or not it is to be used seems not to be determined by the original, instead, it is determined by Chinese, the target language, whose advantages must be taken and will be taken to the full by converting word classes in English.

### 2.1.10 Compare and Analyze 比较与分析

Spring

Springs are not always the same. In some years, April bursts ① upon our Virginia hills in one prodigious leap and all the stage is filled ② at once, whole choruses of tulips, arabesques of forsythia, cadenzas of flowering plum. The trees grow leaves overnight.

In other years, spring tiptoes ③ in. It pauses, overcome by shyness, like my grandchild at the door, peeping ④ in, ducking ⑤ out of sight, giggling in the hallway. "I know you're out there," I cry. "Come in!" and April slips ⑥ into our arms.

The dogwood bud, pale green, isinlaid with russet markings. Within the perfect cup a score of clustered seeds are nestled. One examines the bud in awe: Where were those seeds a month ago? The apples display their milliner's scraps of ivory silk, rose-tinged, all the sleeping things wake up—primrose, baby iris, blue phlox. The earth warms—you can smell it, feel it, crumble April in your hands.

春天

春天并非总是一模一样。四月,有时不知怎的一跃,①**就来到了**弗吉尼亚的山坡上,自然的大舞台上②**转眼**到处生机勃勃。郁金香组成了大合唱,连翘展示出优美的舞姿,洋李奏起了华彩乐章。一夜之间,林木着装,绿叶瑟瑟。

有时,春天会③**悄然而至**,像我的小孙女一样,羞羞答答地依在门外,④**向里探探头**,一闪⑤**又不见了**,只是在门厅里咯咯地笑。"我知道你在那儿藏着呢。"我喊道,"进来!"春天这才悄然⑥**跑进了**我的怀抱。

山茱萸的蓓蕾,淡绿清雅,表面点缀着褐色斑痕。活像一只完美无缺的小杯里,一撮撮种子,半隐半现地藏在里面。人们会敬畏地观察着这蓓蕾,暗自发问:一个月之前,这些种子在什么地方呢?苹果花开,展示出一片片染了玫瑰红的象牙色薄绸。一切冬眠的东西都在苏醒:美丽的樱草花,纤细的蝴蝶花,还有蓝色的草夹竹桃。大地开始变暖——这,你既可以嗅到,也可以触摸到——抓起一把泥土,春天便揉碎在你的手中。

(宋德利 译)

注:《中国翻译》,1988.4.译文稍有修改

**Notes**: This piece is chosen to call our special attention to the conversion of English prepositions and adverbs. In English prose, excellent writers frequently use adverbs and prepositional phrases or idioms to describe actions. This passage is a very good example for us to know the case. So when we come across such pieces, we can convert them into Chinese verbs just as the passage shows us.

## 2.1.11 Exercises 练习

Ⅰ. **Translate the following sentences, paying attention to the underlined words.**

1. Specialization also enables one country to produce some goods more *cheaply* than another country.
2. He is *physically* weak but *mentally* sound.
3. I love having Fridays *off*.
4. I suppose boys think *differently* from girls.
5. How long will she be *away*?
6. This is *where* you are wrong.
7. She *designs* for a famous shop.
8. He *aims* to enter the university next year.
9. He went out *with* his hat on.
10. Party officials worked long hours *on* meager food, *in* cold caves, *by* dimlamps.

Ⅱ. **Passage translation.**

### The Sound of Music

Suddenly I heard quick footsteps behind me, and a full, resonant voice exclaimed, " I see you are looking at my flag."

There he was—the Captain!

The tall, well-dressed gentleman standing before me was certainly a far cry from the old sea wolf of imagination. His air of complete self-assurance and somewhat lordly bearing would have frightened me, had it not been for his warm and hearty handshake.

"I am so glad you have come, Fraulein…"

I filled in, "Maria."

He took me in from top to toe with a quick glance. All of a sudden I became very conscious of my funny dress, and sure enough, there I was diving under my helmet again. But the Captain's eyes rested on my shoes.

We were still standing in the hall when he said, " I want you to meet the children first of all."

Out of his pocket he took an odd-shaped, ornamented brass whistle, on which he piped a series of complicated trills.

I must have looked highly amazed, because he said, a little apologetically," You see it takes so long to call so many children by name, that I've given them each a different whistle."

Of course, I now expected to hear a loud banging of doors and a chorus of giggles and shouts, the scampering feet of youngsters jumping down the steps and sliding down the banister. Instead, let by a sober-faced young girl in her early teens, an almost solemn little procession descended step by step in well-mannered silence—four girls and two boys, all dressed in sailor suits. For an instant we stared at each other in utter amazement. I had never seen such perfect little ladies and gentlemen, and they had never seen such a helmet.

"Here is our new teacher, Fraulein Maria."

"Gruss Gott, Fraulein Maria," six voices echoed in unison. Six perfect bows followed.

That wasn't real. That couldn't be true. I had to shove back that ridiculous hat again. This push, however, was the last. Down came the ugly brown thing, rolled on the shiny parquet floor, and landed at the tiny feet of a very pretty, plump little girl of about five. A delighted giggle cut through the severe silence. The ice was broken. We all laughed.

(Maria Augusta Trapp: *The Sound of Music*)

## 2.2 Omission and Amplification 省词与增词翻译

### 2.2.1 Omission 省词翻译

Omission is one of the translating techniques in which some parts of the original can be omitted when they are translated so that the translation accords with Chinese readers' descriptions. But we have no right to subtract any meaning from the original. In other words, we can't simply cross out the part which we don't understand or omit any part at will. Meanwhile remember that we can't casually cross out the part which should not be omitted. We can say that omission and amplification are a unity of accuracy and economy. In fact, one of the marked differences in syntax between English and Chinese is the disparity in wording. What is regarded as a natural or indispensable element in one language may be regarded as a superfluous or even a stumbling block in the other. Therefore, the technique of omission is the need to get rid of redundant wording to conform to idiomatic Chinese expressions. Now let us further discuss some aspects about omission.

#### 2.2.1.1 Omitting English articles 省略英语冠词

In English language articles are used, but no articles exist in Chinese. Therefore English articles are sometimes omitted while translating English into Chinese.

❖ *A* teacher should have patience in his work.
   教师应当对待工作有耐心。

❖ *A* child needs love.
   孩子都需要爱。

**Comments** Indefinite article "*a*" indicates a class of things or persons as a whole. It is typically used with singular countable nouns. In this case, indefinite article "*a*" can be omitted. As a matter of fact, the first sentence indicates that "*All teachers should have patience in their work*" or "*Any teacher should have patience in his work*". The second one implies that "*All children need love*" or "*Any child needs love*".

❖ *The* horse is a useful animal.

马是有益的动物。

❖ *The* deep-freezer has made life easier for housewives.

冰柜让家庭主妇的生活变得容易得多。

**Comments** The definite article "*the*" in the sentences is used for specific reference to a particular example of a class of animals or things. In this case, we can omit the definite article "*the*" in translation.

❖ *The* moon was slowly rising above the sea.

月亮慢慢从海上升起。

❖ *The* proletariat and *the* peasantry must unite.

无产阶级与农民阶级必须联合起来。

**Comments** In English the definite article is used when the object or group of objects is unique or considered to be unique, and the definite article "*the*" plus adjective represents a class of persons. In this case, we can omit the definite article "*the*" in translation.

But we should notice that articles, including the definite and indefinite articles are not omitted in certain situational contexts when they are used for specific meanings.

❖ He left without saying *a* word.

他一句话不说就走了。

**Comments** As the indefinite article "*a*" indicates "*one*", it cannot be omitted in translation.

❖ The number of vibration *a* second is called the frequency.

**每**秒钟的震动次数称作频率。

**Comments** When the indefinite article "*a*" indicates "*every*", it cannot be omitted in translation.

❖ They saw *the* little party climb ashore.

他们看见**那**一小队人爬上岸去。

**Comments** When the definite article "*the*" denotes "*this*" or "*that*", it cannot be omitted in translation.

### 2.2.1.2 Omitting English pronouns 省略英语代词

Pronouns are more frequently used in English than in Chinese, which is one of the most explicit distinctions between English and Chinese. In English, each sentence usually has its own subject, and the pronoun used as a subject often appears several times. But in Chinese the subject can be used only once and the sentences after that may not have their subjects. Therefore, in E-C translation, repeated English pronouns may be omitted so as to conform the rendering to the accustomed usage of Chinese expressions. Now let us study the following situations.

**1) A English pronoun used as the subject can be omitted in Chinese translation**.

❖ But it's the way *I* am, and try as *I* might; *I* haven't been able to change it.

但**我**就这脾气,(我)虽然几经努力,(我)却未能改过来。

❖ Like his friend *he* had many wonderful ideas, but *he* only put a few into practice.

他像他的朋友一样,虽然有许多美妙的想法,(他)却只将少数想法付诸实践。
- If *I* learn to drive a motorcycle, *I* will certainly buy a new one.
我要是学摩托车的话,(我)就一定去买一辆新的。

**Comments** By comparison, we can easily find the differences between English and Chinese. In English, the same pronoun may be used several times in one sentence, but in Chinese, it may be used just once. That is one of the distinctions in organization of text or in thinking.

**2) But we should clearly notice that when the pronoun used as a subject makes a general reference, it is also often omitted.**

- *We* live and learn.
活到老,学到老。
- *One* must have studied hard before *one* could succeed in mastering a foreign language.
只有勤学苦练,才能精通外语。
- The money *you* pay to school is called school fee.
交给学校的钱叫学费。

**Comments** In the first two sentences, "*we*" and "*one*" actually refer to a general reference, in other words, either of them refers to anyone or all of us. In this case they should be omitted in translation. In the third sentence, "*you*" refers to anyone who enters a school and pays the money.

**3) Possessive pronouns are necessarily retained in English, but sometimes it is unnecessary to have them in Chinese.**

This is a very important distinction between English and Chinese because English-speaking people stress individuals, whereas we Chinese emphasize the comprehensive thinking. Therefore English possessive pronouns are generally omitted in translating.

- Wash *your* hands before the meal.
饭前洗手。
- We are doing *our* physical experiment.
我们正在做物理实验。
- He shrugged *his* shoulders, shook *his* head, cast up *his* eyes, but said nothing.
他耸耸肩头,摇摇脑袋,两眼看天,一句话不说。
- For two weeks, he has been studying the house, looking at *its* rooms, *its* electric wiring, *its* path and *its* garden.
两周以来,他一直注意观察这所房子,查看各个房间的情况,留心电线的走向,了解通道和花园的布局。

**Comments** There are big differences in English and Chinese cultures and values. In the western culture, they intend individualism orientation, but we Chinese maintain the group orientation. Therefore, possessive pronouns are frequently used in English, but they are seldom used in Chinese. Because of such a difference, possessive pronouns are often omitted in Chinese versions.

**4) Sometimes self-pronouns in English used as objects or appositives are usually omitted.**

❖ Why do we feel cooler when we fan *ourselves*?
为什么扇扇子时我们会感到凉快些?

❖ The wings *themselves* are set on the fuselage fairly far back.
机翼是安装在机身后面的。

**Comments** Self-pronouns in English are commonly used for emphasis. But when they are used as objects or appositives they are usually omitted.

**5) In the emphatic construction "*It be…that…*" it is unnecessary for us to translate "*it*" into Chinese.**

❖ *It* is from the sun *that* we get light and heat.
正是太阳才使我们得到了光和热。

❖ *It* is because the book is so useful in my work *that* I bought it.
正因为这本书对我的工作很有用,我才买了它。

**Comments** This construction is often used for force or emphasis. It is our performance that only is the part between "*it*" and "*that*" stood out in Chinese version when we translate it. The pronoun "*it*" does not need rendering.

**6) When the word "*it*", as a non-personal pronoun, expresses time, distance, natural phenomenon or environment, it is often omitted in translating.**

❖ Outside *it* was pitch-dark and *it* was raining cats and dogs.
外面一团漆黑,大雨倾盆。

❖ He glanced at his watch; *it* was 7:15.
他一看表,是七点一刻了。

**7) When "*it*" is used as a formal subject, we may omit it in translating.**

❖ *It* is easy to learn English, but *it* is difficult to attain perfection in it.
英语易学难精。

❖ *It* was necessary that we should make some preparation for it.
我们做些准备工作是必要的。

**Comments** We can easily find that "it" in parts 6 and 7 is used as a non-personal pronoun, expressing time, distance, natural phenomenon and environment, or as a formal subject. In this sense, it may be omitted. When the word "*it*" is used to reason things out, it is omitted. Here is one more sentence for us to study: *It is better to do well than to say well.* 说得好不如做得好。

### 2.2.1.3 Omitting English conjunctions 省略英语连词

In Chinese, conjunctions are seldom used because the language itself is considered an analytic one, whose logical relationship is mainly expressed by its word order. Many conjunctions in structure may seem redundant in Chinese. On the contrary, English language has many conjunctions which connect the contexts. Therefore, omission of the conjunctions is a common practice in English-Chinese translation.

- Mr. Bingley was good-looking *and* gentlemanlike.
  宾利先生仪表堂堂,颇具绅士风度。
- You'll supply financial power, and we'll supply manpower. Isn't that fair *and* square?
  你们出钱,我们出力,这难道还不公平吗?
- Her son was wise and clever, but her daughter was silly *and* foolish.
  她的儿子非常聪明,可她的女儿却很笨。
- She shook *and* trembled with fear.
  她吓得不停地发抖。
- He is a man of culture *and* learning.
  他是个很有学问的人。

**Comments** Both Westerners and Chinese like using synonyms or words with similar meaning or manner to describe something or somebody. Westerners usually use a pair of words connected with "*and*", whereas Chinese often use idioms or set phrases connected to each other without any conjunction. Now that the difference apparently exists between them, we can omit the conjunction "*and*" in Chinese version. All the sentences except the first belong to this case. Although the two words "*good-looking*" and "*gentlemanlike*" are not synonyms in the first sentence, they express a kind of quality about a person. At the same time, we should notice the different habits of expressing between the two cultures, that is, logical relationship in Chinese language is mainly expressed by its word order. So conjunction "*and*" could be omitted in this sentence. Here is one more sentence: *The sun is bright, and the sky is clear.* 阳光灿烂,晴空万里。

- We knew spring was coming *as* (*because*) we had seen a robin.
  我们看见了一只知更鸟,知道春天快要到了。

**Comments** The subordinate conjunction "*as*" or "*because*" expresses the relationship between cause and effect. But in Chinese, word order usually denotes this kind of relationship.

- *If* winter comes, can spring be far behind?
  冬天来了,春天还会远吗?
- *If* you don't go there tomorrow, they'll get angry.
  你明天不去,他们会生气的。

**Comments** The subordinator "*if*", when used to express a kind of condition, is generally omitted in Chinese, especially in spoken Chinese.

- John rose gloomily *as* the train stopped, for he was thinking of his ailing mother.
  火车停了,约翰郁郁地站了起来,因为他想起病中的母亲。

**Comments** The subordinator "*as*" or "*when*", when used to express time, is sometimes omitted when the time sequence is clear or obvious in Chinese version.

### 2.2.1.4 Omitting English prepositions 省略英语介词

Chinese is characterized by its succinctness and prepositions appear less frequently in Chinese than in English. Generally speaking, prepositions relating to place, time and space may be omitted in English-Chinese translation. This is also a common method in translating.

- I have studied English *for* two years.
  我学英语已两年了。
- Smoking is prohibited *in* public places.
  公共场所不准吸烟。
- Rumors had already spread *along* the streets and lanes.
  大街小巷早就传遍了各种流言蜚语。
- We have no school *on* Sundays.
  星期天我们不上学。
- The People's Republic of China was founded *in* 1949.
  1949 年中华人民共和国成立。

**Comments** Here we should pay special attention to the Chinese version in the last sentence. In Chinese, when the adverbial of time is placed in front of a sentence, the English preposition can be omitted. When the adverbial of time stands after the sentence, the Chinese version should be 中华人民共和国成立于 1949 年. This is a good example of different places for the adverbial of time in Chinese translation.

### 2.2.2 Compare and Analyze 比较与分析

| Goodbye to School | 告别学校 |
|---|---|
| Miss Sedley was ①a charming young lady, who deserved all that the head-mistress had written in her praise. ②She has such a kind, generous heart, that ③she won the love of everyone who near her, ④and she had half the school as her particular friends. ⑤Her face blushed with rosy health, and ⑥her lips had the freshest of smiles, ⑦and her eyes sparkled with bright good-nature, except when they were filled with tears, ⑧for she would cry over a dead bird, or over a mouse that the cat had seized and as for saying an unkind word to her—why, even Miss Pinkerton had | 萨克雷<br>赛特笠是①一位迷人的姑娘,对于校长的赞誉之辞她是受之无愧的。②她心地善良,落落大方,③深受身边同事的爱戴,④学校有一半老师都是她的挚友。⑤她的脸色红润健康,⑥嘴角常露出甜蜜(灿烂)的笑容,⑦眼睛晶莹明亮,且透出一丝善意。有时她也会眼含泪水,⑧为一只死去的小鸟而落泪;为一只被猫抓住的耗子而伤感;甚至一 |

given the teachers particular orders to treat her with the greatest gentleness, ⑨as severity was harmful to her.

⑩ When the day of departure came, between her two customs of laughing and crying, Miss Sedley was greatly puzzled how to act. She was glad to go home, and yet dreadfully sad at leaving school. But now the flowers and the presents and the trunks had all been arranged in the carriage, and a very small old box with Miss Sharps' card nailed neatly on it, had been added to the pile. The farewell visit to the headmistress' room having been paid, Miss Sedley was at liberty to leave.

(By W. M. Thackeray)

句不友善的话也会让她难过——这就是为什么连平克顿小姐也曾叮嘱所有老师友好地对她,⑨严厉就会伤害到她。

⑩赛特笠小姐既爱哭又爱笑,所以到了动身的一天却很茫然,不知怎样才好。回家固然是件高兴的事,但离开学校也让人悲痛万分。鲜花、礼物以及**箱具**都已放在车上,一个陈旧的小盒子上工整地别着夏普斯小姐的卡片,也放在行李堆上。向校长道别后,赛特笠小姐就可以随时离开了。

(何三宁 译)

Notes: ①The indefinite article "*a*" here indicates the sense "*one*", so it cannot be omitted.

②③④ The pronoun "*she*" used several times in the original is only employed once in Chinese.

⑤⑥⑦ In the original, the possessive pronoun "*her*" is used three times, but it is used only once in Chinese.

⑧⑨⑩ The conjunctions "*for*", "*as*" and "*when*" express the relationship between cause and effect, condition and time respectively. But in Chinese, word order usually denotes this kind of relationship, condition and time etc. Therefore we don't necessarily translate them literally and put them in the way that Chinese are used to. In other words, they may be omitted in Chinese version.

## 2.2.3 Exercises 练习

Ⅰ. Sentence translation.

1. It was out of *the* question to fly to *the* moon in *the* past.
2. Practically every river has *an* upper, *a* middle, and *a* lower part.
3. *We* cannot see sound waves as they travel through air.
4. The dog is stretching *itself*.
5. He glanced at his watch; *it* was 10:45 already.
6. This is the house in *which* I once lived.
7. *On* July 1, 1997, Hong Kong returned to the People's Republic of China.
8. *In* winter, it is much colder *in* the North than it is *in* the South.
9. Early to rise *and* early to bed makes a man healthy.
10. The day *when* she was born remains unknown.
11. *As* it is late, you had better go home.

Ⅱ. Passage translation.

### The Industrial Revolution

The Industrial Revolution is a long train of changes starting in about 1760. It is not alone: it forms one of a triad of revolutions, of which the other two were the American Revolution that started in 1775, and the French Revolution that started in 1789. It may seem strange to put into the same packet an industrial revolution and two political revolutions. But the fact is that they were all social revolutions. The Industrial Revolution is simply the English way of making those social changes. I think of it as the English Revolution.

What makes it especially English? Obviously, it began in England. England was already the leading manufacturing nation. But the manufacture was cottage industry, and the Industrial Revolution begins in the villages. The men who make it are craftsmen: the millwright, the watchmaker, the canal builder, the blacksmith. What makes the Industrial Revolution so peculiarly English is that it is rooted in the countryside.

During the first half of the eighteenth century, in the old age of Newton and the decline of the Royal Society, England basked in a last Indian summer of village industry and the overseas trade of merchant adventures. The summer faded. Trade grew more competitive. By the end of the century the needs of industry were harsher and more pressing. The organization of work in the cottage was no longer productive enough. Within two generations, roughly between 1760 and 1820, the customary way of running industry changed. Before 1760, it was standard to take work to villagers in their own homes. By 1820, it was standard to bring workers into a factory and have them overseen.

(J. Bronowski: *The Ascent of Man*)

## 2.2.4 Amplification 增词翻译

Amplification, also called addition, is a process in which the original has to be translated into Chinese faithfully and smoothly by amplifying some words on the basis of rhetorical and grammatical requirements, and of accurate comprehension of the original as well. According to the principles in translation, we are not supposed to add any meaning to or subtract any meaning from the original work. However, in practice, it is very necessary for us to employ the technique of amplification. This is because English and Chinese are two entirely different languages and each has its own historical and cultural background. Therefore, many ideas, idiomatic expressions and shorthand words, etc. that are well understood in the country of their origin can hardly make sense to people of the other country. In this case, it is unmanageable for a translator to strick to the original pattern without alteration. Consequently amplification is adopted in dealing with such occasions. In principle, we should follow two points for the technique of amplification. One is to amplify something that doesn't exist in the original but exists in meaning according to the context, logical relationship and habits in writing. The other is to amplify the parts omitted in the original. In order to better manipulate the both languages in translating, we handle this method in a practical way.

## 2.2.4.1 Requirements in rhetoric, logic or meaning 修辞、逻辑、意义等方面的需要

### 1) Amplification of Chinese verbs

- In the evening, after *the banquets*, *the concerts and the table tennis exhibitions*, he would work on the drafting of the final communique.
  晚上,在**参加**宴会、**出席**音乐会、**观看**乒乓球表演之后,他还得起草最后公报。
- There were no *speeches*, no *foreign diplomats*, no ordinary Chinese *with paper flags* and *bouquets of flowers*.
  没有**发表**讲话,没有各国外交官**到场**,也没有普通中国人**挥舞**纸旗、花束的场面。
- He dismissed the meeting without *a closing speech*.
  他没有致闭幕词就**宣布**结束会议。

**Comments** Because of the differences between English and Chinese in sentence structure, thinking and even cultures, some parts are usually omitted in English sentences. In the first sentence, the word "*after*" can be followed by its several objects, which are related to various topics. In spite of the preposition "*after*" used in sentence one, it implies a kind of action. In this sense, it is necessary for a translator to amplify Chinese verbs. In addition, English writing often contains several subjects or objects. "*There be*" construction in English may contain more than two subjects which may refer to several different contents. In Chinese language, however, we have to use different verbs to express different actions. The second example is the case. In the third sentence, the Chinese verbs 致 and 宣布 are amplified for the requirement in logic and meaning.

### 2) Amplification of Chinese adverbs

- The crowds *melted* away.
  人群**渐渐**散开了。
- As he sat down and began talking, *words poured out*.
  他一坐下来就讲开了,**滔滔不绝地**讲个没完。
- I had imagined it to be merely a gesture of affection, but it *seems* it is to smell the lamb and make sure that it is her own. (Ann Blackmore: *Lambing Time*)
  **原来**我以为这不过是一种亲热的表示,但是**现在**看来,这是为了闻一闻羊羔的味道,来断定是不是自己生的。

**Comments** Through reading the first two examples, we clearly notice that English verb phrases "*melted away*" and "*poured out*" connote the meanings of 渐渐 and 滔滔不绝地 in Chinese. So we, while translating, necessarily amplify the deep meaning or suggested concepts of English words, phrases, and even sentences. In the last sentence, the tense in the two clauses is quite different, but Chinese language has no such feature. In order to make the meaning smooth and faithful, it is necessary to add an adverb 现在 in Chinese.

### 3) Amplification of Chinese nouns

- Mary *washed* for a living after her husband died of acute pneumonia.
  玛丽在丈夫患急性肺炎去世后，就靠洗**衣服**维持生活。
- First you *borrow*, then you *beg*.
  头一遭借**钱**，下一遭就讨**饭**。
- At 8:30 every morning, she came to her work—*sweeping*, and *scrubbing* and *cleaning*.
  每天上午8点30分，她都来干活——扫**地**、拖**地板**、收拾**房子**。

**Comments** In English, objects are sometimes omitted, and sometimes unnecessarily to be added in sentences. In this case, the object should be amplified in Chinese version. On the other hand, English language has intransitive verbs, which cannot be followed by their objects. In this case, we may add the objects covered in Chinese. The first two sentences are the case. Here are more examples to show this: *Wash before meal.* 饭前洗手。*Wash after getting up.* 起床洗脸。*Wash before going to bed.* 睡前洗脚。 Although the three verbs in the last sentence are transitive verbs, they are *-ing* forms showing different actions. So we should add nouns to express these actions in order to have clear Chinese.

- This typewriter is indeed *cheap and fine*.
  这部打字机真是**价**廉**物**美。
- He is a *complicated* man—moody, mercurial, with a melancholy streak.
  他是一个**性格**复杂的人——喜怒无常，反复多变，有些郁郁寡欢。

**Comments** Adjectives in English are used to express the features of things or characteristics of persons. When we translate adjectives, we necessarily amplify Chinese nouns before them according to their subjects and modifiers.

- *Oxidization* will make iron and steel rust.
  氧化**作用**会使钢铁生锈。

More examples:
persuasion 说服工作    preparation 准备工作    tension 紧张局势
backwardness 落后状态   madness 疯狂行为      arrogance 自满情绪

- He felt the *patriot* rise within his breast.
  他感到一种爱国**热情**在胸中激荡。
- He allowed *the husband* to be overruled by *the judge*, and declared his wife guilty.
  他让法官的**职责**战胜了丈夫的**角色**，而判决他的妻子有罪。

**Comments** In order to keep with the Chinese habits of expression, Chinese nouns are added after English abstract nouns.

### 4) Clearly express English plurals

- *Correspondents* went flying off to Baghdad for interview last month.

上个月,**记者纷纷**飞到巴格达进行采访。

- In spite of the *difficulties*, we succeeded in finishing the task.
  尽管有**各种困难**,我们仍成功地完成了任务。
- There were *rows* of houses which he had never seen before.
  **一排排**的房子,都是他从来没有见到过的。
- The lion is the king of *animals*.
  狮子是**百兽**之王。
- The very earth trembled as with the tramps of *horses* and murmur of angry *men*.
  大地震动,仿佛**万马奔腾**,**千夫怒吼**。

**Comments** By comparison, plural forms of nouns only exist in English language, in Chinese we need to add some words or phrases else to express plural forms. This difference requires us to clearly express English plurals by amplifying necessary words or phrases. In the first three examples, English words "*correspondents*", "*difficulties*", and "*rows*" are plural forms. So we use 纷纷, 各种, 一排排 to express plural concepts. Sometimes we may use Chinese numerals and other phrases to express English plurals. The last two examples show us this method. Here are more examples like this: *mountains* 群山, *flowers* 朵朵鲜花, *white clouds* 朵朵白云.

### 5) Add Chinese modal particles

- Don't take it seriously. I'm just making fun of you.
  不要认真**嘛**! 我不过开开玩笑**罢了**。
- The eyes were the same color as the sea, cheerful and undefeated.
  那双眼**啊**,像海水一样的颜色,愉快而毫不沮丧。
- How time flies!
  时间过得可真快**啊**!

**Comments** There are many modal particles in Chinese like 吧, 呢, 呀, 吗, 啦, etc. We should correctly and properly use them after reading and figuring out the original with great care when we translate imperative, exclamatory, emphatic sentences and even common ones with this sense.

### 6) Add Chinese classifier measure words

- *A red sun* rose slowly from the calm sea.
  **一轮**红日从风平浪静的海面冉冉升起。
- Into the dim clouds was swimming *a crescent moon*.
  **一钩**新月渐渐隐没在朦胧的云彩里去了。
- *A stream* was winding its way through the valley into the river.
  **一弯**溪水蜿蜒流过山谷,汇合到江里去了。

More examples:

a bike 一辆自行车      a tractor 一台拖拉机      a full moon 一轮满月
a typewriter 一架打字机   a mouth 一张嘴        a bad dream 一场噩梦

❖ Look before you leap.

三思而后行。

❖ The essence retains its identity while appearances may vary.

万变不离其宗。

**Comments** First of all we should know there are no classifier measure words in English. But we Chinese often use them to qualify nouns. This difference requires us to carefully add them in Chinese version. This method is much easier for us to handle in translating. However, some beginners cannot correctly use Chinese classifier measure words when coming across them. Unfortunately, they do not take this aspect seriously. For instance, the version of "*a sheep*" is 一群羊、一头羊 or 一只羊? We have to decide which is better or your favourite in actual translation. Note that we avoid ridiculous collocations in amplification. The last two sentences are different cases and there is not any numeral in the original, but sometimes we should follow the features of Chinese language naturally, esp. Chinese idioms and set phrases if necessary.

**7) Add Chinese generalized words**

❖ Thus he grew in both body and soul.

这样,他身心**两方面**都成长起来了。

❖ China, the United States, England and France are members of the UN Security Council.

中、美、英、法**四国**是联合国安理会成员国。

❖ You and I should not do such a thing.

你我**二人**不该干这种事。

❖ This country is militarily, politically and economically strong.

这个国家在军事、政治、经济**等各方面**都很强大。

❖ The principal functions that may be performed by vacuum tubes are rectification, amplification, oscillation, modulation and detection.

真空管的**五大**主要职能是:整流、放大、振荡、调整和检测。

❖ They talked about inflation, unemployment, financial investment and environmental protection.

他们谈到了通货膨胀、失业、金融投资以及环境保护**等问题**。

**Comments** In Chinese, writers frequently use generalized words to generalize several things paralleled together. The above-mentioned sentences are good examples for us to compare and analyze.

**2.2.4.2 Requirements in sentence structure 句子结构的增词**

**1) Amplify the elliptical verbs of the original**

❖ Reading *makes* a full man; conference a ready man; writing an exact man.

读书使人充实,讨论**使人**机智,写作**使人**准确。

❖ We don't *retreat*; we never have and never will.

我们不后退,我们从没有**后退**过,将来也决不**后退**。

**Comments** In the first original sentence, the verb "*makes*" is omitted twice. We should amplify the elliptical verb when rendering. The situation is the same in the second example, but this time we should pay attention to the verb tense. Here the verb "*retreat*" is left out in the original. Therefore, we have to add it in Chinese version. This is a very practical and common technique in translating.

### 2) Amplify the elliptical part omitted in the original

❖ Students should learn from teachers and *vice versa*.
  学生应当向老师学习,**老师也应当向学生学习**。
❖ *Water evaporates more rapidly* when the temperature is high than when it is low.
  温度高,水就蒸发得快;温度低,**水就蒸发得慢**。
❖ The system of job responsibility can be adopted where the conditions are ripe and *not otherwise*.
  条件成熟的地方可以实行工作责任制,**条件不成熟的地方就不要实行**。
❖ Mars: Do you love me?
  Jackson: Yes, of course, I *do*.
  茉尔斯:你爱我吗?
  杰克逊:是的。当然我**爱你**。

**Comments** This is also a very practical and common technique in translating. In the first sentence, "*vice versa*" refers to the way from that just stated, so we have to add the stated part. In the second sentence, the sense of "*Water evaporates less rapidly when it is low*" is omitted. "*Not otherwise*" in the third sentence means that the system of job responsibility can not be adopted where the conditions are not ripe. The last example tells us that the certain part in answering of the original in English sometimes is not mentioned in speech, but necessarily to be amplified in the target language when it appears in literary works. But it really depends on the manner of speaking and the context in particular. We must show the sense clearly in Chinese version. So we conclude that the part omitted in a sentence should be amplified in Chinese version if necessary.

### 2.2.4.3 Amplification for logic 逻辑性增词

❖ *According to scientists*, it takes nature 500 years to create an inch of topsoil.
  根据科学家们**的看法**,自然界要用 500 年的时间才能形成一英寸厚的表层土壤。
❖ This shows that the *resistance* of an electric conductor is inversely proportional to its *cross-section area*.
  这表明,导体电阻的**大小**与导体横切面的**大小**成反比。
❖ *Basically*, the theory proposed, among other things, that the maximum speed possible in the universe is that of light…
  **就其**基本**内容而言**,这一学说提出的论点包括:光速是宇宙中最快的速度……

- ❖ *Ideally*, one day, researchers will know enough about the genesis of earthquakes and the nature of particular faults to predict quakes directly.

  <u>最理想的**情况是**</u>,有朝一日研究人员能够对地震的成因及具体断层的性质有足够的了解,从而能够直接预报地震。

**Comments** Look at these statements above and we can imagine the effects in Chinese versions without amplified parts. This is a useful and practical method to make versions logically. By amplifying "……的看法","……的大小","就其……内容而言"and"最……的情况是"in Chinese, the versions become much more logical and readable.

### 2.2.4.4 Amplification of necessary cultural background 增补背景知识

- ❖ This great scientist was born in New England.

  这位伟大的科学家出生在<u>美国东北部的</u>新英格兰。

- ❖ The *New York Times*, the *Guardian*, *Le Monde*, the *People's Daily* and the *United Morning Post* all reported the nuclear crises in South Asia.

  <u>美国的</u>《纽约时报》、<u>英国的</u>《卫报》、<u>法国的</u>《世界报》、<u>中国的</u>《人民日报》<u>以及新加坡的</u>《联合早报》都对南亚的核危机进行了报道。

- ❖ Nixon learned that China would welcome a presidential visit.

  尼克松了解到,中国将欢迎<u>美国</u>总统<u>来华</u>访问。

- ❖ Those were the words that were to make the world blossom for, "like Aaron's rod, with flowers." (Helen Adams Keller: *The Story of My Life*)

  后来就是这些词把一个美好的世界展现在我的面前,<u>就像《圣经》上说的</u>"亚伦的杖开了花"一样。

**Comments** If we do not add or amplify the necessary cultural background, it must be very difficult for the reader to understand each Chinese sentence above. Even the reader feels confused and puzzled about the original. Therefore, we, in translating, should well know the source of quotations, names and places, and the reference to the books and other materials. We should completely understand the original so that we can offer the necessary information to the reader.

### 2.2.5 Compare and Analyze 比较与分析

1) The human brain weighs three pounds, but in ① that three pounds are ten billion neurons and a hundred billion smaller cells. (I. Asimov: *The Difference between a Brain and a Computer*)

人脑只有三磅重,但就在这三磅①**物质**中,却包含着一百亿个神经细胞以及一千亿个更小的细胞。

2) The difference between me and these daughters was that they saw me, because of my sex, as destined from birth to become like their

我和这些女儿们的分歧在于:由于性别的缘故,她们认为我生来注定要成为她们父亲那样的人,因而也就成为②**妨碍她们实现**自己愿望的敌人。

fathers, and therefore as an ②enemy to their desires. (S. R. Sanders: *Women and Men*)

3) Some had beautiful eyes, ③others a beautiful nose, others a beautiful mouth and figure: few, if any, had all. (T. Hardy: *Tess of the d'Urbervilles*)

4) I felt madly in love with her, and she④ with me. (R. Zacks: *The Date Father Didn't Keep*)

5) My audiences vary ⑤from tens to thousands. I expected ⑥opposition but got hardly⑦any.

她们有的长着漂亮的眼睛,有的③生着俏丽的鼻子,有的有着妩媚的嘴唇、婀娜的身段;但是,这样样都美的,虽然不能说一个没有,却也是寥寥无几。

我狂热地爱上了她,她④也狂热地爱上了我。

我的听众从几十人到几千人⑤不等,我希望持有异议的人⑥起来跟我辩论,但几乎没有⑦遇到过。

Notes: ① The noun 物质 is amplified in this sentence for smoothness.

② In Chinese version, the part 妨碍她们实现 is amplified for the logic and expressive sake.

③ The verb "*had*" omitted in the original should be amplified in Chinese version.

④ Obviously the phrase "*felt madly in love*" is omitted in the second clause, and so it is necessarily added.

⑤ Words of generalization 不等 is amplified here.

⑥ Some Chinese characters are amplified for logic.

⑦ The elliptical part omitted in the original is amplified in the target language.

## 2.2.6 Exercises 练习

Ⅰ. Sentence translation.

1. After the basketball match, he still has an important conference.
2. She lingered long over his letter. (adverb)
3. The recruit threw the grenade 50 meters.
4. The development of economy remains one of the priorities of the Chinese Government. (noun)
5. White clouds float over the blue sky. (plural)
6. Long-range guns aimed at the position of the enemy.
7. Don't get angry. I am just having a joke with you. (modal particle)
8. How time flies!
9. A red sun rising slowly on the horizon. (classifier measure word)
10. He is so absorbed in the work that he hasn't had a bite since morning.
11. Hydrogen burns in air or oxygen, forming water.
12. More thorough testing might have caught the failure initially.

Ⅱ. Passage translation.

### A School Portrait

I had not visited Eton for many years, when one day passing from the Fellows' Library into Gallery I caught sight of the portrait of my school-friend Digby Dolben hanging just without the door among our most distinguished contemporaries. I was wholly arrested, and as I stood gazing on it, my companion asked me if I knew who it was. I was thinking that, beyond a few whom I could name, I must be almost the only person who would know. Far memories of my boyhood were crowding freshly upon me: he was standing again beside me in the eager promise of his youth; I could hear his voice; nothing of him was changed; while I, wrapt from him in a confused mist of time, was wondering what he would think, could he know that at this actual moment he would have been dead thirty years, and that his memory would be thus preserved and honoured in the beloved school, where his delicate spirit had been so strangely troubled.

This portrait-gallery of old Etonians is very select: preeminent distinction of birth or merit may win you a place there, or again official connection with the school, which rightly lives to keep up an unbroken panorama of its teachers, and to vivify its annals with the faces and figures of the personalities who carried on its traditions. But how came Dolben there? It because he was a poet, that I knew; and yet his poems were not known; they were jealously guarded by his family and a few friends: indeed such of his poems as could have come to the eyes of the authorities who sanctioned this memorial would not justify it. There was another reason; and the portrait bears its own credentials; for though you might not perhaps divine the poet in it, you can see the saint, the soul rapt in contemplation, the habit of stainless life, of devotion, of enthusiasm for high ideals. Such a being must have stood out conspicuously among his fellows; the facts of his life would have been the ground of the faith in his genius; and when his early death endeared and sanctified his memory, loving grief would generously grant him the laurels which he had never worn.

(By Robert Bridges)

## 2.3 Semantic Translation 语义翻译

### 2.3.1 Diction 遣词用字

Vocabulary is the unstable element of a language as it is undergoing constant changes both in form and content. Comparatively, the content is even more unstable than the form. Of course, some meanings remain much the same for a long time because the referents to which they direct us do not change. Furthermore, it is necessary for a translator to know the differences and similarities between English and Chinese languages. The former lays emphasis on hypotaxis(形合) and the latter on parataxis(意合). We should possess a strong awareness of this aspect while translating because it will cause us to be free from the influence of the English syntax on our translation from English into Chinese. In comparison with Chinese, English words are characterized by great vacillation(游移性) and flexibility(灵活性); the meaning of a word may range widely and it depends much on the contextual relationship. That is to say, each word when used in a different context will have a new meaning. Context plays a very important role in understanding the meaning of an English word. Whereas Chinese words, which do not range so widely as English words do, are comparatively rigorous, accurate and fixed in meaning. The vacillation and flexibility of English words are mainly shown by polysemy, therefore, it is often a hard task for a translator to find his Chinese equivalents that are suitable to the occasion. At the same time, we should also pay special attention to English word classes while translating from English into Chinese.

As far as diction is concerned, it is all the time a practical concern and issue that all the translators and English majors encounter in translation. Generally speaking, both English and Chinese words may be classified into five ranks, namely, words in two languages with complete equivalents, words with similar meanings (synonyms), words with various meanings (polysemy), words overlapping in meaning, and words with completely different meanings (antonyms). As to our translators, we are mainly concerned about polysemy, synonyms, words overlapping in meaning and other cases.

By diction we mean the proper choice of words and phrases in translation on the basis of accurate comprehension of the original. In the practice of translation, what perplexes us most frequently is how to find an equivalent in the language to be translated into. Great care is called in the translation of familiar English words into Chinese, as their meanings vary with the change in collocation or context.

### 2.3.1.1 Polysemy 一词多义

Polysemy is a common feature peculiar to all natural languages. This is particularly true of highly developed languages like English. In modern English, an overwhelming majority of words are polysemous. A casual glance of any page of an English dictionary will justify the fact that there are words that have two or three senses, and the most commonly-used ones can have as many as over a hundred. Let us examine just a few words for example. The word "*regular*" may have different meanings on different occasions.

- ❖ regular reading 一般阅读　　　regular job 固定工作
  regular flight 定期航班　　　　regular visitor 常客
  regular speed 匀速　　　　　　regular army 正规军
  regular gasoline 普通汽油

The word "*delicate*" will do the same. Look at the word "*delicate*" carefully in the different situations below.

- ❖ delicate skin 娇嫩的皮肤　　　　delicate porcelain 精致的瓷器
  delicate upbringing 娇生惯养　　　delicate living 奢侈的生活
  delicate health 虚弱的身体　　　　delicate stomach 容易吃坏的胃
  delicate vase 容易碰碎的花瓶　　　delicate diplomatic question 微妙的外交问题
  delicate difference 讲不大清楚的差异　delicate surgical operation 难做的外科手术

delicate ear for music 对音乐有鉴赏力    delicate sense of smell 灵敏的嗅觉
delicate touch 生花妙笔    delicate food 美味的食物

Although numerous definitions have been suggested in dictionaries, scholars still do not think that all of them seem to be perfect. This is because today new words sweep in at a rate much faster than at any other historical period of time. With the rapid development of modern science and technology, with social, economic and political changes, and the influence of other cultures and languages, new words are being invented or introduced every day to express new things and new changes in society. Simultaneously, the present words, because of the changes and influences, have increasingly had other meanings in modern English. So the meanings of the "old words" vary with the changing contexts. Now let us take the word "*identity*" for example.

❖ He also had been demanding that all Irishmen living in Britain be required to carry *identity cards*.

当时,他还一直要求所有居住在大不列颠的爱尔兰人必须携带**身份证**。

❖ Their *sexual identity*, like that of all women competitors, had been officially confirmed by the Olympic Femininity Control Clinic.

她们的**性别鉴定**,像所有的女运动员的性别鉴定一样,已由奥林匹克女性医务监察部正式核实。

❖ Lee has again and again stressed the need for his tiny nation to develop its own Singaporean—as opposed to Chinese—*identity*.

李光耀再三强调他的这个小小国家有必要发展自己的新加坡人的**特点**,以有别于中国人。

❖ In Poland, loyalty to the church became the only means of defending *national identity*.

波兰,效忠教会现成为保护**民族意识**的唯一手段。

❖ A young nation struggling to establish *its identity* produced leaders, such as Jefferson and Jackson, dedicated to a democratic process which, however, excluded Indians and blacks.

年轻的美国在奋力确立**国家体制**之际,产生了诸如杰弗逊和杰克逊那样的领袖,他们致力于民主制度的建立,然而这种民主制度是把印第安人和黑人排除在外的。

**Comments** In translating, polysemy is really a headache for beginners and even old hands. In the above examples, the word "*identity*" has a different sense in each context. Such a phenomenon tells us that word meaning must be judged by the context, instead of simply by a dictionary entry. For instance, "*cards*" in sentence 1 and "*sexual*" in sentence 2 give us a clear hint to decide their definitions. The last three sentences should be carefully read and analyzed by the context, and then we figure out what each sentence mainly talks about, and lastly decide what sense it is in the context.

### 2.3.1.2 Extension 词义引申

The word "extension", also called "generalization", is a term of Latin origin referring to the stretching of meaning. Most words begin as specific names for things. With the passage of time, this precise denotation is lost and the word meaning is extended, generalized or blurred. Extension of meaning is the name given to the widening of meaning, which some words undergo. It is a process by which a word that originally had a specialized meaning becomes generalized. In other words, the term has extended to cover a broader and often less definite concept. A good example is the word "*manuscript*" which now means "any author's writing whether by hand or typed with a type-writer or a word-processor". Its original meaning was "handwriting" only, i.e. writing by hand. Another example is the word "*fox*". Its original meaning is "a kind of doglike animal", but its extended meaning is "a person who deceives others by means of clever tricks".

One more word "*picture*" is given to show extension of meaning. It once meant only a painted picture, then also a drawing, then a photograph, a cinematic picture, an X-ray picture, a TV picture, and now even a radio-telescope picture. While the referent was once a fixed stable object, "*picture*" now names a class of things that can be broken up, reassembled, and dissolved in the case of laser holography, even three-dimensional. Therefore, in translating, we should pay much attention to such a phenomenon. Besides what we have discussed above, we mainly talk about a couple of points below concerning extension.

**1) Extend the word meaning to cover an abstraction concept**

- Every life has its *roses and thorns*.
  每个人的生活都<u>有苦有甜</u>。
- There is a mixture of *the tiger and the ape* in the character of the imperialists.
  帝国主义者的特性是<u>既残暴又狡猾</u>。
- His novel is *a mirror* of the times.
  他的小说是时代的<u>一面镜子</u>。

**Comments** In the first 2 sentences, "*roses and thorns*", "*the tiger and the ape*" are extended to contain abstract concepts expressing the characteristics of these things or animals. In the last sentence, "*a mirror*" is a specific thing used to express the abstraction concept of an exact or close representation. Here "*a mirror*" is not an actual thing but reflects the society that the author wants to describe. In other words, "*His novel is an epitome of the times*". We can find a lot of examples like these: *mend one's fences* 改善关系, *lick one's boots* 巴结某人, *break the ice* 打破僵局, *put one's cards on the table* 表明观点或态度, *eat like a bird* 吃得极少, *catch forty winks* 打个盹儿, etc. In these phrases, some words are specific and countable nouns, but when they are fixed in certain phrases, they should be rendered to cover an abstraction concept or something like that.

- ❖ The OED is *the final court of appeal* in all matters concerning English words.
  《牛津辞典》是英文所有词语方面的问题的**最高权威**。
- ❖ Sam knows he can depend on his family, *rain or shine*.
  萨姆知道**无论境况如何**,他都可以将家庭作为靠山。
  (或:萨姆知道无论下雨还是晴天,他都可以依靠他的家庭。)
- ❖ *See-sawing* between partly good and faintly ominous, the news for the next four weeks was never distinct.
  在那以后的四个星期里,消息时而部分有所好转,时而又有点不妙,**两种情况不断交替出现**。
- ❖ If he is unhappy with her…why doesn't he leave her? She can be happy without him. It is so silly—this *cat-and-dog existence*.
  假使他同她在一块是那么不幸福……他为什么不离开她呢?她没有他还可以幸福的。这是多么无聊啊——**这种经常争吵的生活**。

**Comments** The specific concepts are extended to cover abstract concepts. The specific things or creatures containing in words or phrases will be extended into abstract ones to show their features and symbolization.

**2) Extend the word meaning to cover a specific concept**

- ❖ In two years, he was a national *phenomenon*.
  两年以后,他成了风靡全国的**杰出人物**。
- ❖ Victory always goes to *the strong*.
  胜利永远属于**强者**。
- ❖ Vietnam was his *entree* to the new Administration, his third incarnation as a foreign policy consultant.
  越南战争成了他进入新政府的**敲门砖**,他担任政府的对外政策顾问,那是第三次了。
- ❖ Have you read any *humour* recently?
  近来你读了什么**幽默作品**吗?
- ❖ As a boy, he was *the despair* of all his teachers.
  小时候,他是个使所有老师**失望的孩子**。
- ❖ Public opinion is demanding more and more that *something* be done about noise.
  公众舆论越来越强烈地要求为消除噪音采取**某些措施**。

**Comments** In these sentences, "*phenomenon*", "*the strong*", "*entree*", "*humor*", "*despair*" and "*something*" are all the abstract words or phrases, but in Chinese versions, each of them presents a specific person or thing. So we should know that some abstract English words could be extended into specific concepts in translating in order that we have smooth, understandable and authentic Chinese versions.

### 2.3.1.3 Word classes 一词多性

In English language, there is a phenomenon in which a word can go to several classes. One translator has to pay much attention to this aspect while rendering English materials because a word may have completely different senses when used as different classes.

*milk*: When used as a noun refers to a white liquid produced by human or animal females for feeding their young, but when it is used as a verb, it means to take milk from a cow, goat or other animals.

*manifold*: When used as an adjective means many in number, but it just refers to a pipe when used as a noun. When it is used as a verb, it means to copy.

Therefore, in translating, we have to well know the sentence structure and the key words in the sentence. Meanwhile, we try to understand the figures of speech or word classes. Finally, we should not forget the context so that we can choose the correct meaning. Take the word "*bridge*" for example.

- He pushed his spectacles higher on the *bridge* of his nose.
  他把<u>鼻梁</u>上的眼镜往上推了推。
- The construction workers threw a *bridge* across the river.
  建筑工人在那条河上架起了一座<u>大桥</u>。
- No concession can *bridge* over the chasms between the two groups.
  无论何种让步也不能<u>弥合</u>这两个集团间的裂缝。
- He *bridged* the awkward silence with a funny remark.
  他说了句笑话,<u>打破</u>了尴尬的冷场。

**Comments** In the first two sentences, the word "*bridge*" is a noun, referring to 鼻梁 or 大桥. But it is different in meaning when used as a verb, meaning "*close and break the ice*", just as in the last two sentences. From these examples, we can learn that word meanings will not only be determined by different contexts, but also by parts of speech.

### 2.3.2 Principles in Diction 选词的原则

#### 2.3.2.1 Select word meaning according to word classes 依据词性选择词义

- *Like* charges repel; *unlike* charges attract. (adjective)
  <u>相同的</u>电荷相斥,<u>不同的</u>电荷相吸。
- He *likes* mathematics more than physics. (verb)
  他<u>喜欢</u>数学甚于喜欢物理学。
- In the sunbeam passing through the window there are fine grains of dust shining *like* gold. (preposition)

在射入窗内的阳光里,细微的尘埃**像**金子一般在闪闪发亮。

❖ *Like* knows *like*. (noun)
**英雄**识**英雄**。

**Comments** Everybody knows the word "*like*", but when it is used as different parts of speech, it has different senses in translating. The above-mentioned sentences are good examples in this case.

### 2.3.2.2 Decide word meaning according to the contextual and logical relationship 依据上下文与逻辑关系选择词义

In English, there are two sentences that we should memorize and follow. They are: "No context, no text."(没有上下文,就不能正确理解词义。) and "You know a word by the company it keeps."(理解一个词,要看它的搭配关系。) Let us compare a couple of sentences below.

❖ *The books are closed*, as the company is privately owned.
这是一家私营公司,**账目对外保密**。

❖ *The books are closed* before the dictation gets started.
**书本合上后**再开始听写。(或:请听写时合上书本。)

**Comments** In the two sentences, the context in the first one lies in a privately owned company. The context in the second sentence is, however, in class or a classroom. So the word "*books*" has a different sense in each example because it has a different context. In this sense, a text depends really on the context in translation.

❖ In reading, we must let our eyes rest *once in a while*.
阅读当中,**每隔一段时间**就让眼睛休息一下。

❖ We go for a picnic in the park *once in a while*.
我们**偶尔**去公园野炊。

**Comments** In this pair, "*once in a while*" has different meanings in the different contexts. In sentence one, the phrase indicates "*from time to time*"(每隔一段时间). However, in sentence two, it refers to "*not often*" or "*not regularly*"(偶尔).

❖ "*I'm going to have a class*," the girl said.
那女生说:"我去**听课**。"

❖ "*I'm going to have a class*," the teacher said.
老师说:"我去**给学生讲课**。"

**Comments** In this pair of examples, we can find the same sentence "*I'm going to have a class*", but it has completely different senses in both sentences. This is because the words "*girl*" and "*teacher*" decide the meaning of the sentence "*I'm going to have a class*". From these examples, we can thoroughly understand how important context is in translating.

### 2.3.2.3 Translate literally without any extension 字面直译

❖ The invention of printing was *a milestone* in human progress.

印刷术的发明是人类进步的一个**里程碑**。
- ❖ But when you have learned English, you'll find it *a bridge* to so much knowledge.

但是,当你学会了英语,你就会发现它是通向如此丰富知识的**桥梁**。

**Comments** Sometimes, we can directly make choice of English word meaning in Chinese translation because both languages have the same expressions.

### 2.3.2.4 Suit words or phrases to Chinese description 依汉语的表达习惯译

- ❖ The history teacher told us that making an outline *kills two birds with one stone*. It makes us study the lesson till we understand it, and it gives us notes to review before the test.

  历史老师说列出提纲可以**一箭双雕**,既可帮助我们理解课文,又为我们复习应试提供材料。

- ❖ *He who has a mind to beat his dog will easily find a stick.*

  **欲加之罪,何患无辞**。

**Comments** Some English idioms or set phrases contain the similar implications in Chinese idioms although they express in different ways. In this case, we should render them in Chinese way in order to suit the needs of Chinese readers. For instance, "*kill two birds with one stone*" can be translated into 一箭双雕, not 一石双鸟. The translation of the sentence "*He who has a mind to beat his dog will easily find a stick*" is 欲加之罪,何患无辞. We can not say in Chinese like 想打狗的人很容易找到棍子.

### 2.3.3 Commendatory and Derogatory 词义的褒贬

When the meaning of a word narrows toward a more favorable meaning, it is called elevation or amelioration. For example, "naughty" once meant wicked and depraved. Today it means only mild mischief. "Mischief" itself once meant wicked behavior. Today it can apply to a merely naughty child. At one time, "shrewd" meant depraved or wicked. Today it is somewhat complimentary. Simultaneously, when the meaning of a word narrows toward an unfavorable meaning, it is called degeneration or pejorative change. Some words once respectable may become less so and others once neutral in meaning may acquire a pejorative connotation. For example, the word "peasant" originally was a person who worked on the land, but now it usually refers to a person without education or manners. Such a change has its own historical background, yet we are really required to notice such changes in translation.

In English, it is true that some words are originally used in derogatory sense, some in commendatory sense and others in neutral. When we translate the words in derogatory sense, we have to make them fall into ill reputation, and vice versa. If we know elevation and degeneration of word meaning in mind and follow some principles, everything in this case will be carried out under way in translation.

**1) Directly express meanings of commendatory and derogatory words.**

- He was a man of high *renown*.
  他是位<u>有名望</u>的人。
- His *notoriety* as a rake did not come until his death.
  他作为流氓的<u>恶名</u>是在死后才传开的。
- The tasks carried out by them are *praiseworthy*.
  他们所进行的事业是<u>值得赞扬的</u>。
- Henry keeps *boasting* that he has talked to the President.
  亨利总是<u>吹嘘说</u>他曾同总统谈过话。
- "He was *polite* and always gave advice willingly," she recalled.
  她回忆说:"他<u>彬彬有礼</u>,总是诲人不倦。"
- We were shocked by his *coarse* manners.
  我们对他的<u>粗暴</u>态度感到震惊。
- The boy is appreciated by all his teachers for his *carefulness* in his homework.
  这个男孩因功课做得<u>仔细认真</u>而受到所有老师的赞赏。
- In fact, it is his *meticulousness* that is preventing him from making any progress in his research work.
  事实上,正是因为他的<u>谨小慎微</u>,他的研究工作才得不到任何进展。

**Comments** Carefully studying the above sentences, we will easily identify some of the underlined words are derogatory in meaning, and some are commendatory. The words "renown", "praiseworthy", "carefulness" and "polite" are commendatory in meaning, and "notoriety", "boasting", "meticulousness" and "coarse" are derogatory in meaning. So we are expected to directly express meanings of commendatory and derogatory words in Chinese versions.

**2) When we translate some neutral words, we should decide whether they are commendatory or derogatory according to the context.**

- That young man has a bright *future* before him as a painter.
  那个年轻人当画家的<u>前途</u>十分光明。
  It was time to hold a court and the subject for discussion was the *future* of that prisoner. ( = life in front of somebody)
  开庭时间到了,大家讨论的话题是那名罪犯的<u>下场</u>。
- John was an *aggressive* salesman who did his job quite well. ( = not afraid of opposition)
  约翰是个<u>积极肯干</u>的推销员,他工作干得很出色。
  Hitler pursued an *aggressive* policy after he seized power. ( = always ready to attack)

希特勒夺取了政权之后就推行**侵略**政策。

◆ The *stubborn* boy refused to listen to his parents' advice.

这个<u>犟</u>男孩不肯听父母的忠告。

The invaders met a *stubborn* resistance from the local people.

侵略者遭到了当地人民<u>顽强的</u>抵抗。

◆ The old couple made a *persistent* effort to search for their daughter lost in the earthquake.

这对年老的夫妇<u>执著地</u>寻找着他们在地震中丢失的女儿。

She was vexed by the *persistent* ringing of the phone.

<u>没完没了的</u>电话铃声搞得她心烦意乱。

**Comments** Let us compare the four pairs of sentences above. In the first sentence, the word "*future*" indicates that the young man will become successful and famous. In the second one, the word "*future*" is derogatory in meaning, judging from the context, expressing a life in front of the prisoner. In the second pair of sentences, we also have the same word "*aggressive*", but it is commendatory in the former sentence and derogatory in the latter depending on the context. The word "*stubborn*" in the next pair has the different versions, and the word "*persistent*" in the last pair is also rendered into different translations, although they are neutral in meaning. A neutral word is determined by its context and its mode of behaving in a certain sentence, and then is decided whether derogatory or commendatory in meaning.

## 2.3.4 Compare and Analyze 比较与分析

| | |
|---|---|
| "We all have five to seven mutations," Bombard said. "In the absence of a clinical history, ① <u>the picture</u> is not meaningful and there's a potential for ②<u>harm</u> to be done and the patient wouldn't benefit. That's why we encourage genetic counseling to determine when it is appropriate to do what test." | "我们都有五到七种变异,"鲍姆伯德说,"由于缺乏临床病史记载,①<u>这种说法</u>没有多大意义,②<u>危害身体</u>的可能性对病人没什么好处。这也是我们鼓励进行遗传咨询来确定何时适合进行何种测试的原因。" |

**Notes:** ① Here the translator does not put it literally, whereas he makes choice of the word meaning so carefully that the Chinese version 这种说法 completely is in keeping with Chinese expression and the context.

② It is a word with abstract concept so that it is necessary to add 危害身体 according to the context.

| | |
|---|---|
| Politicians joined thousands of demonstrators on Sunday in a third①<u>straight</u> day of protests against the acquittal of four police officers who killed②<u>unarmed</u> African immigrant Amadon Dialo a year ago in a③<u>a hail of</u> gunshots. | 星期日,即①<u>连续</u>抗议的第三天,政治家们加入了数千人参加的游行队伍,反对无罪释放四名警察,正是他们一年前用枪③<u>一阵狂扫</u>残杀了②<u>手无寸铁的</u>非洲移民阿莫多·迪埃罗。 |

**Notes**: ① The word "*straight*" is translated into 连续, while it has the sense 一直的 literally. By doing so, the Chinese version feels smooth and acceptable.

② Here we should pay much attention to diction or wording in Chinese.

③ The phrase "*a hail of*" means a number of things which strike suddenly with violence, causing pain or damage. Its Chinese version may be 突如其来的袭击, but the translator uses 一阵狂扫, which is very descriptive and vivid. In short, we should notice changes in word meaning while translating.

### 2.3.5 Exercises 练习

Ⅰ. **Sentence translation.**

A) **Translate the following sentences into Chinese according to different word classes.**

1. He *likes* surf-riding.
2. It doesn't look *like* rain.
3. We will never see his *like* again.
4. I can't cook *like* you do.
5. The teacher cannot cite a *like* instance.
6. *Like* enough it will snow.
7. It is not *right* for children to sit up late.
8. The plane was *right* above our heads.
9. In the negative, *right* and left, and black and white are reversed.
10. She tried her best to *right* her husband from the charge of robbery.

B) **Translate the sentences bellow, paying attention to the underlined words in context.**

1. The foreign trade has risen to unprecedented *figures*.
2. Dr. Edward was one of the most reverend *figures* in the world of learning.
3. He saw dim *figures* moving towards him.
4. On the desk there was a bronze *figure* of Plato.
5. Jane was good at *figure* skating.

C) **Translate the following sentences, paying attention to the underlined words with different extensions.**

a. Extend the underlined words or phrases to cover abstraction concepts.

1. Rocks made under water *tell another story*.
2. He is *a rolling stone*.
3. *I have no head* for mathematics.
4. He always *seeks help at the last moment*.
5. Don't dispute over *trifles*.
6. Fatty's Restaurant had become an *institution* in his life in the last seven years.
7. The invention of machinery had brought into the world a new era—the Industrial Age. Money had become *king*.

b. Extend the meaning of underlined words or phrases to cover specific concepts.

8. The Sphinx is *a must* for most foreign visitors to Egypt.

9. It is *a hard nut to crack*.

10. It is hard to get along with a man who *blows hot and cold*.

11. You are really *casting pearls before swine*.

12. If a person *falls into a groove*, he always acts, behaves and thinks in the same way.

D) **Translate the following sentences, paying attention to the underlined parts of commendatory or derogatory.**

1. Hans was too obviously *flattering* the gentleman by saying he was the most courageous man he had ever seen.

2. Mr. Brown felt greatly *flattered* when he received the invitation to deliver a lecture.

3. She is fidgety and *restless*.

4. All the inventors have a *restless* mind.

5. *As luck would have it*, no one was in the building when the explosion occurred.

6. *As luck would have it*, there was rain on the day of the picnic.

7. Many people think that he is one of the most *ambitious* politicians of our times.

8. Although he is very young, he is very *ambitious* in his research work.

II. **Passage translation.**

### How to Grow Old

Some old people are ①*oppressed* by the fear of death. In the young there is a justification for this feeling. Young men who have reason to fear that they will be ②*killed* in battle may justifiably feel bitter in the thought that they have been cheated of the best things that life has to offer. But in an old man who has known human ③*joys and sorrows*, and has achieved whatever work it was in him to do, the fear of death is somewhat ④*abject* and *ignoble*. The best way to overcome it—so at least it seems to me—is to make your interests gradually wider and more impersonal, until bit by bit the walls of the ego recede, and your life becomes increasingly merged in the universal life. An individual human existence should be like a river—small at first, narrowly contained within its banks, and rushing passionately past boulders and over waterfalls. Gradually the river grows wider, the banks recede, the waters flow more quietly, and in the end, without any visible break, they become merged in the sea, and can painlessly lose their individual being. The man who, in old age, can see his life in this way, will not suffer from the fear of death, since the things he cares for will continue. And if, with the ⑤*decay* of vitality, ⑥*weariness* increases, the thought of ⑦ *rest* will be not unwelcome. I should wish to die while still at work, knowing that others will carry on what I can no longer do, and content in the thought that what was possible has been done.

(By Bertrand Russel: *How to Grow Old*, from *Portraits from Memory and Other Essays*)

## 2.4 Number Translation 数字的翻译

When we translate something, especially the materials concerning trade, we have to come across a lot of numerals. In general, it is easy for translators to deal with English numerals and percentage. You can just copy the digits in your translation. But we should still see that it is very easy for us to make errors in translating them. For example, "*Four* out of five earned more than 25,000 dollars a year, two out of five earned more than 50,000 dollars a year, 3 per cent were Jews, 3 per cent black, 22 per cent Catholic, and one fifth of 1 per cent were union officials." The Chinese version for this sentence should be:每5个人当中有4个人的收入每年在25,000美元以上,每5个人当中有2人的收入每年在50,000美元以上。有3%是犹太人,3%是黑人,22%是天主教徒,0.2%是工会官员。This is a very typical English example. There are several numbers in this example. It's easy for us to translate the numbers like 25,000, 50,000, 3 percent, etc. But it's a little bit difficult to put *one fifth of* 1 *per cent* into Chinese.

The best way to correctly translate numerals is to read the original carefully and to proofread it with great care. Meanwhile, we should notice the different expressions underlying the two languages. Now let us talk about some great concerns that all of us should focus on.

### 2.4.1 Some English Numbers 一些英语数字的翻译

There are some common English numbers that are usually used in materials about science and trade. In the first place, we should manage to memorize some commonly used ones like hundred (100 or 百), thousand (1,000 or 千) and million (1,000,000 or 百万). At the same time, we should also know such numbers as *billion*, *trillion*, *quadrillion* and *quintillion*, which are quite different between American use and British use. Now let us look at some sentences with numerals and compare the original and the versions.

- ❖ Foreign funds flowed into China in a spectacular way. The stock of foreign investment grew from under $5 billion in 1989 to nearly $90 billion by 1994.
  外资大量投向中国,外商投资总量由1989年的不足50亿美元增长到1994年的近900亿美元。

- ❖ China has a grassland area of 390 million hectares, of which about 320 million hectares can be used, which places China third in the world in the area of usable grassland.
  中国现有草地面积3.9亿公顷,其中可利用面积3.2亿公顷,居世界第三位。

- ❖ In 1977, the sum total of Chinese imports and exports was less than $15 billion, putting China's share of world trade at 0.6 percent.
  在1977年,中国进出口总额还不到150亿美元,仅占世界贸易总额的0.6%。

In the second place, we should know some common phrases, which are composed of numerals and prepositions, or numerals and other words. They are usually used to indicate the indefinite scope or phenomenon, sometimes to indicate the statue of substances.

by thousands 数以千计;大量          by hundreds 数以百计
by (the) millions 数以百万计         by halves 不完全地

thousands of 数千;数以千计
hundreds of thousands of 几十万;无数的
thousands upon thousands of 成千上万
millions upon millions of 千百万
dozens of 几打;几十个
billions of 几十亿
ten to one 十之八九
nine tenths 十之八九;几乎全部
several millions of 数百万
by one hundred percent 百分之百地;全部
a few tens of 十分之几;有几成
in two twos 转眼;立即
one or two 少许;几个
two over three 2/3
second to none 首屈一指
a decade of 10 个一组
a dozen of 12 个;一打

hundreds of 数百;数以百计
tens of, decades of 数十个
scores of 许多
hundreds of millions 亿万
a hundred and one 许多
a thousand and one 无数的
nine cases out of ten 十之八九
tens of thousands 好几万
fifty-fifty 各半的;对半的;平均
a long hundred 一百多;一百二十
by twos and threes 三三两两;零零散散
at sixes and sevens 乱七八糟
twenty and twenty 许多
first of all 首先
last but one 倒数第二
a score of 20 个一组
a long dozen 13 个

Now look at some sentences with the numeral phrases.

◆ They packed the oranges *in tens*.
他们把橘子<u>十个十个</u>地装成盒。

◆ *Ten to one* she has forgotten it.
她<u>十有八九</u>把这件事给忘了。

◆ We do nothing *by halves*.
我们不会做事<u>不彻底</u>。

◆ Her name ranks *last but one* on the list.
她的名字在名单上排在<u>倒数第二</u>。

◆ Let's go *fifty-fifty* on the dinner check.
餐费咱们<u>均摊</u>吧!

◆ In a few minutes the students began to come in *by twos and threes*.
几分钟之后,学生们<u>三三两两</u>走了进来。

**Comments** From the numbers above, we can see that we should not translate them directly and literally because these numbers indicate the indefinite scope rather than the exact numerals. We, while translating them, should understand their real meanings and conceptions.

## 2.4.2 Translation of Approximate Numbers 约数的翻译

We can find approximate numbers in both English and Chinese, which are used to express indefinite conceptions. For instance, Chinese expressions like 几个、十来个、若干、大约、大概、左右、上下、约有、不到、多于、少于, etc. can be found the equivalent for each in English. Let us carefully look at the following points, which contain very useful English expressions about approximate numbers underlying between English and Chinese.

**1) *More than*, *above*, *over*, *past*, *in excess of*, *or more*, *long*, *odd*, *etc.* can be used to express Chinese 多于、多、超过, etc.**

| | |
|---|---|
| 100 多公斤 | *more than* one hundred kilograms |
| | *above* one hundred kilograms |
| | *over* one hundred kilograms |
| | a hundred kilograms *or more* |
| 1,000 多英里 | a *long* thousand miles |
| 3 个多小时 | three *long* hours |
| 1 公里多 | a *long* kilometer |
| 6 万多 | sixty thousand *odd* |
| 六万几千 | sixty *odd* thousand |
| 八十几厘米 | eighty *odd* centimeters |
| 八百零几克 | eighty hundred *odd* grams |

❖ The weight of this child is said to be *over* one hundred pounds.
  据说这个孩子的体重有 100 **多**磅。

❖ It took me *more than* two hours to finish the homework.
  我花了两个**多**小时才做完家庭作业。

❖ This car has run a *long* thousand miles.
  这辆车已经跑了 1,000 **多**英里。

❖ There are three thousand *odd* students in this normal school.
  这所师范学校有 3,000 **多**名学生。

❖ She is *past* eighty.
  她 80 **多**了。

**2) *Less than*, *under*, *below*, *off*, *or less*, *etc.* can be used to express Chinese 不到、少于、低于, etc.**

| | |
|---|---|
| 不到 80 美元 | *less than* eighty dollars |
| | *under* eighty dollars |
| | *below* eighty dollars |
| | eighty dollars *or less* |

❖ She won't sell this turkey *under* twenty-five dollars.

这只火鸡**低于** 25 美元她是不会卖的。

- The price of that tricycle is *less than* one hundred and eighty-five francs.
  那辆三轮车的售价**还不到** 185 法郎。

- He bought the coffeepot at 6 dollars *off* the list price.
  他以**低于**价目表 6 美元的价格买下了那个咖啡壶。

3) *Or so*, *more or less*, *about*, *in the region of*, *approximately*, *some*, *around*, *etc.* can be used to express Chinese 大约、左右、上下 and others of the like.

| | |
|---|---|
| 11 点钟左右 | *somewhere about* eleven o'clock |
| 约 5 万吨 | *approximately* 50,000 tons |
| 近 3 个月 | three months *or so* |
| 1,000 元左右 | *in the region of* 1,000 yuan |
| 600 公里左右 | 600 kilometers *more or less* |
| 大约两周 | *about* a fortnight |

- The college subscribes to two hundred and fifty magazines *or so*.
  这所学院订阅的杂志**大约**有 250 种。

- Her monthly pay is *in the region of* 400 dollars.
  她的月薪在 400 美元**左右**。

- I get up *around* half past five every morning.
  我每天早上五点半**左右**起床。

4) **We can still use English whole numbers to express approximate Chinese conceptions.**

- I have told you *twenty* times.
  我给你讲过**多少**遍了。

- *A million* thanks for your kindness.
  对你的好意**万分**感谢。

- We have *a hundred* things to do.
  我们还有**许多**事情要做。

- A wonder lasts but *nine days*.
  什么事儿也新鲜不了**多久**。

- She has *fifty* things to tell you.
  她有**许多**话要对你说。

If we want to express the Chinese meanings of 不多不少、刚好、整整, we can employ words such as *flat*, *clear*, *sharp*, *cool*, *just*, *whole*, *exactly*, with whole numbers together.

- He finished the 100-meter dash in 10 seconds *flat*.
  他跑完 100 米**正好**用了 10 秒钟。

- The chief physician treated *cool* 40 patients that day.

  这位主任医生那天治疗的病人<u>整整</u>40人。

**Comments** It is here worth mentioning about the exact numbers for expressing approximate conceptions. Some exact numbers in English, sometimes, show approximate concepts. We may carefully compare the examples in point 4 for further reference.

### 2.4.3 Compare and Analyze 比较与分析

Suppose that we lined up our ①<u>roughly 14 million</u> US businesses in order of size, starting with the smallest, along an imaginary road from San Francisco to New York. There will be 4,500 businesses to the mile, or a little less than one per foot. Suppose further that we planned a flag for each business. The height of the flagpole represents the annual volume of sales and each ②<u>$10,000</u> in sales is shown by one foot of pole.

The line of flagpoles is a very interesting sight. From San Francisco to about Nevada, it is almost unnoticeable, a row of poles about a foot high. From Reno eastward the poles increase in height until, near Columbus, Ohio—③<u>about four-fifths</u> of the way across the nation—flags fly about 10 feet in the air.

But as we approach the eastern terminus, the poles suddenly begin to mount. There are about 300,000 firms in the country with sales ④<u>over $500,000</u>. These corporations occupy the last 75 miles of the 3,000-mile road. There are 200,000 firms with sales ⑤<u>over $1 million</u>. They occupy the last 50 miles. Then there are 1,000 firms with sales of ⑥<u>$50,000,000 or more</u>. They take up ⑦<u>the last quarter mile</u> before the city limits, flags

美国大概有①**1,400万**家商行，假设我们按其规模大小排列，从最小的开始，沿着一条想像的路线从旧金山一直排到纽约。那么，每英里将有4,500家商行，或者说每英尺就将近有一家商行。我们进一步设想为每一家商行树一杆旗帜，旗杆的高度代表商行的年销售量，每一英尺的旗杆表示②**1万美元（10,000美元）**的销售量。

这种旗杆的队列会是一种非常有趣的景象。从旧金山到内华达州的里诺附近，这些高约一英尺的旗杆队列几乎不引人注意。但从里诺一直向东至俄亥俄州的哥伦布市的附近延伸，旗杆高度不断在增加——横跨美国③**大约五分之四**的路程——旗帜便会在大约10英尺高的空中飘扬。

但是，当我们接近东部终点时，旗杆突然开始增高。全国大约有30万家商行的年销售量④**超过50万美元（500,000美元）**。而这些公司就集中在全程3,000英里的最后75英里。20万家公司⑤**超过100万美元**，它们集中在最后50英里。再往前延伸，有1,000家公司的销售量达到或⑥**超过5千万美元（50,000,000美元）**，它们在到达纽约市前的⑦**最后四分之一**英里，这些旗杆在5,000英尺高度的云端飘扬。

flying at cloud height, 5,000 feet up.

　　At the very gates of New York, on the last 100 feet of the last mile, we find the 100 largest industrial firms. They have sales of ⑧ at least ＄1.5 billion, so that their flags are already miles high. Along the last 10 feet of road, there are the 10 largest companies. Their sales are ⑨roughly ＄10 billion and up. Their flags fly 190 miles in the air, literally in the stratosphere.

就在纽约市的边缘，即最后一英里的最后 100 英尺的路上，我们看到 100 家最大的工业公司。它们的年销售量⑧<u>至少达 15 亿美元</u>，它们的旗杆已有一英里之高。在这条想像道路的最后 10 英尺，有 10 家最大的公司。它们的销售量⑨<u>大概有 100 亿美元甚至更高</u>。它们的旗帜会处在 190 英里的高空，几乎可以说是在同温层里飘扬。

注：选自唐述宗，《托福应试大全》，浙江大学出版社，1990。译文有修改。

**Notes**: In this passage, there are many numbers, some of which will be chosen to show the techniques in translating them. Firstly, we should pay attention to English number words like *million*, *billion* and the like, and render them correctly. Secondly, when we translate numbers like ②④⑥, we have two ways: one is to directly put them into Arabic numerals, that is, ＄*10,000—10,000 美元*, ＄*500,000—500,000 美元*, and ＄*50,000,000—50,000,000 美元*; the other is to translate them into Chinese characters, that is, ＄*10,000—1 万美元*, ＄*500,000—50 万美元*, and ＄*50,000,000—5 千万美元*. Thirdly, we correctly and clearly express approximate numbers *roughly*, *about*, *over*, *at least*, *or more*, *and up*, etc. as in expressions ①③④⑤⑥⑧⑨.

## 2.4.4 Exercises 练习

Ⅰ. **Sentence translation.**

1. <u>Ten to one</u>, we will overfulfill our production plan for this month.

2. In fact, <u>a thousand and one</u> mechanical devices waste a great deal of energy in overcoming friction.

3. <u>First of all</u>, our purpose is to apply science and technology in the solution of practical problems.

4. The refrigerator turned out this month must be checked <u>by one hundred percent</u>.

5. The investigation into this traffic accident was done <u>by halves</u>.

6. The sun gives light and heat to the earth <u>by the millions</u>.

7. The recruits were goose-stepping on the drill-ground <u>two by two</u>.

8. <u>Millions of</u> people had seen apples fall, but it was left for Newton to ask why they fall.

9. This table lamp will cost <u>20 dollars odd</u>.

10. That story happened <u>thirty odd years</u> ago.

11. I waited <u>three long hours</u> at the long-distance bus-stop.

12. My jeep has run two thousand kilometers <u>more or less</u>.

13. It weighs <u>above</u> fifteen tons.

14. Helium in the air is a little <u>under</u> 1%.

Ⅱ. Passage translation.

## A Global Economy

President Clinton realized—as all of us must—that today's economy is global. We live in an era in which information, goods and capital speed around the globe, every hour of every day. Whether we like it or not, all of our fortunes are tied together. We are truly interdependent.

America supports international trade because we believe fundamentally that trade will enrich those nations who embrace its discipline. The great promise of trade is its potential to promote mutual prosperity, and to strengthen the bonds between sovereign nations.

The U.S. and China both demonstrate the potential of trade to improve the lives of our people. You know better than I the great achievements of the Chinese economy over the past two decades. In 1977, the sum total of Chinese imports and exports was less than $15 billion, putting China's share of world trade at 0.6 percent. The most populous country in the world, China's exports and imports totaled nearly $200 billion. China had become the world's tenth largest exporter.

Since 1978, when China began opening its economy to increased foreign investment and trade, aggregate output has more than doubled. The growth has occurred in the coastal areas near Hong Kong and opposite Taiwan, where foreign investment and modern production methods have spurred production of both domestic and export goods. Per capita GNP has grown at an average rate of 7.6% from 1980—1992.

The numbers are interesting, but how has this affected the people of China? In the last decade, telephone connection rose more than 60%. Electrical production more than doubled to 621 million kilowatt hours. In short, China has improved the economic well-being of its people.

The people of the United States also have experienced the benefits of world trade. Since World War Ⅱ, the U.S. has been the world's largest economy and, in most years, the world's largest exporter.

But the importance of trade in our economy has exploded in the past three decades. In 1970, the value of two-way trade was equal to just 13% of the U.S. exports (goods and services) have risen by 4 million, to a total of 11 million. That's almost one out of ten American jobs. Last year U.S. trade equaled $1.8 trillion dollars.

Nor is the importance of trade likely to diminish for either China or the United States. China will continue to depend upon lucrative export markets to earn the foreign exchange it needs to develop and grow. At the same time, China's imports will supply the much needed machinery and technology to fuel its continued development.

For the United States, new commercial opportunities will grow most rapidly in the emerging markets. We estimate that three quarters of new export opportunities over the next twenty years—that's an incredible $1.9 trillion in potential exports—will come in the emerging markets of Asia and Latin America. This means jobs for American workers and a higher standard of living for the American people.

(Excerpted from *Remarks by Ambassador Kantor at the University of International Business and Economics*, 1995)

## 2.4.5 Translation of English Multiple 英语倍数的翻译

Multiple is frequently used in English, but it is quite different from Chinese in translation. When we translate English multiple, we should understand and translate it correctly and faithfully or we will make mistakes in translating and even result in great errors.

**2.4.5.1 Some sentence constructions as to increase 用于"增长"常见句型的翻译**

**1)"Multiple + as…as…" construction**

- The grain output of this year is *about three times as great as* that of last year.
  今年的粮食产量**大约**是去年的**三倍**。
  (或:今年的粮食产量比去年**多两倍左右**。)

- Asia is *four times as larger as* Europe.
  亚洲比欧洲**大三倍**。
  (或:亚洲是欧洲的**四倍大**。)

- Were the earth's mass *twice as great as* it is, it would attract an object *twice as strongly as* it does.
  如果地球的质量是它现在的**两倍那么大**,那么地球就能以它现在**两倍**的引力来吸引物体。

- Your room is *three times as large as* mine.
  你的房间比我的房间**大两倍**。
  (或:你的房间是我的房间的**三倍**。)

**2)"Multiple + comparative + than …" construction**

- Mt. Qomolangma is 8,848 meters high, about *two and half times higher than* Mt. Fuji.
  珠穆朗玛峰高8,848米高,比富士山**高一倍半左右**。
  (或:珠穆朗玛峰高8,848米高,**约是**富士山的**两倍半**。)

- Kuwait oil wells yield nearly 500 *times more than* U.S. wells.
  科威特油井的产油量几乎**是**美国油田的**500倍**。

- Iron is almost *three times heavier than* aluminum.
  铁的重量几乎**是**铝的**三倍**。
  (或:铁几乎**比**铝重**两倍**。)

- Your room is *four times larger than* mine.
  你的房间**是**我房间的**四倍**。
  (或:你的房间**比**我的房间大**三倍**。)

- The irrigated area in this prefecture is *four times bigger than* in 1998.
  这个地区的灌溉面积比1998年**增加了三倍**。

### 3) Some verbs + multiple

Verbs like *increase*, *rise*, *exceed*, *grow*, *raise*, *expand*, *go up*, etc. are commonly used to express multiple with the meanings of "increase".

- The number of the students enrolled in evening classes *has increased more than twofold*.
  注册上晚间课的学生人数**增加了一倍多**。
- The total volume of state purchase in the first quarter *rose by 5.2 percent*, compared with the same period of last year.
  和去年同期相比,国家第一季度的总采购量**增加了5.2个百分点**。
- The output of chemical fiber has been *increased three times* as against last year.
  化纤产量比去年**增加了两倍**。
- During this period its territory *increased ten-fold*.
  这个时期它的领土**扩大了9倍**(为原来的10倍)。

### 4) "By a factor of + multiple" construction

This structure is coped with when we have to minus one from the number since the original is not included in Chinese language.

- In case of electronic scanning the beam width is broader *by a factor of two*.
  电子扫描时,波束宽度**增加一倍**。
- Today the speed of our car exceeds the ordinary speed *by a factor of three*.
  今天,我们的汽车速度**超过了**平常速度的**两倍**。
- The population of this county has increased *by a factor of five*.
  这个县的人口已经**增长了四倍**。

### 5) Some words with multiple meaning

Such words with multiple meaning are *double*, *treble*, *quadruple*, etc. in English.

- The output of diesel oil for farm has more than *doubled*.
  农用柴油产量**增加了一倍**多。
- The baby girl *doubled* its weight in a year.
  这个女婴的体重一年中**增加了一倍**。
- Henry *trebled* his money by buying a dog for $50 and selling it for $150.
  亨利花50美元买了一条狗,然后按150美元把狗卖出去,因而使他的钱**增加了两倍**。
- Having the repeater spacing decreased by one half, we made it possible to *quadruple* the bandwidth.
  把中继器间距减少一半,就能使带宽**增加三倍**。
- The output of color TV sets has been *doubled* in the past five years.

彩色电视机的产量在过去五年中**翻了一番**。
- The output of iron and steel is *treble* what it was.
  钢铁的产量是过去的**三倍**。
  (或:钢铁的产量比过去**增加了两倍**。)
- The number of livestock has *quadrupled* this year.
  牲畜的数量今年**增加了三倍**。
- Our population is now *double* what it was thirty-five years ago.
  我国目前的人口**是** 35 年前的**两倍**。

Comments  In this part, the training focus is on some sentence constructions as to increase. But when we translate these constructions, we ought to pay special attention to the different expressions in Chinese versions. In other words, the same original has two Chinese versions. Therefore, we ought to clearly understand the two different versions of the same English expression. In addition, apart from some words, phrases and constructions, we can reach a conclusion that the following sentence structures have the same meanings:

① A is N times bigger than B.
② A is bigger than B by N times.
③ A is N times as big as B.

The exact meaning of the three structures is: A = B × N

### 2.4.5.2 Some words, phrases and structures as to decrease
用于"减少"常见词语和句型的翻译

**1) Some words and phrases**

- The output of cars in Europe last year was 24 *percent less than* in 1996.
  去年欧洲汽车产量比 1996 年**下降了 24%**。
- In this lathe, proper lubrication has *diminished almost three fifths* of the friction.
  把这台车床适当加油润滑,摩擦力**几乎就能减少 3/5**。
- Owing to natural calamities, the wheat output of every *mu* in our village has *decreased from* 500 *kilograms to less than* 350 *kilograms*.
  由于受自然灾害的影响,我们村小麦的亩产量已**从 500 公斤下降到不足 350 公斤**。
- The production cost of electronic organs was *reduced by* 30%.
  电子琴的生产成本**降低了 30%**。
- The depth of water in the first tube is *less than half* that in the other.
  第一支试管内水的深度还**不到**另一支试管的**一半**。
- The leads of the new condenser are *half as long as* those of the old, yet the functions are the same.
  新式电容器的导线**比**旧式电容器**短一半**,但作用是相同的。

- This new method has *halved* the loss of metal.

  这种新方法使金属损耗量<u>减少了一半</u>。

**2）Some structures**

- The length of the designed size was *reduced ten times*.

  设计尺寸的长度<u>缩短到 1/10</u>。

  （或：设计尺寸的长度<u>缩短了 9/10</u>。）

- This kind of film is *twice thinner than* ordinary paper, but its quality is quite good.

  尽管这种薄膜的<u>厚度只是</u>普通纸张的<u>一半</u>，可是质量却相当好。

- Aluminum is almost more than *three times as light as* copper.

  铝几乎<u>比铜轻 2/3</u>。

  （或：铝的重量几乎<u>不到铜的 1/3</u>。）

- We see that the price of the product is *reduced by a factor of* 5.

  可以看到此产品的价格<u>下降了五分之四（4/5）</u>。

**Comments** Besides some words and phrases, we can come to a conclusion that the following sentence structures have the same meanings.

① A is N times smaller than B.

② A is smaller than B by N times.

③ A is N times as small as B.

That is to say, the meaning of the three structures is the same. But when we translate the multiple in decreasing, Chinese character translation is quite different from the multiple in increasing. This is because Chinese character 倍 is only used in increasing, not in decreasing although the word "*times*" is the same in both cases.

## 2.4.6 Compare and Analyze 比较与分析

The population of the world has ①<u>increased more</u> in modern times <u>than</u> in all other ages of history combined. World population ②<u>totaled</u> about 500 million in 1650. It ③<u>doubled</u> in the period from 1650 to 1850. Today the population is more than three billion. Estimates based on research by the United Nations indicate that it will ④<u>more than double</u> in the next twenty-five years, reaching seven billion by the year 2000.

现代世界人口的①<u>增长超过</u>历史上所有其他时期的总和。1650 年世界人口②<u>总数约为 5 亿</u>。1650 年到 1850 年期间这个数字③<u>翻了一番</u>。如今世界人口超过了 30 亿。据联合国调查资料表明，估计在未来的 25 年时间里这个数字将会④<u>增加一倍还不止</u>，到 2000 年世界人口将达到 70 亿。

**Notes：**①The expression *increase more than* means 增长超过 in Chinese.

②*Total*, when used as a verb, implies 总数达 in Chinese.

③④We should express *double* correctly and appropriately, as 是……的两倍, 使……加倍, 翻一番 or 增加一倍 in Chinese. Similarly, *treble*, *quadruple* and other words or phrases with multiple should be exactly rendered like this one.

### 2.4.7 Exercises 练习

#### I. Sentence translation.

1. Jupiter is 5 times far from the sun as is the earth.
2. Cork is 0.25 times as heavy as water; mercury weighs 13.5 times as much as water.
3. The volume of the earth is 49 times larger than that of the moon.
4. This lathe improves the working conditions and raises efficiency fourfold.
5. New boosters can increase the payload by 120%.
6. The speed exceeds the average speed by a factor of 2.5.
7. The sales of industrial electronic products have multiplied six times since 1990.
8. The population of this small town has doubled in the past twenty years.
9. The efficiency of these machines has been more than trebled or quadrupled.
10. The price of mobile phones was reduced by 75%.
11. A is three times smaller than B.

#### II. Passage translation.

All whales fall into two groups, those with teeth and those without. Both beluga and dolphin belong to the suborder of toothed whales known as Odontoceti, along with porpoises, narwhals, pilot whales, killer whales and the largest toothed creature in the world, the sperm whale. Size differences among the Odontoceti are remarkable. A common porpoise will run only 4 to 5 feet in length and 300 pounds in weight; a sperm whale may be 10 times as long and 300 times as heavy. The beluga falls in between, weighing up to 2,000 pounds. And it does chirp. In fact, it makes a great variety of squeaking, whistling, and clicking sounds, which have earned it the name of sea canary.

The toothless, or baleen, whales belong to the suborder of Mysticeti. This is a group of generally large whales, formerly abundant in all the oceans of the world. Though reduced by hunting, most species are still found along the coasts of the United States and Canada. All but two of the Mysticeti reach 40 feet or more at maturity, with the blue whale running up to 100 feet and tipping the scales at up to 130 tons. This whale is by far the largest creature that has ever lived on earth, 4 times the weight of the largest dinosaur, 30 times that of an elephant.

(This passage is taken from TOEFL test in 1988)

# Chapter 3: Syntactic Translation
# 结构翻译

## 3.1 Translation of Negative Sentences 否定句的翻译

It is very important for all of us to learn to deal with the negative sentences in translating. The scope that a negative word governs varies from sentence to sentence. It may cover a whole sentence or part of a sentence. Therefore negation can be generally divided into complete negation, partial negation, double negation, connotative negation, transferred negation, etc. Now let us discuss them one by one.

### 3.1.1 Complete Negation 完全否定

Complete negation can be realized by negative words like *not*, *no*, *none*, *never*, *nobody*, *nothing*, *neither…nor*, *nowhere*, *no one*, etc. Generally speaking, the scope of negation normally extends from the negative word to the end of the sentence.

❖ He is *not* a teacher.
  他**不是**老师。
❖ I'll *never* do so again.
  我再也**不**这样做了。
❖ This problem is so difficult that *none* of us can solve it.
  这个问题太难,我们当中**没人**能解决。
❖ *Neither* of them is at home.
  他俩**都不**在家。
❖ A gas has *neither* definite volume *nor* definite shape.
  气体既**无**一定体积,又**无**一定形状。

Comments When we come across negative words, we should keep in mind whether they are completely negative or not. In this way, we can easily translate them correctly and accurately.

### 3.1.2 Partial Negation 部分否定

In general, some English indefinite pronouns and adverbs are partially negative in meaning, including *some*, *somebody*, *something*, *somewhere*, *somewhat*, *sometimes*, etc. Here is one example: *Some teachers are not experienced*. Its translation "部分教师缺乏经验" shows us that the sentence is partially negative because some of the teachers are not experienced, not the whole although there is a negative word *not*. When we touch upon these words in translation, we should really know the deep meaning. Besides, we should pay attention to some special constructions.

### 3.1.2.1 all (every, each, both, many, everything, everybody...) + not 不定代词/形容词 + not 结构的翻译

- *All* that glitters is *not* gold. ( = Not all that glitters is gold. )
  闪光的东西**不一定都**是金子。(partial negation)
  Compare: None that glitters is gold.
  闪光的都不是金子。(complete negation)

- *All* these metals are *not* good conductors.
  ( = Not all these metals are good conductors. )
  这些金属**并非都**是良导体。(partial negation)
  Compare: None of these metals are good conductors.
  这些金属都不是良导体。(complete negation)

- *Both* of the instruments are *not* precision ones.
  ( = Not both of the instruments are precision ones. )
  这两台仪器**并不都**是精密仪器。(partial negation)
  Compare: Neither of the instruments are precision ones.
  这两台仪器都不是精密仪器。(complete negation)

- *Every* machine here is *not* produced in our factory.
  ( = Not every machine here is produced in our factory. )
  这里的机器**并不全**是我厂生产的。(partial negation)
  Compare: None of the machines here are produced in our factory.
  这里的机器都不是我厂生产的。(complete negation)

- *All* heavy smokers are *not* long-lived.
  ( = Not all heavy smokers are long-lived. )
  烟鬼**并非都能**长寿。(partial negation)
  Compare: None of heavy smokers are long-lived.
  烟鬼都不长寿。(complete negation)

- *Each* side of the streets is *not* clean.
  ( = Not each side of the street is clean. )
  **并非**街道两边都干净。(partial negation)
  Compare: Neither side of the street is clean.
  街道两边都不干净。(complete negation)

- I do *not* want *everything*. ( = I want not everything. )
  我**并不**想什么都要。(partial negation)
  Compare: I do not want anything.

我什么都不想要。(complete negation)

❖ He does *not* like *everybody*. ( = He likes not everybody.)

他**并非**谁都喜欢。(partial negation)

Compare: He does not like anybody.

他谁都不喜欢。(complete negation)

**Comments** Look more carefully at each pair of sentences and compare them. We can find that the first sentence is classified to partial negation in meaning. This is because it contains an indefinite pronoun or adverb plus a negative word. On the other hand, the second sentence is completely negative in meaning. So when rendering the negative sentences, we should not merely notice the negative words, but also pay special attention to those above-mentioned pronouns and adverbs, and their positions in sentences.

However, there are some exceptions in this construction. We should cope with them with great care.

❖ The economic crisis is a mortal wound to the capitalist system, and *all* the remedies in the world *won't* heal it.

Version 1: 经济危机是资本主义制度的致命伤,世上**所有的**药方都治不好这种创伤。

Version 2: 经济危机是资本主义制度的致命伤,**并不是所有**的药方都能治好这种创伤。

**Comments** The original seems to be rendered into two versions according to the construction we have just learned. But when we come across such a sentence, we have to carefully consider it literally—what the writer really means to describe. In this case, what the sentence is meant to say is that none of the remedies in the world will heal it. Therefore, the translation should be version 1.

### 3.1.2.2 always (much, everywhere, entirely, wholly, altogether, often, enough …) + not
副词 + not 结构的翻译

In a certain sense, we can find the equivalent for some phrases in this construction. That is, *not always* equals *sometimes*; *not everywhere* is equal to *somewhere*; *not wholly* equals *in some degree*; *not altogether* is equal to *somewhat*, and so on. All of them remain partially negative in meaning.

❖ It is true that friction is *not always* a disadvantage.

的确摩擦**并不总是**坏事。(partial negation)

Compare: It is true that friction is not a disadvantage.

的确摩擦并不是件坏事。(complete negation)

❖ The rich are *not always* happy.

富人**并不总是**快乐的。(partial negation)

Compare: The rich are not / never happy.

富人并不/决不快乐。(complete negation)

- We *haven't* got *much* information yet.

  我们**尚未**搞到很多情报。(partial negation)

  Compare: We haven't got information yet.

  我们尚未搞到情报。(complete negation)

- I do *not wholly* agree with you.

  我**不完全**同意你的意见。(partial negation)

  Compare: I do not agree with you.

  我不同意你的意见。(complete negation)

- This kind of trees *cannot* be seen *everywhere*.

  这种树**并非到处都能**见到。(partial negation)

  Compare: This kind of trees cannot be seen anywhere.

  这种树哪儿都见不到。(complete negation)

- Tom is *not altogether* satisfied with the result of the experiment.

  汤姆对实验结果**并不完全**满意。(partial negation)

  Compare: Tom is not satisfied with the result of the experiment.

  汤姆对实验结果一点都不满意。(complete negation)

- We do *not often* do morning exercise now.

  现在我们**不常**做早操。(partial negation)

  Compare: We do not do morning exercise now.

  现在我们不做早操。(complete negation)

- The water is not hot *enough*.

  水**不够**热。(partial negation)

  Compare: The water is not hot.

  水不热。(complete negation)

**Comments** Carefully read these pairs of sentences, and we can say that some adverbs like *much*, *everywhere*, *entirely*, *wholly*, *altogether*, *often*, *enough* etc. with negative word "*not*" cause the sentences to be partially negative in meaning.

### 3.1.2.3 not + adverbial (attributive/predicative) + and + adverbial (attributive/predicative)

not + 状语 + and + 状语结构的翻译

In this construction, the two adverbials (attributives or predicatives) are connected by the conjunction "*and*" with negative word "*not*". It is partially negative in meaning. In other words, it negates the part behind "*and*" only.

- This book is *not* instructive *and* interesting.

此书颇有教育意义,但缺乏趣味。
- He did *not* explain it correctly *and* clearly.
 他对此解释得很正确,但不够清楚。

**Comments** Note that the sentences above will be completely negative in meaning if the conjunctive word "*and*" is changed into "*or*". Now let us compare the above with the following.

- This book is *not* instructive *or* interesting.
 此书既无教育意义,又无趣味。
- He did *not* explain it correctly *or* clearly.
 他对此解释得既不正确,又不清楚。

**Comments** We should really concentrate on the distinction of this construction with different conjunction "*and*" or "*or*". In different use of either of the two conjunctions, the translation is quite different.

### 3.1.2.4 "…not … + … as well as…" structure
### "…not … + … as well as…" 结构的翻译

In this construction, it is partially negative in meaning because the negative word "*not*" negates only the part before the conjunction "*as well as*". The part after "*as well as*" is affirmative in meaning.

- Last month reference to computers was *not* found in newspapers *as well as* in magazine and on radio and television.
 关于计算机的参考资料,上个月我在杂志及广播电视上见到过,但报纸上未曾见到。

**Comments** Note that the sentence above will be affirmative in meaning if there is no negative word "*not*" in this construction.

### 3.1.2.5 Some adverbials with partial negation 部分否定意义副词的翻译

At last, we should pay attention to the use of some partial negative adverbials such as *hardly*, *scarcely*, *rarely*, *seldom*, *few*, *little*, etc. because *hardly* and *scarcely* are equal to *almost not*; *rarely* or *seldom* equals *not often*; *few* is equal to *not many* and *little* equals *not much*. In this case, we take it that these adverbials are partially negative in meaning.

- I could *hardly* recognize you.
 我几乎认不出你了。
- He *scarcely* knew the accident.
 他对此事故几乎一无所知。
- He *rarely* speaks to others these days.
 这些天来他很少与别人说话。
- Meetings are *seldom* held recently.
 最近很少开会。
- *Few* of the films are interesting.

Chapter 3: Syntactic Translation

没有几部影片有趣。

❖ There is *little* ink in my pen.
  我的钢笔里<u>几乎没</u>墨水了。

### 3.1.3 Compare and Analyze 比较与分析

According to a law attributed to the savant known only as Murphy, "if anything can go wrong, it will." Corollaries to Murphy's Law suggest themselves as clues to the shoddy goods problems: If anything can break down, it will; if anything can fall apart, it will; if anything can stop running, it will. While Murphy's Law can ①<u>never be wholly defeated</u>, its effects can usually be postponed. Much of human existence consists of efforts aimed at making sure that things ②<u>don't go wrong, fall apart, break down, or stop running</u> until a decent interval has elapsed after their manufacture. Forestalling Murphy's Law as applied to products demands intelligence, skill, and commitment. If these human inputs are assisted by special quality-control instruments, machines, and scientific sampling procedures, so much the better. But gadgets and sampling alone will ③<u>never do the trick</u> since these items are also subject to Murphy's Law. Quality-control instruments need maintenance; ④<u>gauges go out of order</u>; X rays and laser beams need adjustments. No matter how advanced the technology, quality demand intelligent, motivated human thought and action.

根据大学者墨菲的法则,"凡是可能出差错的事终将出差错"。墨菲法则在劣质产品问题中也得到了验证:凡是可能损坏的产品终将损坏;凡是可能破碎的产品终将会破碎;凡是可能出故障的产品终将出故障。墨菲法则①<u>并非无懈可击</u>,它的效应常常可以延迟。人们耗费大量精力,其目的是保证产品在使用相当长一段时间后仍②<u>完好无损</u>。要使墨菲法则在产品中站不住脚,就需要知识、技能、信誉。如果有了人类的这些努力,外加专用的质检工具、机器以及科学的取样程序,情况就会好得多。然而仅靠工具和抽样调查③<u>决不会有效</u>,因为这些工具仍然受墨菲法则的影响。质检工具需要维修;④<u>检测仪器</u>也会损坏;X 光及激光也需要调整。不管技术多么先进,质量仍需要人类的智慧、明确的思想和行动。

(何三宁 译)

注:选自李观仪《新编英语教程》,V5,p97,上海外语教育出版社,2003

Notes: ① In this sentence, we can find the adverb "*wholly*" and the negative word "*never*" used together, which creates partial negation.

②③These two points belong to complete negation.

### 3.1.4 Exercises 练习

Ⅰ. Sentence translation.

1. He is *no* professor.
2. He is *not* humorous at all.

3. I know _none_ of them.
4. _Nobody_ in our college knows Italian.
5. She said _never_ a word the whole afternoon.
6. _Neither_ sentence is correct.
7. The trilingual textbook is _nowhere_ to be bought.
8. _All_ men can _not_ be first.
9. _Every_ composition is _not_ treated in the same way.
10. _Both_ of the substances do _not_ dissolve in water.
11. They are _not always_ in the office on Sundays.
12. The responsibility is _not altogether_ mine.
13. The situation is _not necessarily_ so.
14. This book is _not_ informative _and_ interesting.
15. The boy did _not_ complete the task in time _and_ with care.
16. The students did _not_ clean the windows in the classroom _as well as_ doors.
17. He has seen _little_ of life.
18. I _hardly_ finished it on time.

**Ⅱ. Passage translation.**

    I suspect not everyone who loves the country would be happy living the way we do. It takes a couple of special qualities. One is a tolerance for solitude. Because we are so busy and on such a tight budget, we don't entertain much. During the growing season there is no time for socializing anyway. Jim and Emily are involved in school activities, but they too spend most of their time at home.

    The other requirement is energy—a lot of it. The way to make self-sufficiency work on a small scale is to resist the temptation to buy a tractor and other expensive labor-saving devices. Instead, you do the work yourself. The only machinery we own (not counting the lawn mower) is a little three-horsepower rotary cultivator and a 16-inch chain saw.

    How much longer we'll have enough energy to stay on here is anybody's guess—perhaps for quite a while, perhaps not. When the time comes, we'll leave with a feeling of sorrow but also with a sense of pride at what we've been able to accomplish. We should make a fair profit on the sale of the place, too. We've invested about $35,000 of our own money in it, and we could just about double that if we sold today. But this is not a good time to sell. Once economic conditions improve, however, demand for farms like ours should be strong again.

    We didn't move here primarily to earn money though. We came because we wanted to improve the quality of our lives. When I watch Emily collecting eggs in the evening, fishing with Jim on the river or enjoying an old-fashioned picnic in the orchard with the entire family, I know we've found just what we were looking for. (This is an excerpt from _Exploring Through Writing_, 2nd edition, 1998, published by Cambridge University Press. It first appeared in _Money_ magazine in 1984)

### 3.1.5 Double Negation 双重否定的翻译

Double negation refers to the form in which there are two negative words, one negative word plus "*without*", one negative word with such negative prefixes or suffixes as *un-*, *dis-*, *non-*, *-less* and the like, or one negative word with a connotative negation in one sentence. Let us discuss these constructions with some examples.

- He did it *not without* reason.
  他这样做**不无**理由。
- Japan *cannot* be economically independent *without* trading with foreign countries.
  日本**不**与外国通商,经济上**不可能**独立。
- You *can't* buy things *without* money.
  没钱就买**不到**东西。
- He expected, *not unnaturally*, that his father would help him.
  他指望父亲能来帮助他,这**不是不合情理的**。
- *Nothing is changeless*.
  一成不变的东西是没有的。

**Comments** When we translate such sentences, we can directly render them by using two negative characters in Chinese versions.

But double negative formation cannot always be retained in Chinese versions because there will be repetition and roundabout phenomena in this case. Affirmative formations may be directly employed if necessary.

- There can be *no* sunshine *without* shadow.
  **有**阳光**就有**阴影。
- *No* one has *nothing* to offer to society.
  **人人**都可以为社会奉献点**什么**。
- He *cannot* speak English *without* making mistakes.
  他**一**说英语**就**出错。
- They *never* meet *without* quarrelling.
  他们**每次**见面**肯定**吵架。
- Nowadays it is *not seldom* that a man lives to be seventy years old.
  如今人活到70岁是**常见的**。

**Comments** We need not translate sentences with double negation into ones with two negative words in Chinese all the time. We have another way to translate them into affirmative like the above-mentioned sentences. But note that we have to distinguish between the double negation and the repeated negation. The latter is different from the former. The repeated negation is made up of more than two negative words, which still have negative meaning. The purpose is to emphasize something in a sentence.

Additionally, it is easily concluded that double negative English sentences can be translated in both ways, positive or negative in Chinese, if we want to. Both ways imply emphatic meaning. Which way we choose surely depends on the context of the target text. In the skill of conversion between the positive and the negative, sometimes because the translation is not smooth if it is not converted into negative expressions and sometimes we should translate double negative English sentences in a positive way because positive statements will make the translated text more natural.

### 3.1.6 Connotative Negation 内涵否定的翻译

In English, although there are a lot of words, phrases and structures which have no negative words like *no* or *not*, even some prefixes and suffixes with negative meaning such as *un-*, *non-*, *in-*, *an-*, *dis-* or *-less*, they are still negative in meaning. There are also some English words or phrases, remaining negative, though they have no negative affixations or words, such as *fail*, *refuse*, *free from*, etc. This kind of construction or situation is called connotative negation. It is very important for us to be familiar with connotative negation while we translate them. We should know the following common words and structures.

#### 3.1.6.1 Some words and phrases 含有否定意义词语的翻译

1) **Some common verbs**: *fail*, *neglect*, *exclude*, *overlook*, *miss*, *deny*, *ignore*, *refuse*, *lack*, *keep/prevent/protect...from*, etc.

- ❖ The tool will *fail* to cut effectively as it becomes too worn.
  刀具过度磨损,就<u>不能</u>有效地进行切削了。

- ❖ Painting is the most common way to *protect* metals *from* corrosion.
  涂漆是使金属<u>免受</u>腐蚀的最通用方法。

- ❖ I *doubt* his honesty.
  我<u>不相信</u>他的诚意。

2) **Some common nouns**: *absence*, *ignorance*, *exclusion*, *a fool to*, etc.

- ❖ A vacuum, which is the *absence of* matter, cannot transmit sound.
  真空中<u>没有</u>物质,不能传播声音。

- ❖ This book is *a fool to* that both in plot and execution.
  这本书无论在情节上还是在写作技巧上,<u>都比不上</u>那本书。

3) **Some common adjectives**: *the last*, *the least*, *few*, *little*, *short of*, *free of/from*, *safe from*, *far from*, etc.

- ❖ *Little* is known at present about this oil field.
  目前对此油田的情况<u>几乎一无</u>所知。

- ❖ It is very important that a drawing be *free from* ambiguities and be subject only to a single interpretation.

图纸**不应有**模棱两可的地方，而只能有一种解释，这是很重要的。
- He is *the last* man to accept a bribe.
  他**绝不是**受贿赂的人。

4) **Some common adverbs**：*vainly*，*hardly*，*scarcely*，*in vain*，etc.
- The speed of the satellite *hardly* changes at all.
  这个卫星的速度**几乎没有**任何变化。
- We tried to persuade him to give up the attempt, but *in vain*.
  我们曾劝他放弃这种打算，但是**没用**。

5) **Some common conjunctions**：*than*，*more...than*，*rather...than*，*but*，*but that*，*before*，*unless*，*lest*，*since*，etc.
- *But that* you had helped us, we should have failed.
  **假如**你们**不**帮助我们，我们早就失败了。
- You cannot see any object *unless* light from that object gets into your eyes.
  如果来自物体的光线**不**进入眼帘，你就什么也看不见。
- *Before* I could protest, he got to his feet.
  我**还没来得及**抗议，他已经站了起来。
- It is already three years *since* he was a teacher.
  他**不**当教师已经三年了。
- That's more *than* I can do.
  我干**不**了那事。
- I'd *rather* have tea *than* coffee.
  我宁愿喝茶**而不愿**喝咖啡。

6) **Some prepositions**：*above*，*beyond*，*off*，*against*，*past*，*below*，*beneath*，*behind*，*minus*，*within*，*instead of*，*but for*，*in place of*，*in defect of*，*in default of*，*out of*，*at issue with*，etc.
- *Instead of* the decimal numbering system, the computer uses the binary system.
  计算机**不用**十进位制，而用二进位制。
- I used artificial flowers *in defect of* real ones.
  **没有**真花，我就用了假花。
- *But for* instruments and equipment, the modern marine scientist would be helpless.
  **假如没有**仪器和设备，现代海洋科学家就会一筹莫展。
- It is anything *but* the last word in medical science.
  这些东西**绝不是**医学中的最新成果。
- I was *past* caring now, so I ordered coffee for myself and an ice-cream and coffee for her.

我现在<u>什么都不</u>在乎了。我为自己点了咖啡,为她点了一杯咖啡冰激凌。

- ❖ What you said is *beyond* my ken.
  你的话我<u>不懂</u>。

- ❖ His conduct is *above* reproach.
  他的行为<u>无可</u>指责。

**Comments** The words and phrases mentioned above are just some of the vocabulary in English having connotative negation. We simply collect them one by one in learning, keep them in mind in usage, and only thus can we translate them correctly.

### 3.1.6.2 Some sentence structures 句子结构的否定翻译

**1) It is… that / who…**

- ❖ *It is* a silly fish *that* is caught twice.
  再蠢的鱼<u>也不会</u>上钩两次。

- ❖ *It is* a wise father *that* knows his own child.
  父亲再聪明<u>也不见得</u>了解自己的孩子。

- ❖ *It is* a good divine *that* follows his own instructions.
  善言者<u>未必</u>能行。

- ❖ *It is* a good dog *that* can catch anything.
  什么东西都能抓的狗<u>是不存在的</u>。

- ❖ *It is* a good goose *that* is always dropping.
  世间<u>没有</u>连续下蛋的鹅。(劝人不要过多地向朋友讨东西。)

**2) Some rhetorical questions on special occasions**

- ❖ Am I your slave?
  我<u>才不是</u>你的奴隶呢。

- ❖ Who knows?
  谁<u>都不</u>知道。

- ❖ What is the good of asking a favor of her?
  去求那个女人是<u>没有</u>用的。

**3) Some conditional sentences without main clauses**

- ❖ *If only* he did drive so fast!
  他<u>别</u>把车开得那么快就好了。

- ❖ I am sure! *If* this is English manners!
  我确信这<u>绝不是</u>英国人的礼貌行为。

- ❖ Mercy! *If ever* I heard the like from a lady.
  天哪!一位小姐说出这样的话来,<u>真没听说过</u>。

**4) "More…than…"construction plus subordinate clause with the word "can"**

- That is *more than* I *can* do.
  那是我**办不到的**。
- The beauty of Hangzhou is *more than I can* describe.
  杭州景色之美，**无法**用言语描述。
- He has bitten off *more than he can* chew.
  他承担了**力所不及的事**。

5) Too + adjectives + to

- The patient is *too weak to* be operated on.
  病人太虚弱了，**不能**手术。
- He was *too tired to go* any further.
  他累得再也走**不动了**。
- He was *too careful a scientist to* rush into publication.
  他是一位非常谨慎的科学家，**并不急于**发表著作。

**Comments** As for the structures with connotative negation, there is no special way to follow. They are special expressions in English, which are quite different from Chinese. The best way is to learn them by heart.

### 3.1.7 Compare and Analyze 比较与分析

Suburbs and country areas are, in many ways, even more vulnerable than well-patrolled urban streets. Statistics show the crime rate rising more dramatically in those allegedly tranquil areas than in cities. At any rate, the era of leaving the front door on the latch is ①over.

It has been replaced by dead-bolt locks, security chains, electric alarm system and trip wires hooked up to a police station or private guard firm. Many suburban families have sliding glass doors on their patios, with steel bars elegantly built in so ②no one can pry the door open.

It is③not uncommon, in the most pleasant of homes, to see pasted on the windows small notices announcing that the premises are under surveillance by his security force or that guard company.

The lock is the new symbol of America.

在许多方面，郊区和农村甚至比巡查严密的城市街道更容易受到攻击。统计数字显示，那些据称是治安良好的地区的犯罪率上升得比城镇还要显著。不管怎么说，夜不闭户的时代是①**一去不复返了**。

取而代之的是防盗锁、防护链、电子报警系统以及连接警署或私人保安公司的报警装置。郊区的许多人家在露台上安装了玻璃滑门，并配装有很讲究的钢条，这样就②**无人**能把门撬开。

在最温馨的居家，也③**常常**可以看到窗上贴着小小的告示，声称本宅由某家安全保卫机构或某个保安公司负责监管。

Indeed, a recent public-service advertisement by a large insurance company featured ④ <u>not</u> charts showing how much at risk we are, but a picture of a child's bicycle with the now-usual padlock attached to it. (by Bob Greene, *Learning About College Writing*, 2000)

锁成了美国的新象征。的确如此,最近一家大的保险公司在一则公益广告上④**没有**用图表表明我们的危险有多大,而是用了一幅童车的图片,车身上悬着如今随处可见的挂锁。

注:译文略有修改

**Notes**: ①The word "*over*" here is connotative negation in meaning.

②④The two negative words "*no*" and "*not*" belong to complete negation.

③Occasionally two negatives appear in the same sentence in English, like "*not frequently*", "*a not unattractive girl*", etc. Such double negative phrases are devices of understatement, "*not infrequently*" meaning "*rather frequently*" and "*a not unattractive girl*" meaning "*a fairly attractive girl*". Similarly, the phrase "*not uncommon*" means "*rather common*". In this sense, we can translate the sentences with double negation into the affirmative.

### 3.1.8 Exercises 练习

**Ⅰ. Sentence translation.**

1. The first bombs missed the target.
2. Nothing was left undone.
3. He failed to pass the entrance examination.
4. Never concentrate all your attention on one or two problems, to the exclusion of others.
5. This is the last thing I will do.
6. Such instances are few.
7. There is no smoke without fire.
8. You will never succeed unless you work hard.
9. There is no grammatical rule that does not have exceptions.
10. There is nothing unusual there.
11. The speed of light is too great to be measured with a simple unit.
12. It was more than I could bear.
13. That kind of person is anything but a visiting scholar.
14. The Red Army soldiers would rather die than surrender.
15. Her father is now between jobs.

**Ⅱ. Passage translation.**

### Enchantment of the South Seas

The mighty Pacific washes the shores of the continents—North America, South America, Asia, Australia, and Antarctica. Its waters mingle in the southeast with the Atlantic Ocean and in the southwest with the Indian Ocean. It is not on the shores of continents or in the coastal islands, however, that the soul of the great Pacific is found. It lies far out where the fabled South Sea Islands are scattered over the huge ocean like stars in the sky.

Here great disturbances at the heart of the earth caused mountains and volcanoes to rise above the water. For hundreds of years tiny coral creatures have worked and died to make thousands of ring-shaped islands called atolls.

The air that sweeps the South Sea Islands is fragrant with flowers and spice. Bright warm days follow clear cool nights, and the rolling swells break in a never-ending roar on the shores. Overhead the slender coconut palms whisper their drowsy song.

When white men first came to the Pacific islands, they found that the people living there were like happy children. They were tall men and beautiful women who seemed not to have a care in the world. Coconut palms and breadfruit trees grew at the doors of their huts. The ocean was filled with turtles and fish, ready for the net. The islanders had little need for clothing. There was almost no disease.

Cruel and bloody wars sometimes broke out between neighboring tribes, and canoe raids were sometimes made on nearby islands. The strong warriors enjoyed fighting. Many of the islanders were cannibals, who cooked and ate the enemies they killed. This was part of their law and religion. These savages, however, were usually friendly, courteous, and hospitable. Some of the early explorers were so fascinated with the Pacific islands that they never returned to their own countries. They preferred to stay.

### 3.1.9 Transferred Negation 否定转移

In English, transferred negation refers to a kind of grammatical phenomenon that negative particles may be transferred from one place to another. We should notice that the negative word is generally put in the main clause in English, but in translation, we, in fact, transfer the negative word in the subordinate clause in Chinese.

#### 3.1.9.1 Some english verbs 一些英语动词的翻译

If the main clauses, with negative words, are constructed by such English verbs as *think*, *believe*, *fancy*, *reckon*, *feel*, *suppose* and *imagine*, *consider*, *expect*, the negative words should be transferred into the subordinate clauses introduced by "*that*" in translating. In other words, we should translate this kind of construction according to Chinese expression.

- ❖ I *don't* think that he can operate the new electronic computer.
  我认为他<u>不会</u>操作这台新型电子计算机。
- ❖ She did *not* believe that such things mattered much.
  她认为这种事<u>没多大</u>关系。
- ❖ I *don't* suppose that I'll trouble you again.
  我想<u>不会</u>再麻烦你了。
- ❖ I *don't* imagine that taxes will be reduced this year.
  我认为今年<u>不会</u>降低税收。
- ❖ I had *not* expected things should turn out like this.
  我已经料到事情的结果<u>不应该</u>这样的。

**Comments** In English, when some verbs, used with negative words, introduce the subordinate clauses, the negative words, in this case, negate the subordinate clauses rather than the main clauses. We should be acquainted with this kind of transferred negation in translation.

### 3.1.9.2 "not…because…" construction
### "not…because…"结构的翻译

In English, this construction is usually a hard nut to crack in translation because the negative word "*not*" sometimes negates the verb in the main clause, and sometimes negates the verb of the subordinate clause introduced by "*because*". Therefore when we come cross this kind of construction in translation, we should study and analyze the sentence itself and the context with great care, and manage to translate faithfully. Now let us look at the following examples.

1) **Negate main clauses**

❖ He *cannot* go to school because he is sick.
   他因病**不能**上学。

❖ I did *not* go out because it rained.
   因为下雨,我**没有**出去。

❖ Pure iron is *not* used in industry because it is too soft.
   纯铁因太软而**不**用于工业。

2) **Negative transfer**

❖ The engine did *not* stop because the fuel was finished.
   发动机**不是**因为燃料用完而停止的。

❖ She did *not* come because she wanted to see me.
   她**并非**因为想见我才来。

❖ He did *not* laugh because she was foolish.
   他**并不是**因为她蠢才笑的。

❖ He *didn't* buy the book because he needed it.
   他**并非**由于需要这本书而去买的。

3) **Both cases**

❖ I *didn't* leave home because I was afraid of my father.
   因为我怕父亲,我**没有**离开家。
   (或:我不是因为怕父亲才离开家的。)

❖ We *aren't* using this example because it is ambiguous.
   因为这个例子有歧义,所以我们**不用**。
   (或:我们并不是因为这个例子有歧义才用它的。)

❖ I did *not* marry her because I loved her.
   我因为爱她才**没有**和她结婚。
   (或:我不是因为爱她才和她结婚的。)

**Comments** It is really hard for us to cope with the "*not...because...*" construction in translation because the negative word "*not*", sometimes, can only negate the main clause, and sometimes can only negate the subordinate clause; in some cases however it may negate either of them. Only by carefully and really understanding the original, analyzing and studying the author's intention from the context, can we render it correctly and exactly.

### 3.1.10 Affirmative in Meaning 含有否定词的肯定翻译

In English, although some sentences are negative in form, they are actually affirmative in meaning. So we should pay special attention to these negative sentences in translation. The following phrases and structures should be noticed.

**1) "can + negative word + too / over- " construction**

❖ You *can't* be *too* careful when you drive a car.
  开车时,越小心越好。

❖ *No* man can have *too* much knowledge and practice.
  知识和实践越多越好。

❖ The importance of proper lubrication *cannot* be *over*-emphasized.
  应特别强调适当进行润滑的重要性。

**2) "no/ not/nothing + more/ less + than" construction**

❖ It is *no more than* a beginning.
  这仅仅是个开端。

❖ I had *no sooner* reached home *than* it began to rain.
  我刚一到家,天就下雨了。

❖ *No less than* 150 people were injured in the crash.
  这次飞机失事中,受伤人数竟达 150 名。

**3) "no/ not/ never/ nothing... + but/ except/ until" construction**

❖ Some oil wells produce *nothing but* salt water, while others always remain dry.
  有些油井只产盐水,而另一些油井却总是干的。

❖ She did *not* turn up *until* the meeting was over.
  直到会议结束她才出现。

❖ The molecular formula C6H14 *doesn't* show anything *except* the total number of carbon and hydrogen atoms and hence is seldom used.
  分子式 C6H14 只表示碳原子和氢原子的总数,因此很少使用。

**Comments** Note that the Chinese versions are affirmative in sense though there are negative words in the source language. This is a very good method in translation of such constructions. In English, some phrases appear to have negative words, but they have positive meanings. For instance, "*nothing like*" has the Chinese sense of 没有……比得上; "*no less...than*" is in the sense of 不少于,正好; "*no more than*" has the Chinese meaning of 只有,仅仅; and the expression "*cannot be too*" is in the sense of 无论

怎样……都不过分。Therefore when we translate such phrases or expressions, we should understand their usage in particular.

### 3.1.11 Compare and Analyze 比较与分析

Why do you teach? My friend asked the question when I told him that I didn't want to be considered for an administrative position. He was puzzled that I did not want what was obviously a "step up" toward what all Americans are taught to want when they grow up: money and power.

Certainly ①<u>I don't teach because teaching is easy for me</u>. Teaching is the most difficult of the various ways I have attempted to earn my living: mechanic, carpenter, writer. For me, teaching is a red-eye, sweaty-palm, sinking-stomach profession. Red-eye, because I never feel ready to teach no matter how late I stay up preparing. Sweaty-palm, because I'm always nervous before I enter the classroom, sure that I will be found out for the fool that I am. Sinking-stomach, because I leave the classroom an hour later convinced that I was even more boring than usual.

②<u>Nor do I teach because I think I know answers, or because I have knowledge I feel compelled to share</u>. Sometimes I am amazed that my students actually take notes on what I say in class!

我告诉一位朋友我不想谋求行政职务时,他向我提出这样一个问题:你为什么要教书呢?美国人受的教育是长大成人后应该去追求金钱和权力,而我却偏偏不朝这个方向"发展",这使他大惑不解。

当然,①<u>我之所以教书并不是因为做教师轻松</u>。为了谋生,我做过各种各样的工作:机修工、木工、作家,可教书是最难的行业。就我而言,教书是个令人熬红眼睛、手掌出汗、精神沮丧的职业。说它是熬红眼睛的职业,是因为我晚上无论备课到多晚,总觉得准备得不够充分;说它是令人手掌出汗的职业,是因为我进教室前总是紧张不已,认为学生会发现我原来是个笨蛋;说它是令人精神沮丧的职业,是因为我走出教室一小时后,仍觉得这堂课上得比平常还要平淡无味。

②<u>我之所以教书,不是因为我认为自己能够解答问题,也不是因为我满腹经纶,非得与他人分享不可</u>。有时,学生竟把我课上讲的东西做了笔记,这令我感到很惊异!

注:选自《大学英语》V.3. p46,上海外语教育出版社,1997。译文有修改。

**Notes**: In the short passage, there are two places where transferred negation is used. In sentence ①, "*don't*" does not negate the main clause, rather it negates the subordinate clause "*because teaching is easy for me*". In sentence ②, instead of negating the main clause "*do I teach*", "*nor*" actually negates because-clause.

### 3.1.12 Exercises 练习

Ⅰ. **Sentence translation.**

A) **Translate the following, paying attention to connotative negation.**

1. I have failed to convince him of his error. (verb—be unsuccessful in)
2. Under fifty people were there. (preposition—less than, fewer than)
3. She always seemed too busy in the house. (too—more than enough)
4. The stranger had already gone before he hurried to the hotel. (before—earlier than the time when...)
5. I'll do it now before I forget it. (conjunction)
6. The point slipped my attention. (verb)
7. He is not stupid, merely ignorant. (adjective)
8. The explanation is pretty thin. (adjective)
9. It was beyond his power to sign such a contract. (preposition)
10. He is above corruption. (preposition)
11. I will not go unless I hear from him. (conjunction)
12. The guerrillas would fight to death before they surrendered. (conjunction)
13. I should do the work rather than you. (conjunction)
14. I love you more than I could say. (conjunction)

**B) Translate the following, paying attention to the underlined parts.**

1. Suddenly he heard a sound behind him, and realized he was *not alone* in the garage. (there was someone else besides him)
2. You can *never be too* careful about English-Chinese translation. (more than enough)
3. It was *not until* 1972 that Charles Chaplin was welcome back to receive an award—the award of an Oscar. (later than the time when...)
4. The American leaders believed that their cause could *not win unless* they had the confidence of other peoples.
5. The effects of some medicine are *not immediate*.
6. There is *nothing like* jogging as a means of exercise.
7. She is *no less* diligent *than* her sister.
8. I have *no more than* ten dollars in my pocket.
9. We *cannot be too* careful in doing experiments.

**C) Translate the following for smoothness.**

1. The doubt was still *unsolved* after his repeated explanation. (verb)
2. He *carelessly* glanced through the note and got away. (adverb)
3. All the articles are *untouchable* in the museum. (adjective)
4. He manifested a strong *dislike* for his father's business. (noun)
5. *Don't lose time in* posting this letter. (phrase)
6. Students, *with no exception*, are to hand in their papers this afternoon. (phrase)
7. Metals do *not* melt *until* heated to a definite temperature. (conjunction)

**II. Passage translation.**

### The Future of International Trade

In spite of the difficulties of predicting future trends in world trade, we can specify factors that will be important.

Although feeding the world's population will be a major problem, the world is probably not headed for disaster. First, the world's arable acreage can be expanded greatly. Second, the distribution of food and the yield of food per acre can be improved. Third, population growth can be controlled. Historical evidence shows that birth and death rates level off as countries move into the industrial stage.

If population growth continues at its present pace, the future balance between food demand and supply may become dependent on new dietary patterns. Reduced consumption of meat, increased use of new high protein food made from soybeans, and development of ocean resources for food are some alternatives that must be considered.

Growth of trade will depend greatly on availability of energy sources. There may still be a trillion barrels of recoverable oil in the Middle East. But the oil crisis of 1974 has led to renewed interest in coal and to a search for alternative sources of energy. Solar, geothermal, and nuclear energy will play a large role in the years to come.

In future trade the key development to watch is the relationship between the industrialized and the developing nations. Third World countries export their mineral deposits and tropical agricultural products, which bring them desired foreign exchange. Tourism has also been greatly responsible for the rapid development of some developing nations. Many Third World nations with high unemployment and low wages have seen an emigration of workers to the developed nations. Western Europe has received millions of such workers from Mediterranean countries. The developing nations profit when these workers bring their savings and their acquired technical skills back home. Many developing nations benefit when Western nations establish manufacturing in their countries to take advantage of cheap labor.

International monetary cooperation will have a significant impact on future trade. If the IMF (International Monetary Fund) countries are not able to agree upon a new international monetary order in the years to come, international trade may become too risky for some companies to get involved in. If the IMF is unable to create sufficient international liquidity reserves in the future, there may not be enough liquidity to sustain growth in trade.

## 3.2 Translation of Passive Sentences 被动句的翻译

As we know, English has two voice forms: the active voice and the passive-voice. The former is much easier for all translators to cope with in translating. So our discussion will be focused on the passive voice which is the more problematic and thus more intriguing of the two voice forms.

Many actions involve two persons or things—one that performs the action and the other affected by the action. The former is referred to as the "agent" and the latter the "recipient".

In English, the passive-voice is much more often used than in Chinese, especially when the text involves economic and scientific matters; besides, there are quite a lot of differences between Chinese and English in the expression of passive meaning. Therefore when we translate between the two languages, we should pay attention to their differences in the expressions of passive meaning and in the use of the passive-voice. Here we'll talk about some common methods regarding English passive sentences.

### 3.2.1 Common Methods of Translating the Passive-Voice 被动句的翻译方法

The extensive use of passive-voice sentences is a distinct characteristic of English language. They are used in English when: 1) it is not necessary or not appropriate to mention the agent of the action; 2) it is impossible to mention the agent of the action; 3) the focus of the sentence is on the recipient of the action. Passive-voice sentences are also used to improve the coherence of the context or to make a better arrangement of sentences. In the scientific and technological papers, which are characterized by objectivity and impartiality, passive-voice sentences are more frequently used. So in order to do a good job in English-Chinese translation, we should master the skill of translating English passive-voice sentences properly. There are several methods of handling English passive-voice sentences in translation.

#### 3.2.1.1 Convert the passive-voice English into the active-voice Chinese 英语被动句转换成汉语主动句

**1) The subject of a SL sentence is kept intact and the SL sentence is translated into a Chinese active sentence.**

Even if some English passive-voice sentences are translated into Chinese active sentences without using such words as 被, 受, the active meaning of the TL sentences is still explicit. Under such circumstances, we can keep intact the subject of the SL sentence, and translate the SL sentence into a Chinese sentence which is active in form but passive in meaning.

❖ Other questions *will be discussed* briefly.

   其他问题将简单地<u>加以讨论</u>。

**Comments** The subject of the original English is translated into the subject of an active-voice Chinese sentence.

❖ His house *is located* on the edge of the city.

   他的房屋<u>坐落</u>在市区的边缘。

**Comments** When the passive-form verb of the original sentence roughly equals an intransitive verb in semantics, we can directly translate the English sentence into an active-voice Chinese sentence.

❖ During the World Cup our streets *were filled with* football fans.

   世界杯比赛期间,街上<u>挤满了</u>足球迷。

**Comments** When the passive form of an English sentence expresses a state in semantics, we can directly render the sentence into an active-voice Chinese one.

❖ Candidates *are required* to present themselves fifteen minutes before the examination begins.

考生**应**于考试前15分钟到达考场。

**Comments** When the passive form of an English sentence expresses an obligation or duty, we can directly convert it into active-voice Chinese.

**2) The subject of the SL sentence is used as the object of the TL sentence in translation.**

In handling English passive-voice sentences, we can convert the subject of the SL sentence into the object of the TL sentence and translate the SL prepositional object which is equivalent to the agent of the action into the subject of the TL sentence. If necessary, we can add general-reference subjects such as 人们，我们，大家，有人，部分人, etc. in the translation.

❖ 1,200 people had *been saved* by soldiers in the earthquake.

在地震中，战士们已**救出**1,200人。

**Comments** The by-agent, the logical subject of the original English, is translated into the subject of an active-voice Chinese sentence, while the subject of the original is converted into the object of the Chinese sentence.

❖ English *is spoken* in Britain, the U.S. and some other countries.

英国、美国和其他一些国家**讲**英语。

**Comments** The subject of the original is used as the object of an active-voice Chinese sentence in the translation, while the adverbial of place in the original is used as the subject of the Chinese sentence.

❖ *It is suggested* that meeting be put off till next Monday.

**有人建议**会议推迟到下星期一举行。

**Comments**: When "*it*" is used as the formal subject of a passive-voice English sentence, we can translate the sentence by adding a logical subject to the Chinese version. This logical subject is often a pronoun of general-reference such as 人们，大家 etc.

❖ All metals *are found* not to conduct electricity equally well.

**人们发现**，并非所有的金属都能同样好地导电。

**Comments** In the TL sentence, a general-reference subject 人们 is added and the subject of the SL sentence is converted into the object of the predicate verb in the translation.

**3.2.1.2 Convert passive-voice English sentences into be-verb Chinese sentences 英语被动句转换成含"是"的汉语句**

In Chinese, we often use "……是……的" to show a fact about people or things. Such a structure often has a passive meaning in Chinese, equivalent to a passive-voice English sentence. So some passive-voice English sentences can be conveniently rendered into be-verb Chinese sentences by adding 是 in the translation.

❖ In the old society, women *were looked down upon*.

在旧社会，妇女们**是受歧视的**。

- History *is made by the people*.
  历史**是**人民创造**的**。
- Some plastics *have been discovered by accident*.
  某些种类的塑料**是**偶然发现**的**。
- The Statue of Liberty *was presented to the U. S.* in the nineteenth century *by the people of France*.
  自由女神雕像**是**法国人民在19世纪**送给美国的**。
- Rainbows *are formed* when sunlight passes through small drops of water in the sky.
  彩虹**是**阳光穿过天空中的小水滴时**形成的**。
- Rome *was not built* in a day.
  罗马**不是一天建成的**。
- Concrete *is made of* cement, sand, stones and water.
  混凝土**是**用水泥、沙子、石子和水**制成的**。

**Comments** In the above translations, the Chinese sentence pattern of "……是……的" is used to describe the objective circumstances of persons or things. It usually has a passive meaning in Chinese so that it is equivalent to the English passive form.

### 3.2.1.3 Convert passive-voice English sentences into subjectless Chinese sentences 英语被动句转换成汉语无主语句

English sentences always have their subjects except for imperative sentences, but Chinese sentences can have no subject (subjectless sentences). This is an important difference between the two languages. Therefore, passive-voice English sentences can be converted into subjectless Chinese sentences when it is not necessary to tell readers the agent of an action. As a rule, a passive-voice English sentence without a by-agent but with a modal verb (auxiliary) can be translated into a subjectless sentence.

- Great efforts should *be made* to inform young people especially the dreadful consequences of taking up the habit.
  应该尽最大努力告诫年轻人危害，特别是沾上这个习惯后的可怕后果。
- Smokers must *be warned* that doctors have reached the conclusion that smoking increases the possibility of lung cancer.
  必须警告吸烟者，医生已得出结论，吸烟会增加患肺癌的可能性。

**Comments** As is shown in the translation of the above two sentences, we can convert the subjects of the original English sentence into the objects of subjectless Chinese sentences, and place them behind the predicate verbs.

- New source of energy must *be found*, and this will take time.
  必须找到新的能源，这需要时间。

**Comments** The subject and the predicate of the original English sentence are placed together, and translated into a Chinese predicate and an object, but the sentence is without a subject.

❖ Water *can be shown* as containing impurities.
可以证明水含有杂质。

Comments The subject of the original English sentence can be translated into the sub-subject of Chinese.

❖ Wrongs *must be righted* when they are discovered.
发现了错误一定要改正。

Comments The subjects in the main clause and the subordinate clause of the original English sentence are the same. So when this English sentence is translated into a subjectless Chinese sentence, 错误 serves as both the object of 发现 and 改正.

### 3.2.1.4 Convert passive-voice English sentences into passive-form Chinese sentences 用含有被动概念的词翻译英语被动句

In Chinese, we also have certain passive-form sentences that emphasize the passiveness of the action. If the original passive-voice English sentence is translated directly into a passive-voice Chinese sentence, the latter usually has the effect of emphasis. We can translate these kinds of sentences by adding Chinese functional words such as 被、受、使、把、给、遭、由、为, etc. in the translation.

1) "被……"、"给……"、"叫……"

❖ The thief *was arrested* by the policeman.
小偷被警察抓住了。

❖ Over the years, tools and technology themselves as a source of fundamental innovation have largely *been ignored* by historians and philosophers of science.
工具和技术本身作为根本性创新的源泉多年来在很大程度上被科学史学家和科学思想家们忽视了。

❖ Running water has long *been used* to turn the wheels of industry.
很久以来，流水就被用来转动工业上用的轮子。

❖ Part or all of the light may *be reflected, absorbed, or transmitted* by the thing or object that comes into its way.
一部分的光或全部的光可能给挡住其去路的东西或物体所反射、吸收或透射。

2) "遭……"、"受……"、"遭受……"

❖ Our roof *was damaged* in last night's storm.
在昨夜的暴风雨中，我家的屋顶遭到了破坏。

❖ Our foreign policy *is supported* by the people all over the world.
我们的对外政策受到了世界人民的支持。

❖ The success of our economic development *is continually lauded*.
我国经济发展所取的成功不断受到人们的赞扬。

- Last year the region *was visited* by the worst drought in 60 years.
  去年这个地区**遭受到** 60 年来最严重的旱灾。

3)"为……所……"
- Socialist ideology has *been accepted* by the people of the whole country.
  社会主义思想体系已**为**全国人民**所接受**。
- Only a small part of the sun's energy reaching the earth *is used* by us.
  传到地球的太阳能只有一小部分**为**我们**所利用**。
- The atomic theory *was* not *accepted* until the last century.
  原子学说直到上世纪才**为**人们**所接受**。

4)"(是)由"、"让"
- Natural light or "white light" *is* actually *made up* of many colours.
  自然光或者"白光"实际上**是由**许多种颜色**组成**的。
- History *is made* by the people.
  历史**是由**人民**创造**的。
- Most letters from home *are read* to him by his girlfriend.
  他的家信大多数**是让**女友**读**给他听的。

5)"予以……"、"加以……"
- The problem must *be dealt with* at the appropriate time.
  这个问题必须在适当的时候**予以处理**。
- The subject will *be discussed* briefly later.
  那个主题稍后将简单地**加以讨论**。

**Comments** These kinds of translation in the above sentences are frequently used to emphasize the actions of passiveness or to lay stress on the by-agents.

### 3.2.1.5 Convert by-agent and recipient into cause-and-effect
行为者与接受者转换成因果关系

If the by-agent is an inanimate noun, not an animate one, not a person or animal, the by-agent and the recipient can be translated into a cause-and-effect relationship in Chinese. This treatment renders the translation natural and smooth in conformity to Chinese habitual way of expression.

- In that sense the characters are called into existence *by the demands of the plot*.
  从这个意义上说,人物**由于情节的需要**而产生出来。
- The use of English in international diplomacy is strengthened *by its acceptance as one of the official languages of the United Nations*.
  **由于英语被接受为联合国的官方语言之一**,这就使英语在国际外交场合使用更为广泛。

**Comments** Such a situation indeed requires us to carefully analyze the original and comprehend it and see whether it contains a cause-and-effect relationship between the agent and the recipient.

### 3.2.1.6 Some useful patterns 一些常用的句型

| | |
|---|---|
| It is said that… | 据说,有人说 |
| It is well known that… | 众所周知 |
| It is hoped that… | 希望,有人希望 |
| It is believed that… | 大家相信,有人相信 |
| It is reported that… | 据报道 |
| It is learned that… | 据闻,已经查明 |
| It is found that… | 据发现,人们认为 |
| It is claimed that… | 据说,有人说 |
| It is supposed that… | 据推测,人们猜测 |
| It is considered that… | 据估计,人们认为 |
| It is thought that… | 有人认为 |
| It has been announced that… | 已经宣布 |
| It is asserted that… | 有人主张 |
| It is rumoured that… | 听说,谣传 |
| It is universally accepted that… | 人们普遍认为 |
| It is taken that… | 人们认为,有人认为 |
| It is regarded that… | 人们认为 |
| It is suggested that… | 建议,有人建议 |
| It is demonstrated that… | 据证实,已经证明 |
| It is recommended that… | 有人建议 |
| It is proposed that… | 有人提出 |
| It will be seen from this that… | 由此可见,因此可知 |
| It was noticed above that… | 人们注意到,前面已指出 |
| It must be admitted that… | 必须承认,老实说 |
| It has been illustrated that… | 据说明,据图示 |
| It is stressed that… | 人们/有人强调说 |
| It cannot be denied that… | 不可否认 |
| It is sometimes asked that… | 人们有时会问 |
| It was felt that… | 有人感觉到了 |
| It is calculated that… | 据计算 |
| It should be realized that… | 我们应该认识到 |

It is pointed out that…          有人指出，人们指出
The principle of… is outlined…   本文概述了……的原则
The apparatus for… is described… 本文描述了……的装置
Automation of… is discussed…    本文讨论了……的自动化
An account of… is given…        本文叙述了……
The use of… is addressed…       本文论述了……的应用
The mechanism of… is established… 本文探讨了……的机制
The dependence of… is established… 本文确定了……的关系
An analysis of… was carried out… 本文对……做了分析

### 3.2.2 Compare and Analyze 比较与分析

The conversion of mechanical energy to heat is by no means new to us. We are also familiar with other transformations of energy. ① <u>Chemical energy is converted into heat</u> when fuel burns. Electrical energy is transformed into heat and light in electrical lamps and electrical stoves. Radiant energy turns into heat when sunlight strikes an object which absorbs it. "All contradictory things are interconnected; not only do they coexist in a single entity in given conditions, but in other given conditions, they also transform themselves into each other." In a word, all energies may be converted from one form into another and what is more, they all can transform into heat by themselves. Heat is an energy of irregular motion of particles in a substance; at ordinary temperature it is less usable than any of the other energies.

However, at high temperatures heat energy may be converted into energy of more usable forms. ② <u>Different kinds of machines have been made to convert heat into mechanical energy.</u> ③ <u>Diesel and gasoline engines are designed to convert heat</u> ④<u>that is developed by the burning of fuel into mechanical energy for running tractors, trucks, and cars.</u> ⑤ The mechanical energy is

机械能转换为热能对我们而言一点也不生疏。我们也熟悉其他的能量转换形式。①**燃料燃烧时，化学能就转换成热能**。在电灯及电炉中，电能转换为光能和热能。太阳光照到吸收光的物体上时，辐射能就转换为热能。"一切矛盾着的东西都互相联系着，不但在一定的条件之下共处于一个统一体中，而且在一定条件之下互相转化。"总而言之，一切能都可以从一种形式转换成另一种形式，并且它们自己都能转换成热能。热能是物质内的微粒无规则运动所产生的能量，在常温下它比其他各种能的用处都小。

然而在高温下，热能可转换成更有用的能量。②**人们已经制造出把热能转换为机械能的各种机器。**③**柴油发动机和汽油发动机被设计用来把**④**燃烧燃料产生的热能转换成机械能，用来开动拖拉机、卡车和汽车。**

converted from heat energy by steam turbine generators. And the generators, in turn, convert the mechanical energy into electrical energy. All these transformations are taking place every minute and everywhere in our daily life and production.

⑤蒸汽涡轮机把热能转换为机械能,使发电机运转。而发电机又把机械能转换为电能。这些能量转换在我们的日常生活和生产中时时处处都在发生着。

Notes：①The original passive sentence is translated into an active-voice Chinese sentence. The original subject is retained in the Chinese sentence while the verb is used in the active voice. This is the main technique used to translate most of the passive-voice sentences in this passage.

②The original passive-voice sentence is translated into an active-voice sentence by converting the original subject into an object and by adding a new subject 人们 which is a pronoun of general-reference.

③The main clause of the original English sentence is in passive voice. It is translated into a passive-voice Chinese sentence by using 被 which is a typical marker of passive structure in Chinese.

④This attributive clause is also in passive voice. Since it introduces the agent of the action by using "*by…*" structure, the translator translates it into an active voice structure by converting the agent "*burning of fuel*" into a subject.

⑤The original passive-voice sentence is translated into an active-voice sentence by converting the agent of the action "*steam turbine generators*" into the subject of the Chinese sentence, while the subject of the original sentence "*the mechanical energy*" is converted into the object of the predicate verb in the Chinese sentence.

A current search of the files indicates that the letter is no longer in this bureau's possession. ① It is noted that ② the letter was received two months ago, and after study, ③ returned to your office. In view of the foregoing, ④ it is regretted that your office has no record of its receipt. If ⑤ the letter is found, ⑥ it would be appreciated if this bureau ⑦ was notified at once.

最近查找了卷宗,发现本局并无此信。①根据记录,②信是两个月前收到的,经研究后,已③寄还贵处。有鉴于此,贵处似无收信的记录,④甚为遗憾。如能⑤找到此信,请立即⑦通知本局,⑥不胜感谢。

Notes：This is a letter in which there are several passive sentences. The translation completely follows the Chinese language writing style and features so that it is very fluent and natural when reading.

### 3.2.3 Exercises 练习

Ⅰ. Sentence translation.

1. The boy student was criticized yesterday morning.
2. The compass was invented by Chinese long ago.
3. Such books are written for children.
4. This help-the-poor policy has been successfully carried out.
5. Sometimes the communication would be seriously disturbed by solar spots.

6. A railway bridge is being built by the workers.

7. Mechanical energy can be changed back into electrical energy through a generator.

8. You are wanted on the phone.

9. He was considered quite qualified for the job.

10. Visitors are requested to deposit their bags before entering the exhibition hall.

11. Life cannot be understood without much charity.

12. Measures have been taken to prevent the epidemic from spreading quickly.

13. Attention should be paid to safety in handling exploders.

14. The price of tape recorders has been cut again.

15. That city is well supplied with water.

16. This limousine will be equipped with safety belts.

17. Shelley's poems have been translated into many languages.

18. It is stressed that the field of science may be divided into two major areas: natural science and social science.

19. It should be pointed out that this process is oxidation.

**II. Passage translation.**

The protons and neutrons in the nuclei of most common atoms are strongly held together. The nuclei of these atoms are said to be stable. On the other hand, the nuclei of some atoms especially the bigger ones like uranium, are not so stable. This is partly due to the large number of protons and neutrons present in their nuclei.

Large unstable nuclei have a tendency to break up, on their own, into small nuclei. They can also be made to break up, or split, into smaller nuclei if they are bombarded with very small particles. The splitting of the nucleus of an atom is called fission. But what is the importance of fission? When fission of, say, a uranium nucleus occurs, the nucleus splits up into small nuclei of other atoms and gives off neutrons and a large amount of nuclear energy in the form of heat. The energy given off from the fission of just one kilograms of uranium is equivalent to the energy we can obtain from burning over 900,000 kilograms of coal! Just imagine what a tremendous amount of energy we can get from nuclear fission.

## 3.3 Translation of Long Sentences 长句的翻译

English and Chinese languages are sharply different in their sentential structures. Most English sentences are hypotactic in nature, while most Chinese sentences are paratactic in nature. By hypotactic, we mean that the sentential constituents are interlinked by formal linguistic means, such as prepositions, conjunctions and other connectives, and the grammatical and logical relationships within the sentence are explicitly indicated by connectives and grammatical markers. For this reason, in English, there are often long sentences that consist of a main clause and numerous subordinate clauses (i.e. attributive clauses, adverbial clauses and objective clauses) and phrases

(i. e. infinitive phrases, nominal phrases and prepositional phrases), involving complicated grammatical and logical relationships within the sentence. Chinese sentences are mostly paratactic which lack grammatical markers or connectives to organize sentential constituents, and therefore the grammatical and logical relationships within the sentence are often implicit, but generally inferable from the context. As a result, Chinese sentences are mostly short and simple in structure. Chinese sentences do not have complex hierarchies as English sentences do. By contrast, it is very convenient to build long sentences by means of subordinate clauses, phrases, connectives and grammatical markers in English language. Due to this difference in English and Chinese sentence structures, the translation of English long sentences is a difficult point we should attach great importance to. In this part, we will have an exhaustive discussion on the translation of long English sentences in English-Chinese translation.

### 3.3.1 General Procedures of Translating Long English Sentences
### 长句翻译的总体原则

The translation of long English sentences is often "a hard nut to crack" for translators, since long English sentences are very complicated in structure, involving various logical and grammatical relationships. It is not easy to distinguish a long sentence's structure at a glance. For example, a modifier in a long sentence is sometimes separated from its headword by intervening words or phrases, and such a phenomenon often leads to misunderstanding of the entire sentence. Still, a modifier may qualify several headwords or a headword may be qualified by several modifiers. Even if the translator can fully comprehend the SL sentence, it is not easy to convey its meaning in fluent Chinese. In spite of such difficulties, it is still possible to translate long English sentences well if we adopt the follow procedures to handle them:

1. Divide a long English sentence into meaningful groups and identify the main clause and the subordinate clauses.

2. Distinguish the logical relationships between modifiers and their headwords, determine whether other elements are inserted between modifiers and their headwords, find out whether a headword is qualified by several modifiers or whether a modifier qualifies several headwords.

3. Analyze the logical relationships among the meaningful groups (including the time order of actions).

4. Translate the meaningful groups into individual Chinese short sentences.

5. Based on the logical relationships among the meaningful groups of the SL

sentence, rearrange the Chinese short sentences in logical order, adding necessary connectives and deleting redundant words so as to make the translation cohesive and concise.

6. Revise and polish the translation by referring to the SL sentence.

### 3.3.2 Some Techniques of Translating Long English Sentences
### 长句翻译的方法

Apart from the above six steps we can generally follow in dealing with long English sentences, there are several commonly used techniques mostly related to the stage of representing the original meaning in the translating process.

#### 3.3.2.1 Synchronizing 顺译法

Just as its name implies, *synchronizing* refers to the translation method that follows the order of time, plot and logic for the original English sentences. In other words, when the structural order of the SL sentence is the same as the logical order of an equivalent Chinese sentence, we can translate the SL sentence sequentially, and arrange the Chinese version in the same order as the original sentence. Now analyze the following sentences and finger out how the method goes.

- ❖ Visual cues from audience members can indicate that a speech is dragging, that the speaker is dwelling on a particular point for too long, or that a particular point requires further explanation.

  听众的眼神可以表明,演说过于拖沓,演说者在某一点上讲得太多,或者在某一点上还需要作进一步的解释。

**Comments** The main clause of the SL sentence is "*Visual cues from audience members can indicate…*" The predicate verb has three coordinate objective clauses that are organized in the same order as an equivalent Chinese sentence. So we can translate the original sentence sequentially.

- ❖ But art history focuses on much more than this because art reflects not only the political values of a people, but also religious beliefs, emotions, and psychology.

  但是艺术历史注意的不仅仅是这些,因为艺术反映的不单是一个民族的政治价值观,而且还有他们的宗教信仰、情感和心理特点。

**Comments** The SL sentence is a complex sentence containing an adverbial clause of cause. Such a logical order of "*result*" followed by "*cause*" is in conformity to that of Chinese language, so the original sentence can be translated sequentially.

- ❖ One widely held belief is that a sharp fright will end a troublesome bout of hiccups, but many people prefer just waiting for them to go away as this "cure" is often worse than the ailment itself.

一种普遍为人们接受的观点是，猛然的惊吓会止住一阵讨厌的打嗝，但是许多人宁愿等打嗝自然过去，因为这种"止嗝的方法"往往比打嗝本身更糟。

**Comments** This sentence can be divided into three meaningful groups: "*One widely held belief is that a sharp fright will end a troublesome bout of hiccups*"; "*but many people prefer just waiting for them to go away*"; "*as this 'cure' is often worse than the ailment itself*". There is a strict logical sequence among these groups. Rendering the SL sentence sequentially will make the translation smooth and accurate.

### 3.3.2.2 Reversing 倒译法

If the structural order of a long English sentence is just the opposite of that of an equivalent Chinese sentence, the SL sentence should be tackled in a reverse order in translation, i.e. we should start our translation from the back of the original sentence. So the TL sentence will be organized in the opposite order in relation to the SL sentence. Its purpose is to accord with Chinese expression. In practice, reverse-order translation is more frequent than sequential-order translation.

- *He did not remember his father* who died when he was three years old.
  
  他3岁时父亲就死了，<u>所以记不起父亲的样子</u>。

- *Can you answer a question* which I want to ask and which is puzzling me?
  
  我有一个问题弄不懂，想请教您，<u>您能回答吗</u>？

- *And I take heart from the fact* that the enemy, which boasts that it can occupy that strategic point in a couple of hours, has not yet been able to take even the outlying regions, because of the stiff resistance that gets in the way.
  
  吹嘘能在几小时内就占领战略要地的敌人，由于一路受到顽强抵抗，甚至还没占领外围地带。<u>这一事实使我增强了信心</u>。

**Comments** The above sentences are translated in reversing way in order to be agreeable with Chinese writing features. In the first sentence, the part "*He did not remember his father*" is translated after the second part. If the second sentence is translated in the synchronizing or sequential-order method into 你能回答一个我要问你的而使我弄不清楚的问题吗？ it is little bit unnatural and hard for us Chinese to read.

- It remains to be seen whether the reserves of raw materials would be sufficient to supply world economy which would have grown by 500 percent.
  
  如果世界经济真的以5倍于现有的速度增长，那么原材料的储备是否能充分满足其需求，尚不得而知。

**Comments**: In the SL sentence, "*whether the reserves of ... by 500 percent*" is a subjective clause, and "*it*" is a formal subject. Such a structure of "*It remains to be seen whether...*" ensures an end weight of the sentence. But if this sentence is translated sequentially, it is impossible to represent the original meaning conveniently in Chinese. So we should translate the attributive clause "*which would have grown by 500 percent...*" first and convert it into a Chinese adverbial clause of condition in order to make the rendering fluent.

- That our environment had little, if anything, to do with our abilities, characteristics and behavior is central to this theory.

  这种理论的核心是,我们的环境同我们的才能、性格特征和行为即使有什么关系的话,也是微不足道的。

Comments in the SL sentence, "*That our environment had… and behavior*" is a subjective clause. If we start translating the sentence from the beginning, the resulting Chinese version will be out of balance—the beginning part of the sentence will be too long while the ending part will be too short. It is preferable to translate the original sentence in a reverse order.

- He flew in just the day before from Georgia where he had spent his vacation basking in Caucasian sun after the completion of the construction job he had been engaged on in the South.

  他本来在南方从事一项建筑工程;任务完成后,他就去格鲁吉亚度假,享受高加索的阳光,昨天才坐飞机回来。

Comments In the original sentence, "*where …*" introduces an attributive clause followed by a prepositional phrase "*after the completion of the construction job…*" containing another attributive clause. We have to break up the original construction and translate it chronologically according to Chinese habitual way of narrating an event. So the TL sentence is in a reverse order in comparison with the SL sentence.

### 3.3.2.3 Embedding 包孕法

The method *embedding* is mainly used for English attributive structures, which is translated as Chinese structure "……的……".

- In 1970, he was placed under house arrest *when he refused to use massive force in suppressing worker riots on the seacoast*.

  1970年他因拒绝使用大规模武力镇压沿海城市的工人骚乱而被软禁。

- Congress has made laws requiring most pressure groups to give information *about how much they spend and how they spend it, the amount and sources of funds, membership, and names and salaries of their representatives*.

  国会已制定法律,要求大部分压力团体呈报他们花费了多少钱,怎样花的,款项的总额以及来源、成员人数、代表的姓名和薪金等情况。

Comments It is easy for us to learn and master this method, but we should know the point that when an English attributive structure is too long, this method can not be used because it probably results in a tedious and inexpressive Chinese sentence. It is suggested that other methods should be used to cope with it.

### 3.3.2.4 Cutting 切分法

*Cutting* method can be explained by two ways. *One is called division*, which means that modifiers in a long English sentence often consist of attributives, adverbials, attributive and adverbial clauses etc. If a modifier is too long to deal with, we can divide it into several parts, and then translate them into Chinese clauses. The other is cutting, in which English sentences will be cut into several parts according to sense group, and then add necessary words or phrases before the new sentence in order to keep Chinese complete and fluent.

❖ The idea of ‖ a fish being able to generate electricity strong enough to light small bulbs, even to run an electric motor, ‖ is almost unbelievable.

鱼能发电,其强度足以点亮小灯泡,甚至能开动马达。‖ 这种想法简直令人难以置信。

**Comments** The focus of the sentence is the modifier of the word "*idea*". That is to say, the attributive is too long to be translated easily. If we divide the long attributive into three Chinese clauses, the Chinese version would be natural and smooth.

❖ There are swift flowing rivers, ‖ slow, sluggish rivers, ‖ mighty rivers with several mouths, ‖ rivers that carry vast loads of alluvium to the sea, ‖ clear, limpid rivers, ‖ rivers that at some seasons of the year have very much more water than at others.

有的河水流湍急;‖ 有的河流速缓慢;‖ 有的河河口有好几处;‖ 有的河带着大量冲击土入海;‖ 有的河清澈见底;‖ 有的河水量在一年中的某些季节较少,而在某些季节却多得很。

**Comments** The basic structure of the sentence is "there are + compound subjects". Here are six subjects that have their own attributives. We can translate them into six parallel clauses in order to make the translation as smooth and expressive as natural Chinese.

❖ Intellectually emancipated at a time when women of good family were not encouraged to do anything more ambitious than dabble in the arts, ‖ she became the editor of a review entitled *Modern Women* ‖ in which she was bold enough to publish essays by the revolutionaries.

当时,对有教养人家的女子,至多不过让她们对艺术稍事涉猎,并不鼓励她们做比这更有抱负的事情。‖ 但她不受旧思想的约束,担任了一家名叫《现代妇女》的杂志的编辑。‖ 她大胆地在这个刊物上发表革命人士的文章。

**Comments**: The central part of the sentence is "*she became the editor*". Before and after the essential part, there are several modifiers, which may be divided into three parts to be translated conveniently into Chinese. The first part gives the background information; the second is the essential part of the sentence, and the third gives further explanation.

❖ He visited many places, in all of which he was received with the usual enthusiasm ‖ *which* attached his arduous labors.

他走访了很多地方,常常受到热情的欢迎,**这都是他**努力的结果。

❖ ‖ Human beings have distinguished themselves from other animals, ‖ and in doing so ensured their survival, ‖ by the ability to observe and understand their environment ‖ and then either to adapt to that environment or to control and adapt it to their own needs. ‖

人类把自己和其他动物区别开来。‖ 与此同时，人类还具有观察和了解周围环境的能力。‖ 他们或控制环境，或根据自身的需要改造环境。‖ 人类就这样一代代地生存下去。

**Comments**: The last two sentences belong to the second explanation. It is very clear for us to notice that the long sentences are cut into several parts, which are then translated one by one. Here we should pay attention to the aspect that something coherent between parts should be added. The first sentence is cut into two parts, and the pronoun "*which*" in the second part should be really understood, and then translated into 这都是他. The last sentence is cut into four parts, and 人类 and 他们 are added after we completely figure out the relationship between the subject and predicate.

### 3.3.2.5 Splitting 拆译法

The so-called *splitting* refers to the method that a certain part, including a word, a phrase or a clause, in a sentence is drawn out. This part can be translated in to a Chinese sentence alone, which can be placed at the end of the entire sentence or in front of it.

❖ It is a NATO matter; any comment on it should *appropriately* come from NATO.
这是北约组织的事宜，对此事的任何评论应该由北约组织决定，这才是恰当的。

❖ Young men who have reason to fear that they will be killed in battle may *justifiably* feel bitter in the thought that they have been cheated of the best things that life has to offer.
如果年轻人由于某种原因认为自己有可能在战斗中死去，想到生活所能提供的最美好的东西自己全部无法享受，觉得受了骗而感到痛苦，这是无可指责的。

❖ An outsider's success could even *curiously* help two parties to get the agreement they want.
说来奇怪，一个局外人取得的成功竟然能够促使双方达成一项他们希望得到的协议。

**Comments**: Here are three examples. In the first example, the word "*appropriately*" is drawn out, translated into 这才是恰当的, and then put at the end of the whole sentence. In the second example, the same method is used, and the Chinese version 这是无可指责的 for "*justifiably*" is placed at the end of the whole sentence. Although the same method is used in the last sentence, the Chinese version 说来奇怪 for "*curiously*" is placed in the front of the whole sentence.

### 3.3.2.6 Recasting 重组法

*Recasting* refers to the method requiring the translator to accurately comprehend and grasp the long sentence, to deconstruct the sentence, and then to adjust and recast it by using his or her own words to appropriately express the information, meaning and core style and features of the original. It is little bit difficult for the translator to master this method, which needs him or her to be acquainted to both languages and to have the ability of rewriting and organizing.

- ② In practice, ③ the selected interval thickness is usually **a compromise between the need** ①for a thin interval to maximize the resolution and thick interval to minimize the error.

  ①为保证最大分辨率必须选用薄层,为使误差最小却需选用厚层,②实际上③通常选择介于两者之间最佳厚度。

- ④ What the New Yorker would find missing is ③ what many outsiders find oppressive and distasteful about ①New York—its rawness, tension, urgency; its bracing competitiveness; ② the rigor(寒战,发冷) of its judgment; and the congested, democratic presence of so many other New Yorkers encased in their own world.

  ①纽约的粗犷、紧张,那种急迫感和催人奋进的竞争性,②它的是非观念之严酷无情,纽约市的那种各色人等的熙熙攘攘,兼容并蓄于各自的天地之中的格局,③所有这些都使那些非纽约人感到厌恶和窒息;④而这一切,又是纽约人所眷恋的。

**Comments**: As the definition of this skill has been mentioned, this skill requires the translator to accurately comprehend the long sentence, to deconstruct it, and then to adjust and recast it. The examples mentioned above are good ones for us to understand the method. Carefully reading and analyzing them, we have clearly noticed that the Chinese versions adapt to our understanding and thinking (the marked numbers can be paid attention to), the English sentences (the numbers are disordered), however, are quite different in writing and organizing from Chinese ones. This is because there exist different writing styles and features between the two languages. One more thing we should pay attention to is that the information and meaning of the original have to be maintained when we use this method.

### 3.3.2.7 Inserting 插入法

If we have trouble reorganizing the split-up components of the original version when translating long sentences, we can use brackets or dash to insert such items as descriptive attributive, adverbial, and appositive and parenthesis into the TL sentence. Such inserted elements generally supply necessary additional or background information. This technique can make the Chinese version smooth and expressive, and avoid translationese.

- When I went to Yan'an in the summer of 1946, the Anti-Japanese War, *and the Second World War of which it was a part*, had been over for just a year.

  1946年夏天去延安的时候,抗日战争(抗日战争是第二次世界大战的组成部分)才刚刚结束一年。

**Comments** The attributive clause in the original sentence "*...of which it was a part*," can be separately translated and inserted into the TL sentence by means of a bracket to give additional information.

- The second aspect is the application by all members of society *from the government official to the ordinary citizen*, of the special methods of thought and action that scientists use in their work.

  第二个方面是全体社会成员(从政府官员到普通公民)都使用科学家们在工作中所采用的那种特殊的思考方法和行为方法。

**Comments** The prepositional phrase "*from...to...*" can be separately translated and inserted after 社会成员 in the Chinese version to give further explanation.

- The method was largely developed by physicists, chemists and biologists; it was later adopted by people working in such areas as education, psychology and sociology, *where the subjects of research were often people.*

  这种方法在很大程度上先是由物理学家、化学家和生物学家使用,后来为在教育学、心理学和社会学等领域内(其研究对象是人)工作的研究人员所采纳而发展起来的。

**Comments** The non-restrictive attributive clause of the original sentence "*where the subjects...*" is translated as an inserted element and placed behind the noun it modifies to give an explanation.

Of course, we just introduce this method and know that we can have many ways to deal with the explanatory parts in long sentences. As all we know, scholars and experts have different opinions about the inserting method. Some think that the certain parts for the further explanation in such long sentences can be translated in the way that the original goes without using the brackets because it is part of the sentence. If you persist in doing so, the bracketed part will become the translator's voice. Others believe that the methods in translation are many-sided and open-ended, and the translator should employ as many methods as he or she can to render the original in order to embody translational artistry.

### 3.3.2.8 Integrating 综合法

It often happens in the translation of long sentences that we cannot handle a long English sentence properly by using a single skill only. Under such circumstances, we have to make a comprehensive use of the above skills: Some parts of the SL sentence may be translated in a sequential order; other parts may be rendered in a reverse order. Some elements of the original sentence may be handled by means of division or insertion; others may be dealt with by the use of brackets or dashes. This is called *integrating*. In this way, we will be able to make a smooth rendering of the original sentence. Look at the following examples.

- But without Adolf Hitler, who was possessed of a demoniac personality, a granite will, uncanny instincts, a cold ruthlessness, a remarkable intellect, a soaring imagination and until toward the end, when drunk with power and success, he overreached himself an amazing capacity to size up people and situations, there almost certainly would never have been a Third Reich.

然而,如果没有阿道夫·希特勒,那就几乎可以肯定不会有第三帝国。因为阿道夫·希特勒有着恶魔般的性格、花岗石般的意志、不可思议的本能、无情的冷酷、杰出的智力、深远的想象力以及对人和局势惊人的判断力。这种判断力和胜利使他冲昏了头脑而自不量力,终于弄巧成拙。

Comments  The main clause of the original sentence is "*there almost certainly would never have been a Third Reich*". The prepositional phrase "*without Adolf Hitler*" is followed by a non-restrictive attributive clause "*who…*" which contains an adverbial clause "*until…*" This inserted adverbial clause serves to give supplementary information. So it can be translated and placed at the end of the TL sentence according to the logical relationship within the SL sentence. Other parts of the sentence are in the same logical order as the TL sentence. Therefore there are both sequential-order and inverse-order treatments in the translation of the original sentence.

❖ Energy is the currency of the ecological system and life becomes possible only when food is converted into energy which in turn is used to seek more food to grow, to reproduce and to survive.

能量是生态系统的货币,只有当食物变为能量,能量再用来获取更多的食物以供生长、繁殖和生存,生命才成为可能。

Comments: The original sentence is a compound sentence made up of two coordinate clauses. The second coordinate clause contains an adverbial clause of time introduced by "*only when…*" and a non-restrictive attributive clause. We use inverse-order translation to move ahead the adverbial clause of time, and translate the non-restrictive attributive clause by means of division.

❖ By the middle of the year, he warned, the Soviet Union would overtake the United States in the number of land-based strategic missiles, the result of a massive Soviet effort beginning in the mid 1960s, after the Cuban fiasco, to achieve at least parity and possibly superiority in nuclear weapons.

他警告说,到本年年中,苏联将在陆上发射的战略导弹的数量上超过美国,因为苏联在古巴事件失败后,从20世纪60年代中期起就大力发展导弹,目的是为了在核武器方面至少达到同美国均等,并力争超过美国。

Comments: The original sentence is a simple sentence containing a parenthesis which can be moved ahead in translation. There is also a nominal phrase expressing consequence, which contains a prepositional adverbial and an infinitive. On the basis of the logical relationship among these sentential constituents, this nominal phrase can be translated as a clause of reason in the Chinese version.

## 3.3.3 Compare and Analyze 比较与分析

① In addition, one class of family reasons shares a border with the following category, namely, having children in order to maintain or improve a marriage; to hold the husband or occupy the wife; to repair or rejuvenate the marriage; to increase the number of children on the assumption that family happiness lies that way. The point is underlined by its converse: in some societies the failure to bear children (or males) is a threat to the marriage and a ready cause for divorce.

Beyond all that is the profound significance of children to the very institutions of the family itself. To many people, husband and wife alone do not seem a proper family—they need children to enrich the circle, to validate its family character, to gather the redemptive influence of offspring. ②Children need the family, but the family seems also to need children, as the social institution uniquely available, at least in principle, for security, comfort, assurance, and direction in a changing, often hostile, world.

①此外，还有一些家庭方面的原因与下面的这种动机有关，也就是想通过生孩子来维持或改善婚姻状况；或者是用孩子来拴住丈夫或妻子；或者是通过生孩子来修复婚姻或给婚姻注入活力；或者是因为有多子多福的想法，所以想多生孩子。这种愿望可以从相反的情况得到强调：在某些社会中，如果夫妻不育或不能生育男孩，就会对婚姻产生威胁，也可以成为离婚的正当理由。

除了上述所有原因以外，人们还认为生育后代对家庭制度至关重要。对很多人来说，只有丈夫和妻子的家庭似乎是不健全的，还需要有孩子来丰富家庭的生活，体现家庭的特点，并且孩子会对婚姻产生补偿作用。②孩子需要家庭，但家庭好像也同样需要孩子，养育后代似乎是一种独特的社会习俗。至少从原则上说，只要遵从这种社会习俗，即使人们生活在多变而险恶的环境中，也能够得到安全感，获得慰藉，增强信心，并使自己的生活有明确的目标。

**Notes**: ①The original sentence contains a series of coordinate infinitive phrases which are used to express the different reasons of having children. These infinitives are translated into a string of short Chinese clauses which are linked by a repetition of "或者".

②The original long sentence contains two coordinate main clauses. The second one is far more complex than the first one. So it is divided into several meaningful groups according to its structure: "*but the family seems…*", "*as the social…*", "*at least in principle*", "*for security, comfort*", etc. And each is translated into a Chinese clause. Notice that in this process, new words are added to make the expressions more complete in meaning, such as "获得慰藉", etc. Besides, the word order of the original sentence is also partially altered to suit to the linguistic habit of Chinese.

## 3.3.4 Exercises 练习

### I. Sentence translation.

1. The Civil War, lasting four years and costing at least a million lives civilian and military, was the most extensive war ever fought on the soil of the New World, a war that proved to the planters in a revolutionary way that human beings in America could no longer be bought or sold, worked and killed at will to serve the profit of parasitic landowners.

2. If you reach Chicago by train and spend only an hour or two there you will feel the light wind off the lake gives it the name "Windy City".

3. The contrast between this knowledge and understanding of Kissinger's tactics and this uncertainty about his strategy is characteristic of the most of what is written and said, not just about his role in the Middle East but about a whole range of Kissinger's ventures, including the most important one he has undertaken.

4. The global economy that boomed in the 1960s, growing at an average of 5.5 percent a year, and pushed ahead at a 4.5 percent-a-year rate in the mid-1970s, simply stopped growing in 1981—1982.

5. Of the guests, none except the American notices this or sees the boy place a bowl of milk on the veranda just outside the open doors.

6. The 25-year teaching veteran says he was denied a promotion and pay rise last year because he hadn't published a sufficient number of research papers.

7. A man may usually be known by the books he reads as well as by the company he keeps; for there is a companionship of books as well as of men; and one should always live in the best company, whether it be of books or of men.

8. And raising good cotton, riding well, shooting straight, dancing lightly, squiring the ladies with elegance and carrying one's liquor like a gentleman were the things that mattered.

9. Anyone who has ridden on a railroad train knows how rapidly another train flashes by when it is traveling in the opposite direction and conversely how it may look almost motionless when it is moving in the same direction.

### II. Passage translation.

Washington—A group of 20 U.S. and Russian scientists are preparing to launch an unprecedented expedition that will involve being set adrift on an ice floe for five months off the frozen coast of Antarctica, following roughly the same path as the ill-fated expedition of a British explorer nearly eight decades earlier.

In February the scientists, together with 12 support personnel, are due to disembark from the Russian ice breaking research ship Akademik Federov onto an ice floe at the southern end of the Weddell Sea, about 2,000 kilometers south of the tip of South America.

Camped in a nest of prefabricated huts on a chunk of ice about a half kilometer wide and three meters thick, they'll drift northward for about 650 kilometers to gather the extensive data on the poorly understood interactions of ocean, ice and atmosphere in the Weddell Sea. The delicate balance of this system has a strong impact on global climate and ocean currents.

The floe's trajectory will take the scientists through the western part of the Weddell Sea, a region that has been largely off limits to researchers because of its perpetual ice. But in a 1993 meeting of Antarctic scientists in St. Petersburg, Russian scientists suggested a slow but sure way to get a research station into the western Weddell: rely on the natural drift of the ice floes.

# Chapter 4: Cultural Translation
# 文化翻译

## 4.1 Differences between "Culture" in English and 文化 in Chinese 汉英文化的差异

The term "culture" in English does not correspond perfectly with Chinese term 文化. Chinese people think that 文化 is the concept that the instructions and civilized governing have been carried out since the ancient China. Whereas the term "culture" in English, coming from Latin, refers to planting, cultivating or tilling the land in old English, and it was later extended to the concept of civilization, including mental, moral, aesthetic, educational and intellectual activities. In Modern English its original meaning is still retained. In contrast, 文化 is a native word in Chinese. 文 and 化 were used together when the Warring States fought against each other. When the both Chinese characters are used together, they mean 以文教化. They were combined into one word in the Han Dynasty, with its meaning contrasted with "nature" on the one hand and "primitiveness" and "savage" on the other hand. So 文化 was originally associated with mental activities alone.

The different definitions from some reference books may be helpful to show clearly the distinctions between the two terms.

《现代汉语词典》(北京:商务印书馆,1996.1318)defines "文化":

1. 人类社会历史发展过程中所创造的物质财富和精神财富的总和,特指精神财富,如文学、艺术、教育、科学等。

2. 考古学用语,指一个历史时期的不以分布地点为转移的遗迹、遗物的综合体。同样的工具、用具,同样的制造技术等是同一种文化的特征,如仰韶文化、龙山文化。

3. 指运用文字的能力及一般知识:学习文化,文化水平。

*Webster's Ninth New Collegiate Dictionary* (Beijing: World Publishing Corporation, 1988.314) gives "*culture*" the following definitions:

When the term "culture" is used as a noun, it includes:

1. cultivation, tillage

2. the act of developing intellectual and moral faculties, esp. by education

3. expert care and training(beauty culture)

4. a: enlightenment and excellence of taste acquired by intellectual and aesthetic

training; b: acquaintance with and taste in fine arts, humanities, and broad aspects of science as distinguished from vocational and technical skills

5. a: the intellectual pattern of human knowledge, beliefs, and behavior that depends upon man's capacity for learning and transmitting knowledge to succeeding generations; b: the customary beliefs, social forms, and material traits of a racial, religious or social group

6. cultivation of living material in prepared nutrient media; also: a product of such cultivation

When the term "culture" is used as a verb, it has the following definitions:

1. cultivate

2. a: to grow in a prepared medium; b: to start to culture from

Comparing the definitions mentioned above, we can clearly find at least the following differences between "culture" in English and 文化 in Chinese:

1. Though the word class of 文化 is not specified, it is seldom used as a verb in Chinese, whereas "culture" can be used as a verb in English to refer to physical activities.

2. Senses 2 and 3 of 文化 correspond to none of the senses of "culture" in English.

3. Sense 1 of 文化 is more inclusive than any of the senses of "culture" and it stresses the academic development. As will be discussed shortly, literature, arts, social sciences, education and natural sciences belong to academic culture.

4. Senses 1 and 6 of "culture" have no equivalent in the dictionary entry for 文化.

5. "Culture" emphasizes the moral, aesthetic, intellectual changes experienced by individual members of a group and the patterns of knowledge, beliefs and behavior.

These are differences in the everyday senses of the two terms. We would like to make sure that in their everyday senses "culture" and 文化 are not to be equated.

## 4.2 Relationship between Culture and Language 文化与语言的关系

Language is part of culture. It cannot be equated with culture. We do not know the exact period of time when language and culture appeared, but we can say for sure they appeared at the same time. There is no culture that has no language as its part. Language and culture are not separable. We can say that culture is the general environment of different activities in language. Language is strongly influenced and shaped by culture just as a mirror. Culture is reflected in language, and at the same time it exists in the intellectual structures that a certain group use their language. In this sense, we ought to really pay special attention to cultural aspects when we are engaged in the task of translation. However, the relationship between them is not just that between a part and the whole. It is much more complex than that. Language is the carrier and container of culture and it also exerts its influence on culture. Human knowledge and experience are described and stored in language. Customs, habits and behavioral patterns can be described and analyzed in language. Social institutions, value systems, beliefs, world views can be described, analyzed and evaluated in language. Even the visual arts like painting, sculpture, and dancing and the auditory arts such as music and singing can be described and evaluated in language. To be sure, culture can exist in the form of materials. But language as the medium of communication is indispensable in their production and use. It is concluded that language and culture are closely related, influencing and shaping each other. To learn a foreign language implies to learn the culture in which it is spoken. A language can never be learned in a cultural vacuum. Culture is learned through language. Without language as the medium for formal or informal instruction, no culture could ever be learned.

Social scientists tell us that cultures differ from one another and each culture is unique. As cultures are diverse, languages are diverse. It is only natural then that with differences in cultures and differences in languages, difficulties often arise in translating between cultures and across cultures. Understanding is not always easy. Learning a foreign language well means more than merely mastering the pronunciation, grammar, words and idioms. It also means to see the world as native speakers of that language see it, learning the ways in which their language reflects the ideas, customs, and behaviors of their society, learning to understand their "language of the mind". Learning a language, in fact, is inseparable from learning its culture.

Due to the relationship and characteristics between culture and language, translation, in other words, is the process of rendering the culture underlying the language. It is not simply understood as an activity on linguistic facet. We hold that to translate from one language into another, in a sense, is to translate the culture of the language.

## 4.3 Translation and Culture 翻译与文化

The term "culture" addresses three salient categories of human activity: the "personal," whereby we as individuals think and function as such; the "collective," whereby we function in a social context; and the "expressive," whereby society expresses itself. Language is the only social institution without which no other social institution can function; it therefore underpins the three pillars upon which culture is built.

Translation, involving the transposition of thoughts expressed in one language by one social group into the appropriate expression of another group, entails a process of cultural decoding, recoding and encoding. As cultures are increasingly brought into greater contact with one another, multicultural considerations are brought to bear to an ever-increasing degree. Now, how do all these changes influence us when we are trying to comprehend a text before finally translating it? We are not just dealing with words written in a certain time, space and sociopolitical situation; most importantly it is the cultural aspect of the text that we should take into account. The process of transfer, i. e., recoding across cultures, should consequently allocate corresponding attributes vis-a-vis the target culture to ensure credibility in the eyes of the target reader.

Multiculturalism, which is a present-day phenomenon, plays a role here, because it has had an impact on almost all peoples worldwide as well as on the international relations emerging from the current new world order. Moreover, as technology develops and grows at a hectic pace, nations and their cultures have, as a result, started a merging process whose end is difficult to predict. We are at the threshold of a new international paradigm. Boundaries are disappearing and distinctions are being lost. The sharp outlines that were once distinctive now fade and become blurred.

As translators we are faced with an alien culture, which requires that its message be conveyed in anything but an alien way. That culture expresses its idiosyncrasies in a way which is called "culture-bound": cultural words, proverbs and of course idiomatic expressions, whose origin and use are intrinsically and uniquely bound to the culture concerned. So we are called upon to do a cross-cultural translation whose success will depend on our understanding of the culture we are working with.

Is it our task to focus primarily on the source culture or the target culture? The answer is not clear-cut. Nevertheless, the dominant criterion is the communicative function of the target text.

Finally, attention is drawn to the fact that among the variety of translation approaches, the "integrated approach" seems to be the most appropriate. This approach follows the global paradigm in which having a global vision of the text at hand has a primary importance. Such an approach focuses from the macro to the micro level in accordance with the Gestalt-principle, which states that an analysis of parts cannot provide an understanding of the whole; thus translation studies are essentially concerned with a web of relationships, the importance of individual items being decided by their relevance within the larger context: text, situation and culture.

In conclusion, it can be pointed out that the trans-coding (decoding, recoding and encoding) process should be focused not merely on language transfer but also—and most importantly—on cultural transposition. As an inevitable consequence of the previous statement, translators must be both bilingual and bicultural if not multicultural.

## 4.4 Lexical Translation in Culture 文化中的词义翻译

Chinese is a member of the Sino-Tibetan family, which consists of more than 400 languages and dialects and is the most popular and most used family. Chinese is obviously standing out in it. English belongs to the Indo-European family, which contains over 100 languages. It is the most world-wide used language on earth. Each has its own features.

English is a kind of synthetic language, whose feature is inflection. That is to say, English language has plurals, tenses, genders, and a lot of derivatives as well in words. Meanwhile, its feature is symbolized in word order and auxiliaries in constructing sentences. Take the sentence "He works well." for example. The words in this sentence cannot be converted in order at random. But only can we change the order when it is changed into a question or an emphatic sentence. The changed sentences should be "Does he study well?" or "He does study well."

Chinese, strictly speaking, is a kind of analytic and agglutinative language, whose phrases are constructed and linked with individual characters. For instance, 光 and 明 constitutes the phrase 光明, 正 and 大 constitutes 正大 and then the two phrases when placed together form a new phrase 光明正大. Another feature of Chinese is that there is no inflection. In other words, the nouns in Chinese cannot be changed in form, the verbs have no different tenses, and there is no gender change in words. The formation of phrases relies on word order and empty words, and others.

As far as vocabulary is concerned, both languages process plenty of vocabulary. Each has its own ways to express in words. Because of different environments, different ways of thinking, different histories and traditions, both languages remain a lot of words with little corresponding meanings. The most difference is the lexical gap(词义空缺).

❖ hill, mountain, landmass, alp, leap—山
 hen, chick, cock, rooster—鸡
 blue, green—青
 hare, rabbit—兔
 mouse, rat—鼠

**Comments** Carefully compare English and Chinese in this column and we find that the English words on the left cannot generalize the single word on the right.

❖ 你,您—you    江,河—river    父,母—parent
 枪,炮—gun    嫁,娶—marry    夫,妻—spouse

**Comments** Similarly, the English word on the right of each line cannot accurately express the Chinese characters on the left. It is this difference that leads to big difficulties in translating. This requires us to get acquainted with the characteristics underlying the two languages and cultures.

As for word classes, or parts of speech, there are 10 classes in English. They are noun, verb, adjective, pronoun, adverb, numeral, conjunction, preposition, article and interjection. There are also, roughly speaking, 10 parts of speech in Chinese. They are noun, verb, adjective, pronoun, adverb, numeral (plus Chinese classifier measure words), conjunction, preposition, auxiliary and interjection. Comparing the parts of speech, we conclude that English has its article alone, and Chinese owns its classifier measure words alone.

The classification of parts of speech in English is based on grammar, word classes and elements of a sentence. They have strictly corresponding relations. But the classification of parts of speech in Chinese is mainly based on word meaning, that is, notional and empty, dynamic and static, concrete and abstract in word meaning. Because of the differences, some points should be paid attention to. Firstly, in English-Chinese translation, we should apply some techniques to amplify, omit, interpret, transliterate etc. Secondly, we cannot be tied down by the literal meanings and should attach importance on the general meaning, and discourse meaning, and deal with the material flexibly. Thirdly, because of different classes, we may employ the technique of conversion so that we make the translation version various.

❖ She went away with *satisfaction*.

She went away *satisfied*.

She *satisfactorily* went away.

她满意地走了。

**Comments** The three English sentences show us the features of sentence structure. But we can only use one Chinese sentence to translate each of them.

### 4.4.1 Words and Conceptual Meaning 单词与概念意义

English has developed and has been used in English speaking countries that have geographical, historical and other cultural features that cannot be found in Chinese culture. Thus many English words referring to these culture-specific features convey the conceptual meaning that does not exist in Chinese culture. Even if there are translation equivalents in Chinese to these English words, they are only used to refer to specific features of English culture. For example, we may read the English words or phrases like "crocodile tears", "olive branch", "sour grapes", "white pollution", "Internet", "e-commerce", etc. Their equivalents are 鳄鱼眼泪,橄榄枝,酸葡萄,白色污染,因特

网,电子商务. Actually, they are a coincidence on the one hand, and people live on the same earth and have some similarities in the two cultures on the other hand. We, of course, also realize that cultures among nations are influenced and infiltrated with each other.

Many English words are related with geography, history, politics, Christianity and living styles. This is because each language is spoken within its geographical boundaries. There are many words in each language that refer to geography related features, such as places in these areas and plants and animals living in this climate. For instance, "the Mississippi" stands for a long river located in the States, and its version is 密西西比河, "London" is the capital of the UK, so we may translate it into 伦敦, and "kangaroo" is a kind of animal originally living in Australia, so we can translate it into 袋鼠.

Each culture has its own history, which is represented in language. When we come across the word "hippie"(嬉皮士), we ought to know its background. It has been referred to a young man or woman who rejects authority, existing institutions and conventional attitudes towards morality, style of dress, etc. in the U.S. since the 1960s. The word "castle"(城堡) means a fortified building or a group of buildings within a defensive wall in ancient England.

Some words illustrate the relationship between words and politics. The word "congress", for example, is the federal legislature of the U.S. The Chinese version is 美国国会. The term "Prime Minister" is the leader of the British government. So its Chinese version is 英国首相.

In English many words are related to Christianity and holidays which are sometimes foreign to most of the Chinese people. The word "trinity"(三位一体), for example, is the union in one Godhead of three persons, Father(圣父), Son(圣子) and Holy Ghost (圣灵). The holiday "Boxing Day" is the first weekday after Christmas, a legal holiday in England, Wales, Northern Ireland, New Zealand, Australia and South Africa. Christmas boxes are traditionally given to dustmen, postmen and a few other public servants. We, therefore, translate it into 节礼日 rather than 拳击日. "Easter" should be translated into 复活节 instead of 东方人.

Many English words reflect the living style of English speakers. First of all, native speakers of English normally live on what we call western-style food and drink. A few instances are cited to show the importance of this point. "Pudding"(布丁) is a sweet dish typically composed of fruit and flour and fat, boiled or streamed, or of fruit baked with pastry, or of cereals baked in milk, or of creams, custards, etc. "Cocktail"(鸡尾酒) is a drink of spirits mixed with others or with various flavorings. We make every effort to be familiar with such words related to the living style. It is easy for us to handle these words in English. But sometimes it is a little bit difficult for us to deal with some words reflecting the living style. The word "privacy" in English readily reflects the principal contrast between English and traditional Chinese cultures. "Privacy", interpreted as "freedom from undesirable intrusions" and regarded as a human right, has no appropriate equivalents in Chinese. Even though 隐私 is used as its translation equivalent, the Chinese term does not sound so pleasant to the majority of the Chinese people. It may imply that some secret is purposefully kept from those who have the right to know it. The Chinese saying 好事不怕人,怕人没好事 is still frequently heard, which leaves no room for "privacy". We suggest the translation version of "privacy" 私事 rather than 隐私. It is just like the English term "love store" which should be translated into 色情商店 instead of 爱情商店."Striptease" is 脱衣舞 not 布条取乐. Chinese who know only a smattering of English have been known to introduce a companion as "my lover", which causes foreigners to stare in surprise. Actually, the companion is not a lover, but the person's spouse, not 情妇,情夫, but 爱人,丈夫 or 妻子. The term 爱人, literally meaning the person one loves, obviously needs a different rendering in English—simply "husband, wife, fiancé or fiancée". Here let us compare some of English words and what may be mistaken for their equivalents in Chinese:

| | | |
|---|---|---|
| black sheep | 败类,恶棍 | (not 黑羊) |
| high school | 高中 | (not 高等学校) |
| busybody | 爱管闲事的人 | (not 大忙人) |
| busywork | 无用功 | (not 忙碌的工作) |
| cooker | 炊事用具 | (not 厨师) |
| dog days | 三伏天 | (not 狗的日子) |
| donkeywork | 苦役 | (not 驴干的活) |
| Dutch wife | 藤制睡具 | (not 荷兰老婆) |
| first-lady | 总统夫人 | (not 原配夫人) |
| free-love | 公开同居 | (not 自由恋爱) |
| freshman | 大一学生 | (not 新鲜男子) |
| goose step | 正步走 | (not 鹅步) |
| greenhouse | 温室 | (not 绿色的房子) |
| hen-party | 妇女聚会 | (not 母鸡派对) |
| ladybird | 瓢虫 | (not 女士鸟) |
| lover | 情人 | (not 爱人) |

| | | |
|---|---|---|
| night-cart | 粪车 | (not 夜车) |
| pigtail | 辫子 | (not 猪尾巴) |
| political campaign | 竞选活动 | (not 政治活动) |
| restroom | 洗手间 | (not 休息室) |
| service station | 加油站 | (not 服务站) |
| wester | 西风 | (not 西方人) |

Just a few are here listed for words and conceptual meanings. In fact there are a great number of words like these in English. This requires us to concentrate on words and their conceptual meanings while translating. We cannot understand and use them literally and directly.

Here it is worthwhile to mention that some words are generally considered pejorative in one language, but not generally in the other. For example, "ambitious" (野心勃勃) and "equalitarian" (平均主义的) are pejorative in Chinese but positive or neutral to most Americans. On the contrary, "propaganda" (宣传) and "do-gooder" (社会改良家) are pejorative to most Americans, but positive or neutral in Chinese.

### 4.4.2 Words and Associative Meaning 单词与联想意义

For students of a foreign language, it is essential that they know not only the conceptual meaning of words, but also their associative meaning, which is, generally, peripheral in lexical meaning, though. Many English words, since they appeared, have had associative meaning, including connotative, social, affective, reflected, and collocational. If connotations of words, varying from culture to culture, are ignored, serious misunderstandings may occur in cross-cultural communication or translation. The connotations of a great many English words are different from those of their translation equivalents in Chinese. Therefore it is very important for a translator to well know this point. Only a couple of words are mentioned here for example. The word "book" refers to "a number of printed pages fastened together and enclosed in a cover". This is universally true. But for the Chinese people books contain knowledge and wisdom for people, especially, the youth, to learn, while for English speakers, they express ideas for people to consider, to agree or disagree, and to comment. The word "sexy" means "sexually suggestive or stimulating" or "generally attractive or interesting". It is a positive term in English. To be sexy is to possess a positive human quality. Mothers want their daughters to be sexy and girls hope to be sexy, too. However, the sex morality in China is different. We all know that, before the door-open policy, the compliment "You are pretty" by a strange male might hurt a Chinese girl. Even though Chinese culture is changing rapidly, the sentence "You are sexy" might not be taken as a compliment in Chinese because 性感

connotes loose sex morality which is generally rejected in Chinese culture.

### 4.4.2.1 Colors associated with culture and their translation
### 色彩的文化内含及其翻译

Science research shows that there are more than hundreds of colors in the world. The words and expressions of colors vary from culture to culture and their classifications are quite different. But the basic classifications of colors between China and English-speaking countries are roughly the same. They are red, orange, yellow, green, blue, indigo and violet(赤、橙、黄、绿、青、蓝、紫). Because of physical, mental and psychological reasons, the semantic meaning remains different in different customs, habits, and expressions. Now let us look at the following colors and distinguish their associative meaning between English and Chinese.

"Red" is usually associated with celebrations, happiness, delight and joyful occasions. This is true in both English-speaking countries and China. We usually find antithetical couplets written on scrolls in red on both sides of doors during the Spring Festival in China, the brides often wear red clothes in weddings, and when people meet their animal years every twelve years, they frequently wear red belts and red underwear so as to be lucky and dispel misfortunes. Similarly Westerners also like the "red" color, which is still associated with the same pleasant meaning as Chinese do. They regard Christmas and other holidays as "red-letter days"(纪念日,吉日). When they invite the summit leaders of other nations, they use "the red carpet"(隆重的欢迎) in the airport as the most courteous reception.

The word "red", however, sometimes may give us a kind of unpleasant feeling when reading.

❖ a red battle 一场血战　　　　red hands 沾满鲜血的双手
　 red tape 繁文缛节　　　　　 red herring 让人分心的东西
　 red-light district 红灯区　　　red ink 赤字
　 in the red 亏本　　　　　　　paint the town red 狂欢,痛饮

Meanwhile, the "red" color can symbolize health and emotion in both English and Chinese.

❖ A fine old man came to me, with a face as *red* as a rose.
　一位<u>红光</u>满面,精神矍铄的老人朝我走来。

❖ The maxim was that when a married couple saw *red* lawyers saw green.
　俗话说,夫妇吵得<u>面红耳赤</u>之时,便是律师招财进宝之日。

Comments  The word "*red*" in the first sentence implies being healthy and the "*red*" in the second represents a sort of emotion. Here we should pay more attention to the second meaning. English words "see red" expresses the meaning of getting extremely angry or losing one's temper. It is quite different from Chinese Characters 见红, which suggests the bleeding before childbirth or in the first sexual intercourse.

In addition, 红 in ancient China represents beauty. 红颜, 红粉, 红闺, 红楼 are cited as some examples. 红颜 in Chinese means "a beautiful girl" or "a pretty face", 红粉 can be rendered into "a gaily dressed girl". 红闺 may be translated into "a lady's room". 红楼 is "a boudoir".

"Green" has different associative meanings between English and Chinese. In English, it is often used to express "envy and jealousy". For this reason, we can find such phrases as "green with envy" (眼红), "green as jealousy" (妒忌) and "the green-eyed monster" (害了红眼病) in English.

❖ Alice's girl friends were *green with envy* when they saw her new dress.
爱丽丝的女友看到她的新衣时,心里充满了**妒忌**。

**Comments** In Chinese, however this concept is expressed as 红眼, which is really opposite to the English meaning. If we translate it into "red-eyed", we indeed make a big mistake.

Sometimes "*green*" is used to express "an inexperienced or untrained person" or "something undeveloped or gullible".

❖ Smith is a boy who is still *green* at his job.
史密斯是一个对其工作**尚无经验**的青年。

❖ "My eyes, how *green*!" exclaimed the young gentleman. (C. Dickens: *Oliver Twist*)
"啊唷,多么**幼稚**!"小绅士喊道。

By comparison, the Chinese character 绿 is extended to imply that someone's wife has adultery or illicit intercourse with other male, whose expression is 戴绿帽子. If we translate it into "to wear a green hat", native English-speakers may misunderstand it as 头戴一顶绿色的帽子. Actually the Chinese express 戴绿帽子 should be translated into "to be a cuckold" in English instead.

"Green" is sometimes associated with paper money or currency (纸币) as in the phrase "long or folding green".

黄 in Chinese is used to denote something pornographic, filthy, vulgar, trashy, old or obscene. So there appear some expressions like 黄色电影,黄色书刊,黄色音乐,黄色软件 in Chinese. Their English versions should be "obscene films", "filthy publications", "vulgar music", and "trashy software" respectively. Instead in English the word "blue" is used to express such concepts whereas the English word "yellow" has nothing to do with these concepts. We can find expressions in English like "yellow pages"

(黄页电话簿)which refer to the phone directory, and "the yellow press"(耸人听闻的报纸)which refers to the newspapers which present news in a sensational way. "Yellow boy"(金币) refers to gold coin. Sometimes the associative meaning of "yellow" is "cowardly or timid". For instance, "He is too yellow to stand up and fight." is translated into 他太软弱,不敢起来斗争.

But we should know that 黄 was treated as the highest position in ancient China. For one thing, it is pronounced the same as 皇, which stands for an emperor and everything related to him. And for another, 黄 presents harvest in autumn because everything turns yellow at that time.

"Blue" is used to present "tranquility" and "the color of the clear sky in late fall or of the deep sea on a fine day" both in English and Chinese. However, the associative meanings of this word in English are more than in Chinese. In English, it is figuratively used to imply "sadness and hopelessness" as in the phrases "in a blue mood", and "to have the blues".

❖ "You look *blue* today. What's the matter with you?"
　"She is in *holiday blue*."
　"你今天显得闷闷不乐,出了什么事情?"
　"她得了假期忧郁症。"

Comments In the short dialogue above, the first "blue" means "sad", the other is a phrase equal to "winter holiday depression", which refers to the sad and lonely mood before the Christmas.

In addition, the word "blue" in English is applied to denote "pornographic, or vulgar". The phase "a blue film" is translated into 黄色电影, and the Chinese version of "to make a blue joke" is 讲黄段子 or 开下流玩笑.

❖ By one survey, more than 20 million Americans now watch at least one *blue* video each week.
　据一项调查显示,现在美国有两千多万人每周至少观看一部黄色录像片。

"White", whose associative meaning is very similar in both English and Chinese, figuratively connotes "purity or innocence". That is why the brides are dressed in white in western countries. However, "white" in some English phrases does not denote 白 in Chinese.

❖ a white lie 善意的谎言　　　　　the white coffee 牛奶咖啡
　white collar 脑力劳动者　　　　white elephant 大而无用的东西
　white feather 丧失斗志,胆怯　　white hope 令人寄以厚望的人
　white magic 善意的法术　　　　white slavery 拐卖妇女的行业
　white wash 掩饰,粉饰

The colour "black" symbolizes "death, hardship and sorrow" both in English and Chinese. Therefore, English-speaking people usually wear black clothes or garments when attending a funeral. The Chinese people also wear weeds when mourning over the death of someone. So "black tidings" should be translated into 噩耗 or 不幸的销息. The version of "the Black Friday" is 凶险不祥的日子. Further examples in English may include "blacklist"(黑名单), "black market"(黑市), "a black-letter day"(倒霉的一天).

The "black" color is also associated with "anger or rage" in English. For instance, "black in the face" and "to look black at somebody" can be respectively translated into 脸色铁青 and 怒目而视.

❖ I got some *black looks* from the shopkeeper when I cancelled my order.
  当我撤销订单时,店老板对我怒目而视。
❖ The slightest order was received with *a black look*, and grudgingly and carelessly obeyed. (R. L. Stevenson:*Treasure Island*)
  就是让他们做一点小事,那些人也会怒目而视,干起活来也是勉勉强强,马马虎虎。

Sometimes, "black" symbolizes "evil" as in "black-hearted"(坏心肠) and "blackguard"(恶棍). It sometimes implies "very sad feelings, behaviors, news etc." For example, "The bad news we've been getting means that things look black for us." can be translated into 我们得到的这些坏消息意味着情况很不乐观.

### 4.4.2.2 Animal and plant words and their translation 动植物名称及其翻译

Languages of all nations contain a lot of words denoting animals and plants, and so are English and Chinese. However, because of different cultures, different environments, different histories, different customs, etc., animals and plants have been given different meanings in different languages. So some animal and plant phenomena in translation should be paid special attention to, so as to make our translations more accurate and more excellent.

Animals and plants are our neighbors, and companions living together. With the development and progress of human society, many animals and plants become domestic, serving people. Our human beings cannot live without them. So animals and plants widely and deeply affect the whole human society from material to culture. Animal and plant words in all the languages are a typical example of this phenomenon; however animals and plants in different nations, areas or languages have different associations and cultural connotations, which may bring about some trouble in our translation tasks and communications between different cultures. So, we'd better know about different ideas of animals and plants of different peoples.

Let us firstly talk about some animals in detail, and compare the different connotations between English and Chinese.

"Dog" will be taken for example. A dog, in English culture, is a pet which can even be considered a family member. Dog is the best friend of man. So English-speaking people would say, "Don't bother getting a dog. In today's world, the computer is clearly your best friend."(不要麻烦养狗了！如今这个世界，计算机无疑才是你最好的朋友。) This implies that a computer is as helpful and useful as a dog in today's world. Some other English words and phrases can be also found to express such passion to dogs：

- a jolly dog 快活的人　　　　　a lucky dog 幸运儿
  a water dog 水性好的人　　　　as faithful as a dog 像狗一样忠实
  cat and dog life 经常吵闹的生活　top dog 重要人物，有权势的人
  dress up like a dog's dinner 穿着极其讲究
- Every dog has its day.
  人皆有得意之日/瓦片也有翻身时。
- Give a dog a bad name.
  欲加之罪，何患无辞。
- Help a lame dog over a stile.
  助人于危难之中。
- Love me, love my dog.
  爱屋及乌(爱我就爱我的狗)。
- You can't teach an old dog new tricks.
  习性难改。

While in China, a dog is sometimes thought to be something unpleasant and disliked. It is very pejorative in meaning in Chinese. This can be readily illustrated by the Chinese words and idiomatic expressions：走狗、癞皮狗、丧家狗、狗奴才、狗腿子、狗仗人势、狐朋狗友、挂羊头卖狗肉、狗改不了吃屎、狗嘴里吐不出象牙。Many others can be added to this list, but they are enough to exemplify the negative attitudes of the Chinese people towards these creatures.

Another typical Chinese word 龙 will be taken for another example. As long as we talk about Chinese culture, it is inevitably to refer to "dragon". As we all know, dragon is a totem in China's history. And totem, something relevant to religion and mythology, is usually considered to be kin to the nation, as a symbol of the nation. Chinese dragon has such a supernatural power that it can walk；fly, swim, make clouds move and rain fall. On the account of its supernatural power, emperors and common people worshiped it as an auspicious animal. Emperors in ancient China regarded dragon as themselves, and manage to be the real dragon, the son of the heaven, in the sake of bonding and domesticating the common people's mind, to secure his country and manage the state affairs. Common people worship the dragon, and manage to be the descendants of dragon, because they want to get bless from the Manito. So, in the Chinese culture, dragon has become a god that could give benefits to all, in the charge of rainfall. So people worship it for good weather and big harvest. Dragon becomes a symbol of auspiciousness and the spirit of China. Consequently, there are many phrases of good meanings denoting dragon in Chinese, such as: 龙凤呈祥,藏龙卧虎,画龙点睛,生龙活虎,龙飞凤舞,望子成龙,龙盘虎踞. And some people like to put 龙 in their children's names, showing their great expectation to their offsprings, for example, 李小龙, 成龙, 金龙 etc. However, in English, "dragon" comes from the Greek word "drakōn", with the meaning of "to see", "to wash and flash". A dragon is a fabulous winged crocodile, usually represented as of large size, with a serpent tail. Thus, it is always confused with snake. In Revelation, Satan was imaged as the great Dragon. In the literature of Christian, dragon is related to snake, Satan, and evilness. So, in English, if you call a woman a dragon, you mean that she is fierce and unpleasant.

Some researches show that some animals have similar connotations between English and Chinese cultures, and some are quite different. Now let us look at some other animals and their connotations between English and Chinese.

Connotations of some animals are similar in both languages.

| Animal | Connotations in English | Connotations in Chinese |
| --- | --- | --- |
| ant | frugality or forecast | 节俭,预测 |
| ape | imitation | 模仿 |
| ass/donkey | stupidity /a foolish person | 愚笨,蠢人 |
| bantam cock | brave or self-glorification | 自我显示 |
| bat | blindness | 盲目,瞎 |
| bee | hardworking | 勤劳 |
| bull | strength or straightness | 力量,直率,勤奋 |
| butterfly | sportiveness, living in pleasure | 美丽,欢快 |
| camel | domestication | 勤俭持家 |
| cock | vigilance or overbearing insolence | 报晓,守时 |
| crocodile | hypocritical | 虚伪,假慈悲 |
| dog | faithful or dirty | 忠实,肮脏 |
| dove | innocence | 清白,无辜 |
| fox | craftiness or trick | 精明,狡猾 |
| goats | lasciviousness | 好色 |
| hawk | rapacity or penetration | 强取,掠夺 |
| hen | mother's love | 母爱 |
| hog | impurity | 肮脏 |
| horse | speed, benefaction or grace | 速度 |

| | | |
|---|---|---|
| lamb | an innocent person or sacrifice | 无辜者 |
| lion | nobleness or bravery | 勇敢 |
| monkey | trick | 精明；机警 |
| ox | patience, strength or pride | 勤奋；任劳任怨 |
| pig | bigotry, dirty or greedy | 肮脏，馋，懒 |
| swan | gracefulness | 优雅；高贵 |
| tiger | ferocity | 凶猛；霸道 |
| wolf | barbarity or ferocity | 凶残，狡诈，贪婪 |
| worm | cringing | 畏缩；卑躬屈膝 |

Connotations of some animals are different in both languages.

| Animal | Connotations in English | Connotations in Chinese |
|---|---|---|
| bat | evil | 洪福 |
| bear | ill-temper or uncouthness | 愚笨，无能 |
| bull | ill-temper or bellicose | 勤劳，无私 |
| calf | lumpishness or cowardice | 骁勇，勤劳 |
| cat | cheating | 馋嘴，不忠 |
| cow | longevity | 勤劳，勇敢 |
| cuckoo | cuckoldry, adultery of one's wife | 美丽，守时 |
| dragon | Satan and his crew | 高贵 |
| duck | cheating | 笨拙 |
| eagle | majesty, inspiration | 敏锐，远大 |
| elephant | sagacity, ponderosity | 高大 |
| fly | fragile, insignificant | 肮脏 |
| goose | priggish and foolish | 高贵，忠实 |
| lamb | Christ | 温顺 |
| lark | happiness | 悦耳动听 |
| mule | pertinacity | 力量，负重 |
| nightingale | sadness | 清脆婉转的歌声 |
| owl | wisdom | 灾难，死亡 |
| parrot | mocking verbosity | 学舌，效仿 |
| peacock | pride, arrogance | 吉利，美丽 |
| puppy | conceit | 忠实 |
| rabbit | fecundity | 敏捷；机警 |
| serpent | wisdom | 邪恶 |
| turtle | chastity | 长寿 |

Here are some phrases, expressions and sentences with animal words. We should note that the majority of them are usually compared to people, but the references between the original and the Chinese versions are quite different.

❖ 
| | |
|---|---|
| a bear market 熊市 | a bull in a china shop 举止粗鲁的人 |
| a cold fish 死气沉沉的人 | a drowned rat 落汤鸡 |
| a dull fish 笨蛋 | a fly in the ointment 一颗老鼠屎,坏了一锅汤 |
| a lion in the way 拦路虎 | a loose fish 道德放荡不羁的人 |
| a poor fish 可怜的人 | a queer fish 怪人 |
| a snake in the grass 阴险的人 | a talkative as a magpie 唧唧喳喳像麻雀 |
| a wolf-whistle 调情口哨 | an ass in a lion's skin 狐假虎威 |
| as blind as bat 有眼无珠;瞎眼 | as craft as a fox 像狐狸一样狡猾 |
| as faithful as a dog 像狗一样忠实 | as greedy as a wolf 像狼一样贪婪 |
| as happy as a cow 快乐得像只百灵鸟 | as hoarse as a crow 公鸭嗓子 |
| as majestic as a lion 虎彪彪 | as mute as a fish 噤若寒蝉 |
| as rude as a bear 像熊一样笨拙 | as strong as a horse 力大如牛 |
| as stupid as a donkey 像驴一样蠢 | beard the lion 虎口拔牙 |
| beard the lion in his den 敢在太岁头上动土 | |
| black sheep 害群之马 | break a butterfly on a wheel 杀鸡用牛刀 |
| cast pearls before swine 对牛弹琴 | chicken-hearted 胆小如鼠 |
| cock of the school 高才生 | crazy as a bat 精神失常;发疯 |
| cry wolf 狼来了 | dirty dog 坏蛋 |
| drink like a fish 畅饮 | eat like a pig 喧闹而贪婪地大吃大喝 |
| fish in troubled waters 浑水摸鱼 | have bats in the belfry 异想天开 |
| hold a wolf by the ears 骑虎难下 | hungry as a bear 饿得像狼 |
| in like a lion, out like a lamb 虎头蛇尾 | industrious as an ant 像蜜蜂一样勤劳 |
| lead a cat and dog life 争吵不休的生活 | |
| let the cat out of the bag 说走了嘴 | like a cat on hot bricks 如坐针毡;热锅上的蚂蚁 |
| like a drowned rat 像只落汤鸡 | like a duck to water 如鱼得水 |
| make a pig of oneself 狼吞虎咽 | mole 在黑暗中工作的人 |
| pigs in clover 行为卑鄙或粗鲁的有钱人 | |
| poor snake 干苦力的人 | rain cats and dogs 倾盆大雨 |
| rat in a hole 瓮中之鳖 | set a fox to keep one's geese 引狼入室 |
| swim like a duck 游得像条鱼 | talk horse 吹牛 |
| the lion's share 最大的份额 | throw somebody to the wolves 使某人陷入虎口 |
| whip the cat 一毛不拔;爱财如命 | wolf in sheep's clothing 披着羊皮的狼 |

work like a horse 像老黄牛一样干活

❖ A bird is known by its note, and a man by his talk.
听音知鸟，闻言知人。

❖ The camel is the ship of the desert.
骆驼是沙漠之舟。

❖ A good horse should be seldom spurred.
好马无需多加鞭。

❖ When the weasel and cat make a marriage, it is a very ill presage.
黄鼠狼与猫结亲，不是好兆头。

❖ Better be the head of an ass than the tail of a horse.
宁为鸡首，不为牛后。

As far as plant words are concerned, different cultures have words with different connotations because these words are used in different geographical areas and districts. Human beings have been living on plants on earth, which have been endowed with certain implications according to their colors, shapes or qualities. In English, "olive branch"（橄榄枝）symbolizes "peace"（和平），"white chrysanthemum"（白菊）represents "truth"（真理）. "Acacia"（刺槐）stands for "friendship"（友谊），just a few to be mentioned here. In Chinese, plants similarly have connotations in language. We can find a lot of idiomatic phrases with plant words, like 雨后春笋，寸草春晖，岁寒松柏，豆蔻年华，松鹤延年 etc.

Some words, phrases and sentences in English are mentioned below to show this point.

❖ a big potato 大人物
a sucked orange 血汗被榨干了的人；被充分利用而如今不再需要的人
apple of the eye 掌上明珠         banana oil 花言巧语
bean ball 投手投向击球手头部的球    bean 脑袋瓜
cherry 童男；童女；无经验的士兵     forbidden fruit 禁果
full of beans 精力充沛             garlic-burner 意大利产的摩托车
gild the lily 多此一举；徒劳无益    lemon 质量极差的汽车
nut 怪人；疯子；傻子；花花公子      old bean 老兄
orange sunshine 迷幻药             peach 迷人的女子；出众的人/事
pepper 精力；活力                  pineapple 手榴弹；小型炸弹
plum 最好的东西；声望好待遇高的轻松工作；意外的收获
polish the apple 送礼；讨好；拍马屁  sour grapes 酸葡萄
spill the beans 泄露秘密           spinach 胡说八道；无用之物

swallow a watermelon seed 怀孕　　the Big Apple 纽约市
the clean potato 正派的人；正经的事　the movie nut 电影迷
a hard nut to crack 棘手的问题；难对付的人
top/second banana 最出色/二流的喜剧演员
under the rose 秘密地，私下里（比喻偷偷摸摸的行为或勾当）
yellow tulip 爱情　　　　York-and-Lancaster rose 战争
zinnia 思念离别的朋友

❖ Mary is an *apple-polisher*, she will do anything for the boss.
玛丽是个<u>马屁精</u>，老板叫她干啥她就干啥。

❖ Michael's *such dead nuts* on her that he's getting dull.
迈克尔爱她爱得<u>发狂</u>，以致变得木头木脑。

❖ I am glad the tax accountant *knows his onions*.
我很高兴税收会计<u>十分胜任他的工作</u>。

❖ He is practically *off his onion* about her.
他对她简直<u>神魂颠倒</u>了。

**Comments** In the last four sentences, we can find that "*apple-polisher*" originates from the phrase "to polish the apple". That is to say, some of plant words or phrases can be changed in form. "*To be (dead) nuts on*" is a phrase meaning "to like something very much, or love something/somebody madly". Some other phrases with nut are "to be nuts to somebody" meaning greatly satisfy somebody, "off one's nut" meaning mad, "do one's nut" meaning be very worried or angry, and "a hard nut to crack" meaning a difficult problem, person, etc. to deal with. "*Know one's onions*" means "to have knowledge based on experience". "*Off one's onion*" means "mentally unbalanced".

### 4.4.3 Compare and Analyze 比较与分析

| | |
|---|---|
| Mr. Brown is a ① <u>white</u> man. He was looking rather ② <u>green</u> the other day. He has been feeling ③<u>blue</u> lately. When I saw him he was in a ④ <u>brown</u> study. I hope he'll soon be in the ⑤ <u>pink</u> again. | 布朗先生是个非常①<u>忠实可靠的</u>人。那天，他脸上颇有②<u>病容</u>。近来他③<u>闷闷不乐</u>，我看到他时他在④<u>沉思</u>之中。希望他早日恢复⑤<u>健康</u>。 |

注：选自包惠南，《文化语境与语言翻译》，2001.140

**Notes**：① The word "*white*" when used as slang means "honest, faithful or trustful".

② The word "*green*" here means "unhealthily pale in the face, as though from sickness, fear, etc."

③ The word "*blue*" in this sentence means "sad and without hope of people and conditions".

④ The word "*brown*" in this sentence is placed in the phrase "to be in a brown study", which means "in quiet thought, fantasy or idle dream".

⑤ "*Pink*" when used as an adjective primarily denotes a color that is pale red. But when it is used in the phrase "in the pink (of conditions or health)", it means "in perfect health, very well" in a humorous way.

### 4.4.4 Exercises 练习

Ⅰ. **Translate the following expressions into Chinese**.

1. red meat, reds under the bed, to run a business in the red, wave a red flag, red handed, red blooded, red hunter, red alert

2. a white Christmas, a white-collar job, a white night, white smith, white room, white alert

3. a black day, a black spot, a black sheep, a black comedy, to run a company in the black, a black and white, black tea, black beetle

4. having the blues, blue Monday, a blue fit, a blue ribbon, a bluestocking, blue collar jobs, blue water, blue alert

5. green line, green room, green-eyed monsters, a greenhorn, a greengrocer, green fingers, a green old age, green light

6. yellow journalism, yellow pages, yellow dog

7. a grey day, grey-haired, a grey market, a grey list, grey cloth, grey mare

8. in the pink of health, pink-collar employees, pink elephants, pink tea, pinkeye

9. from the purple families, a purple passage, purple medic

Ⅱ. **Passage translation.**

How men first learned to invent words is unknown; in other words, the origin of language is a mystery. All we really know is that men, unlike animals, somehow invented certain sounds to express thoughts and feelings, actions and things, so that they could communicate with each other; and that later they agreed upon certain signs, called letters, which could be combined to represent those sounds, and which could be written down. Those sounds, whether spoken, or written in letters, we call words.

The power of words, then, lies in their associations—the things they bring up before our minds. Words become filled with meaning for us by experience; and the longer we live, the more certain words recall to us the glad and sad events of our past; and the more we read and learn, the more number of words that mean something to us increases.

Great writers are those who not only have great thoughts but also express these thoughts in words which appeal powerfully to our minds and emotions. This charming and telling use of words is what we call literary style. Above all, the real poet is a master of words. He can convey his meaning in words which sing like music and which by their position and association can move men to tears. We should, therefore, learn to choose our words carefully and use them accurately, or they will make our speech silly and vulgar.

## 4.5 Cultural Connotations of the Idiomatic Phrases and Their Translation
习语的文化内涵与翻译

English idiomatic phrases, including set phrases(成语), proverbs(谚语), sayings

(格言), colloquialisms(俗语), allusions(典故), and slang(俚语), are an important part of the English language and English culture. To learners of English as a foreign language they are often hard to understand and harder to use or translate correctly because they are rich language items in culture. To learn them means to learn not only words and grammars but also the underlying culture. This is by no means easy. However, their proper use or translation is often a mark of one's command of English. It is worthwhile to make effort to learn how to translate them.

There are a great number of idiomatic phrases in both English and Chinese, which are a very strong nature of culture, the essence of a certain language, and the crystallization of long and practical use of the language. Generally speaking, they are characterized with the qualities of vividness, harmony, rhythm, shortness, easy remembering, and simplicity.

### 4.5.1 Set Phrases and Their Translation 成语的翻译

#### 1) Characteristics of set phrases

When we read some set phrases in English and Chinese, we can find a surprising coincidence between them that some of them are extremely similar, and even identical in meaning and form. This shows us the fact that human beings are living on the same earth, have experienced similar developmental procedures in history, and have shared the material and resource so that they have some similarities in their languages as well. Now let us compare the following.

❖ to strike while the iron is hot 趁热打铁
  to be on the thin ice 如履薄冰
  to pour oil on the flame 火上浇油
  to fish in the troubled waters 浑水摸鱼
  as light as a feather 轻如鸿毛
  to sit on pins and needles 如坐针毡
  an eye for an eye, a tooth for a tooth 以眼还眼,以牙还牙
  great oaks grow from little acorns 合抱之木,生于毫末
  knit one's brow 紧锁眉头

However, the differences between the two cultures account for the majority of set phrases. This is because many of these idioms are closely related to their culture. English set phrases are too numerous to be discussed one by one here. The following are only some of them cited as illustrations and loosely classified into several categories.

Set phrases in English are related to mannerisms. Let us discuss a couple of examples. "To ride one's high horse" means "to be haughty, arrogant, and proud". This set phrase corresponds to 趾高气扬 in Chinese, though it may be associated with 春风得意马蹄疾 if it is interpreted somewhat literally. Both the set phrases in English and Chinese are pejorative, relying on images. But the images concerned are different. Another contrast is that the English phrase is colloquial, while the Chinese is literary. "To pull somebody's leg" is saying something in a joking way, "to tease, or deceive somebody temporarily". From the interpretation we can see that the phrase does not correspond to 扯某人后腿 in Chinese. When we translate it like that, we try to prevent him from advancing or making progress. In fact, the English set phrase corresponds to 愚弄某人 or 开某人的玩笑. Again the meaning is expressed figuratively in English, but in a straight forward way in Chinese.

Set phrases in English are related to philosophy. For example, "A big fish in a small pond" refers to a person whose importance and influence are great only in a restricted situation or small community. It may correspond to 鹤立鸡群 in Chinese. This set phrase is very figurative. The difference lies only in the fact that in the two languages a person is compared to different animals. In other words, in English, a person is compared to a fish, whereas he is compared to 鹤 and 鸡 in Chinese. We can see more examples like " to play the flute to a cow"(对牛弹琴), "love me, love my dog"(爱屋及乌), "as strong as a horse"(健壮如牛), "to have a head like a sieve"(心猿意马) and so on.

Set phrases in English are also related to love and marriages. A couple of examples are here cited to show this point. "To love at first sight" means "to fall in love with somebody on the first occasion of seeing or meeting". It is a true equivalent to 一见钟情 in Chinese. "The marriage of true minds" refers to any alliance or relationship based on mutual respect, identity of interests, beliefs held in common. This idiom is not limited to marriage in the literal sense of the word. It may correspond to 真诚的联合 or 珠联璧合 in Chinese.

Set phrases in English sometimes lie in other cases. Look at some examples. "A nine days wonder" refers to a person or event that attracts a lot of notice and is the subject of much talk for a short time but is soon forgotten. It corresponds to 昙花一现 in Chinese. The English idiom is somewhat descriptive, while the Chinese one is mainly figurative, alluding to "broadleaved epiphyll", a plant whose beautiful flowers last briefly. "Between Scylla and Charybdis" denotes the situation between two equally hazardous alternatives. It is derived from Scylla and Charybdis, two monsters in Greco-Roman mythology, which corresponds to 腹背受敌,进退两难 in Chinese. And "to know something like the palm of one's hand" means to be thoroughly familiar with the nature and details of something. This idiom is a true equivalent to the Chinese four-character expression 了如指掌, except that the English one is colloquial, while the Chinese one is literary.

### 2) Methods of translating set phrases

**A. Metaphrase(直译)**: Because of some similarities between the two cultures, we may find their equivalents in the target language, and we can employ the technique of literal translation so as to completely retain their meanings and forms in both cultures, that is, retain the original images.

- a castle in the air 空中楼阁　　go through fire and water 赴汤蹈火
  turn a blind eye to 熟视无睹
  kill two birds with one stone 一石二鸟;一箭双雕
  heart and soul 全心全意　　turn a deaf ear to 充耳不闻
  wash one's hands of 金盆洗手　　as easy as turning over one's hand 易如反掌
  go all out 全力以赴　　smooth tongue 油嘴滑舌
  blow one's own horn 自吹自擂　　burn the boat 破釜沉舟
  a bolt from the blue 晴天霹雳　　six of one and half a dozen of the other 半斤八两
  hang by a hair 千钧一发　　show the cloven hoof 露出原形
  after one's own heart 正中下怀　　have pity on somebody 同情某人
  laugh in sb's face 当面嘲笑　　last but not least 最后但不是最不重要的一点
- Misfortunes never come singly.
  祸不单行。
- Walls have ears.
  隔墙有耳。

**B. Substitution(套译)**: When the equivalents of some set phrases can not be located in the target language, a substitute may be applied in the translation. This translation should be understood by the readers and retain the image anyway. In other words, the form between the two cultures is different though, the meaning between them is the same.

- have an axe to grind 别有用心　　talk through one's hat 胡言乱语
  neither fish nor fowl 不伦不类　　a fly in the ointment 美中不足
  by the skin of one's teeth 九死一生　　call a spade a spade 直言不讳
  hole and corner 鬼鬼祟祟　　leave no stone unturned 想方设法;千方百计
  kill the goose that lays the golden eggs 杀鸡取卵
  diamond cut diamond, crook cut crook 棋逢对手,将遇良才

**C. Paraphrase(意译)**: In the case that the reader can not literally understand some of set phrases in the source language when translated into Chinese, the method of paraphrase can be used to deal with them.

- in a pig's whisper 低声地 　　　　　　　draw blood 伤人感情;惹人生气
  hang on sb's sleeve 依赖某人;任某人做主
  hang on sb's lips 言听计从 　　　　　　　make a monkey of 愚弄
  to be full of beans 精神旺盛;精力充沛
  bend an ear to 倾听;聚精会神地听
  get cold feet 开始感到怀疑、胆怯或害怕
  a skeleton at the feast 扫兴的人或物 　　a skeleton in the cupboard/closet 家丑
  bury one's head in the sand 采取鸵鸟政策
  child's play 简单的东西;容易的事情 　　eat one's words 承认自己说错了话
  move heaven and earth 想方设法;千方百计

**D. Multiple translations(译文的多样性)**: In practical translation, we may come across such a phenomenon that one set phrase in English has multiple translations in Chinese and vice versa. We can choose the one we prefer, or pick up the one appropriately fitting in the context. Examine the following carefully and we find that each of the set phrases in English on the left can match any of the set phrases on the right in Chinese, and each on the right can match any on the left.

- fish in the air 水中捞月
  cry for the moon 挑雪填井
  plough the sands 扬汤止沸
  make a wild goose chase 缘木求鱼
  hold a candle to the sun 钻冰求酥
  catch at shadows 以冰致蝇
  lash the waves 以狸饵鼠
  beat the air 隔靴搔痒

### 4.5.2 Proverbs and Their Translation 谚语的翻译

#### 1) Characteristics of proverbs

As defined in dictionaries, a proverb is a brief familiar maxim of folk wisdom, usually compressed in form, often involving a bold image and frequently a jingle that catches the memory. For a proverb to become popular it must be outstandingly wise and it must contain enduring wisdom. So some people call them as "the daughters of daily experience". Proverbs contain folk wisdom rather than scientific accuracy and therefore they provide interesting glimpses or clues to a people's geography, history, social organization, social views and attitudes. In a word, proverbs reflect a people's living and living environment. For this reason proverbs are culture-specific. People who live along sea coast and whose livelihood is dependent upon the sea will have proverbs about sailing and about the weather in the sea. Nomadic people will have proverbs about pastureland, about castles, sheep, and horses and about wolves.

As we know, religion is an important source of proverbs. So it is simply natural that many English proverbs are related to Christianity in one way or another.

❖ Each cross hath its own inscription.
每个十字架都有自己的铭文。

❖ God helps those who help themselves.
自助者天助之。

❖ God sends meat and the devil sends cooks.
上帝赐予食物,魔鬼派来厨师。

❖ He that serves God for money will serve the devil for better wages.
为金钱而侍奉上帝的人会为更多的报酬服侍魔鬼。

❖ Man proposes, God disposes.
谋事在人,成事在天。

❖ Mills of God grind slowly but sure./The mills of God grind slowly.
天网恢恢,疏而不漏。

❖ Whom God would ruin, he first deprives of reason.
上帝要毁灭谁,必先夺其理性。

❖ Whom the Gods love die young.
上帝的宠儿早夭折。

Some proverbs in English are derived from *The Bible* and other masterpieces. *The Bible* is one of the most extensively-read books and the most influential religious classic work in the West, including English-speaking countries. It is also regarded as a wonderful literary work. Although it was originally written in Hebrew, English speakers have had English versions for almost 1,000 years. And the proverbial sayings in it have become a major component of the popular wisdom.

❖ A rose by any other name would smell as sweet.
玫瑰无论叫什么名字都是香的。

- All are of the dust, and all turn to the dust again.
  人人来自泥土,又回归泥土。
- Gossiping and lying go hand in hand.
  闲话与谎言结伴而行。
- Great men are not always wise.
  伟人并非事事聪明。/智者千虑,必有一失。
- It is better to be a beggar than a fool.
  做乞丐胜过做傻瓜。
- Judge not according to appearance.
  不要以貌取人。
- Life is but a walking shadow.
  人生不过是移动的影子。
- Never cast your pearls before swine.
  不可对牛弹琴。
- Pride goes before a fall.
  骄兵必败。

Some English proverbs are related to geography. A nation's geographical environment is a framework in which a language and culture have been developing. The geographical features of a country are inevitably reflected in the national language in general and proverbs in particular. For example, the Chinese proverb 不到黄河心不死 is apparently related to the Yellow River, the second longest river in China and the cradle of Chinese civilization. 不到长城非好汉 is clearly related to the Great Wall, one of the well-known scenic spots in China. Place names can also be observed in English proverbs.

- Carry coals to Newcastle.
  背煤上煤都,多此一举。
- England is the ringing island.
  英国是充满钟声的岛屿。
- Oxford for learning, London for wit, Hull for women and York for horses.
  牛津人学问好,伦敦人才智高,哈勒的女人美,约克的马匹好。

Some English proverbs are related to navigation. This is because the U.K. is an insular country, detached from the continental Europe. For this reason navigation has been and is very important to the Englishmen. They frequently use words of navigation in proverbs.

- A great ship asks deep water.
  大船深水行。

- A small leak will sink a great ship.
  小漏沉大船。/蝼蚁之穴能溃千里之堤。
- A smooth sea never made a skillful mariner.
  海水平静难造就优秀水手。
- Any port in a storm.
  船在暴风雨中不择港口。/慌不择路。
- It is a hard sailing when there is no wind.
  无风难驶船。/巧妇难为无米之炊。
- Let another's shipwreck be your seamark.
  别人的沉船就是你的航标。/前车之鉴。
- Little boats must keep to the shore.
  小船随岸行。
- Many drops of water will sink the ship.
  积漏成多会沉掉航船。
- Rats desert a sinking ship.
  船沉鼠要逃。/树倒猢狲散。
- The good seaman is known in bad weather.
  天气恶劣才能显出优秀航海家。

Some English proverbs are related to sexism, which refers to discrimination against females. Though sexism is unfair, we can find it in either English or Chinese. For example, we Chinese often say 红颜薄命,女子无才便是德 and something like that to show sexism. The following proverbs reflect sexism in English.

- Beware of the forepart of a woman, the hind part of a mule, and all sides of a priest.
  当心女人的美貌、骡子的后蹄和牧师的一切。
- Dally not with money or woman.
  金钱、美女玩弄不得。
- Gaming, woman, and wine, while they laugh, they make men pine.
  赌博、女人和酒,使男人在笑声中消瘦。
- Maids want nothing but husbands, and when they have them they want everything.
  姑娘除了丈夫什么都不要;一旦有了丈夫,她们什么都要。
- The more women look in their glass, the less they look to their house.
  女人镜子照得越多,家务做得越少。
- Wives and children are bills of charges.

妻子和孩子是账单。

Some English proverbs are related to the history of England. Each nation has its own history. Since proverbs are historical products, they may reflect some aspects of the national history. For example, the English proverbs below are apparently related to the history of England.

❖ It is as hard to please a knave as a knight.
   取悦坏蛋和骑士同样困难。
❖ Kings' chaff is worth other men's corn.
   国王的糠胜似百姓的粮。
❖ All Stuarts are not sib to the king.
   与国王同姓的不是皇亲。
❖ From whipping post to pillory.
   鞭打之后又披枷。

Some English proverbs are related to thrift. English speakers value thrift. A nonverbal example is that when treating guests at home, the hostess normally prepares food according to the number of persons at table, while Chinese hostess may prepare more than enough food on similar occasions. English abounds with proverbs telling the merits of thrift. The following are just a few of them.

❖ From saving comes having.
   富裕来自节俭。
❖ Frugality is an estate alone.
   节俭本身就是财富。
❖ Thrift is good revenue.
   节俭就是收入。
❖ Thrift is philosopher's stone.
   节俭犹如点金石。

2) **Methods of translating English proverbs**

A. **Literal translation(直译)**: This method can be firstly employed in translating proverbs if they are easy to be understood as the version 良好的开端等于成功的一半 of "Well begun is half done." This is because most of English proverbs appear vivid and figurative. We should manage to clearly show the qualities of the original.

❖ A bird in the hand is worth two in the bush.
   双鸟在林不如一鸟在手。
❖ A good beginning makes a good ending.
   有良好的开端,才有良好的结果。

- A lazy youth, a lousy age.
  少壮不努力,老大徒伤悲。
- Beauty lies in the lover's eyes.
  情人眼里出美人(西施)。
- Better be the head of an ass than the tail of a horse.
  宁为驴头,不做马尾。
- Better late than never.
  迟做总比不做好。
- Bitter pills may have wholesome effects.
  良药苦口。
- Example is better than precept.
  以身作则胜于口头教诲。
- Forbidden fruit is sweet.
  禁果格外甜。
- Grasp all, lose all.
  贪多必失。
- Half a loaf is better than no bread.
  有总比没有好。
- He laughs best who laughs last.
  谁笑到最后,谁笑得最好。
- If you run after two hares, you will catch neither.
  同时追俩兔,全都抓不住。
- In the country of the blind the one-eyed man is king.
  盲人国中独眼称雄。
- Looker-on see more than players.
  当局者迷,旁观者清。
- More haste, less speed.
  欲速则不达。
- No mill, no meal.
  不磨面,没得饭。/不劳无获。
- Self do, self have.
  自作自受。
- Speech is silver, silence is gold.
  雄辩是银,沉默是金。
- The proof of the budding is in the eating.

布丁好不好，一尝就知道。
- No news is good news.

  没有消息就是好消息。

**B. Substitution（套译）**：Secondly, if we can not translate English proverbs by means of literal translation, we may employ the method of substitution. In other words, when a proverb is very similar in meaning, and figure of speech between English and Chinese, we may search a substitute in the target language for the source language. Carefully compare the following.

- Fish begins to stink at the head.

  上梁不正下梁歪。
- Give a thief enough ropes and he'll hang himself.

  多行不义必自毙。
- It is never too late to mend.

  亡羊补牢，未为迟也。
- Many straws may bind an elephant.

  烂麻搓成绳，也能拉千斤。
- Nothing venture, nothing have.

  不入虎穴，焉得虎子。
- One boy is a boy, two boys half a boy, three boys no boys.

  一个和尚挑水吃，两个和尚抬水吃，三个和尚没水吃。
- One man may steal a horse, while another may not look over the hedge.

  只许州官放火，不许百姓点灯。
- Spare the rod and spoil the child.

  孩子不打不成器。
- Time and tide wait for no man.

  时不我与。
- Where there is life, there is hope.

  留得青山在，不怕没柴烧。
- When shepherds quarrel, the wolf has a winning game.

  鹬蚌相争，渔人得利。

**C. Liberal translation（意译）**：As we know, proverbs are closely related to national culture, which are attached to strong national color. In this case, literal translation can not be applied because the translation version will be sorry-reading, and its meaning is to be farfetched and hard to understand. Therefore, liberal translation may be used. Besides, the proverbs with strong national color are not rendered generally by the method of substitution. In other words, the names of people and places in English proverbs can never be directly copied in Chinese versions; similarly the Chinese names and places can not be used in the English versions.

- ❖ A quiet conscience sleeps in thunder.
  白日不做亏心事，半夜敲门心不惊。
- ❖ All work and no play makes Jack a dull boy.
  只工作不玩耍，聪明孩子也变傻。
- ❖ Do as the Romans do.
  入乡随俗。
- ❖ Every man has a fool in his sleeve.
  人人都有糊涂的时候。
- ❖ He that sups with the devil must have a long spoon.
  和坏人打交道必须提高警惕。
- ❖ When Greek meets Greek, then comes the tug of war.
  两雄相遇，其斗必烈。
- ❖ Don't put the cart before the horse.
  切勿本末倒置。
- ❖ It is no use crying over spilt milk.
  覆水难收，哭亦无用。

**D. Combination of literal and liberal translation**(直译与意译并用)：Sometimes the two methods can be used together in translating English proverbs. We may receive better effects in this way.

- ❖ You can take a horse to the water, but you can't make it drink.
  牵马河边易，逼马饮水难。
- ❖ Still water runs deep.
  静水深流，大智若愚。
- ❖ Who has never tasted bitter, knows not what is sweet.
  不尝黄连苦，哪知蜂蜜甜。
- ❖ Men may meet but mountain never.
  山与山无法碰头，人和人总会相遇。

**E. Colloquialism and easy-reading**(口语体且上口)：Proverbs are a sort of language form that is extensively handed down in everyday communications. They are characterized with colloquialism and easy-reading. Therefore in translating proverbs, we should manage to maintain the qualities of simplicity, shortness, antithesis, smooth-reading and easy-remembering, and even rhythm.

- Easy come, easy go.
  来得容易去得快。
- Like father, like son.
  有其父必有其子。
- Look before you leap.
  三思而后行。
- Out of sight, out of mind.
  眼不见,心不烦。
- The leopard can't change its spots.
  江山易改,秉性难移。
- Wonder is the laughter of ignorance.
  少见多怪。

When we translate proverbs, we ought to keep in mind the following three points.

A. The names of people and places in English proverbs can never be directly copied in the Chinese versions; similarly the Chinese names and places can not be used in the English versions. Appropriate adaptations will be made to be beneficial to the readers' understanding and reception to the original.

B. The translation of English proverbs should be colloquial and easy-reading.

C. The translation versions need logic and artistry.

### 4.5.3 Allusions and Their Translation 典故的翻译

#### 1) Characteristics of allusions

An allusion in English, according to some reference books, means an implied or indirect reference, especially when used in literature or literary quotation, from history or old classics. But the definition of a Chinese allusion is a bit different from the one mentioned above. 典故 in Chinese lays emphasis on the historical reference like 名落孙山,朝三暮四,一鸣惊人 etc., each of which has a story serving as an instruction or implication. Allusions can be loosely classified into the following categories.

Some allusions originate in historical stories or events. Every culture has its own well-known historical stories and events. People began to describe them in a brief way, and then formed allusions. The allusion "burn one's boats or bridge" originally referred to the story that the army of Gaius Julius Caesar burned their boats after crossing the river Rubicon, by which he just wanted to tell his soldiers that they had to fight with their enemy, and there was no way to withdraw. This allusion is just the same as the Chinese allusion 破釜沉舟. Some allusions came from mythology, esp. from Roman and Greek myths and legends. For example, "Prometheus"(普罗米修斯,为人类偷窃火种而受惩

罚的人) says that Prometheus, the son of Uranus disobeyed Zeus's (宙斯,宇宙的主宰) great power to steal fire as the gift for benefiting the earth. Some allusions came from folk legends that refer to the illustrations for a certain person or event handed down in spoken form. For instance, it was said that a swan uttered sad and nice sounds to express the feeling reluctant to die before its death. So the allusion "swan song" appeared. Later it is to be used to figuratively denote the last show or last piece of poets, musicians and others. Its Chinese version should be 辞世之作,告别演出 or 绝唱.

Some allusions originate from literary works or fables. The allusion "kill the goose to get the gold eggs"(杀鸡取卵) came from a Greek fable. It was said that once there was a villager having a goose that could lay gold eggs. The villager was eager to be rich quickly, and killed it for more. But he got nothing in the end. Another allusion "cherish a snake in one's bosom", originating from *Aesop's Fables*, telling the story that a snake was saved by a farmer, but it bit him after coming to life. This allusion implies a person who requites kindness with enmity, teaching people not to tolerate evil, or show mercy to an evildoer. Some allusions are actually the culturally-loaded names of fictional figures and heroes. For example, "Uncle Tom"(汤姆大叔), a fictional figure, is a black person who is very friendly to white people and meekly submits to oppression, maltreatment, etc. "Superman"(超人) is a film figure who can do something incredible.

Some allusions come from folk customs and practices. In both English and Chinese, such birds as owls and black birds are treated as ill omen. So we can find the allusion "a bird of ill omen" in English, which refers to a person who may bring bad news.

Some allusions come from sports games in English, which are comparatively unknown in many other countries. For example, "to carry the ball" is an expression originated in American football meaning to have the main responsibility for getting a certain task or job done. Its Chinese version should be 负起责任;承担领导责任. "To not get to first base", coming from baseball, means to fail early or at the very beginning of an attempt, which can be translated into 出师不利. "To be down and out", originated from boxing, means in a hopeless situation after trying. Therefore we may translate it into 彻底垮了;虽经努力但无济于事. Some more examples from sports are as follows.

❖ to give somebody a punch 打击某人
　　to play one's trump card 出绝招;打出王牌
　　to have two strikes against one 处境不利;形势不妙

2) Methods of translating allusions

A. **Literal translation**(直译): It is used to retain the image of the original. This method can be beneficial to the communication and mixture between English and Chinese cultures.

- a Judas kiss 犹大的吻（比喻背叛行为）
  crocodile tears 鳄鱼的眼泪（比喻假慈悲）
  Eden 伊甸园（比喻乐园、安乐土）
  forbidden fruit 禁果（比喻非法的逸乐或不正当的两性关系）
  sour grapes 酸葡萄（把得不到的东西说成是不好的）
  stick and carrot 大棒与胡萝卜（比喻软硬兼施）
  the tower of ivory 象牙之塔（比喻脱离现实的小天地）
  the Trojan horse 特洛伊木马（比喻暗藏的敌人或危险）
  Watergate 水门（比喻为击败政治对手而滥用国家权力）
  Waterloo 滑铁卢（比喻惨败或致命的打击）
  a kiss of death 死亡之吻（比喻胜败之事）
  put someone in check 将他一军（比喻为难某人）
  hellfire 地狱之火（比喻苦受煎熬的事）
  a Sphinx's riddle 斯芬克司之谜（比喻难解之谜）
  the Fifth Column 第五纵队（比喻间谍）

**B. Image-rendering（形象翻译）**：This method is used to not only show the original image but also amplify some words.

- like a dog in the manger 占着茅坑不拉屎
  a Aladdin's cave 宝库（比喻藏有巨大财富的地方）
  Achilles' heel 死穴（比喻唯一致命的弱点）

**C. Substitution（套译）**：It is used to shift the references to the ones that the reader gets acquainted with so that the source language is easily expressed and understood.

- be besieged on all sides 四面楚歌
  gild the lily 画蛇添足
  trust to chance and windfalls 守株待兔
  at one's wits' end 黔驴技穷
  make a frantic last minute effort 临时抱佛脚
  cast pearls before swine 对牛弹琴

**D. Paraphrase（意译）**：Some allusions in one language are quite different from those in the other. The reader may not understand the associative meaning when allusions are translated in the above ways. So we can only give up the image and then render the figurative meaning.

- a Solomon 聪明人;贤人　　　　a Pandora's box 灾祸的源头
  the sword of Damocles 即将来临的危险
  a Catch 22 situation 左右为难的尴尬局面;无法摆脱的困境
  an Uncle Tom 逆来顺受的人　　　squeeze play 施加压力;穷追猛打
  to hit below the belt 不择手段　　an Aladdin's ring 制胜法宝

**E. Note-adding(加注)**: It is a very useful method to translate some allusions that can not be clearly rendered in the target language. We suggest adding notes behind the version or endnotes at the bottom of the page if necessary.

- Falstaff: I am as poor as Job, my lord, but not so patient. (W. Shakespeare: *Henry IV*)
  福斯塔夫:我是像约伯一样的穷人,大人,可是却没有他那样的好耐性。
  (注:约伯,以忍耐贫穷著称的圣徒,见《圣经约伯记》)

## 4.6 Cultural Connotations of Euphemisms and Their Translation
委婉语的文化内涵与翻译
### 4.6.1 General View to Euphemisms 委婉语概述

Euphemisms are pleasant, polite or harmless sounding words or expressions used to mask harsh, rude or infamous truths. Perhaps, in all cultures there seem to be certain notions or things that people try to avoid mentioning directly, though there are such terms in the language. When these notions or things have to be referred to, people tend to use words or expressions that sound better. These words or expressions are termed as euphemisms.

One of the terms that are universally avoided in verbal communication is "death". Even though it is well-known that death is the inevitable end of any living organism, human beings, generally, have a negative feeling toward it and try many words or expressions that can be used to refer to "death" or "die" indirectly. The following is a list of euphemisms that can be used to substitute "death" or "die".

- abandon the world 谢世;弃世　　　be in Abraham's bosom 在天国
  be no longer with us 不和我们在一起了　be no more 殁了;不在了
  breathe one's last 停止了呼吸;咽气　　close one's eyes 闭眼;合眼
  cross the bar 去世　　　　　　　　decrease 牺牲

depart from life 辞世;去世　　　　depart from the world forever 与世长辞
end one's day 天年已尽　　　　　expire 断气;寿终
go out of this world 逝世　　　　 go the way of all flesh 上路了
go to heaven 去极乐世界　　　　 go to sleep 正寝;长眠
go to the better world 去太平极乐世界　go to the beyond 到了另一个世界
go to the upper regions 去天国;升天　go west 归西
go 走了;殁了　　　　　　　　　lay down one's life 献身;捐躯
lose somebody 失去某人　　　　 meet one's end 遇难
pass away 过世　　　　　　　　 pass on 去世
pay the debt of nature 了结尘缘　　rest 长眠
return to dust 入土　　　　　　　to kingdom come 上天国

❖ One's heart stopped beating.
　某人心脏停止了跳动。
❖ One's life came to an end.
　某人生命走到了尽头。

This list contains only the commonly-used English euphemisms for "death" or "die". Let us take another term "pregnant" for example. English-speaking people would not like to use it in everyday English. We may find some euphemisms for it.

❖ a lady-in-waiting 待产的女人　　　a mother-to-be 准妈妈;要做母亲的人
　to be big-bellied 大肚子　　　　　to be big with young 怀有小生命
　to be going to have a baby 要生娃娃了　to be in the family way 身子不方便
　to be in an interesting condition 有孕在身　to be expecting 怀孕
　to be in a delicate condition 行动不方便　to be baby-bound 有孕
　to carry a baby 怀胎

**4.6.2 Methods of Translating Euphemisms 委婉语的翻译方法**

**1) Commendatory expression**(褒义表达): Because of the nature that euphemisms are pleasant, polite or harmless sounding words or expressions are normally used to mask harsh, rude or infamous truths. As we know, some professions or jobs in the world stand in high social status, but some in a low position. For this reason people usually do not directly use these terms of jobs in low social position, and instead choose some other terms of professions in high social status in a commendatory way. When we translate them, we manage to avoid the harsh, rude or infamous truths in the original and render them by means of commendatory expressions.

| Originals | Euphemisms |
|---|---|
| undertaker(殡葬工) | mortician 丧葬师;葬礼指导 |
| hairdresser(女理发师) | beautician/cosmetician 美容师;美容专家 |
| shoemaker(鞋匠) | shoetrician 鞋靴专家 |
| garbage collector(垃圾清运工) | sanitation engineer 环卫工程师 |
| plumber(管道工) | heating engineer 供暖工程师 |
| dry cleaner(干洗工) | dry cleaning engineer 干洗工程师 |
| foreman(工头,领班) | supervisor 领导 |
| pressman(印刷工) | press operator 出版工作者 |
| gardener(花匠,园丁) | landscape technician 风景技师 |
| cook(厨师) | chef 烹饪大师 |
| secretary(秘书) | administrative assistant 行政助手 |
| teacher(教师) | educator 教育工作者 |
| janitor(房屋管理员) | maintenance engineer 维护工程师 |
| | superintendent 房屋主管 |
| floor walker(巡视员) | aisle manager 大堂经理 |
| film projectionist(电影放映员) | multimedia systems technician 多媒体技师 |

**2) Understated expression**(含蓄表达): In any language, there are euphemisms and taboos. The former are the indirect references, and the later are direct ones. The both seem to be different but similar in form, and their meanings are closely related. If euphemisms are directly mentioned in writing or speech, those who say them may be regarded as impolite, rude, or uneducated. In order to avoid mentioning euphemisms directly, the understated translation is indeed needed in rendering. For example, people don't often say "go to the lavatory"(去厕所), "pass urine"(撒尿) or "defecate"(拉屎) in everyday communication, instead many euphemisms for them are used: washroom, bathroom, restroom, comfort station, powder room, ladies', gents', men's, WC, and toilet.

| Originals | Euphemisms |
|---|---|
| back(落后) | underdeveloped 欠发达的 |
| blind(瞎的) | visually retarded 视觉迟钝的 |
| condom(避孕套) | French letter 法国信 |
| fat(肥胖) | plump 丰满, stout 强壮, |
| | full-figure 体态丰腴, outsize 超过标准尺寸 |

| | |
|---|---|
| handicapped(残废的) | disabled 丧失能力的 |
| illiterate(文盲) | verbally deficient 词语方面有缺陷 |
| imbecile(低能儿) | educable 可教育的, trainable 可培训的 |
| lazy(懒惰) | underachieved 未能充分发挥潜力 |
| leprosy(麻风病) | Hansen's disease 汉森氏病 |
| mental hospital(精神病院) | clinic for the emotionally disadvantaged 情绪不稳定者诊所 |
| old(年老的) | senior 阅历较深的, past one's prime 已过壮年, feel one's age 感觉上了年纪 |
| poor(贫穷的) | underprivileged 无特权的,社会地位低下的 |
| prison(监狱) | correctional therapeutic communities 纠正治疗社区 |
| rape(强奸) | assault 袭击, violate 侮辱, force 强迫 |
| sick(生病) | be under the weather 不舒服, feel bad 感觉不大好 |
| slow(迟钝的) | do better work with help 在别人的帮助下可以做得更好些 |
| cheat in class(作弊) | depend on others to his/her work 依靠别人做事 |

**3）Image-rendering(形象表达)**：Image is the feature of euphemisms. It is the translator's task to show their images so as to embody the rhetorical effects of vividness and humor in euphemisms.

| **Originals** | **Euphemisms** |
|---|---|
| an illegitimate child(私生子) | a son under the rose 玫瑰丛下的孩子 |
| go to lavatory(上厕所) | go to number one 去一号 |
| die(死) | be under the sod 命归黄泉;赴黄泉 |
| be pregnant(怀孕) | wear the apron high 围裙系得高高的 |
| cancer(癌症) | big C; terminally ill 晚期;晚期病 |
| opium(鸦片) | drug; big O 禁药;罂粟 |

## 4.7 Compare and Analyze 比较与分析

After a long wait, the doctor called me into the office. I waited for him to ask me what was wrong. After a few minutes, he said, "What's the matter, ①the cat's got your tongue?"

"No," I said. "I haven't been feeling well

等了许久之后,医生让我进了诊断室。我等他给我看病,过了一会儿,他问道:"怎么了,①为什么不讲话?"

"不是的,"我说,"最近感觉不

lately. I don't have a cat, and my tongue is fine. I have a sore throat and my knee hurts."

"I was only ②pulling your leg," said Dr. Ruby. "I'm ③ all thumbs when it comes to jokes."

"If you were standing over there," I said, "how could you have pulled my leg? Anyway, my knee hurts; please don't pull my leg. And your hand looks fine to me," I continued. "I see ten fingers, not all thumbs."

"Oh,④ what a pain in the neck," said Dr. Ruby. "This patient is really ⑤bullheaded."

I answered, "Is that why I have a pain in the neck, because it's turning into a bull? I thought the pain was from the sore throat."

"You're giving me a pain in the neck," shouted Dr. Ruby. "Do you ⑥have a chip on my shoulder or something? Just laugh!"

"I don't have a chip on my shoulder. Nothing is broken. I told you I have a sore throat and a pain in my knee."

"My knee only hurts when dance," said the doctor. "That's because I ⑦have two left feet."

"Your feet look all right to me," I answered. Dr. Ruby shook his head and left the room.

"Is Dr. Ruby speaking English?" I murmured. "I can't understand anything he says. What a dumb doctor!"

As I said "dumb doctor", Dr. Ruby entered the room.

"You⑧ put your foot in your mouth this time, young man!" he said.

舒服。我没有养猫,舌头也没有毛病。我的嗓子发炎,膝盖有点痛。"

"我只是②和你开玩笑,"鲁比大夫说,"我③笨得连玩笑都不会开了。"

"你站在那边,怎么能扯到我的腿呢?我的膝盖倒是伤了,千万别扯我的腿。"我继续说道:"你的手没事嘛,10个指头很正常,不全是大拇指呀。"

"哎呀,④讨厌的家伙。"鲁比说,"这个病人真是⑤顽固。"

我回答说:"我的脖子痛是因为撞到牛了?我想我是嗓子疼。"

"真让人讨厌。"鲁比大夫吼道,"你是不是⑥成心找不愉快?真是可笑!"

"我的肩膀没有屑片,没有骨折。我说了我的嗓子发炎,膝盖痛。"

"跳舞时我的膝盖才痛,"鲁比大夫说,"那是因为我⑦笨手笨脚。"

"你的腿看上去很好呀。"我回答道。鲁比大夫摇摇头离开了房间。

"鲁比大夫讲的是英语吗?"我嘟囔着,"我没法理解他的话。真是个蠢医生!"

在我说"蠢医生"的当儿,鲁比大夫走了进来。

"这回你可⑧讲坏话了,年轻人!"他说。

"But I can't put my foot in my mouth because my knee hurts!"

Before I knew it, the doctor told me to get dressed, go home, buy some medicine, and stay in bed for two days. As he wrote his bill, he said, "Just ⑨keep your nose to the grindstone, learn some English, and you'll get by, even if it's only ⑩ by the skin of your teeth."

As I left, I saw the doctor trying to pull his hair out.

"可我没法把脚放在嘴里,我的膝盖有伤!"

我还没有明白是怎么回事,这名大夫就让我穿衣服回家,买一些药,在家休息两天。在写处方时,他说:"⑨**刻苦学习**吧,掌握了英语你就会明白的,只有这样⑩**才行**(会成功)。"

我离开的时候,我看见那位大夫生气地撕扯着头发。

**Notes:**

① "*The cat's got your tongue*" means "you're very quiet" or "you don't speak".

② "*Pulling one's leg*" means "joking or teasing".

③ "*To be all thumbs*" means "to be clumsy or to be bad at doing something".

④ "*What a pain in the neck*" is a slang, which refers to a feeling of annoyance or displeasure.

⑤ The conceptual meaning of "*bullheaded*" seems to be literally related to a bull, but actually it has nothing to do with it.

⑥ "*Have a chip on my shoulder*" means "to have an angry attitude".

⑦ "*Have two left feet*" means "to be clumsy or not graceful".

⑧ "*Put your foot in your mouth*" means "to say something embarrassing".

⑨ "*Keep your nose to the grindstone*" means "continue working hard".

⑩ "*By the skin of your teeth*" means "just make it".

This is a conversation between a doctor whose tongue is English, and a foreign student who is not familiar with English idiomatic phrases. Apparently, the foreign student's trouble is caused by the idiomatic phrases listed above. He interprets them literally while the relationship between idioms and their meaning is arbitrary.

## 4.8 Exercises 练习

I. **Phrase and sentence translation.**

A) **Translate the set phrases by means of dictionaries.**

1. make one's flesh creep
2. just what the doctor ordered
3. not for all the tea in China
4. a marriage of convenience
5. mince one's words
6. with honey on one's lips and murder in one's heart
7. look for a needle in a haystack

8. bat an eye
9. keep one's own company
10. make bricks without straw
11. keep one's nose clean

**B) Translate the proverbs by using dictionaries.**

1. Far from Jupiter, far from thunder.
2. Wine and wenches empty men's purses.
3. Tell money after your own father.

**C) Translate the allusions below by means of dictionaries.**

1. an Oliver Twist; a Shylock; a pound of flesh; a Romeo; a Cinderella
2. Friday; Venus; Atlantic; Europe; Uranium
3. the old Adam; the Garden of Eden; David and Goliath
4. marathon; Hancock; a Napoleon
5. kick off; knock out; throw me a curve ball; play one's triumph/winning cards

**D) Translate the following sentences, paying attention to the underlined parts with euphemisms.**

1. That boy is an *underachiever*.
2. My daughter had *tummy trouble* last night.
3. This bride is too *plump* to fit into the new dress.
4. His wife is seven months *gone*.
5. It was said that there had been a *massive exchange* in Kashmir.
6. Her husband swore that he *had had* no *connection with* any other woman.
7. After nearly ten years of married life, she *was heavy with child*.
8. The old lady is *hard of hearing*.
9. Jane *has got the flags out*.
10. Olivia *was in a bad way* and asked for three days leave.
11. Are you a *S*, *D* or *W*? (S = separated; D = divorced; W = widowed)

**II. Passage translation.**

Can man be credited with choosing the right path when he knows only one? Can he be congratulated for his wise decision when only one judgment is possible? If he knows nothing of vice, is he to be praised for adhering to virtue?

From the day when the first man tasted the forbidden fruit, he has been struggling with the choice between good and evil, but without his full awareness of the pleasing taste of that apple, or even of its existence, could he be worthy of praise for forbearing to eat it?

Wisdom consists of the deliberate exercise of judgment; knowledge comes in the discrimination between those known alternatives. Weighing these alternatives is the way of maturity. Only then does man have the strength to follow his choice without wavering, since that choice is based firmly on knowledge rather than on an uncertain, dangerously shallow foundation of ignorance.

# Chapter 5: Literary Translation
# 文学翻译

## 5.1 Definition of Literary Translation 文学翻译的定义

It has been acknowledged for a long time that there exist two large species of translations: documental and scientific translation, and literary translation. Literary translation is a big topic to talk about because people like to put it alone. Before we touch the subject to give any precise definition, we may first ask a closely-related question: What is Literature? Since literary translation is the translation of literature, it is reasonable to assume that the answer of this question will be enlightening to the question we have as the title of this chapter.

So what is literature? Though we may read volumes of books or tons of classics and easily point out that they are literature, it is still helpful to think of the denotation of literature without having concrete things in front.

Obviously, literature has various forms. A book is the common form of literature but a letter also can be. And not every book can rank as literature just as not every letter does. Sometimes there will be some unexpected members fall into the scope of literature, for example, philosophical books like *DaoDeJing*. Unlike many other Chinese philosophic books dusted on shelf, this Chinese classic is reread again and again for its poetic and ambiguous language and thought-provoking content. Its mysterious philosophic cloak does not prevent it being appreciated and interpreted as a piece of famous literary work. Instead it lends the book written two thousand years ago more life to endure the long passage of time to come yet alive in this fast-changing age.

Thus if we want to seize the essence of literature, form is not the proper standard or to be exactly not the sufficient stick-yard for judgment. Form matters indeed anyhow. The things about genre, that is to say, labels like prose, novel are needed to distinguish literature from non-literature. But sometimes these formal standards are not clear and effective enough to make a clear distinction between yes and no. More often than not, they are not broad enough to include some widely-recognized literary pieces. For instance, the *Declaration of Independence* can hardly be attributed to any existing category of literature. It is neither prose nor poem, neither drama nor fiction. After all it is regarded as an influential literary and political piece.

Just forget about those formal constrains then. Let's get to the core of literature. According to some scholars, the following three qualities constitute what we normally accept as literature:

1. Having language as artistic medium and of imaginative nature;
2. Self-contained as a whole;
3. Preferably with something central to the whole or with a soul in a sense.

In a word, literature is above all an art that attempts to tell the truth by means of language. Remember these literary elements and try to demonstrate them when translating, then we may say it is literary translation.

## 5.2 The Domain of Literary Translation 文学翻译的范畴

Translation can be roughly classified into two forms, literary translation and non-literary translation. Literary studies have always, explicitly or implicitly, presupposed a certain notion of "literariness" with which it has been able to delimit its domain, specify, and sanction its methodologies and approaches to its subject. This notion of "literariness" is crucial for the theoretical thinking about literary translation. According to the traditional discussion, literature is considered as an autonomous and independent domain. According to Wang Hongyin (王宏印, 2006:143-149), literature can be divided into *primary type*, which includes novels, prose, poetry and dramas, and *secondary type*, which includes epic, biography, prose poem, words of a song and poetic drama. Primary type is the basic one in literary typology and the ratified type in aesthetics. Secondary type derives and comes from the primary type.

The traditional discussion of literary translation considers finding equivalents not just for lexis, syntax or concepts, but also for features like style, genre, figurative language, historical stylistic dimensions, polyvalence, connotations as well as denotations, cultural items and culture-specific concepts and values. The choices made by the translators like the decision whether to retain stylistic features of the source language text or whether to retain the historical stylistic dimension of the original become all the more important in the case of literary translation.

According to Peter Bush, "Literary translation is the work of literary translators. That is a truism which has to serve as a starting point for a description of literary translation, an original subjective activity at the centre of a complex network of social and cultural practices." (Taken from *Routledge Encyclopedia of Translation Studies*, 2004)

There often are discussions about which one of the two types: documental and scientific translation and literary translation, offers greater difficulties. Some people sustain that the scientific-technical translation is more difficult because of the experience and knowledge it requires in different disciplines and, therefore, a stronger specialization. Others are of the opinion that literary translation is more difficult because of the language quality required here for the original as well as the translated texts. In our opinion, literary translation is no less important and difficult as documental and scientific translation. This is because each requires its own experience and knowledge and both need to solve their problems in translating.

## 5.3 The Criteria of Literary Translation 文学翻译的标准

As to this point, many translators and scholars hold that *faithfulness to the original* and *smoothness and expressiveness of the translated text* are the two aspects about translation criteria (See Chapter 1). However, they are not enough for literary translation because literary works are not only the narration of objects and notions, but also the artistic conception and image to attract the reader. Meanwhile, creativity and translation are inseparable, especially in literary rendition. A translator should always be resourceful in terms of vocabulary and syntactic structures in order to handle repetitions in the ST. Literary translators in particular need to be also creative in translating the "formalities" of the ST. Creativity in translation can be defined as coming up with novel strategies for dealing with familiar or common problems, whether on the lexical, syntactic or formal levels. The translator is, however, torn between the form and the content of the ST and the limits of freedom and idiomaticity in the TL. Thus, he or she is bound to be creative in terms of his or her knowledge of the TL and what TL-receivers would not baulk at. Moreover, according to Knittlova (2000: 72-73), translator's creativity must have its limits. She maintains that: Judging its right degree might lie within the scope of modern translatology, which approaches the translation from the holistic point of view and which can with advantage use the principles of text linguistics. These might be of some use just because translation should keep all the text parameters or textuality standards unchanged as far as possible with adequate adaptation to the conventions of the target language.

Translation itself is considered as a creative process for a number of reasons: 1) Translation is not merely a transformation of an original text into a literal equivalent, but also successfully conveys the overall meaning of the original, including that text's surrounding cultural significance; 2) The process of searching out a target-language counterpart to a difficult source-language word or phrase is often creative.

Neubert (1997: 17-19) further maintains that: A translation is not created from nothing; it is woven from a semantic pattern taken from another text, but the threads—the TL linguistic forms, structures, syntactic sequences, etc. In the course of achieving something new, mediators (translators and interpreters) have to resort to novel ways of encoding an old message. They are forced to creativity because the means of the TL are not identical with those of the SL. To arrive at an adequate TL version, new resources have to be tapped. In these efforts, creativity plays a prominent role. Creative uses of the target language are the result of the various problem-solving strategies applied to any piece of SL text.

Moreover, the model of creativity in translation comprises four steps (Niska, 1998):

A. Preparation: the first stage in the process, where the problem is investigated, i.e. accumulating knowledge about the problem to be solved, from memory and other sources;

B. Incubation: a resting phase where the problem is temporarily put aside, if the solution is not found immediately;

C. Illumination: a stage where an idea of a solution comes to mind, as a "flash" or "click" as the culmination of a successful train of association;

D. Verification: a stage where alternative solutions are tested and their usability is measured. It is at this stage that the creative product is born.

## 5.4 The Procedures of Literary Translation 文学翻译的过程

Generally speaking, translating is made up of three steps: understanding, expressing and proofreading, and literary translation still need to follow the procedures. At the same time, the procedure *verifying* needs to be added in literary translation.

Understanding: Besides what we have mentioned in Chapter 1, analysis is considered while understanding the original. In other words, the translator should analyze the facial, deep and stylistic meanings, and understand content and form of the text, including lexis, syntax and rhetoric, and the author's attitude, views, writing devices, and connotations of some words and phrases.

Verifying: According to Mao Dun (茅盾, 1951), "The translator has experienced the author's artistic creativity by means of SL itself and verified it in his or her own thought, emotion and life experience. Then he or she uses the literary language of the original to reproduce the content and form of ST correctly and completely. Such a translation procedure will put the author in harmony with the translator so that the translation seems to be written by another foreign language."（译者通过原作的语言外形，深刻地体会了原作者的艺术创造的过程，把握住原作的精神，在自己的思想、感

情、生活体验中找到最适合的印证,然后运用适合于原作风格的文学语言,把原作的内容与形式正确无遗地再现出来。这样的翻译过程,是译者和原作者合二为一,好像原作者用另外一国文字写自己的作品。)

Expressing: On the basis of understanding and verifying, the translator should employ literary language and tries his or her best to thoroughly reproduce content, form and style of the original so as to make content and form achieve dialectical unity. As we all know, literary translation lays emphasis on the reproduction of the original spirit and linguistic style. It has been acknowledged that literary translation is referred to as an art and creativity. Therefore the translator is required to not only comprehend the original and really grasp its gist, but also have an aesthetic judgment and appreciation to the original.

Proofreading: It is indispensable to proofread the translation version. The procedure of proofreading is to read and correct the translator's proofs, so that the mistakes can be put right before the proper version printing is done. (See Chapter 1)

## 5.5 Attentions for Literary Translation 文学翻译需要注意的方面

The essence of literature is a kind of linguistic art, in which, by means of language, characters are well depicted, scenes are finely described, language is delicately employed, structure and movements are deliberately organized and idiomatical phrases and rhetorical devices are properly used. Therefore, these aspects should be paid special attention to in translating literary works for a beginner. These points with examples are one by one listed below.

### 5.5.1 Character Depiction 人物刻画

❖ She remembered how in Nascosta even the most beautiful fell quickly under the darkness of time, like flowers without care; how even the most beautiful became bent and toothless, their dark clothes smelling, as the mamma's did, of smoke and manure. But in this country she could have forever white teeth and color in her hair. Until the day she died she would have shoes with heel and rings on her fingers, and the attention of men, for in this new world one lived ten lifetimes and never felt the pinch of age, no, never. She would marry Joe. She would stay here and live ten lives, with a skin like marble and always the teeth with which to bite meat. (excerpt from *Clementina* by American writer John Cheever)

她想起,在那斯科斯塔,最美的娇娃因为不堪时艰很快便姿容消退,就像无人护理的花朵一样;绝色美人很快就弯腰驼背,皓齿尽落,一身皂衣,就像老妈妈一样,散发着炊烟和粪肥的臭味。但是在这个国度,她可以永葆洁齿,头顶青丝。一直到她辞世那一天,她都可穿着高跟鞋,戴着戒指,还有许多男人向她献殷勤。在这新世界里,人生十世仍不感时世艰辛;不会的,永远不会。她要嫁给乔。她要留下来,带着一身白皙如玉的皮肤,两排专门吃肉的皓牙,好好地过它十辈子。

**Comments**: As we all know, style can be thought of as the linguistic characteristics of a particular text. One of the tasks of literary texts is to depict the characters appearing in a piece of fiction. Character depiction, therefore, is often adopted to achieve an aesthetic effect through language. In the above text, the author depicts the character who was once "*the most beautiful*", but then "*fell quickly under the darkness of time*" and "*became bent and toothless*" "*like flowers without care*" (rhetorical device simile). It requires careful attention to realize that before her death "*she could have forever white teeth and color in her hair*", and "*she would have shoes with heel and rings on her fingers, and the attention of men*" "*with a skin like marble and always the teeth with which to bite meat*". Through the linguistic depiction, a vivid and lifelike character turns up in front of us. Therefore the translator accurately realizes this kind of depiction and well correspondingly translates the text.

## 5.5.2 Scene Description 景色描写

❖ It was she who had stopped the car where the common rose steeply to the left, and a narrow strip of larch and beech, with here and there a pine, stretched out to the right, towards the valley between the road and the first long high hill of the full moor. She was looking for a place where they might lunch, for Ashurst never looked for anything; and this, between the golden furze and the feathery green larches smelling of lemons in the last sun of April—this, with a view into the deep valley and up to the long moor heights, seems fitting to the decisive nature of one who sketched in water-colors, and loved romantic spots. Grasping her paint box, she got out. (excerpt from *The Apple Tree* by British writer John Galsworthy)

正是她叫车停了下来。这儿,左边但见那块公有地陡峭地向上升起,右边是狭狭的一溜落叶松和山毛榉林子,还疏疏落落地长着几棵松树,直向介于公路和整个荒原上的第一座又长又高的山岗中间的山谷伸展过去。她在寻找一个可以让他们坐下来吃东西的地方,艾舍斯特是什么也不寻找的;而现在这个地方,处于金黄的金雀花和在四月的斜阳里散发着柠檬味儿的绿色蓬松的落叶松之间,可以眺望深深的山谷,仰望长长的荒原群丘,似乎适合一个热爱奇景异迹的水彩画家的有决定意义的天性。拿起画箱,她跨出车来。

**Comments**: Our first impression of this passage is of a meticulously detailed setting of the scene. The description is clearly etched, so that we can reconstruct, in our mind's eyes, the whole topography. But more than this, we have a vivid sense of the loneliness of the human observer, set apart from the surroundings "*where the common rose steeply to the left, and a narrow strip of larch and beech, with here and there a pine, stretched out to the right, towards the valley between the road and the first long high hill of the full moor.*" Furthermore, the scene is detailedly described that "*this, between the golden furze and* the feathery green larches smelling of lemons in the last sun of April—this, with a view into the deep valley and up to the long moor heights, seems fitting to the decisive nature of one who sketched in water-colors, and loved romantic spots." Additionally, quite long sentences are suitably used to describe a scene, and the effect of the placing the shorter sentence at the end is powerful: whereas other sentences relate the setting to the observer, the last one relates the observer to the setting, and thereby summarizes what has been implied

### 5.5.3 Linguistic Art 语言艺术

❖ The poor pupil young man hesitated and procrastinated: it cost him such an effort to broach the subject of terms, to speak of money to a person who spoke only of feelings and, as it were, of the aristocracy. Yet he was unwilling to take leave, treating his engagement as settled, without some more conventional glance in that direction than he could find an opening for in the manner of the large, affable lady who sat there drawing a pair of soiled *gantè de Suede* through a fat, jeweled hand and, at once pressing and gliding, repeated over and over everything but the thing he would have liked to hear. He would have liked to hear the figure of his salary; but just as he was nervously about to sound that note the little boy came back—the little boy Mrs. Moreen had sent out of the room to fetch her fan. He came back without the fan, only with the casual observation that he couldn't find it. As he dropped this cynical confession he looked straight and hard at the candidate for the honour of taking his education in hand. This personage reflected, somewhat grimly, that the first thing he should have to teach his little charge would be to appear to address himself to his mother when he spoke to her—especially not make her such an improper answer as that.

(excerpt from *The Pupil* by Henry James)

那位可怜的年轻人犹豫不决，错失良机。向一位似乎只谈感情和贵族的人提条件，或提钱的事真是难于启齿。然而，他不情愿就此离开，认为这是定好的约会，只是朝那个方向瞟了一眼，但见在一个空位处，那位体态臃肿、和蔼可亲的夫人坐在那里，用戴有珠宝的胖手扯拉着一副污损的鹿皮手套，喋喋不休地谈论着别的事，唯独不提钱的事情。他想听到他该拿多少薪水，可就在他急切想听到酬劳时，那个小男孩回来了。刚才摩热恩夫人打发他去屋外为她拿扇子，扇子没有取回来，小男孩只是漫不经心地看了看，说他没有找到。他还承认自己的讥诮行为，并直眼瞪着要给他上课的年轻人。这个男孩的反应多少有点冷漠，这说明他首先要教会小男孩在和母亲讲话时，应学会问候，而不能像这样做不礼貌的回答。

**Comments** About lexical features, this passage has a rather low frequency of nouns; moreover, over half of these nouns are abstract, referring to entities which exist on a social or psychological plane: effort, subject, terms, money, feelings and aristocracy all occur in the first sentence. James makes sparse use of adjectives, and of those that occur, many have nothing to do with physical attributes: *unwilling*, *conventional*, *affable*, *casual*, *cynical*, etc. verbs are particularly frequent in the passage; but this does not mean that it is full of action. The most notable classes of adverb are those of manner (*straight*, *nervously*, etc.) and of degree (*somewhat*). James seems to prefer rather more formal Latinate terms: *procrastinated*, *reflected*, *observation*, *confession*, etc. It is easy to find more simple language in which the same ideas might have been expressed in a more humdrum context: delay for procrastinate, for example. The loftier tone of these words blends with a certain tendency to affection ( the Gallicism *gantè de Suede*), and to euphemism (payment is referred to by terms). There is also a tendency towards circumlocution, particularly in combinations of a verb with an abstract object, as in "*take leave*", "*sound that note*", and "*dropped this cynical confession*". About grammatical features, James's sentences are on the average much shorter and the syntax is more involved. This may be caused to some extent by the general abstractness of the language; but it is also a matter of the kinds of syntactic presentation and complexity. As a result, his syntax becomes meaningful in the light of an appraisal of his particular concern with psychological realism. In short, literary stylistics has, implicitly or explicitly, the goal of explaining the relation between language and artistic function, and an aesthetic effect is achieved through language as well.

### 5.5.4 Narrative Movements 情节发展的层次

❖ The boy went out. They had eaten with no light on the table and the old man took off his trousers and went to bed in the dark. He rolled his trousers up to make a pillow, putting the newspapers inside them. He rolled himself in the blanket and slept on the other old newspaper that covered the springs of the bed.

He was asleep in a short time and he dreamed of Africa when he was a boy and the long golden beaches and the white beaches, so white they hurt your eyes, and the high capes and the great brown mountains. He lived along that coast now every night and in his dreams heard the surf roar and saw the native boats come riding through it. He smelled the tar and oakum of the deck as he slept and he smelled the smell of Africa that the land breeze brought at morning.

(excerpt from *The Old Man and the Sea* by American writer Hemingway)

孩子去了。他俩吃饭的时候,桌子上连个灯都没有。孩子走开以后,老头儿脱掉裤子,摸黑上了床。他把裤子卷成枕头,把报纸塞在里边,然后用军毯裹住身子,睡在破床弹簧上面的旧报纸上。

他不久就睡着了,梦见了他儿童时代所看到的非洲,长长的金黄色的海滩和白色的刺眼的海滩、高耸的海岬和褐色的大山。现在,他每晚住在海边,在梦中听到了海潮的怒号,看见了本地的小船从海潮中穿梭来去。睡着的时候,他闻见到了甲板上的柏油和填絮的味道,闻到了地面上的风在早晨送来的非洲的气息。

**Comments**: When writing a narrative, one of the attentions *narrative movements* should be kept in mind to present the events of our narration in a logical and coherent order. The time sequence in narration is usually chronological. We may want to use an occasional "flashback," that is, inserting an event from past in the midst of a chronological flow. Events should be linked by smooth transitions. In this passage, our impression is that Hemingway tends to use short sentences and arranges narration quite well, which is primarily organized in logical and time order although there few connectives. It is very clear to find out the narrative movements in the first paragraph, in which the actions like "*took off*" and "*went to bed*", "*rolled*", "*putting*" and "*slept*" happen in the logical order. In order to conform the narrative movements, the translator add the phrase 孩子走开以后 and 然后. In the second paragraph, the narrative movements are arranged in time order. At the same time, the flashback can been found "*in his dreams*".

## 5.6 Exercises 练习

**Passage translation.**

My wife has brown hair, dark eyes, and a gentle disposition. Because of her gentle disposition, I sometimes think that she spoils the children. She can't refuse them anything. They always get around her. Ethel and I have been married for ten years. We both come from Morristown, New Jersey, and I can't even remember when I first met her. Our marriage has always seemed happy and resourceful to me. We live in a walk-up in the East Fifties. Our son, Carl, who is six, goes to a good private school, and our daughter, who is four, won't go to school until next year. We often find fault with the way we were educated, but we seem to be struggling to raise our children along the same lines, and when the time comes, I suppose they'll go to the same school and colleges that we went to.

(Excerpt from *The Season of Divorce* by American writer John Cheever)

# Chapter 6: Translation of Scientific Texts
# 科学文本翻译

## 6.1 Text Types and Domain of Scientific Translation 科学翻译的文本类型和范畴

Scientific Translation is comparatively and relatively discussed with literary translation. Different people have different views on text types. According to functionalist approaches (Reiss, 1977/1989; Nord, 1996/2001), there are three main text-types: expressive texts, informative texts and operative texts. Each text-type is identified by its semantic, lexical, grammatical and stylistic features, which influence the way a text is translated and also serve as a basis for translation criticism. In the case of each text-type, these features reflect the primary function which the text serves, which should be preserved in the translation.

The major characteristics of texts of the *expressive type* is that they include an aesthetic component, as the author exploits the expressive and associative possibilities of the language in order to communicate his thoughts in an artistic, creative way. This means that when translating such texts the translator should try to produce an analogous aesthetic effect, as well as reproduce the semantic content of the original. The expressive text-type is exemplified to different extents by poetry, novel and biographies. (Shuttleworth & Cowie, 2004:56)

In the case of *informative texts* the primary aim is one of conveying information to the receiver. This means that a translator should concentrate on establishing semantic equivalence, and only then turn to other kinds, such as connotative or aesthetic. Similarly, a translation which is deemed to fulfill this function of reproducing in TL the informative content of SL should be judged to be successful. Reference books, business letters, official documents and academic articles all represent this text-type to varying degrees. (Shuttleworth & Cowie, 2004:79)

*Operative texts* contain messages which are intended to persuade the receiver to undertake a certain course of action, such as buying a specific product or voting for a particular political party. In other words, in such a text both content and form are subordinated to the extralinguistic effect which the text is designed to achieve. This means that a translator's main aim should be produce a TT which has an equivalence persuasive force to that of the original. However, besides transmitting similar impulses to action, the translation process will also entail preserving the basic semantic nature. Political manifestos, advertisements and sermons are all examples of this type of text. (Shuttleworth & Cowie, 2004: 117)

In addition, Reiss uses a subsidiary text-type, multi-medial text, which supplements her three basic text typology. *The multi-medial category* consists of texts in which the verbal content is supplemented by elements in other media; however, all such texts will also simultaneously belong to one of the other, main text-types. Reiss argues that this text-type forms a superstructure over the other three, as the special requirements of this type take precedence over whatever basic text type a given text otherwise belongs to. Songs, comic strips, plays, and writing for radio or television are all examples of this type, and the translator of such texts will need to ensure that the translation is equally suited as the original for use in the relevant medium. (Shuttleworth & Cowie, 2004: 109-110)

In our view, it is acceptable to classify text-types according to text functions, which is helpful to figure out a guideline for translators and to help in the process of translation criticism. The domain for science translation contains such text-types as science and technology, social science, popular science, etc. With the development of science and technology in the present-day world, the quantities of documents dealing with science and technology such as journal papers, books, scientific reports, patent documents, proceedings are multiplying at an accelerated rate. Most of these scientific and technological texts are written in English which is the most widely used international language in the world. As a result, the so-called EST or English for Science and Technology has now become an important variety of English that has its unique stylistic characteristics. Therefore we should take account of these characteristics in the translation of English for Science and Technology.

## 6.2 Characteristics of Scientific Texts 科学文本的特点

### 6.2.1 Lexical Characteristics 词法特点

**1) Vocabulary categories**

A. Pure technical terms (specialized technical terms): used only in certain disciplines, fields and branches of learning, for example, hydroxide 氢氧化合物, diode 二极管, isotope 同位素.

B. General-purpose technical terms: used in more or less the same sense in a great variety of disciplines, fields and branches of learning, for example, frequency 频率, density 密度, energy 能量, magnetism 磁性, feedback 反馈, transmission 传送.

C. Semi-technical words: used in different disciplines, fields and branches of learning. For instance, the primary meaning of "feed" is 喂养, but it can mean 加电, 供水, 输送, 加载, 进刀 or 电源 in different contexts or fields. The word "service" can carry the sense of 运转, 操作, 维修, 设备 or 使用 in different technical fields instead of the basic meaning 服务.

D. Abstract nouns: derived from verbs or adjectives, for example, insulate—insulation, expand—expansion, move—movement, leak—leakage, stable—stability, humid—humidity and so on. The use of abstract nouns serves to achieve concision and formalness which characterize Scientific English.

E. Words with affixation: some examples with prefix *hydra-*: hydra-beating, hydrability, hydracids, hydra-cyclone, hydragoga, etc. and some words with suffix *-meter*: barometer, chronometer, thermometer, spectrometer, micrometer, etc. The extensive use of affixation is intended to name the multitude of new concepts that keep springing up each day in the world of science and technology.

F. Abbreviations: for example, RADCM (radar countermeasure), CTF (certificate), LADAR (laser radar), AWACS (airborne warning and control system), and PPC (program planning and control). The extensive use of abbreviations is also intended to meet the requirements of concision and economy in Scientific English.

G. Common words: used in the same way as in everyday English.

## 2) Lexical characteristics

A. Some scientific English words are monotonous and stable in meaning and usage as compared with ordinary English. For example, "make" is seldom used in its basic meaning of 做, 制造, but often has the following two collocations: one is *make + action noun*, for example, "make a calculation", "make a change", "make a correction", "make a measurement" etc., the other *make + direct object + indirect object*, for example, "make something done", "make something a tool" etc..

B. Abstract nouns denoting actions or states are extensively used. They are mostly derived from verbs or adjectives, such as "transmission", "evaluation", and "resistance". This is known as "the trend of nominalization" in English for Science and Technology. "The trend of nominalization" is intended to achieve the concision and formality of expression, and the simplicity of structure, for example, "the utilization of salinity power by reverse electro-dialysis and other methods" (盐动力是通过逆电渗发和别的方法来利用的) is commonly used instead of "Salinity power is utilized by reverse electro-dialysis and other methods".

C. Scientific English is characterized by formalness and solemnity. It tends to use formal words instead of informal or colloquial words in terms of its diction. Here are five pairs of synonyms below, the first one is an informal word while the second one is a formal word which is likely to occur in English for Science and Technology.

- send—transmit　　change—convert　　enough—sufficient
  better—superior　　use up—consume

D. A feature "the continuous use of nouns" in English for Science and Technology means that a headword is modified by several nouns. This is also referred to as "Expanded Noun Modifiers". "The continuous use of noun" can effectively simplify sentential structure.

- power transmission relay system = a relay system for power transmission
  送电中继系统
- illumination intensity determination = determination of the intensity of illumination
  照明强度测定

E. The frequent use of connectives such as conjunctions or prepositions. This is due to the emphasis on logical relations and logical reasoning in English for Science and Technology.

## 6.2.2 Syntactical Characteristics 句法特点

### 1) Frequent use of present tense

The tendency of using present tense, especially present simple tense is used in scientific English to denote "permanence", "universality" or "truism" in the description of natural occurrence, processes or general laws, so the tense is generally timeless.

- One of the most striking characteristics of modern science has been the increasing trend toward closer cooperation between scientists and scientific institutions all over the world.
  现代科学最显著的特点之一，就是全世界科学家及科学机构之间不断发展更密切的合作的趋势。

**Comments** The original sentence is in present perfect progressive tense to denote a trend which started in the past and which will continue into the future.

### 2) Frequent use of passive voice

A. Passive voice can highlight the object of description or discussion without any reference to human agent, which is characteristic of scientific language.

- All business decisions must be made in the light of the market.
  所有企业都必须根据市场来做出决策。

**Comments** It is neither possible nor necessary to specify who make these "*business decisions*" in the SL sentence. In the TL sentence, we can use 企业 as the subject of the sentence according to Chinese linguistic habits.

- ❖ No work can be done without energy.

  没有能量就不能做功。

**Comments** The original sentence is in passive voice since it describes a universal truth without any involvement of human agents. In the translation, we can convert the SL sentence into a subjectless sentence that frequently occurs in Chinese.

B. Passive voice can avoid subjectivity and achieve objectivity which is a prominent feature of scientific language.

- ❖ All sorts of necessities of life can be made of plastics.

  各种日常用品都能用塑料制造。

**Comments** The use of passive voice helps to achieve objectivity in the original sentence.

- ❖ An example is given to.../A discussion is presented to...

  本文举例(说明……)/ 本文讨论了……

**Comments** The original sentence typically occurs in the abstract of a scientific paper. Passive voice is used here to avoid such expressions as "The author gives an example of..." which has a little bit subjectivity. But equivalent Chinese versions 本文举例(说明……)/ 本文讨论了…… are normally adopted in such text type.

C. Passive voice is used to serve the purpose of concision and economy.

D. Passive voice is sometimes used for smooth cohesion of discourse.

- ❖ When the radiation energy of the sun falls on the earth, it is changed into heat energy to warm the earth.

  当太阳的辐射能到地球时就转化为热能,从而使大地暖和起来。

**Comments** The use of passive voice in the main clause enhances its cohesion with the subordinate clause "When the radiation energy…"

### 3) Frequent use of nominal structures

In scientific writings, a noun phrase is often used in place of a sentence. Such noun phrases are known as nominal structures. They are clear, concise, compact and information intensive in place of long clauses and sentences.

- ❖ *The discovery of the constant speed of light regardless of the motion of its source by Einstein* threw some interesting light on the study of theoretical physics.

  爱因斯坦发现:无论光源是否运动,光的速度都恒定不变,这一发现给理论物理的研究带来了发人深省的启迪。

**Comments** The underlined part of the sentence is a typical nominal construction. It is equivalent to a long sentence meaning "Einstein discovered that the speed of light is constant, no matter how fast its source is moving".

❖ *The testing of machines by this method* entails some loss of power.

用这种方法试验机器，会浪费一些能量。

**Comments** "*The testing of machines by this method*" in the original sentence is equivalent to an adverbial clause of condition "If machines are tested by this method".

❖ *Continued exposure of the eye to light of high intensity* would cause loss of sight.

眼睛持续暴露在强光中会导致失明。

**Comments**: "*Continued exposure of the eye to light of high intensity*" in the original sentence is equivalent to an adverbial clause of condition "If the eye is continuously exposed to light of high intensity".

### 4) Ellipsis, inversions and separations often used

This phenomenon is due to the rhetorical and stylistic need in scientific English. Ellipsis can achieve concision and brevity. Inversions can foreground a certain element. Separations make a sentence well-balanced and symmetrical.

❖ All bodies consist of molecules and *molecules of atoms*.

所有的物体都由分子组成，而分子又由原子组成。

**Comments** The underlined part of the sentence is an ellipsis. Its complete form should be "all molecules consist of atoms".

❖ All these forces the platform must be able to withstand without changing its operating characteristics.

平台必须能承受所有这些力，而其作用性能不得有所改变。

**Comments** This is a typical inverted sentence. Its normal order should be "The platform must be able to withstand all these forces without changing its operating characteristics". This sentence is inverted in order to highlight "*All these forces*".

❖ The distance to the sun, from where we are on the earth, is about 1 million walking days.

假如从地球步行到太阳，约需一百万天。

**Comments** In this sentence, "*the distance*" is separated from "*from where we are on the earth*" to keep the sentence well-balanced and to avoid ambiguity. The normal order of the sentence should be "The distance from where we are on the earth to the sun is…".

### 5) Frequent use of long and complicated sentences

Such long sentences usually consist of a variety of clauses, phrases and other subordinate constituents. Such a sentential structure is intended to express the different logical relationships between the things that are described in the paper explicitly and precisely. Now let us look at the following sentence.

❖ Only by studying such cases of human intelligence with all the details and by comparing the results of exact investigation with the solutions of AI (Artificial

Intelligence) usually given in the elementary books on computer science can a computer engineer acquire a thorough understanding of theory and method in AI, develop intelligent computer programs that work in a humanlike way, and apply them to solving more complex and difficult problems that present computer can't.

只有很详细地研究这些人类智能的情况,并把实际研究得出的结果与计算机科学基础论著上所提出的人工智能解决方案相比较,计算机工程师才能彻底地了解人工智能的理论和方法,开发出具有人类智能的计算机程序,并将其用于解决目前计算机不能解决的更为复杂和困难的问题。

**Comments** The original long sentence is in inverted order. The general structure of this sentence is "Only by doing… and by doing …can a computer engineer…" There are three coordinate predicates in this sentence: "*acquire…*", "*develop…*" and "*apply…*" But there are also two attributive clauses: "*that work in a humanlike way*" and "*that present computer can't*", and a past participle phrase "*given in the elementary books on computer science*" and several prepositional phrases that are also modifiers. This is characteristic of English sentential structure that is hypotactic in nature. Since Chinese sentences are mostly paratactic in contrast to English sentences, in translating long sentences, we often need to break them up into short parts and convert them into correspondent short Chinese clauses.

### 6.2.3 Organizational and Rhetorical Characteristics 结构与修辞特点

Scientific writings deal with matters related to science and technology. So its style is plain and simple. Rhetorical devices which are commonly employed in literary English are not very frequently used in scientific writings, except for popular science writings. However, English for Science and Technology often adopts a formulaic style of writing in its textual format to attain clarity and accuracy. Firstly, in respect of its textual format, apart from the title and abstract, a scientific text is usually divided into three parts: *introduction*, *main body* and *conclusion*. The introduction gives the background information and the significance of the research. The main body contains a detailed discussion on the research. The conclusion makes a summary of the discussion and puts forward suggestions for future research. As far as sentences are concerned, scientific English often adopts a "forward position" sentence pattern, that means, the main information is placed ahead as much as possible so that the reader can catch the gist of the message and grasp the writer's line of thought. Let us look at the following sentence.

❖ Seawater can be used for a supply of drinkable water if it can be separated from the salt dissolved in it.

如果海水中的盐能分离出去海水就可用作饮用水。

**Comments**: In this sentence, the main information is contained in the first part of the sentence that is put ahead of the subordinate clause "*if it can…*" So the reader can quickly grasp the key point of the sentence.

In scientific writings, some writing formulas and sentence patterns, which refer to stylistic rules, layouts and expressions in texts alike, are commonly used. For instance, a research paper generally contains title, abstract, introduction, materials and methods (equipment and test/experiment procedure), result, discussion, summary, acknowledgements and references. In addition, sentence patterns tend to be fixed and regular. Some common sentence patterns are listed as follows.

**1) Some patterns in the beginning of scientific texts are as follows.**

The patent describes... 本专利叙述……

The present invention is related to... 本发明介绍……

The method of ...is discussed in the report 本报告讨论……的方法

An overview is presented of ...in this article 本文概述……

An examination is made of ...in the article 本文研究……

This paper deals with... 本文讨论……

**2) Some common sentence patterns are as follows.**

The principle of ⎫　　　⎧is outlined 本文概述了……的原则
The apparatus for ⎪　　　⎪is described 本文描述了……的装置
Automation of ⎪　　　⎪is discussed 本文讨论了……的自动化
The use of ⎬ ... ⎨is addressed 本文论述了……的应用
The mechanism of ⎪　　　⎪is examined 本文探讨了……的机理
The dependence of ⎪　　　⎪was established 本文确定了……的关系
An analysis of ⎭　　　⎩was carried out 本文作了……的分析

In the technical standard texts, the use of certain standards will be clearly and definitely specified. Some commonly-used patterns are as follows.

The term "This method" is commonly used as the subject of a sentence in method standard.

This method $\begin{cases} \text{covers}\ldots \\ \text{is intended for}\ldots \\ \text{is (not) suitable for}\ldots \\ \text{describes}\ldots \end{cases}$ 适用于……
(不)适用于……
描述……

Although rhetorical devices are not frequently used in scientific English texts, they are still to be paid attention to deal with while translating because rhetorical devices are here and there appearing in such texts. *Simile* is sometimes used to make a comparison between two thing using the words "like", "as", or "as if" to clarify a kind of logic. *Metaphor* is used to describe one thing by stating another thing to create an association. For example, the words "windows", "menus" and "network" in computer, and "traffic" (通信) and "tunnel" (信道) in IT, etc. *Personification* is used to represent something that is without life as a human being or as having human qualities. The words "memory" (记忆器), instructions" (指令) and "data processing" (数据处理) in computer, and "arm" (手臂), "robot-cop" (机器人警察), "robonurse" (机器人护士) and others are good examples. *Rhyme* is usually used in literary texts, but it is sometimes used in scientific texts, especially in titles and an introduction, for example, "solar system search from space" (从太空探索太阳系) and "tracing disease to trace minerals" (疾病的微量矿物质探源). Actually, other rhetorical devices like *metonymy*, *parallelism*, *repetition*, etc. may be used every once in a while.

### 6.2.4 Scientific Translation Techniques 科学翻译的方法
#### 6.2.4.1 Attentions on word translation 注意词语翻译

Word translation is the most important part in the translation of scientific English texts because a word is the basic unit of meaning and it is also the basic building block of language. The correct understanding and rendering of words lays the basis for success in translating. In translating an EST word, the translator should take its context into account. Besides, he should also consider the branch of learning in which this word is used. For this reason, he or she should have a basic knowledge of the field he or she is translating. To be more specific, the translator should pay attention to the following points in translating words.

**1) A word should be translated according to the branch of learning in which it is used.**

As we have pointed out before, the exact meaning of a word in EST often depends on the field in which it is used. This is especially true of semi-technical words, which account for the bulk of vocabulary in EST. Therefore, we have to take account of this factor in rendering EST words. Let's take the word *power* for example. This semi-technical word can be translated in different senses depending on the following branches of learning in which it is used:

❖ Mathematics: The sixth *power* of two is 64. 2 的 6 次方是 64。
　Physics: horse *power* 马力（功率）　rated *power* 额定功率
　Optics: 1,000 *power* microscope 千倍显微镜
　Electrology: *power* network 电力网；电源开关
　Chemistry: chemical *power* 化学能　combining *power* 化合力
　Mechanics: *power* shaft 传动轴　brake *power* 制动力

The word "*system*" also has different senses in a variety of fields, so it should be translated differently.

❖ Electrics: electric light *system* 电照明系统　*system* fault 电力网故障
　　　　　　charging *system* 装料装置　loading *system* 装载设备
　Mathematics: *system* of equations 主程组
　Mechanics: *system* of forces 力系
　Chemistry: acid *system* 酸法
　Philosophy: ideological *system* 思想体系
　Sociology: industrial *system* 工业体系　social *system* 社会制度
　　　　　　a new *system* of teaching English 一套新的外语教学法

**2) A word should be translated according to its collocation.**

Collocation refers to the habitual concurrence of words in a language. A word might have different meanings when it collocates with different words. In English-Chinese translation, there are two types of collocation which should be particularly paid attention to.

The first type of collocation is "*adj. + noun*", for example:

❖ The patient is in a *critical condition*.
　病人处于**病危状态**。
❖ The *critical pressure* is the pressure under which gases can be liquefied.
　**临界压力**指气体液化时所需的压力。
❖ They are at a *critical time*.
　他们正处于**危急的关头**。
❖ In order to meet the *critical service requirement*, scientists are still looking for better materials.
　为了满足**紧迫的使用要求**，科学家仍在寻求更好的材料。
❖ These components are more *critical* for the latter than for the former.
　后者对这些部件的要求比前者更为**严格**。
❖ Scientists should look on every new invention with a *critical eye*.

科学家应该用**挑剔的眼光**看待每一种新发明。

The second type of collocation is "*verb + noun*", in which we need to pay special attention to the same word with different meanings. Let us look at the following examples.

❖ Exercises *develop* health bodies. 运动**有益**健康。

*develop* a new method **发明**一种新方法

*develop* a new energy source **开发**新能源

*develop* a large amount of heat **产生**大量的热

*develop* a new product **研制**新产品

*develop* heart problem **得(罹患)**心脏病

*develop* a photo **洗**照片

*develop* a theory **创立**一种理论

*develop* a new species of wheat **培育**新品种小麦

*develop* one's abilities **培养**能力

In addition, a word should be translated according to its context. A renowned British linguist once remarked on the importance of context to the meaning of a word, "Every word is a new word in a new context." To comprehend and render a word in consideration of its context is a fundamental principle in translation. When translating an EST word, we should not follow mechanically its definition in dictionary. Instead, we should flexibly comprehend its meaning according to its context and re-express its contextual meaning in Chinese.

❖ Scientific discoveries and inventions have often been *translated* rapidly into practical devices.

科学发现和发明常常迅速地**转化**成实用器件。

❖ The weight of a *typical* man is around 65 kg.

**普通**人的体重大约是65公斤。

❖ Some species are *killed* in survival competition.

有些物种在生存竞争中被**淘汰**了。

❖ Head gear is *protective clothing*.

安全帽是一种**劳保用品**。

❖ This volcano has not been *active* for thousands of years. It is an *inactive* volcano.

这座火山已有几千年没有**喷发**,是一座**死**火山。

❖ *Old* energy sources will continue to play a major role in industrial *activity*.

**传统的**能源将继续在工业**生产**中起到重要作用。

**Comments** In the first sentence, the word "*translate*" usually means 翻译. But in this sentence, its literal meaning is extended into 转化 which is in accordance with its context. In the second sentence, the word "*typical*" usually means 典型的. But its literal meaning is extended into 普通 which is in accordance with its context. This contextual meaning is nonexistent in dictionaries. In the third sentence, if "*kill*" is translated as 杀死, it will distort the original meaning and cause misunderstanding on the part of the reader. In the forth sentence, the phrase "*protective clothing*" should not be rendered literally as 保护衣服. In the fifth sentence, the word "*active*" is translated as 喷发 and "*inactive*" as 死 according to the context. In the last sentence, the word "*old*" should not be rendered literally as 老的 and "*activity*" should not be translated as 活动.

### 6.2.4.2 Attentions on other skills 注意其他技巧

About translation skills and methods, we can still adopt the ones mentioned in Chapter 2 and Chapter 3, in which the translation methods and skills are discussed in detail. That is to say, in EST translation, we also need to employ such methods and skills as addition or amplification, omission, conversion, diction principles in lexical translation, and the methods and skills in syntactic translation.

**1) Lexical addition**: To be specific, in translating scientific English, addition is employed according to the context to make the rendering clear and complete in meaning or to adapt to the linguistic norms of Chinese. Addition can only be used in EST translation when it is required for semantic, grammatical or logical reasons. We should not add words whose meanings are nonexistent in the original. The aim of lexical addition is to allow the meanings or concepts of original English lexical items to be reproduced intact in Chinese. For instance, Chinese nouns have no marker of plurality, which have to be inferred from the context. In EST translation, when it is necessary to indicate the plurality of a noun in Chinese, we have to add words for this purpose. Let us look at the following example.

❖ The first electronic *computers* went into operation in 1946.
第一批电子计算机于1946年投入使用。

**Comments** In the above Chinese version, 批 is added to indicate the plurality of "*computers*". By contrast, in the English version, the plurality is marked by the plural suffix -s.

Abstract nouns are changed into concrete noun. As has been stated before, in English for Science and Technology, there is a profuse use of abstract nouns derived from adjectives or verbs. These abstract nouns often express concrete concepts. Under such circumstances, when these abstract nouns are translated into Chinese, it is necessary to add other nouns to indicate their concrete concepts or categories. The added nouns are known as category nouns.

❖ absorption 吸收作用/吸水性            administration 管理部门
   compromise 妥协办法/折中方案    confusion 混乱状态
   constraint 约束条件                      display 显示值
   application 使用场合/适用范围    evaporation 蒸发过程

computation 计算**技术**/计算**结果**  　　choice 选择**对象**
characteristics 特性**曲线**  　　　　　emedy 治疗**方案**
option 选择**余地**  　　　　　　　　penetration 穿透**能力**
organization 编排**方式**  　　　　　　repair 检修**措施**
damage 损坏**程度**  　　　　　　　　imagination 想象**力**
transition 过渡**时期**

**Comments** In the above Chinese versions, the underlined words are category words that are collocated with nouns to form concrete concepts.

Grammatical addition is sometimes needed in translating scientific English. English grammatical structure is quite different from Chinese language. English language possesses grammatical marker—suffixes to indicate tense, voice, mood etc. In EST translation, these grammatical meanings often have to be re-expressed in Chinese by lexical means, i.e. by addition of words. Generally speaking, the following circumstances require grammatical addition. Addition is needed to express the logical meaning in non-predicate verbs such as infinitives, gerunds, present and past participles. These non-predicate verbs carry add-on logical meanings such as cause, effect, intention, means, condition, supposition, etc. These add-on logical meanings often need to be re-expressed in the Chinese version by means of addition.

❖ *Not having been discovered*, many laws of nature do exit.
　**虽然**许多自然规律尚未发现，**但**它们确实存在。

❖ Lung cancer, *diagnosed early*, can be successfully treated by surgery.
　肺癌**如果能及早诊断**，就能获得满意的手术治疗。

**Comments** In the first sentence, the non-predicate verb phrase "*Not having been discovered*" implies a logical meaning of concession. This logical meaning is made explicit in the Chinese version by adding 虽然……但. In the second sentence, the non-predicate verb phrase "*diagnosed early*" implies a logical meaning of condition or supposition. In the Chinese rendering, this logical meaning is re-expressed by the added words 如果.

Addition is needed to indicate tense. The concept of tense in English is indicated by verb changes. In Chinese, there is generally no need to highlight the tense of verbs which can be inferred from the context. But in some cases when it is necessary to clarify the concept of tense, we will have to add words to express this meaning.

❖ People *thought* that the sun revolved around the earth.
　人们**曾经认为**太阳围绕地球旋转。

❖ Pollution *was, is and will still be* a major problem in human society.
　污染**过去是、现在是、将来仍然是**人类社会的主要问题。

**Comments** In the first sentence, 曾经 is a necessary addition to suggest that people no long think so now. In the second sentence, it is necessary to highlight the concept of time that is also emphasized in the original. This concept of time is expressed by 过去,现在,将来.

Addition can be used to indicate the concept of moods. In English, there are three moods: declarative, imperative and subjunctive. The declarative moods usually do not need to be re-expressed in Chinese, but in the case of imperative and subjunctive moods, it is often necessary to signify these concepts by means of adding such words like 注意, 请, 务必, 必须, 切勿, 假定, 如果.

❖ *Should* troubles occur, contact your supplier.

<u>如果</u>出现问题,<u>请</u>与供应商联系。

❖ Do not leave dead batteries in the battery box as this may cause malfunction.

<u>注意</u>不要将废电池留在电池槽内,以免引起故障。

**Comments** The subordinate clause in the original English sentence is in a subjunctive mood that expresses a condition and the main clause is in an imperative mood that expresses a request. Since there is no such subjunctive mood or imperative mood in Chinese, we have to add 如果 and 请 in the first sentence to compensate for this inadequacy. The second English sentence is in an imperative mood. So in the Chinese version, we add 注意 to express a polite request.

Addition can be used to render English elliptical structures into Chinese. Elliptical structures often occur in EST for the purpose of concision. When translating these elliptical structures into Chinese, we often have to add words to conform to Chinese syntactical norms and to avoid loss of meaning in the Chinese version.

❖ Yes, sport events are worth watching on television; you can often see them better *if you were there in person*.

是的,体育比赛在电视上看是不错,但是假如能亲临现场观赏就更好了。

**Comments** In the adverbial clause of comparison (the underlined part), the words "you could see them" is omitted. It is almost a norm in English to omit the subject and the link verb "be" of an adverbial clause of time, condition, or concession if the subject of the adverbial clause is the same as that of the main clause. In an adverbial clause of comparison, what is omitted is generally the part which is the same as that of the main. But in the Chinese version, we have to supplement the omitted part of the original to make the meaning complete.

English for Science and Technology is in general plain and simple, but it is also logical and rational since it is used to convey the logical reasoning of science. In EST translation, clarity, accuracy and logicality are primary requirements for the Chinese version. But due to the differences in linguistic norms and thinking habits between Chinese and English, some English sentences which in the original are logical might be very awkward when transferred into Chinese. Under such circumstances, we have to add words to make them smooth and natural in terms of Chinese linguistic logics. This is known as logical addition.

- The leakage current of capacitor is an important measure of its quality.

  电容器漏电流的**大小**,是衡量电容器质量**好坏**的重要尺度。

- Atomic cells are very small and light as compared to ordinary dry ones.

  与普通干电池相比,原子电池**体积**小、**重量**轻。

Comments If the underlined words are not added, the real meaning of the sentences will be lost in the Chinese version.

**2) Lexical omission**: Omission, which is often used in scientific English, means to omit words which are redundant in Chinese, or which are incompatible with Chinese linguistic or logic norms. Proper use of this EST translation technique can make the Chinese version smooth, clear and concise. But we should be careful not to omit the essential meaning of the original. The Chinese version should remain equivalent to the original in meaning and spirit, even though one or more original words have no counterparts in the rendering. Lexical omission, mainly has prepositional omission, pronoun omission and verb omission.

- Vitamin A is toxic *in* high doses.

  大剂量维生素 A 可能引起中毒。

Comments In the Chinese version, the original English preposition "*in*" is omitted. If it is retained in the Chinese version, the rendering will be very clumsy.

- *You* can retrieve information on Internet when you need it.

  在因特网上,可根据需要检索信息。

- Animals can protect *themselves* from the heat of summer.

  动物能躲避夏日的炎热。

Comments In the first English sentence, the word "*you*" refers to an indefinitely specified person. On such occasions, "you" should be omitted in Chinese. In the second sentence, the original self-pronoun "*themselves*" is omitted to achieve brevity.

- Some substances, such as glass *offer* a very high resistance.

  某些物质,比如玻璃的阻值极高。

- The spacecraft *made* a soft landing on the moon.

  这架空间飞行器在月球上软着陆。

Comments The Chinese versions are smooth and concise verb-free sentences. The verbs "*offer*", "*made*" are omitted.

- Radioactivity may cause illness that could *be passed on to our children and grand children*.

  放射线可引起遗传性疾病。

**Comments** The underlined part of the original is simplified as 遗传性 for logical omission which is fully equivalent to its counterpart in the English version. Due to the differences in linguistic norms and thinking habits between Chinese and English languages, if an English sentence is translated word-for-word under certain circumstances, it may lead to logical redundancy. In this case, it is necessary to omit certain words to make the Chinese version accurate and clear.

**3) Syntactical translation:** One of the characteristics in EST is the presence of long sentences that are very complicated in their structures, consisting of a variety of clauses, phrases and constructions. English sentences are hypotactic in nature, which means that they possess rich means of structural organization, such as suffixes, grammatical markers, and syntactic rules. This makes it possible to construct long and complicated sentences in English. Besides, English for Science and Technology is used to express abstruse logical reasoning involving a great variety of logical relations in scientific research. Long sentences can be used to meet the need of describing these relations. These two reasons account for the abundant presence of long sentences in English. By contrast, Chinese sentences are paratactic in nature. Chinese sentences are generally short and simple in structure. This is because Chinese language lacks the overt syntactic means to organize involved sentence structures. Therefore, in EST translation, we often need to break a long English sentence into several segments, and translate each segment into a Chinese short sentence. This technique is known as splitting in EST translation. Details about the translation methods of long sentences can refer to Chapter 3. Here are a couple of points that are emphatically mentioned, of utilizing this technique.

A. Sequential-order splitting: When the logical order of expression in a long English sentence is the same as that in Chinese, we can split this sentence into several sections, and translate each section into a Chinese short sentence and arrange these short sentences in the original order.

❖ ①Only by studying such cases of human intelligence with all the details② and by comparing the results of exact investigation with the solutions of AI (Artificial Intelligence) usually given in the elementary books on computer science③ can a computer engineer acquire a thorough understanding of theory and method in AI, ④develop intelligent computer programs that work in a humanlike way, ⑤and apply them to solving more complex and difficult problems that present computer can't.

①只有很详细地研究这些人类智能的情况,②并把实际研究得出的结果与计算机科学基础论著上所提出的人工智能解决方案相比较,③计算机工程师才能彻底地了解人工智能的理论和方法,④开发出具有人类智能的计算机程

序,⑤并将其用于解决目前计算机不能解决的更为复杂和困难的问题。

**Comments** The original sentence is in an inverted order; it consists of two adverbial clauses (① and ②) and three coordinate predicates (③, ④ and ⑤). Accordingly it is divided into 5 corresponding segments, each of which is translated into a Chinese short sentence. Since the logical order of description in the original is the same as in Chinese, the short Chinese sentences are organized in the same order as they are in the original.

❖ ①In his special theory of Relativity, presented in 1905 ②and evolved in his spare time while he worked as an examiner at the Swiss patent office, ③ Einstein proposed a new fundamental view of the universe, ④based on an extension of the quantum theory.

①爱因斯坦的相对论发表于1905年,②并在他担任瑞士专利局审查员的工作之余,得以完善,③该理论提出了一种全新的基本宇宙观,④这种观点的基础是对量子理论的进一步推导。

**Comments** Apart from the main clause, the above original English long sentence consists of a prepositional phrase, another past participial phrase (which contains an adverbial clause of time), and another past participial phrase. According to the components of information in this sentence, we divide this sentence into 4 segments marked with ①, ②, ③ and ④, and translate them into Chinese short sentences which are organized in the same order (i.e. time order) as in the original sentence.

B. Reverse-order splitting: In some long English sentences, the part that conveys primary information is placed at the head, while the part that contains secondary information is positioned in the end. This order is generally reverse in relation to Chinese way of logic thinking. In dealing with these long English sentences, we can break them into small sections which are translated into corresponding Chinese short sentences and reorganized in a reverse order.

❖ ①The increasing speed of scientific development is quite extraordinary② if we consider ③that computer, satellite and television, which are taken for granted now ④ would have seemed fantastic⑤ to people who lived in the 1920's.

⑤对于生活在20世纪20年代的人来说,④计算机、卫星、电视还似乎是不可思议的东西,③而这些东西在今天早已司空见惯,②考虑到这一点,①科学发展的速度之快的确令人惊叹。

**Comments** According to its informational structure, the original sentence is split into 5 components which are translated into 5 corresponding short Chinese sentences. But in consideration of Chinese habitual mode of thinking, they are reorganized in a reversed order in relation to the original English sentence.

❖ ①A student of mathematics must become familiar with all the signs and symbols commonly used in mathematics and bear them in mind and be well versed in the definitions, formulas as well as the technical terms in the field of mathematics, in order that ②he may be able to build up the foundation of the mathematical subject and master it well for pursuing advanced study.

②为了能打好数学基础,掌握好数学,以利于深造,①学数学的学生必须熟悉和牢记数学中常用的符号和代号,精通数学方面的定义、公式和术语。

**Comments** According to Chinese habitual way of thinking, we generally express conditions first and facts or results next, or purposes first and actions next.

C. Altered-order splitting: Some English sentences are quite different from Chinese sentences in their sentence order, information structure and logical focus. On these occasions, we should alter the order of the original sentence and rearrange the split components of the sentence according to the Chinese habitual mode of logical reasoning. The Chinese version is neither in a sequential order nor in a reverse order as compared with the original English sentence. Instead, it is in an altered order.

❖ ①Scientific studies may be divided into pure science ②which primarily deal with theoretical work and ③applied science ④which is more concerned with applied research.

①科学研究可以分成理论科学和③应用科学,②前者以理论研究为主,④而后者更注重于应用研究。

**Comments** The original long sentence consists of two attributive clauses which modify two prepositional objects "*pure science*" and "*applied science*" respectively. In the Chinese version, we split the original sentence into several parts (see the marked number). And regroup and reorganize them in an altered order and add the necessary words 前者 and 后者 to make the sentences more coherent.

❖ ①Ginevan says ② it's reasonable, therefore, ③to expect that the vulnerability of the studied bees ④ is indicative of what may be occurring ⑤ in small bees important to pollination, such as honeybees.

①吉凡尼说,③既然发现所研究的这些蜂容易受到伤害,②所以人们就有理由担心,⑤对于植物授粉有重要作用的小型蜂(如蜜蜂),④也可能会有类似的遭遇。

**Comments** The original English sentence is split (see the marked numbers) and regrouped in an altered order according to Chinese habit of logical reasoning and then translated into Chinese.

## 6.3 Compare and Analyze 比较与分析

①Fibre-optic lines will form most of the backbone of the information highway, just as they do for the phone system today. Fibre-optic cable is made of long, thin strands of glass

①光纤电缆构成了今日电话系统的主干线,同样,它也将构成未来信息公路的主干线。光纤电缆的制造材料是细长的玻璃丝而

rather than wire, and it transmits information in the form of digitized pulses of laser light rather than the radio waves used by coaxial cable. Because light pulses have shorter wavelengths than radio waves, engineers can ②cram much more data into fibre-optic lines than into other kinds of cables and wires. A single fibre, for example, can handle a ③mind-boggling 5,000 video signals or more than 500,000 voice conversations simultaneously. This huge capacity allows it to transmit all signals digitally, so noise or static easily can be filtered out. Finally, because glass is an inherently more efficient medium for transmitting information than other materials, a fiber-optic line can transmit a signal thousands of miles without much "signal loss". Fiber-optic cable, simply put, is the method ④of choice for transmitting massive quantities of information over long distances.

Another key is "digital compression"—a variety of methods for reducing the amount of digital code (streams of ones and zeros) needed to represent a piece of information—whether it is a document, a still picture, a movie or a sound. Digital compression is most critical for transmitting video, because digitized video consumes enormous amounts of space. Just four seconds of a digitized film, for example, would completely fill a 100 megabyte hard drive. A feature film of typical length, if uncompressed, would occupy more than 350 ordinary compact discs.

Compression techniques achieve their gains ⑤by recording only the changes from one frame to the next. The background image in a movie

不是金属导线，它的信息传输方式是激光数字脉冲而不是同轴电缆使用的无线电波。由于光脉冲的波长比无线电波的波长短，因而工程师可以②**输入光纤电缆的信息量之大**令其他类型的电缆和导线望尘莫及。例如，一根光纤电缆可同时处理五千个电视信号或50多万次电话通话，③**简直令人惊奇**。这种巨大的能力使它可以实现全部信号传输数字化，从而轻而易举地滤掉噪音或静电干扰。最后要指出的是，玻璃作为媒介，它本身的传输效率便高于其他材料，因而一条光纤电缆可将一个信号传输数千英里而几乎没有"信号流失"。简而言之，光纤电缆是远距离传输大量信息的④**最佳方式**。

另一关键技术是"数字压缩"技术——即减少数码（一连串的1和0）数量的各种方法，这种数码用来表示某种信息，如一份文件、一张静止图片、一部电影或一种声音。数字压缩技术对影像传送来说至关重要，因为数字化影像会占据大量的存储空间。例如，仅仅四秒钟的数字化影片，便要占据一百兆的硬盘存储空间。一部普通长度的故事片，如果未经压缩，要占350多张普通光盘。

⑤**数据压缩技术只记录一个画面与下一个画面之间的变化**，从而实现其功能。例如，电影场景的背景图像在一个画面转为另一个

| | |
|---|---|
| scene, for example, typically does not change much from one frame to another. In a digital compression scheme, the background would be recorded only once; after that, only the actors movements would be captured. | 画面时通常是不变的,在数字压缩系统中,背景图像只被记录一次,此后便只记录演员的动作。数据压缩技术使可供选择的有线电视频道从几十个增加到几百个,数字压缩技术还能使数据更容易通过本不是用于传送数据的媒体线传送——特别是电话线。 |
| One result is more choices—hundreds of channels coming through your cable TV line instead of dozens. Digital compression also makes it easier to piggyback data onto media that were not designed with data in mind: in particular, phone lines. | |

**Notes:**

① The word order of the original sentence is reversed in the Chinese version, since Chinese tends to place the focus of information at the end of a sentence.

② "*Cram*" is used creatively in the original. But it is very hard to find an equivalent that is of the same vivid effect in Chinese. So this word is interpreted as 输入量大(数据) in the Chinese version.

③ "*Mind-boggling*" is taken out from the original sentence, and converted into a Chinese sentence.

④ "*Of choice*" in the original sentence means "of the best choice".

⑤ The "*by*" clause in the original sentence is split from the main clause in translation, and placed before the main clause of the original sentence according to Chinese linguistic habit.

## 6.4 Exercises 练习

**I. Sentence translation.**

1. A magnet's poles always points north and south.

2. The craters on the moon looks like deep pits.

3. The major problem in "fabrication" is the control of contamination and foreign material.

4. We will be tracing slow acquisition of knowledge about material world by scientists in many different cultures.

5. The whale, swimming like a fish, is a mammal.

6. Since ancient times, various ideas have been suggested on the nature of dreams.

7. Handle with care.

8. The experiment should succeed and would if no mistake occurred.

9. The best clock cannot but entail a certain error.

10. These side effects can be overcome by slight adjustment.

11. There are many kinds of bacteria which vary in shapes and sizes.

12. The brain is the center of our nerve system.

13. The present process of making steel from iron is only about 100 years old.

## II. Passage translation.

Neuro-computer architecture is modeled on current understanding of the way the human brain encodes and processes information. Nodes in a neural network, called processing elements, model individual nerve cells, or neurons, in the human nervous system. In the brain, each neuron receives electrochemical impulses from thousands of other neurons. If the sum of the signals received is strong enough, the neuron sends it onto another nerve cell or to a muscle or organ. Laboratory scientists are now trying to determine how the organic network of nerve cells is arranged and what happens within a neuron when learning takes place.

Neural network simulation software lets developers work with some of the dozens or so best-known theories of brain organization and learning. They can experiment with processing elements and the strengths of signals between the elements. The brain is a massively parallel processor, working on many inputs at once; neuron-computers are also inherently parallel. But most currently available products are software packages of add-in boards that simulate neural networks in conventional serial computers.

# Chapter 7: Translation of Applied Texts
# 应用文本翻译

## 7.1 Professional Translation 行业翻译

Generally speaking, translation, according to text types, can be roughly divided into the following types: literary translation, scientific translation, applied translation and oral translation. Applied translation can be further classified into professional translation, practical translation, multimedia translation and others. Professional translation here refers to the translation of a certain field, which roughly contains legal documents, journalism, trades, finance, physical education, medicine, tourism, etc. Practical translation refers to the translation of the fields that are very commonly applied and used in everyday English such as practical writings, street signs, advertisements, trademarks and others. Multimedia translation refers to the translation of such aspects as film and television translation, voice-over and dubbing, and captioning and subtitling, website and internet and so on.

### 7.1.1 Legal Translation 法律翻译

Legal documents, including statutes, agreements, contracts etc., are written in a style of English known as "legal English", "legal language" or "language of the law". This variety of English is developed on the basis of common English but it also has its own characteristics specifically related to the legal profession. It has its own terminology and is characterized by accuracy and preciseness. Such a style of legal English is sometimes known as "frozen style". The language of legal documents should meet strict requirements in lexical, syntactical, textual structures. Therefore the translator should take these stylistic features into consideration in order to do a good job in his translation.

#### 7.1.1.1 Lexical features of legal documents and their translation
#### 法律文献的用词特点及其翻译

Legal documents are very particular about the preciseness and formalness in diction in order to avoid ambiguity. In translation of lexical items in legal documents, we should be very careful about the concision and smoothness of the Chinese version. Besides, we should pay attention to the wording so as to ensure the preciseness of the expressions. The following are some key points in this respect, which we should keep in mind in translating legal documents.

### 1) Choose standard legal terms and keep the style appropriate

In legal documents, specialized legal terms are often used instead of common words, including those legal jargons and set phrases that are no longer used in other varieties of English. In the translation of legal documents, we should take care to use standard legal terms as much as possible. In addition, in consideration of the formal style of the wording in legal documents, we should refrain from using colloquial words in preference to formal words as far as we can. In order to achieve the solemnity in wording, we can choose, when necessary, traditional Chinese expressions in translation.

❖ The bank authorised by the *holder* to receive payment shall be liable only for *crediting* the sum on the *bill* to the *holder's* account according to the items specified in the bill. The bank which the *drawee* authorised to make payment shall be liable only for paying the sum on the *bill* from the *drawee's* account according to the items specified in the bill.

受**持票人**委托进行收款的银行的责任限于按照汇票上记载的事项将**汇票**金额**贷记**入**持票人**账户。受**受票人**委托付款的银行的责任限于按照**汇票**上记载的事项从**受票人**账户支付**汇票**金额。

**Comments** The word "*holder*" in the original text can only be rendered as 持票人 instead of 持有人, "*credit*" as 贷记 instead of 信用, "*drawee*" as 受票人, and "*bill*" as 汇票 instead of 账单 in line with the legal terminology.

❖ *In consideration of you* making a loan available to the *Borrower*: ____, we *hereby issue* this *Guarantee* for the account of the Borrower and agree as follows…

**鉴于你方**向**借款人**:____提供了一笔贷款,我行**特此为**借款人**出具保函**并保证如下……

**Comments** In translating the above fragment of a legal document, the translator is very careful in his choice of words for the Chinese version, especially with regard to the rendering of the underlined parts of the original: instead of using 考虑到 to render "*in consideration of*"; the translator chooses 鉴于 which is more formal and more commonly used in similar official legal documents in Chinese; the translator chooses 你方 which is a legal term in preference to 你们 which is more informal. The same is also true of 借款人 instead of 借钱人, 保函 instead of 保证人 and 出具 instead of 写. "*Hereby*" in the original is a typical frozen-style word which is seldom used in common English. So the translator chooses 特此 which is of an equivalent stylistic effect in Chinese. As a result, the Chinese version is faithful to the original not only in meaning but also in style.

❖ *In witness whereof*, *the Bank* *has caused this Guarantee to be executed* by its duly authorized representative on the date *first above written*.

我行已派遣充分授权的代表于<u>前述</u>日期<u>签署此保函</u>，以资证明。

**Comments** This is the concluding sentence of a bank guarantee（银行保单）."*In witness whereof*" is a cliché commonly used at the end of a legal document to offer proof for a legal matter. This is an archaism which should be translated into the same style. We can render it as 以资证明。"*First above written*" is also a cliché which can be translated as 前述的。"*Has caused this Guarantee to be executed*" is an official way of saying "sign this Guarantee". We should not take it for granted by translating as "执行这一保单"。"*The Bank*" is a modest reference to the issuer of this Guarantee, which can be translated as 我行。

❖ *I*, undersigned, *hereby* certify that the goods to be supplied are produced in Japan.

下列<u>签署人兹</u>保证所供之货物系在日本国内制造。

**Comments** In the above English sentence, "*I*" refers to the signatory of the certificate, which is a legal person. So "*I*" should not be translated as 我。In this example, "*hereby*" is translated as 兹 which is the same as 特此 in meaning and in style. Besides, the Chinese version uses traditional Chinese word 之 and 系 to achieve a formal and official style.

❖ This Law is *formulated* for the purpose of *standardizing* negotiable instrument acts, protecting the legal rights of parties concerned in negotiable instrument activities, *maintaining* the socialist market economy.

为了<u>规范</u>票据行为，保障票据活动中当事人的合法权益，<u>维护</u>社会主义市场经济的发展，<u>制订</u>本法。

**Comments** Such words as "*formulate*", "*standardize*", "*maintain*" are very formal bookish words. In addition, such words as "in accordance with", "in consistency with", "in compliance with" which are very formal words often appear in legal documents, while in ordinary English, the same meanings are expressed by "according to", "be consistent with", "comply with" which are less formal.

In order to render legal terms accurately and appropriately, the translator should have a knowledge of legal profession. English lexicons are rich in meanings. One word often carries different senses in a variety of field. As is shown below, many ordinary words have different meanings in everyday English and legal English. If we do not know this distinction, we are apt to make mistakes in legal English translation.

| English word | Ordinary meaning | Legal meaning |
| --- | --- | --- |
| action | 行为 | 诉讼 |
| appeal | 恳求，吸引 | 上诉 |
| award | 奖品 | 裁决,判决 |
| minor | 较小的 | 未成年人 |
| dock | 码头 | 被告席 |
| deed | 行为 | 契约 |
| immunity | 免疫力 | 豁免权 |

| | | |
|---|---|---|
| leave | 离开 | 休庭 |
| warrant | 保证 | 拘捕令 |
| sentence | 句子 | 判决 |

In this connection, another interesting phenomenon is that many legal terms occur in pairs. The knowledge of this regularity is helpful to the proper translation of legal English.

❖ offerer 要约人　　　　　　　offeree 受约人
　mortgagor 抵押人　　　　　mortgagee 承受抵押人
　pledgor 质押人　　　　　　　pledgee 承受质押人
　indorser 背书人　　　　　　　indorsee 被背书人
　insurer 保险商　　　　　　　 insured 投保人
　accuser 控方　　　　　　　　accused 被告

### 2) Use abbreviations in legal documents

Abbreviations are frequently used in legal English to achieve concision. These abbreviations are often shorthand forms of legal jargons. So in translating legal documents, the translator should be well acquainted with the meanings of these abbreviations or he can turn for help to specialized glossaries or dictionaries of abbreviations of legal terms. The following are some examples of commonly used abbreviations in legal documents.

　A. F. B 空运提单　　　　　　ADB 亚洲开发银行
　amt. 金额　　　　　　　　　　A/S 记账销售
　atty. 代理人　　　　　　　　　B. D. 银行汇票
　B/N 现钞　　　　　　　　　　C. B. 现金账簿
　CD 存款凭证　　　　　　　　Cis 负债证明书
　DO 交货单,交割单,出货单　D/Y 交货,交割
　FA 面额　　　　　　　　　　　FX 外汇
　FV 面值　　　　　　　　　　　I/C 进口托收,内向托收
　ISP. 商品检验　　　　　　　　L/G 担保函,保函,保证书
　L/H 质押证书,押汇质权书　　NBB 抵押赎回债券
　OD 透支　　　　　　　　　　　P/N 期票
　P/O 付款委托书　　　　　　　ROA 资产盈利率
　S/N 装货通知

### 3) Adhere to the principle of "consistency" of legal terms

The precision of diction is highly emphasized in legal documents. By contrast, the variety of diction, i. e. the use of alternative words that denote the same concept is not advocated. As a result, it often happens that the same word may be repeated in a text, a paragraph or even a sentence time and again. This is the principle of "consistency" in the use of legal terms. This principle is intended to ensure precision against possible ambiguity or vagueness. This principle should also be followed in legal translation. Except when necessary, the repeated word in the original English text should also be rendered into a Chinese word.

> ❖ *Housing loans*, whether secured with uncompleted or completed buildings, are those under which *mortgagor* warrants that *mortgagee* is the first beneficiary of the *mortgage* and that *mortgagor* will fulfil all obligations hereunder.
> 楼花和**现房抵押(按揭)贷款**的**抵押(按揭)人**保证该**抵押(按揭)贷款**的第一受益人是**抵押(按揭)权人**且**抵押(按揭)人**将保证履行本合同全部条款。

**Comments** "*Mortgagor*","*mortgagee*" and "*mortgage*" can be translated as 抵押人, 抵押权人, 抵押贷款, or they can be translated as 按揭人, 按揭权人, 按揭贷款. Choosing whether the first group of renderings or the second group, we should keep the consistency of the Chinese rendering throughout this legal document in compliance with the principle of the "consistency" of legal terms. It is not allowed of translating "*mortgagor*" first as 抵押人, and then as 按揭人. Otherwise, there might be vagueness as a result.

### 4) Ascertain the meanings of the original words in accordance with relevant professional knowledge and context

The wording of legal documents is precise and strict. In translating legal documents, we should not take the meaning of the original words at face value. The translator should be versed in basic legal knowledge and infer the meaning in accordance with relevant professional knowledge and surrounding context.

> ❖ We regret to inform you that there is short weight of 4.5M/T *only*. Therefore, we lodge a claim against you for the short weight of 4.5M/T as follows…
> 我们遗憾地通知你们,(来货)短缺4.5公吨整。因此,我们就此短缺4.5公吨一事提出索赔如下……

**Comments** In the above fragment of a legal document which lodges a claim for a short weight of cargo, the meaning of "*only*" is very subtle. We should not take it for granted that "*only*" simply means 仅仅. Otherwise this meaning will constitute a logical contradiction with its context: If the short weight is "*only*" 4.5 M/T, why should "*we*" bother to lodge a claim for this loss? This interpretation of "*only*" will leave a pitfall which might be taken advantage of by the other party against this claim for loss. As a matter of fact, here "*only*" means "no more or less than" (整整/正好). That is why "*only*" is put behind the noun it modifies.

In some statutes, regulation, agreements, contracts or other types of legal documents, the text is organized in clause-by-clause manner. The contents of these articles are interlinked and interlocked with each other. In this case, the translator must bear in mind the entire context when translating individual words and phrases so as to render their exact contextual meaning properly.

❖ Subject to the provisions of Clause 9.3.5 liquidated damages for which the Contractor is liable under Clause 9.3.2 shall be calculated in accordance with the following.

承包方按9.3.2条款中有责任支付的预定违约罚金采用下述方法计算。进一步的规定在9.3.5条款中给出。

**Comments** If the translator does not consider the content of Clause 9.3.5, it is hard to ascertain the meaning of "*Subject to*" in this sentence. Note that the content of Clause 9.3.5 is as follows:

Notwithstanding the provisions of Clause 9.3.2 and 9.3.4 the Contractor's total liability for liquidated damage under those clauses shall not exceed ＿＿＿＿＿% of the Contract Price and…

It turns out that the content of Clause 9.3.5 sets further restriction on the Contractor's total liability for liquidated damage, i.e. Clause 9.3.5 stipulates the highest limit of the total liability.

### 7.1.1.2 Syntactical features of legal documents and their translation
### 法律文献的句法特点及其翻译

One of the problems in translating legal documents is the handling of complicated syntactical structures. The first step in the precise understanding of the original and the faithful representation of its meaning in the Chinese version is to make a thorough syntactical analysis of long and complicated sentences in a legal document.

**1) Use of "shall/may" in legal documents**

The structure of predicate verbs in legal English is relatively simple. Since legal documents are mainly intended to stipulate what ought (not) to be done and what can (not) be done, apart from the use of the simple present tense, the most commonly used structures of predicate verbs in legal English are as follows:

*shall* (*should*) + *verb*    *may* (*might*) + *verb*

In translating these structures, the translator should try to keep the Chinese version in conformity to the English source text with regard to the tone of sentences.

❖ This Guarantee *shall* become effective on the date hereof and shall expire on ＿＿＿ date of the Loan Agreement. Following each repayment of principle under the Loan Agreement, our liability hereunder *shall* be reduced accordingly. Our liability hereunder *shall* not be affected by…

本保函自开立之日起生效,直至＿＿＿失效。随着贷款协议项下本金的每一期偿还,我行的担保责任亦相应递减。我行在本保函项下的担保责任将不受下列事件的影响……

**Comments** In this excerpt, the sentences all contain "shall + verb" predicate verb structure.

❖ No allowance of time by you or any other act or omission by you which for this provision *might* exonerate or discharge the Bank *shall* in any way release the Bank from any liability hereunder.

你方所允许的时限或做出的任何行为或发生的疏漏,尽管可能免责或解脱银行,都不能解除银行的此项责任。

**Comments** "*Might*" in this sentence suggests a possibility. It should not be translated as 可以。"*Shall in any way*" in this sentence expresses a permission, so it is translated as 不能。

### 2) Structural characteristics in legal documents

The chief characteristic of sentential structure in legal English is their lengthiness and complicatedness. The sentences in legal English tend to be extraordinarily long and complicated, consisting of a string of clauses, phrases at different ranks. To translate such a long run-on sentence in legal English, the translator should first make a thorough analysis of the internal structure and logical relations within the sentence, identifying the progression of ideas from beginning to end. Then the translator should divide this long sentence into a number of small units according to Chinese syntactical characteristic, each of which is then translated into a Chinese short sentence. Finally, these short sentences should be rearranged in a proper order.

❖ ① On the Supplier's failure of the faithful performance of all the contract documents and modifications, amendments, additions and alterations thereof that may hereafter be made, ②including replacement and/or making good of defective goods (hereinafter called the failure of performance) as determined by you and notwithstanding any objection by the Supplier, ③the Bank shall, on your demand in a written notification stating the effect of the failure of performance by the Supplier, ④pay you such amount or amounts as required by you⑤ not exceeding in aggregate amount of guarantee in the manner specified in the said statement.

①如果供货方未能按合同及其后可能做出的合同变更、合同修改、合同变动,②包括对不合格商品的更换或修补条款履行责任(以下简称违约),违约由你方认定,而供货方对此提出的异议无效,③则我行在收到你方指出供货方违约的书面通知后,④向你方支付索赔书上所要求的一笔或数笔款项,⑤但不超过本保函担保的总金额(担保金额)。

**Comments**: This is a typical long sentence in legal document. But under close examination, we can see it contains primarily two adverbial phrases (*On the Supplier's failure of*...; *on your demand*...) which state the conditions of the Bank's paying the amount of guarantee, and a main clauses which states that the Bank will pay the amount of guarantee. These phrases and clauses contain respectively internal clauses and phrases. In view of this analysis, we divide this sentence into 5 units (see the marked numbers) which are translated and rearranged in the original order.

❖ ①If an applicant claims that a required document is forged or materially fraudulent ② or that honour of the presentation would facilitate a material fraud by the beneficiary on the issuer or applicant, ③a court of competent jurisdiction may temporarily or permanently enjoin the issuer from honouring a presentation ④or grant similar relief against the issuer or other persons ⑤only if the court finds that …

①如果申请人宣称某项必要单据属于伪造或具有实质上的欺诈性,②或者兑付提示将为受益人对开证人或申请人进行实质性欺诈提供便利,⑤只要法院发现下述情况,③有管辖权的法院可以暂时或永久禁止开证人兑付某一提示,④或者针对开证人或其他人采取其他类似的补救方法……

**Comments** This long sentence also consists mainly of two adverbial clauses of condition (*If an applicant claims*…; *only if the court finds that*…) and a main clause. The first adverbial clause contains two coordinate object clauses. The main clause contains two coordinate predicates. Accordingly this sentence is broken up into 5 parts, each of which is translated into a Chinese short sentence. The last clause (marked with number ⑤) is moved ahead in the Chinese version in accordance with the logical order of Chinese sentences.

❖ *Any clause, covenant, or agreement* in a contract of carriage relieving *the carrier or the ship* from liability for *loss or damage* to, or *in connection with*, goods arising from *negligence, fault, or failure* in *duties and obligations* provided in this article or lessening such liability otherwise than provided in these rules shall be *null and void* and of *no effect*.

运输契约中<u>任何条款、约定或协议</u>,凡解除<u>承运人或船舶</u>由于<u>疏忽、过失或未履行本条款规定的责任和义务</u>,因而引起货物或关于货物的<u>丢失或损害</u>责任的;或在本公约以外减轻这种责任的,都应<u>作废或无效</u>。

**Comments** As is shown in this example, there are often coordinate elements (the underlined parts) for the purpose of precision and accuracy. These coordinate elements tend to be bewilderingly complicated, blurring the structure of the sentence. So the translator should first identify the main clause in the sentence and infer the interrelationship between the coordinate elements before translating the whole sentence. Take this sentence for example, the main clause is "*Any clause, covenant, or agreement*…*shall be null and void*". And "*relieving*" and "*lessening*" introduce respectively two subordinate clauses of restrictive condition. On the basis of this structural analysis, the translator can perceive various semantic relations within this long sentence.

### 3) Use of conditional clauses in legal English

In legal English, there is a rich use of conditional clauses to set restriction on certain matters. In the same legal document, different ways of expressing conditions are often used to avoid redundancy. The following are some common conditional expressions in legal English:

(1) in case of        (2) only if        (3) only after
(4) provided         (5) unless         (6) if

(7) in view　　　　(8) on condition that　　(9) providing that

- *In case of* transfer, document No. ＿＿＿＿ is no more required *provided that* the Bank of China, Lianyungang certifies it has transferred the credit.

**如果**进行转账，**只要**中国银行连云港支行证明该行已进行转账操作，就不再需要第＿＿＿＿号文件。

Comments　This sentence contains two conditional clauses introduced respectively by "*in case of*" and "*provided that*". Accordingly, they are translated respectively as 如果 and 只要.

- *Where* statute operates in the law of torts, its function is usually to reform or to limit the common law.

**如果**成文法在民事侵权行为法律范畴内运行，其功能通常是改良或限定不成文法。

Comments　Here "*where*" actually introduces an adverbial clause of condition. So it is equivalent to "if" in function.

### 4) Use of passive voice in legal English

Passive voice is extensively used in legal English. This is because in a passive sentence, the object of discussion is put in a prominent position which can draw readers' attention. Besides, a passive sentence is flexible in structure that allows for free extension of its information. Furthermore, a passive sentence is relatively formal and solemn in correspondence to the stylistic feature of legal English.

- The advising bank is requested to notify the beneficiary without adding their confirmation.

我们(开证行)请求通知行通知受益人而没有增加他们的保兑。

Comments　Since passive sentences are not so often used in Chinese, this sentence is translated into an active sentence by adding a subject 我们 in Chinese.

### 5) Use of formulaic expressions

The translation of legal documents should comply with the formulaic expressions used habitually in such documents. Since legal English strives for accuracy to avoid ambiguity, there are often formulaic expressions that have been patterned in legal English. In translation, such formulaic expressions should be converted into their Chinese equivalents that are so patterned.

- We the undersigned hereby certify that…

签名如下以示证明……

- Wang Gang and Li Xia are hereby married of their will. Upon due examination it is found in conformity with the articles of…

根据彼此意愿，王刚和李霞结为夫妻，经审查，符合……

### 6) Some patterns for certain meanings

Some patterns for Chinese meaning "根据……"
in accordance with…         according to …
pursuant to…                to be formulated to…
in line with…               on the basis of…
based on …

Some patterns for Chinese meaning "为了……"
to + v.                     in order to …
with a view + v. -ing       in the view to…
for the purpose(s) of…

Some patterns for Chinese meaning "实施"
to put into effect/force    to come into effect/force
to go into effect/force

## 7.1.2 Compare and Analyze 比较与分析

<table>
<tr><td>Plant Construction Contract</td><td>工厂建造合同</td></tr>
<tr><td>

**Article 1—Definitions**

①"The <u>Owner</u>" shall mean ___.
"The Contractor" shall mean ___.
"The Plant" shall mean all or any part of the machinery, equipment and materials forming ② the <u>permanent installation</u> as specified in Appendix(…)
"The Site" shall mean all the land where the plant is to be constructed in accordance with this Contract.
"The Works" shall mean the works to be done by the Contractor under this Contract.
"The Contract Price" shall mean the total sum payable to the Contractor by the Owner for the Works.

**Article 2—Contractor's Responsibilities**

1. The Contractor ③ <u>shall</u> design, engineer, and construct the Plant at ④<u>the Site</u>.
2. The Contractor shall provide all equipment, materials, tools, facilities, labor and services necessary for the successful construction of the Plant except those items and facilities to be supplied by the Owner under Article (…).
3. The Contractor shall perform the Works in

</td><td>

第一条　定义
①"业主"指_____。
"承包商"指_____。
"工厂"指在附录×中指定的构成②<u>固定设备</u>的全部或部分机器、设备和材料。
"工地"指按本合同用于建造工厂的全部地皮。
"工程"指承包商按本合同实施的工程。
"合同价格"指业主向承包商支付的全部工程款项。

第二条　承包商的职责

1. 承包商③<u>应</u>负责设计、筹划以及在④<u>指定工地</u>上建造工厂。
2. 除了业主根据第×条提供的物品和设施以外，承包商应提供所有为使工厂成功建造所必需的设备、材料、工具、设施、劳工和服务。
3. 承包商应根据附录×中的

</td></tr>
</table>

accordance with the Schedule in Appendix ( … )

4. The Contractor shall provide the Owner's personnel with training of operation and maintenance of the ⑤Plant in accordance with Appendix ( … )

5. The Contractor shall supply the Owner with the spare parts specified in Appendix ( … )

6. The Contractor shall supply the Owner with the maintenance equipment specified in equipment specified in Appendix ( … )

**Article 3—Owner's Responsibilities**

1. The Owner shall make available the Site and grant the Contractor free and uninterrupted access ⑥thereto throughout the duration of this Contract.

2. The Owner shall provide those items and facilities specified in Appendix ( … ) at the time therein established.

3. The Owner will obtain from the relevant Authorities those licenses and permits necessary to construct and operate the Plant on the Site including work permit for the Contractor's employees.

4. The Owner shall pay the Contractor for the Works performed the Contract Price set out in Article ( … )

**Article 4—Contract Price**

1. Within ( … ) days after the effective date of this Contract, the Owner shall pay the Contractor ⑦as full and complete compensation for accomplishing the Works and assuming all obligations under this Contract the Contract Price in the amount of ＿＿＿.

2. The Contract Price is not subject to escalation, and the cost of executing the Works shall be the risk of the Contractor who shall be deemed to have obtained all information and taken into account all circumstances which may affect the cost in agreeing the Contract Price.

日程安排施工。

4. 承包商应根据附录×中的规定为业主培训⑤工厂设备的操作和维修人员。

5. 承包商应向业主提供附录×中规定的备件。

6. 承包商应向业主提供附录×中指定的维修设备。

**第三条　业主的职责**

1. 业主应提供工地，并在本合同有效期内允许承包商自由地、不受干扰地⑥出入该工地。

2. 业主应按时提供附录×中指定的物件和设施。

3. 业主将从有关部门获取为工厂建造、设备运行所必需的执照和许可证，包括承包商雇员的工作许可证。

4. 业主应按第×条中规定的合同价格向承包商支付工程款项。

**第四条　合同价格**

1. 在本合同生效后××天内，业主应向承包商支付金额为××的⑦合同价格，作为承包商完成该工程并承担本合同规定的所有义务的全部报酬。

2. 合同价格不再上调，完成工程的成本风险应由承包商承担，商定合同价格时应认为承包商已获得全部信息并已把所有可能影响成本的因素估计在内。

**Notes:**

①Here "*owner*" should be translated as 业主 instead of 拥有者.

②Here "*permanent installation*" should not be translated literally as 永久装置.

③In this sentence, "*shall*" indicates an obligation instead of "future", so it is translated as 应.

④Here the meaning of "*the*" should be highlighted in the Chinese version 指定的 in order to eliminate ambiguity.

⑤The addition of 设备 in the Chinese version is intended to make the meaning more accurate and complete.

⑥Here "*thereto*" is an archaism which is typical of the diction in legal English. It simply means "to".

⑦Be careful that between "*pay*" and its object "*the Contract Price in the amount of…*", there is a long element separating them. Such a construction often occurs in legal English. But in the Chinese version, the object of "*pay*" should follow its verb immediately.

## 7.1.3 Exercises 练习

### Ⅰ. Sentence translation.

1. This Law is promulgated with the purpose of regulating insurance activities, protecting the legitimate rights and interests of the parties involved, strengthening supervision and regulation of the insurance industry and promoting its healthy development.

2. The various kinds of taxable payments referred to in the proceeding paragraph include payments in cash, payments by remittance, payments through transfer accounts and payments in marketable securities or in kind, which are rendered into equivalent amount money.

3. The Publisher shall pay the Author ____ in advance, which shall be a charge of all sums to the Author under this Agreement.

4. If the bill of lading contains particulars concerning the general nature, leading marks, number of packages or pieces, weight or quantity of the goods which the carrier or other person issuing the bill of lading on his behalf knows or has reasonable grounds to suspect do not accurately represent the goods actually taken over or, where a shipped bill of lading issues, loaded, or if he has no reasonable means of checking such particulars, the carrier or such other person must insert in the bill of lading a reservation specifying these inaccuracies, grounds of suspicion of the absence of reasonable means of checking.

### Ⅱ. Passage translation.

PART Ⅰ  SPHERE OF APPLICATION AND GENERAL PROVISIONS

CHAPTER Ⅰ  SPHERE OF APPLICATION

**Article 1**

(1) This Convention applies to contracts of sale of goods between parties whose places of business are in different States:

(a) when the States are Contracting States; or

(b) when the rules of private international law lead to the application of the law of a Contracting State.

(2) The fact that the parties have their places of business in different States is to be disregarded whenever this fact does not appear either from the contract or from any dealings between, or from information disclosed by, the parties at any time before or at the conclusion of the contract.

(3) Neither the nationality of the parties nor the civil or commercial character of the parties or of the contract is to be taken into consideration in determining the application of this Convention.

**Article 2**

This Convention does not apply to sales:

(a) of goods bought for personal, family or household use, unless the seller, at any time before or at the conclusion of the contract, neither knew nor ought to have know that the goods were bought for any such use;

(b) by auction;

(c) on execution or otherwise by authority of law;

(d) of stocks, shares, investment securities, negotiable instruments or money;

(e) of ships, vessels, hovercrafts or aircrafts;

...

### 7.1.4 Tourist Translation 旅游翻译
### 7.1.4.1 What is tourism 什么是旅游

Speaking of tourism, we think primarily of people who are visiting a particular place for sightseeing, visiting friends and relatives, taking a vacation, and having a good time. They may spend leisure time engaging in various sports, sunbathing, talking, singing, taking rides, touring, reading, or simply enjoying the environment. If we consider the subject further, we may include in our definition of tourism people who are participating in a convention, a business conference, or some other kind of business or professional activity, as well as those who are taking a study tour under an expert guide or doing some kind of scientific research or study. Actually, it is hard to define tourism because different people have different views on it. One has only to consider the multidimensional aspects of tourism and its interaction with other activities to understand why it is difficult to come up with a meaningful definition that will be universally accepted. Anyone who attempts to define tourism or to describe its scope fully has to consider the various groups that participate in and are affected by this industry. Four different perspectives of tourism can be identified: the tourist, the business providing tourist goods and services, the government of the host community or area, and the host community. Thus, tourism may be defined as the sum of the phenomena and relationships arising from the interaction of tourists, business suppliers, host governments, and communities in the process of attracting and hosting these tourists and other visitors.

Francis Bacon wrote in his prose *Of Travel*, "Travel, in the younger sort, is a part of education; in the elder, a part of experience." This idea coincides with an old Chinese saying: A better way to acquire knowledge is to travel ten thousand li rather than read ten thousand volumes.

Travel has always been regarded as a very effective way of obtaining knowledge and enriching lives worldwide. Nowadays, under the pressure of hectic daily life, many people choose to tour outside the home environment or abroad to relax. Almost everyone has some rough idea about tourism.

One of the first attempts to define tourism was made by Professors Hunziker and Krapf of Berne University. They held that tourism should be defined as "the sum of the phenomena and relationships arising from the travel and stay of non-residents, in so far as they do not lead permanent residence and are not connected to any earning activity".

In 1981, an international conference on Leisure-Recreation-Tourism, held by the International Association of Scientific Experts in Tourism and the Tourism Society in Cardiff, formulated a broader definition, "Tourism may be defined in terms of particular activities selected by choice and undertaken outside the home environment. Tourism may or may not involve an overnight stay away from home."

In 1991, the World Tourism Organization endorsed the statement, "Tourism comprises the activities of persons traveling to and staying in places outside their usual environment for not more than one consecutive year for leisure, business or other purposes."

International tourism is thus defined by the World Tourism Organization as "travel across international borders for more than 24 hours for the purpose of business or pleasure".

### 7.1.4.2 Cultural translation and translating culture 文化翻译与翻译文化

When we discuss the translation of tourist texts from one language to another, first of all, it is very important to make a distinction between the two terms, "translating culture" and "cultural translation". Translating culture, in a narrow sense, refers to the act of transferring meaning from one specific culture-bearing language to another. Cultural translation refers to a dynamic process where everyone and everything that are a part of the interaction in translation undergoes change, where notions are constructed about other cultures and about oneself. We believe that translating culture is an act only in translation and cultural translation is the understanding and rendering of cultural concepts. Translating tourist texts is not merely translating culture, but also involves cultural translation. In a sense, translating tourist texts means translating the source culture for the reader.

As we know, culture is the "integrated pattern of human knowledge, beliefs, and behavior that is both a result of and integral to the human capacity for learning and transmitting knowledge to succeeding generations. Culture thus consists of language, ideas, beliefs, customs, taboos, codes, institutions, tools, techniques, works of art, rituals, ceremonies, symbols." (Stevens, M. A., et al, 2008:430) Tourist attractions are often deeply rooted in the culture of a country. Every society, on every level, has its own culture influenced by its history. Therefore, the aim of tourist text translating should be not only cultural rendering but also translating culture.

Nowadays people are becoming more and more familiar with the term "cultural tourism", which reflects the close relationship between tourism and culture. Tourism is a kind of cultural phenomenon, and cultural communication is the purpose of tourism activities. Firstly, the hope to understand different cultures is the fundamental motive of tourism. People always feel curious about what they are not familiar with. The nature of pursuing newness and beauty urges people to go out for adventures. These adventures bring about cultural exchanges and thus, tourism, as a special industry, comes into being. Secondly, culture is the most important implication of tourist resources. Generally speaking, tourist resources are composed of natural resources and artificial resources. The latter is the reflection of culture, which includes historical relics, festivities, man-made tourist scenery and so on. The natural resources, though from nature, are explored by human beings and characterized by human cultural consciousness.

### 7.1.4.3 Qualities of tourist texts 旅游文本的特性

Tourist texts mainly feature the expressive, the informative and the vocative functions. Their purpose is to introduce the scenic spots, and to convey the related information so as to enable the viewers to understand and enjoy the spots. The expressive function works as the mind of the speaker, the writer, or the originator of the text. He or she uses it to express the feelings irrespective of any response. The core of the informative function is an external aspect, the facts of a topic, that is, reality outside language, including reported ideas or theories. The core of the vocative function is the readership, the addressee. The term "vocative" is used in the sense of "calling upon" readership to act, think or feel, in fact to "react" in the way intended by the text. Nowadays, vocative texts are more often addressed to a readership than a reader. (Newmark, 1988:40-45). Actually, the vocative function is the goal while the informative function is the premise. This is because tourist texts are some kind of popular reading materials for ordinary people. The purpose is to draw the tourist's attention, arouse their interest and give them aesthetic impression, so that they may be persuaded to visit the tourist attraction and gain the knowledge of the nature, culture, history and customs of the tourist attraction after reading the text. Therefore, the vocative function is of utmost importance.

As a result, a number of factors need to be taken into account. As Newmark points out, "The first factor in all vocative texts is the relationship between the writer and the readership. The second factor is that these texts must be written in a language that is immediately comprehensible to the readership." (Newmark, 1988: 41) However, this effort can be achieved only through the provision of sufficient background information. Before potential visitors make up their minds to go sightseeing, they may want to obtain some relevant information about the tourist destination such as the location, historical importance, and cultural traditions. A detailed, accurate and attractive description will strengthen visitors' resolve to go; therefore, to be informative is also another important consideration. According to Newmark, both informative text and vocative text belong to communicative translation, while the expressive text to semantic translation. In his opinion, communicative translation attempts to render the exact contextual meaning of the original text in such a way that both content and language are readily acceptable and comprehensible to the readership (Newmark, 1988: 48-49). At the same time, the expressive function should not be neglected either. As a result of reading a well-translated tourist text, people can sense a national pride and a warm welcome exuding from the host country's guidebooks.

Apart from the above-mentioned functions, tourist texts still possess "the aesthetic function" (Chen Hongwei, 1998: 273) and the cultural values. Speaking of aesthetic function, it is evident that the tourist text is often very short and well-organized in structure, and succinct and lively in language. As far as the cultural value is concerned, it primarily manifests in three aspects: the inherent values accumulated in natural views like rivers, lakes, mountains and so on; the traditional values long-established in heritage like habits, traditions, practices, social structures, arts and crafts, etc. ; and the artificial values held in man-made sights like palaces and temples, imperial tombs and underground museums, architecture and gardens, and others. The translation of such texts is characterized by a special intention but disadvantaged by inadequate cultural equivalents. As we know, the ideal tourist texts should maintain such qualities as being informative, intriguing, realistic, practical, cultural, educational, humorous and even poetic.

Thanks to the above-mentioned qualities and their functions, the translator has to think of "genre conventions" and follows the target reader's reading habits and feelings when translating the text. Nord said, "Genre conventions are the result of the standardization of communication practices. As certain kinds of text are used repeatedly in certain situations with more or less the same function, these texts acquire conventional forms that are sometimes even raised to the status of social norms."(Nord, 2001:53) In this context, the translation of a tourist text should attach importance to the equivalence of the informative contents and stylistic functions between the original and the translated texts, rather than the equivalence in linguistic forms.

Translation of tourist texts is a kind of publicity activity. Its essence is that the translator should attempt to produce the same effect on the target language readers as is produced by the original on the source language readers. Chinese readers seldom have difficulty in understanding the original because they share the same cultural background with the writer. But cultural discrepancies will hinder foreign readers from understanding those texts properly. Therefore, translators should adopt a proper method to adjust the version so as to help readers apprehend the texts. Otherwise, "they will find the translation requiring so much effort to understand that they are likely to stop reading, unless they are very highly motivated."(Jin Di & Nida, 1984:102)

To sum up, when translating tourist texts, we are not just dealing with words written in a certain time, space and sociopolitical situation; most importantly is the cultural aspects of the text that we should take into account. There are at least five kinds of influences that we need to consider on the translation of tourist texts from one language to another, and they are: (1) the influence of associative and connotative meanings; (2) the influence of different understandings and thoughts, (3) the influence of metaphors and expressions; (4) the influence of religions and myths; and (5) the influence of values and life style. Therefore, translation of tourist texts should be tourist-oriented, culture-specific, and concept-based.

### 7.1.4.4 Strategies of translating tourist texts 旅游文本翻译的策略
#### 1) Domesticating

The domesticating strategy was first put forward by Schleimacher, (1838/1963:47) and developed by Lawrence Venuti (1995: 19-20). It "entails translating in a transparent, fluent, 'invisible' style in order to minimize the foreignness of the TT." (Munday, 2001:146) In the West, "the domesticating strategies have been implemented at least since ancient Rome." "Such strategies find their strongest and most influential advocates in the French and English translation traditions, particularly during the early modern period." (Baker, ed. 2004:240-244) This is because, in my view, they share much more similarities such as beliefs, traditions, habits, etc. than they do with Asians. Therefore Western scholars and translators preferentially apply domesticating strategies to render texts. They are also used when translating between Chinese and English, for instance, the translation of the place name "the Marco Polo Bridge" for Lugouqiao(卢沟桥), is a typical example of domesticating. Lugouqiao is a bridge near Beijing with special historical significance. The literal transliteration into "Lugou Bridge" simply tells where it is but the English reader does not know its historical significance and meaning. If it is translated as "the Marco Polo Bridge", the English reader may understand it more clearly and more easily. Similarly, "the Marco Polo Bridge Incident" was a battle between Japan's Imperial Army and China's National Revolutionary Army, marking the beginning of the Sino-Japanese War (1937—1945). This incident happened there and was very similar to the battle at the Marco Polo Bridge in France. Our purpose to translate such texts is to keep it understandable for the TL reader. The tourist-centered approach should be, therefore, considered essential. However, in this translation, the historical incident is found, but the cultural element itself is lost. The reader does not know from the translation the cultural value of the bridge itself, which is an architectural work of eleven arches, restored by the Kangxi Emperor (1662—1722, A. D.) during the Qing Dynasty.

Due to the many voids and differences between Chinese and English, cultural factors are often lost after translating tourist texts. To understand Chinese culture, the translator needs to focus on the many untranslatable words and phrases. These untranslatable words and phrases sometimes can be seen as small signs of what is lost in translation. Take the Chinese term Bao Zheng (包拯) for example, he was a historical Chinese figure in Northern Song Dynasty (960—1127, A. D.) who enforced the law strictly and impartially, impartial and incorruptible, dared to state outright and remonstrate with the emperor. Because of this, he has been called Bao Gong(包公) or Bao Daren(包大人) that shows people's respect for him. Nowadays Gong (公) or Daren(大人) in this term is translated into "Lord" and the full name "Lord Bao", which refers to a man who has a rank in aristocracy especially in Britain or a man in medieval Europe who was very powerful and owned a lot of land. In this case, the equivalence in form is found between the two languages. Unfortunately, the Chinese cultural elements in it will be lost if we directly and simply translate it because the English word "lord" cannot reflect the people's respect for him or tell what Bao Zheng did at that time. Actually this term can be put as "the revered Mr. Bao" or "His Excellency Bao Zheng" which contains the respect for Bao Zheng, but "lord" is ambiguous here. These words embody a rich and varied part of our culture. In this context, we will make every effort to figure out what a tourist destination should have and introduce its culture and history to the reader when translating such tourist texts. Translating tourist texts is a valuable clue to what one culture finds of interest in another, more exactly to what some individuals and groups in a given culture find of interest in another. Therefore, if such terms containing strong historical and cultural implications are superficially put into "Lord Bao", connotations among them will be lost in translation. The reader by no means understands what this term should imply. This paper holds that such terms should be translated according to their annotations or connotations, and the tourist-oriented approach should be followed. Perhaps you may ask what the difference is between the domesticating and the tourist-oriented approaches. In fact, they are only slightly different in meaning. The former refers to the translation that the effect of the original term is exactly the same as the effect of the translated version; the latter is a strategy that is fully considerate of the reader, and may employ such methods as addition, deletion and others to satisfy and comply with the reader's needs.

In short, the domesticating strategy is an essential way of translating tourist texts, but it cannot solve all the problems existing in culture-specific tourist texts. We need to find the similarities in culture when translating between languages from the East and the West. The advantages of domesticating include maintaining the terseness of the TL text, obtaining an understanding of the SL text, and gaining the interest of the TL reader. The biggest weakness is that the cultural and historical elements of the original text could be lost in translation.

**2) Foreignizing**

"Foreignizing entails choosing a foreign text and developing a translation method along lines which are excluded by dominant cultural values in the target language." (Venuti, 1997:242; Baker, ed. 2004:242). As far as the foreignizing strategy is concerned, it should center on the cultural and historical items underlying the tourist text. In other words, we should stick to the culture-specific strategies when translating the text. In principle, faithfulness is the top priority in translating tourist texts. This is because such translation should be faithful to the central ideas of the SL text such as cultural background, historical facts, geographical settings, aesthetic values, man-made attractions and natural landscapes. In order to adhere to faithfulness, as far as Chinese texts are concerned, the foreignizing strategy is primarily employed. According to Venuti, "Strategies in producing translations inevitably emerge in response to domestic cultural situations. But some are deliberately domesticating in their handling of the foreign text, while others can be described as foreignizing, motivated by an impulse to preserve linguistic and cultural differences by deviating from prevailing domestic values." (Venuti, 1995:240-244) In actual translation, we usually use *pinyin* to translate some culture-specific items indicating names, places or events. The Peking opera, for example, is a traditional Chinese opera form that dates back to the year 1790 when four local opera troupes of Anhui Province came to Beijing on a performance tour on the order of the imperial court. *Jiaozi*(饺子), a very popular food, enjoyed by most Chinese is supposed to bring good fortune. Because of semantic voids between Chinese and English, it cannot be simply translated as "dumplings" or "Chinese dumplings". This is because dumplings and *jiaozi* are quite different in meaning and quality. Another typical example is *kungfu*, or *wushu*, which is also known in the West. There is no need to domesticate it to translate it into "Chinese martial arts". This is because most people in the world have heard of *kungfu*. Even though the term "Chinese martial arts" is sometimes used, it is impossible to tell the reader about the origin, the function, and the essence of the cultural heritage. It is concluded that the unique items in the ST can be translated by means of the foreignizing strategy. Chinese musical instruments, some dish names and other culture-specific items can be put in *pinyin*.

Technically, we can use both of the strategies to tackle the cultural elements in translating tourist texts. Tourist texts should be primarily translated by means of foreignizing so as to maintain the original cultural factors. Only in the situation that we cannot deal with do we use the domesticating strategy, in other words, allowing the alien to be seen, or as Schleiermacher famously put it, bringing the reader to the text rather than the other way round. The problem is that if a translation is successful, in the sense of reading it as if it was written in the target language, then its creator and its original culture become invisible. For this reason, the domesticating strategy should be applied as little as possible when translating tourist texts. This is because the purpose of tourist texts is to spread the foreign or different cultures to the reader, and the translator is responsible for disseminating the original culture to the TL reader.

To sum up, the foreignizing strategy is a favorable approach to translating tourist texts. The advantages include revealing the cultural and historical factors of the ST, disseminating the culture and customs of the original, and showing the equality between languages and between cultures. The disadvantages include neglecting the reader's emotion and understanding. In other words, the functions of disseminating the ST cultures are found, but the effects of attracting the tourists are likely lost when employing such a strategy.

### 7.1.4.5 A new strategy—neutralizing 新策略——中立化

#### 1) Definition

Due to the special nature of tourist texts and the functions of their special text-types, the translation of tourist texts should serve the purpose of arousing the interest of the TL reader and motivating them to visit the tourist destination described in the text. The translator has more freedom in tourist translation than in other types of translation.

Some theorists and scholars have held that the domesticating and foreignizing strategies cannot be employed together in one text. Andre Lefevere (1992:149) is of the opinion that domesticating and foreignizing are completely different strategies in translation, and cannot be combined to translate one text. However, this is not feasible in actual practice because our purpose in translating tourist texts is not only to translate the source language into the target language, but also to translate the exotic elements of the SL into the target text. Neither domesticating nor foreignizing can provide the solution to cope with the tourist text.

In fact, the domesticating and the foreignizing are a paradox in translation studies. It is very hard for the translator to clearly distinguish between them and use them in translating. As Sun Yingchun (2004:67) said, "As for the priority of the domesticating or that of the foreignizing strategies used in translation, it is probably inappropriate to say which is prior before the specific translation is analyzed. This is because translation is an act of intention or skopos and its purpose constantly changes with the specific situation." So does the translation of tourist texts.

According to Nida (1986), no translation is ever completely equivalent. A number of different translations can in fact represent varying degrees of equivalence. This means that "equivalence" cannot be understood in its mathematical meaning of identity, but only in terms of proximity, i.e. on the basis of degrees of closeness to functional identity.

Functional equivalence implies a different degree of adequacy from minimal to maximal effectiveness on the basis of both cognitive and experiential factors. A minimal, realistic definition of functional equivalence could be stated as "The readers of a translated text should be able to comprehend it to the point that they can conceive how the original readers of the text must have understood and appreciated it." Anything less than this degree of equivalence should be unacceptable. A maximal, ideal definition could be stated as "The readers of a translated text should be able to essentially understand and appreciate it in the same manner as the original readers did." (Nida, 2001:87) The maximal definition implies a high degree of language-culture correspondence between the source language and target language.

It is clear that the domesticating or the foreignizing strategies cannot solve all the problems in translating tourist texts. A new strategy, namely, neutralizing, may be able to be put forward as the criterion for the translation of tourist texts and can help promote cultural exchange because the translator should try their best to transfer the cultural message from the original text to the target text while retaining readability and acceptability of the translation. Here the neutralizing strategy does not simply mean the mixture of the domesticating and the foreignizing. It refers to the act and process of constantly modulating their own awareness of what they translate, to satisfy the reader's needs and to achieve correlative equivalents between the ST and the TT. In other words, the translation of tourist texts does not rely on either strategy and the translator fully takes into account all the cultural elements existing in the text whenever necessary. Newmark, who put forward the "correlative approach to translation", states that "The more important the language of the original or source language text, the more closely it should be translated." According to this approach, seven methods are suggested to cope with different kinds of texts: component analysis, modulation, descriptive equivalent, functional equivalent, cultural equivalent, synonymy and paraphrase (Newmark, 1991: 1: 33). The degree of compatibility in the first method is highest and the last is the lowest. Different texts and different contents of the same text can be translated by different methods. As translators for tourist texts, they may follow the three step approach for neutralizing. The first step is to modulate the translator's awareness of what features a tourist text possesses, and constantly judge what kinds of texts is being translated and what differences and similarities may exist between the original text and the target text. From there the translator should analyse what the target reader may feel when reading the translation. The second step is to satisfy the reader's needs. In other words, the translator should follow the tourist-oriented strategy and understands what the reader needs may entail and then manage to meet such needs. The last is to achieve different equivalents between the ST and the TT, terms of equivalence in information, equivalent in concept, equivalent in aesthetics according to the qualities of the source text.

## 2) The information-oriented principle

According to the qualities of tourist texts, transferring information is one of the most important functions in translation. In order to perform such a function, the translator has to follow the information-oriented principle, supply the reader with enough information from the original text and help them understand the culture and history of the ST. In other words, the translator should always think of what the target reader may be thinking, ascertain as much as possible what the reader may wish to find in the tourist text, and supply them with enough information to supplement what they already have. The purpose is to reach an equivalent in information.

## 3) The association-applied principle

Newmark (1981:39-48) once remarked, "Communicative translation addresses itself solely to the second reader, who does not anticipate difficulties or obscurities, and would expect a generous transfer of foreign elements into his own culture as well as his language where necessary." The translator is here required to transfer foreign elements into the readers own culture. But this is not all that he or she does in translating. We also take retaining the original culture into consideration. In other words, the domesticating and foreignizing methods should be simultaneously used so as to maintain both cultures. Such association principle, especially in C-E translation, can help close and bridge the cultural voids or gaps, create the association with them and perform the vocative function as well. *Liang Shanbo*（梁山伯）*and Zhu Yingtai*（祝英台）, for instance, is a folk legend, which tells the story about a young man and a woman who were deeply in love, and they turned into two butterflies and flew away wing to wing because their parents were opposed to their marriage. We cannot use transliteration here because it's a moving love story. It was once translated into "The Butterfly Lovers" or "The Romance of the Butterfly", which is a good translation. We also can follow the association principle to translate "Liang Shanbo and Zhu Yingtai" into English "the Romeo and Juliet of China".

This example clearly tells us that the association principle can help the reader create association with their own culture and history, and improve the mutual understanding between the two cultures in tourist texts. In this case, the translations show consideration for the foreign reader's cognitive settings, textual effect due to the correlativeness, and favorably disseminate the traditional Chinese culture to the world.

### 4) The concept-based principle

The concept-based principle is primarily used for the words or phrases of the tourist texts bearing cultural or historical elements, which cannot reflect the culture-specific conceptual meanings. It is employed to supply what the ST should have but does not have and to establish communication with the target reader. Its function is to directly convey the concepts of history and culture of the source text, disseminate the culture of the original, and draw the reader's focus on the scenic spot. "Trinity College" in the city of Oxford, for example, should be translated into 三一学院, not 特里尼蒂学院 because the word "Trinity" has an important position in Westerners' minds, and bears the cultural background. Such examples as "All Souls"（万灵学院）, Madame Tussand's（图索德夫人蜡像馆）, Stonehenge（巨石阵）, etc. also can show this case.

C-E translation also can follow this principle. The City of Nanjing, for instance, is famous for its *yuhuashi*（雨花石）, which is a kind of colourful and beautiful stone made of quartzite, opal and chalcedony and usually sold in tourist shops. But it has several English translations, e.g., "Rain Flower Stone", "*Yuhua* Pebbles", "*Yuhua* Stones" and "Rain Flower Pebbles" as found in tourist texts. Some foreign readers may be puzzled about these and think that it might be different stones. The translator has to put himself or herself in the reader's position. To English-speaking readers, stone and pebble are quite different. The word "stone" refers to "the hard compact non-metallic material of which rocks are made" (Hanks, 1979:1432) and "pebble" refers to "a small usually round stone especially when worn and rounded by the action of water" (Gove, P. B. et al, 2002) on the seashore or a riverbed. First of all, the translator has to make a correct choice between the two words. According to geological survey, the *Yangtze* River ran by this area during the tertiary period and the pretty-looking stones gradually accumulated through time to become small, roundish, and smooth due to the action of water. The river changed its course because of the crustal movement and the pebbles were deposited in this area. So it is evident that choosing "pebble" is the correct choice. What about the translation of *Yuhua*? It was once suggested that *yuhuashi* should be translated into "*Yuhua* stones" (*Wang Qiusheng*, 2004:77). This version is not very good because it doesn't show the connotative meaning of *Yuhua*. Foreign readers do not know what *Yuhua* or *yuhuashi* is. Tradition had it that the eminent monk, Yun Guang(云光), in *Nan* Dynasty (420-589, A. D.) preached a sermon in Nanjing and incessantly talked about Buddhism. The audience was intoxicated with his profound knowledge and eloquence. The Heaven was moved to tears, and then dropped flower rain to the ground, which turned multicolored stones that were later called *Yuhuashi*. According to the legend, it may be translated into "Flower-rain Pebbles". If it appears in the tourist text rather than the title, it is also necessary to illustrate it and even explain it by the legend.

### 7.1.4.6 Common methods in translating tourist texts 旅游文本翻译的常用方法

To be honest, there mainly exist two sorts of difficulties facing the translator in translating tourist texts. One is the difficulty caused by the lexical voids and cultural impact between two languages. Because of the different histories, geographical conditions, faiths and customs, some mismatch words, also called culture-loaded words or culture-bound words, definitely appear between two languages. The other is the difficulty caused by the different style and rhetoric of writing between two languages. As a result, some translation methods should be used in translating tourist texts.

#### 1) Choice of words

The accurate and proper choice of words is actually needed in translation. Vocabulary is the unstable element of a language as it undergoes constant changes both in form and content. In comparison with Chinese, English words are characterized by greater vacillation and flexibility. In other words, each English word when used in different contexts will have somewhat different meanings, whereas Chinese words are more rigorous, accurate and fixed in meaning. Sometimes it is hard for a translator to select its meaning when encountering a tricky word, which really requires accuracy in translation.

❖ Whichever way you choose to visit Zhengzhou, you will reach here quickly and enjoy a comfortable *stay*, because Zhengzhou has a wide range of accommodation to suit all *budgets* and *tastes*... (Sapna Nayyar, *Beijing Review*)
无论乘坐何种交通工具都能迅速抵达郑州,<u>下榻此处</u>会让你备感舒适,这里的住宿条件能充分满足各种<u>档次</u>和<u>品位</u>的要求……

**Comments** In this short passage, the underlined words "*stay*", "*budgets*" and "*tastes*" are very common in English. Instead of the literal translations 逗留、预算 and 口味, they should be translated, by means of proper choice of words, into 下榻, 档次 and 品位. This requires the translator to be faithful to the original and pay special attention to the polysemy or the indeterminacy of the English language in choosing Chinese words, so that he or she can improve the translation quality. So we can say that translation quality of tourist texts is strongly influenced by accuracy and faithfulness to the original and by the fidelity of the words we choose.

**2) Addition or Amplification**

The translation methods addition or amplification has been in detail discussed in Chapter 2. Some other contents about it will be supplemented in this section. Aiming at translation of tourist texts, we will supplement *rhetorical amplification* and *amplification by notes* which are often used in translating tourist texts. A couple of examples are analyzed below.

❖ Tower, domes, balanced rocks, and arches have been formed over millions of years of weathering and erosion, and the process continues, constantly reshaping this fantastical rock garden. (Arches National Park, *National Geographic*)
岁月沧桑,风化雨蚀,造就了这里奇特的山体风貌:漫山"巨塔"高耸,"穹丘"浑圆,"不倒翁"摇摇欲坠,"大拱门"凌空而起,奇形怪状,自然天成。大自然造物不尽,还在不断创造新的神奇。

**Comments**: The original text is terse and simple, which suits English style of writing. But we can not translate it completely according to its writing manner and sequence. Instead, the method rhetorical amplification can be used here in Chinese version so as to accord with Chinese writing style. If we read and compare the source and target texts for several times, the functional equivalence has been achieved not only by rhetorical effect but also by vivid expression.

❖ City Cruises Plc Dose Not Accept Liability for Any Loss (including theft), Damage to Belongs or Personal Injury Unless We Are Legally Responsible.
泰晤士河游轮公司对于<u>物品</u>遗失(包括失窃)、财产损失以及个人伤害所造成的<u>任何损伤概</u>不承担责任,除非另有法律<u>规定</u>。

**Comments** This is a sign of tourist attraction beside Thames in London. This sign clearly lists the three situations, *any loss (including theft)*, *damage to belongs or personal injury*, that they are *not accept liability for*, and claims that *unless we are legally responsible* as well. It is terse and accurate in language, and simple and formal in syntax. But literal translation can't be used here because the Chinese version is not expressive nor communicative. Therefore, rhetorical amplification is needed. The underlined parts 物品、任何损伤概、规定 are necessarily added.

### 3) Structural division and combination

Because of the differences in structure between English and Chinese, it is impossible for us to ensure their complete correspondence. This requires us to cope with the structure of target texts by means of division and combination. Now look at the following examples.

- *The fanciful names* at Arches National Park like Fiery Furnace, The Gossip, Marching Men, Dark Angels, etc. *do justice to* the *otherworldly* rock *formations* they denote. (*Arches National Park*, *National Geographic*)

  石拱门国家公园内**各景点**的名称可谓**五花八门、极富创新**:"火炉烈焰"、"三个女人一台戏"、"进行者"、"黑天使"等等。**这些名称用来形容那满山造型怪异的山石群像**可谓**名副其实、惟妙惟肖**。

**Comments** The original only has one well-organized sentence. But we should divide it into two parts in the translation, instead of the original structure, and add the part 这些名称用来 to combine the two sentences.

- Although the state (Hawaii) is located in the tropical zone, its climate is comfortable because of the ocean currents that pass its shores and winds that blow across the land from the northeast. The temperature usually remains close to the annual average of 24 degrees Centigrade.

  夏威夷地处热带,气候却温和宜人,年均温度常年在摄氏 24 度左右。岛上时时刮过的东北风,伴着太平洋吹来的阵阵海风,让人备感凉爽舒适。

**Comments**: The first sentence of the original is well-organized but a little bit long. It should be divided to be translated according to Chinese writing style, and so the part "*close to the annual average of 24 degrees Centigrade*" is placed near the front so that the semantic meaning becomes clear. In addition, the part 让人备感凉爽舒适 is added in the end in order to keep the meaning expressive and natural.

### 4) Textual adjustment and adaptation

Textual adjustment and adaptation refers to the method that the whole translated text should be adjusted to suit the reader's reading habit and to highlight the expressive and vocative functions to the reader. It had better be done in one paragraph. It has the following advantages: connection and coherence, logical relationship between sentences, reconstruction and adaptation of the translated text, consideration of the translated text as a whole.

◆ Cape Breton Highlands National Park stretches across the northern part of Nova Scotia's Cape Breton Island, embracing the best the island has to offer. Franked on the east by the Atlantic Ocean and on the west by the Gulf of St. Lawrence, this magnificent preserve of highland plateau offers steep headlands, rich bogs, and windblown barrens (home to rare arctic and alpine plants), crystalline lakes and swift-running streams sandy beaches, Acadian forests, and deep canyons. Made of some of the oldest visible rock on the planet, this rugged land was shaped by uplift, erosion, and glaciers, beginning between one billion and 345 million ago. (*Cape Breton Highlands National Park*, *National Geographic*)

布里多尼角国家高地公园位于加拿大布里多尼岛,东边为大西洋,西边为圣劳伦斯海湾,地处该岛最佳位置,范围覆盖新斯科舍省北部全境。岛上景色壮丽,一派原始山地高原风光:海岬陡峭,泥沼肥沃,深峡幽谷,碧涧清潭,急流走溪水,沙滩遍海滨,那山风肆虐的荒坡是稀有的北极高山植物家园,那大片的林地是著名的阿卡迪亚原始森林。该岛由地球上仅存的最古老岩石构成,3.45亿年到10亿年前经地壳隆起、自然风化和冰川的作用,形成了岛上巨岩叠嶂的崎岖山地风貌。

**Comments** The translator uses the method inversion to adjust the order of the original and then reorganize the translated text. The order is that the geographical position is first, the specific scenic spot is second, and the sentence order are then rearranged according to Chinese writing style. The purpose is to keep the translated text rhythmical, fluid and expressive. Additionally, the words and phrases "*preserve*", "*visible*" and "*windblown barrens*" are put into 原始的、仅存的、山风肆虐的荒坡 respectively, which seem to be appropriate.

### 7.1.5 Compare and Analyze 比较与分析

Hawaii

The eight major islands and over 100 small islets of Hawaii—like a chain of beads some 2575 kilometers long—lie upon the Pacific, southeast to northwest. Although the state is located in the tropical zone, its climate is comfortable because of the ocean currents that pass its shores and winds that blow across the land from the northeast. The temperature usually remains close to the annual average of 24 degrees Centigrade.

Rough, black rocks of lava just out of the

夏威夷

由8座大岛和100多个小岛组成的夏威夷群岛,像一串珍珠从南到北撒落在方圆2575公里的太平洋洋面上。夏威夷地处热带,气候却温和宜人,年均温度常年在摄氏24度左右。岛上时时刮过的东北风,伴着太平洋吹来的阵阵海风,让人备感凉爽舒适。

部分海岸馋岩叠嶂,熔岩乌黑,断崖绝壁破水而出。而有的地方,则海滨地平缓,一路伸向东南。那

water along parts of the coastline. In some places, cliffs rise almost straight from the water's edge. Along the gentle sloping land areas to the southeast are beaches of yellow, white and black sands.

The largest island, Hawaii, lies at the southeastern end of the chain and is almost twice as large as all the others combined. Five volcanoes gave the island its form; two are still alive: Kilauea and Mauna Loa. Mauna Loa the world's largest active volcano, towers about the scenic Hawaii National Park which stretches from the 4250-meter mountain peak across the sea to neighboring Maui, the valley island. Tropical plants, sandy desert, waterfalls, craters and caves make the 78-square-kilometer park a tourist attraction.

里黄沙似金,白沙似银,黑沙如铅,煞是好看。

最大的岛屿要数夏威夷岛,它位于群岛的东南端,面积为其他各岛总合的两倍。全岛由5座火山构成,其中基拉韦厄和莫纳罗亚火山还在熔岩喷涌。莫纳罗亚火山是全球最大的活火山,顶峰高达4250米,高耸在夏威夷国家森林公园之上。该公园面积780平方公里,范围从莫纳罗亚火山顶峰顺山谷跨海延伸至相邻的毛伊岛,是著名的旅游胜地。园内热带植物茂密,沙地荒滩,飞瀑流泉点缀其间,还有神奇的火山口、山中洞穴常年供游人观赏。

### 7.1.6 Exercises 练习

**Passage translation.**

China has long been famous for its tourism resources, such as famous mountains, numerous relics and historical sites, and colorful folklores. To give full play to the great potential of these resources and to feed the needs of international tourist market, we have developed a series of new products combining sightseeing and holiday making. In 1992, the State Council ratified to establish 12 State-level holiday resorts, leading to the establishment of a number of provincial-level holiday resorts. After three years of development and construction, some of the holiday resorts have been taken shape and will be put into use. After successful organization of China Landscape '93, China Heritage '94 and China Folklore '95, China National Tourism Administration is launch another activity entitled China Holiday Resort '96.

During the China Holiday Resort '96, tourist from overseas can choose as ideal place for their holiday, during which time they can participate in various activities.

## 7.2 Practical Translation 实用翻译

Practical texts refer to texts which are used for practical purposes in people's daily life. They affect almost every aspect of people's everyday life such as politics, economy, science and technology, but excluding literature. The translation of practical texts is quite different from the translation of literary texts. There are three reasons for this difference:

First, the language used in such practical texts often has its unique linguistic characteristics. Secondly, the translation of practical texts aims at practical purposes, such as the communication of scientific information or the promotion of a product. Thirdly, the translation of practical texts often targets at particular groups of readers, such as experts, businessmen or consumers. These three factors should be taken into account when we undertake practical translation. Generally speaking, the most typical varieties of practical texts are official documents, public signs, advertisements, trademarks, product manuals, etc.

### 7.2.1 Translation of Signs 公示语翻译

#### 7.2.1.1 An introduction in brief 简要介绍

A sign refers to a lettered board or other public display placed on or before a building, room, shop or office to advertise business there transacted or the name of person or firm conducting it (*Webster's Third New International Dictionary*). Sign is a broad term, widely used in public facilities, ranging from traveling, catering, accommodation, recreation, shopping to medical service, educational institution and financial service. Signs, which belong to social phraseology, cover a wide range from environmental communication signs (way-finding/directing signs, information signs, notices, and warnings), street signs, traffic signs or road signs, road markers, parking signs, school signs, no-smoking signs, construction signs, travel signs, instructional notices and so on. They are, with their social communicative functions, widely used by the public on all kinds of occasions. Signs are everywhere in our lives. They make our lives easier and more exciting when we are familiar with them. But sometimes they also bring problems to us. For example, a tourist might not be able to understand signs in a foreign country. Although much research has been directed to automatic speech recognition, handwriting recognition, optical character recognition (OCR), speech and text translation, little attention has been paid to automatic sign recognition and translation. Sign translation along with spoken language translation can help international tourists to overcome language barriers.

#### 7.2.1.2 The principle of translating signs 公示语翻译原则

Skopos theory, proposed in the late 1970's and early 1980's by Reiss and Vermeer, is the core theory of functionalism, which is a broad term for various theories focusing on the function or functions of texts. Skopos theory stresses the interactional, pragmatic aspects of translation, arguing that the shape of TT should above all be determined by the function or skopos that it is intended to fulfill in the target context. Reiss and Vermeer formulate this principle into two skopos rules: an interaction is determined by (or is a function of) its purpose and the skopos can be said to vary according to the recipient.

From these principles, it follows that the translator should use the translation strategies which are most appropriate to achieving the purpose for which TT is intended, irrespective of which whether they are considered to be the "standard way" to proceed in a particular translation context; in short, when producing a TT "the end justifies the means". An awareness of the requirements of the skopos thus expands the possibilities of translation, increases the range of possible translation strategies, and releases the translator from the corset of an enforced—and hence often meaningless—literalness. (Shutteworth & Cowie, 2004:156)

The framework of the theory is that any form of translation action, including therefore translation itself, may be conceived as an action, as the name implies. Any action has an aim, a purpose. The word "skopos", then is a technical term for the aim or purpose of a translation, an action (which) leads to a result, a new situation or event, and possibly to a "new" object. (Nord, 2001:12) A translational action may involve a variety of purposes, which may be related to each other in a hierarchical order. Three possible kinds of purposes in translation may be: the general purpose aimed at by the translator in the translation process, the communicative purpose aimed at by the target text, and the purpose aimed at by a particular translation strategy or procedure. That is to say, when translating a sign, the translator should above all know what his or her purpose is, what function (indicating, prompting, restricting or compelling) the sign has, and what strategy determined by the purpose (literal or free, domesticating or foreignizing, etc. ) he or she use according to the features of signs.

### 7.2.1.3 The basic functions of signs 公示语的基本功能

Signs perform the four basic functions: indicating, promoting, restricting and compelling. As its meaning suggests, *indicating*(指示) is to indicate or guide readers. Signs as such are also called instructive/directive/guiding notices which give readers detailed information with no prohibition and restriction. Indicating is the most basic function performed in sign language. Indicating signs generally give readers relevant information about what it is and what service it provides. This is a basic function of sign language. Each type of signs has indicating function, such as "Toilet for Men" (男厕所), and "Toilet for Women"(女厕所).

*Prompting*(提示) has no striking difference from indicating except that the former carries the tone of warning. It aims at reminding readers of paying considerable attention to signs. You may see a sign saying "Wet Paint" (油漆未干) near the recently painted bench, implying "Don't touch the bench, or you will get painted". And "Mind Your Head When Rising from Seat" (起立时谨防碰头) to warn you to be careful.

*Restricting*(限制)signs, unlike the two functions mentioned above, put restrictions and constraints to readers, who are expected to abide by certain rules in the interest of public. Restricting signs are to keep or confine within limits. "Please Give This Seat, If A Handicapped or Elderly Person Needs It"(请让座给伤残人或老年人) and "30 Minutes Parking"(限停 30 分钟) are good examples.

　　*Compelling*(强制)signs have great power and potency to induce action on brief. With its tough tone, negative words and comparatively uniform sentence structures, there is little possibility of alternatives. Imperatives are preferred in this circumstance. For example, "No Smoking"(严禁吸烟), "No Littering"(严禁乱扔垃圾), "Dog Must Be Kept on a Leash"(狗须用皮带牵住) and "Construction Area, No Pedestrians Beyond This Point"(施工重地,行人不得入内).

### 7.2.1.4 Features of signs and their translation 公示语特点及其翻译

　　Signs belong to functional varieties. They are distinguished from other types of languages by their unique features embodied in their applied circumstances. Generally speaking, there are five features, which are *conciseness*(for example, "Don't Touch" or "Hands Off" 勿动展品 instead of "Please Don't Touch The Exhibits", "Night Bell" 夜间有事,请按此铃 rather than a translated sentence); *directness*(for example, "No Passengers on Trucks" 严禁客货混装 instead of "Don't Put Passengers and Cargoes Together"); *suitable mood*, suggesting instruction, order, request and warning (for example, "Keep Distance" 保持车距,"Handle with Care" 小心轻放, "Fire Alarm" 火警, "No Driving after Drinking" 禁止酒后开车); *combining letters with pictures*; and *capitalization of English signs* as in the examples mentioned above.

　　Therefore, the translator should adhere to the functions and the features of signs in translating signs, and overcomes their functional and Pragmatic deficiencies in Chinese versions. More examples are listed below to show the features and functions in sign translation.

- ❖ Clean Up After Your Dog 清理您爱犬的粪便(prompting, concise)
- ❖ Way Out to Montague Place 去 Montague Place 的出口(indicating, concise)
- ❖ Silence Please 请保持肃静(restricting, suitable mood)
- ❖ No Entry 禁止进入(compelling, concise, direct)

### 7.2.2 Exercises 练习

**I. Translate the following signs into Chinese.**

1. Arrivals Lounges (By Invitation Only)
2. First Aid Point
3. No Alcohol to be Consumed in This Area

4. No Pigeon Feeding (Do Not Feed the Pigeons)

5. Dog Must be Kept on a Lead

6. No Skateboarding or Rollerblading

7. Youth Hostel 400yds

8. No Ball Games Allowed

9. For Your Comfort & Safety Please Wear the Seatbelt Provided

10. This Area Closed

11. Please Follow the Visitor Route Indicated in Your Guide Ticket (Cambridge Residents & Members of the University May Enter Free of Charge)

12. No Bicycles, Dogs, Radios or Picnics Allowed

Ⅱ. **Translate the following signs into English.**

| 游客止步 | 仅限紧急情况下使用 | 租车服务 |
| 外卖服务 | 客满 | 售完 |
| 让路 | 凭票入场 | (限速)60 公里/小时 |
| 残疾人通道 | 排队等候 | 小心碰头 |
| 教师休息室 | 打折销售 | 现在营业 |
| 退房 | 国际直拨 | 贵宾室 |
| 小心轻放 | 请勿打扰 | |

## 7.2.3 Advertising Translation 广告翻译

Advertising is one of the marketing strategies in the international business activities. Advertisements exist everywhere and influence us every day. According to a statistics, one third of the present-day newspaper's space is used for advertising in England. Advertisement is a widely used medium of communication in business activities. If we want to do a good job in English advertisement translation, it is necessary for us to know something of advertisements' characteristics.

The goal of advertisements can be summarized as follows: *Attention*, *Interest*, *Credibility*, *Desire*, and *Action*. To be more accurate, advertisements must attract people's attention—for example, by using bold type and eye-catching pictures. Next, advertisements must arouse the prospective customers' interest in the product and build credibility for the product. Then advertisements should be able to arouse a buying desire that finally leads to a purchasing action. If the translation of an advertisement cannot achieve these effects of the original, it will be a failure. The general principles of advertisement translation should be: smoothness, precision and conciseness.

*Smoothness* means to use smooth and natural Chinese expressions that Chinese customers can accept to give the information about a product. Whether the translation of an English advertisement is excellent or not depends on the response of its receivers. Only when the Chinese readers' response to the translation is similar to the original readers' response to the original advertisement, will the translation achieve its purpose. To achieve this, the first step is to translate the original with smooth Chinese expressions.

*Precision* is also demanded by the advertisement's functions. If the meaning of the original advertisement were altered in the translation, the consumers would be misled by the Chinese version.

*Conciseness* means the translator should use informative and concise diction and sentence structures. The education levels of the readers are varied, so far too complicated or difficult diction or sentence structures in translation may make it hard for its intended readers to comprehend its information.

### 7.2.3.1 Lexical characteristics of English advertisements 英文广告的词法特点

The words and phrases in advertisements are colorful and lively, and the only purpose of choosing a word in writing an advertisement is to "promote products". Therefore, these phrases are usually intriguing and appealing. The lexical characteristics of English advertisements can be summarized in the following aspects:

#### 1) The abundant use of modifiers

In advertisements, there is an abundant use of modifiers to highlight the merits of a product, to describe vividly the special features of the product and to enhance its appeal to the prospective customer. To attract more customers to buy their products, advertisements often highlight their unique merits with the use of comparative and superlative degree modifiers, though they don't belittle other similar products directly.

- ❖ *Famous world-wide gourmet* cuisine. *Excellent daily* specials and *mouth-watering* desserts.

  <u>世界有名的</u>美食烹调，<u>精美的每日</u>特色饭菜和令人垂涎的点心。

- ❖ For the first time, there's a remarkable gel that can give your hair any look you want—*sleeker, fuller, straighter, curlier, more natural*, even wet—without a drop of alcohol or oil.

  一种前所未有，不同寻常的发乳问世了。它可以使您的头发随心所愿——<u>更光滑，更丰茂，更平直，更卷曲，更自然</u>，甚至保持湿度——都不含一滴酒精或油脂。

- ❖ Vaseline Intensive Care "Aloe & Lanolin" combines *natural* aloe with skin softening lanolin and a *fresh* herbal scent to soothe and condition *rough, dry* skin. Absorbs fast with *no greasy* after-feel. Helps restore your skin's natural softness. In just seconds, you'll see and feel the difference. *Great year-round* skin care for the whole family.

  <u>天然</u>芦荟及羊脂配方凡士林特效润肤露，蕴含丰富的滋润成分和<u>新鲜</u>草本

香味，**不油不腻**，补充肌肤因**干燥**而失去的水分，快速渗透，发挥滋润效果，**全年适用**。（注：译文为编译）

**Comments** The first example is a restaurant advertisement. We can see that the adjectives account for one half of the words used in the advertisement. They show the restaurant's features to its customers. In the second advertisement, the use of five successive comparative degrees adjectives, i. e. "*sleeker*, *fuller*, *straighter*, *curlier*, *more natural*", suggests that this kind of gel is better than other gels and meet consumers' different demands. The original English version of the last advertisement contains a number of modifiers such as "*natural*", "*fresh*", "*rough*", "*dry*" etc. which help to describe vividly the fine quality and effect of this product.

### 2) Intentional wrong spellings

Intentional wrong-spellings in English advertisements can arouse people's sense of curiosity about the advertisement and impress people deeply.

❖ Drinka Pinta Milka Day.

**Comments** This is a milk advertisement. The normal form of the expression should be: Drink a Pint of Milk a Day. This intentional misspelling is intended to induce prospective customer's curiosity, and it reads rhyming and rhythmic. Besides it uses four words that have no grammatical relation with each other to express a complete concept. This purposeful wrong spelling is used much to the advantage. However, it is not easy to translate this advertisement, or rather, it cannot be translated literally, because as for the Chinese characters, we cannot add any stroke to them. So we can only translate its basic message as：一天请喝一品脱牛奶。If we try to reproduce the rhythmic effect of this advertisement with some unconventional methods, how about this version：一日请喝一品牛奶？This translation uses two homophonic Chinese characters 瓶 and 品 to achieve an effect of rhyme. Also, for the people who know English well, they will think of 品 as a derivative of "pint（品脱）". For the people who do not know English, they will reflect that the Chinese character 瓶 was wrongly replaced by the Chinese character 品. If so, the translation attracts people's attention with this play on word. To a certain degree, the effect is more or less equivalent to the original advertisement because it can arouse the same curiosity and leave a deep impression on readers.

### 3) The use of coined and strange words

Advertisements often invent new words and strange words to highlight products' characteristics: novel, creative and original, so that they can satisfy the consumers who are fond of following fashion. When we translate these new coinages and strange words into Chinese, we should bring our imagination into full play because we can't find their equivalents in dictionaries.

❖ Give a *Timex* to all, to all a good Time.

**Comments** This is a watch advertisement. The watch's brand name is Timex. Timex is a new coinage: a mix of "Time" and "excellence". The formation of this coinage helps to associate 时间 with 优秀 in our mind. To translate the brand name well, we should endeavor to reproduce the meaning and originality of the new coinage. To that end, we translate it by both transliteration and free translation：给诸君一块"天美时"表,各位就掌握了好时光。On the one hand, the translation of "*Timex*" as 天美时—has a pronunciation similar to "*Timex*" and it sounds harmonious. On the other hand, the translation conveys the connotation of the coinage "*Timex*"：The watch is of good appearance and superior quality. These three Chinese characters 天美时 allude to the excellence of this product to Chinese customers.

### 4) The use of abbreviations and compound words

Copywriters often try to shorten the length of advertisements to cut down its cost. For this purpose, abbreviations and compound words are frequently used in many advertisements. The translator should make sure of the meaning of such words and substitute them with their natural equivalents in translation.

- ❖ Where to leave your troubles when you fly *JAL*.
  
  乘坐**日航班机**,一路无烦恼。

- ❖ Even at just over $100 per person per day, our *thrill-of-a-lifetime* trips are cheap.
  
  即使每人每天一百多美元,我们那**令人终生难忘的极富刺激性的**旅行仍然便宜。

- ❖ The Myst is multimedia intrigue at its best, exploiting the *CD-ROM* format like no other entertainment software. (The Myst)
  
  美斯特,最优秀的多媒体软件,它对**光盘只读存储器**格式的开发利用是其他任何娱乐软件无法比拟的。(美斯特软件)

**Comments** "*JAL*" in the first example is the abbreviation of Japan Airlines. "*Thrill-of-a-lifetime*" in the second is a shorthand phrase in place of a lengthy clause：a trip which will brings the passenger a thrill for his lifetime. In the original advertisement of the last, "*CD*" is an abbreviation of "compact disk", and "*ROM*" is an abbreviation of "read-only memory". But since most Chinese readers do not recognize these abbreviations, they should be explained fully in the translation.

### 7.2.3.2 Syntactical characteristics of English advertisements 英文广告的句法特点

#### 1) Concise and short sentences

Conciseness is a common characteristic of most advertisements. Their sentences are generally short and succinct. This is because complex sentences are not easy to understand and they will dull readers' interest in the advertisement, while brief and short sentences are vivid, eye-catching and readable. So we should also use short Chinese sentences to translate such advertisements.

- ❖ Coca-Cola is it.
  
  还是可口可乐好!

- ❖ Fresh Up with Seven-Up.
  
  请饮七喜,倍添精神。

**Comments** These are two advertisements of beverages. The copywriters use just three or four words to highlight the excellence of the products. The advertisements are not only easy to remember but also boosting the brands' images. The translator uses Chinese four-character structure so that the Chinese versions are as succinct, readable, vivid and eye-catching as the original.

Many such short-form advertisements (or slogans) are so popular that they have become almost household words, such as "Can't beat the real feeling! —Coca-Cola"(挡不住的诱惑！——可口可乐), "Good to the last drop. —Maxwell House Coffee"(滴滴香浓，意犹未尽。——麦斯威尔咖啡) and "A diamond is forever. —de Beers"(钻石恒久远，一颗永流传。——戴比尔斯钻戒).

### 2) Elliptical sentences

The plentiful use of elliptical sentences in advertisements is in compliance with the principle of conciseness. Besides, elliptical sentences can emphasize the key information in the advertisements.

❖ —Arthritis Pains?
　—All your need is Bayer Aspirins!
　—您正在忍受关节炎的痛苦吗?
　—贝尔阿司匹林使你药到病除!

**Comments** As is shown in the above example, in translating elliptical sentences in English advertisements, the translator sometimes needs to make necessary addition to make the Chinese version fully informative to the TL readers.

### 3) Imperative sentences

The purpose of advertisements is to appeal to consumers to buy the advertised goods. The use of imperative sentences enhances the appellative function of advertisements. Translators can also use imperative sentences to translate the originals so that the translation can achieve the same effect as the original.

❖ If you are looking for lifelike sound from small, beautiful and durable speakers, listen to our Bose Speakers, and begin to live your life to music.
　如果您正在寻找一台漂亮又耐用的音响效果逼真的小型扬声器，那就听一听我们的"博士"扬声器，让您的生活伴着音乐开始吧!

**Comments**: This advertisement uses two imperative sentences, i.e., "*listen to…*" and "*begin to…*" It is meant to persuade consumers to buy the advertised product. The translator also uses an equivalent imperative sentence in the translation to arouse the buying desire of the consumers who are still hesitant. The following are some other such examples.

### 4) Interrogative sentences

The use of interrogative sentences shortens the psychological distance between advertisers and readers by requiring readers' response to communicate with readers. Some interrogative sentences such as rhetorical questions are not really raising questions since they don't need answers. This kind of interrogative sentences reminds readers of the advertisement's purpose and attracts people's attention.

❖ DERWENT Scientific and Patent Information
  Fluent in French?
  An excellent communicator?
  A good organizer?
  Then develop your career within this sales support role.
  德温特科技专利信息
  法语说得流利吗?
  非常善于交际吗?
  是个优秀的组织者吗?
  如果是的话,就请到我们这个销售领域,拓展您的事业吧!

Comments  When translating the above advertisement, translators have to consider the function of interrogative sentences and try to achieve the same function in the translation. This translation also uses interrogative sentences to communicate the advertisement's information and achieve an equivalent effect.

### 7.2.3.3 Rhetorical devices used in English advertisements 英文广告的修辞方法

Rhetorical devices are often used to strengthen the expressive effect of language and enrich the signification of an utterance in English advertisements. In the course of translation, rhetorical devices are also used to achieve an equivalent effect. The following rhetorical devices are often adopted in advertisements:

**1) Simile**

Simile is the use of an expression which describes one thing by directly comparing it to another by using such words as "as" or "like" in English. In Chinese, we often use 如、好像、就像、犹如 and so on for the same purpose.

❖ Featherwater: light *as* a feather.
  法泽瓦特眼镜——轻如鸿毛。
  Today, Sakura Bank is *like* a thriving sakura.
  如今,樱花银行就如一棵茂盛的樱花树。
  Light *as* a breeze, soft *as* a cloud.
  轻如风,柔如云。

Comments  The first example is an advertisement of spectacles. In this advertisement, the weight of Featherwater spectacles is compared to that of a feather. People who wear spectacles certainly think that the lighter a pair of spectacles is, the better and more comfortable it is. So the translator employs the same rhetorical style: 法泽瓦特眼镜——轻如鸿毛 to achieve a similar effect in translation. The second is an advertisement of Japan's Sakura Bank, which is compared to a blooming sakura (the pronunciation of the Japanese word which means cherry blossom). While translating this advertisement, we should also transfer this simile to the Chinese version to keep intact the original expressive effect. The last one is an advertisement of a garment. It describes the material of the garment is "as light as a breeze" and "as soft as a cloud". Such a vivid simile informs the consumer of the softness and comfort of this garment and arouses his purchasing desire. This rhetorical device is translated literally into the Chinese version for it is both acceptable and effective for Chinese consumers as well.

### 2) Metaphor

Unlike simile, metaphor doesn't explain the reason of comparison and doesn't compare two things directly by using "like" or "as". It induces the readers to think about its deep meaning.

❖ EBEL—the architects of time.

**Comments** EBEL is the brand name of a watch produced in Switzerland. This advertisement reflects the watch's excellent quality by comparing the watch to the architect of time. We can translate it literally as follows: 依贝尔手表——时间的缔造者. This Chinese translation does not use such words as 犹如, because Chinese readers can understand the metaphorical meaning of 时间的缔造者, which also alludes to the watch's fine quality of keeping time punctually.

❖ You're better off under the Umbrella.

在"伞"的保护下,你可以无忧无虑地享受旅行的乐趣。

**Comments** This is the advertisement of a travel insurance company. A traveler always cares about his safety on his journey. This advertisement makes use of this psychology and likens itself to an "umbrella" to imply that if you buy its insurance, you can enjoy your journey with no concern for accident.

### 3) Pun

Pun is a humorous play on words in which a word is used in two meanings, or two words with the same pronunciation but different meanings. It is difficult to translate puns used in English advertisements. English and Chinese are two radically different languages and the two cultural traditions are different. These differences pose difficulties for translating English puns literally. But we can handle the original puns with other methods than literal translation.

❖ I'm *More* satisfied.

摩尔香烟,我更满意。

❖ Ask for *More*.

再来一支,还吸摩尔。

**Comments** These are two advertisements of More Cigarette. They are typical examples of puns. The advertisements take advantage of the two meanings of "*more*" ingeniously: "more", as an adverb, means 更加,更多; here, it is also the name of a brand. These two advertisements leave a deep impression on readers: This product is better than others and more satisfactory to consumers. The translator uses Chinese four-character structure which is very smooth and elegant to translate the puns freely. We must point out that the formal feature of the original pun is lost. But this loss is inevitable in translation.

### 4) Parallelism

Parallelism is to use a series of the same or similar sentential structures to pass on certain information. The use of parallelism can enhance the expressive effect of message and highlight the advertisement's purpose. It is rhythmical and symmetrical. So translators should also recreate the original effect by using similar parallelism in Chinese.

❖ I want the body of a Greek god.
   I want to work out in a huge fitness centre.
   I want to stay in the heart of the Central Business District.
   I want a room with a view of three countries.
   Everything I want is at the world's tallest hotel.
   The Westin Stamford & Westin Plaza, Singapore
   我想有希腊神之身躯
   我想在巨大的健身中心锻炼
   我想住在商业中心地带
   我想入住能眺望三个国家的房间
   我最想住在世界上最高的宾馆里
   新加坡威斯汀·斯坦福/威斯汀广场

**Comments** This is an advertisement of Singapore's Westin Hotel. In the advertisement, "*I want*" is repeated four times. It expresses an assumed customer's eager desire to enjoy staying in this hotel. The translator should use similar parallelism in translation to achieve the same effect as the original.

❖ Designed with a computer. Silenced by a laser. Built by a robot. (Volvo)
   电脑设计，激光消音，机器人制造。(沃尔沃汽车)

**Comments** This advertisement is made up of three perfect parallel structures. This feature is replicated in the Chinese translation.

### 5) Personification

Personification is to treat inanimate things as animate beings by associating them with speeches, deeds or thoughts and feelings of human beings. International business advertisements often use personification which leaves an impression of originality on consumers.

❖ Unlike me, my Rolex never needs a rest.
   不像我，我的劳力士从不休息。

❖ Flowers by Interflora speak from the heart.
   英特福劳拉花店培育的鲜花倾诉人的心里话。

**Comments** Example one is an advertisement of Rolex Watch. We know that people need rest but a watch does not. However, this advertisement personifies Rolex Watch and says it "*never needs a rest*". It underscores Rolex's good quality of precision and durability. This advertisement can be translated according to the original meaning. This translation is vivid and interesting and retains the original appeal. Example two is **an** advertisement of a flower shop. In this advertisement, "*flowers*" is personified, it can "*speak from the heart*", so when you present a flower bought in this shop to others, the flower can speak on your behalf.

### 6) Rhyme

English advertisements sometimes employ rhyme such as alliteration or end-rhyme to make the advertisement pleasant-sounding. Alliteration appears in English advertisements more than end-rhyme. But it is difficult to translate them into the same rhetorical device in Chinese. Because English and Chinese are different in linguistic structure, rhyme in English may not be translated literally into Chinese.

- Sea, sun, sand, seclusion—and Spain!
  You can have all this when you visit the new hotel Caliente.
  大海、太阳、沙滩、幽静——西班牙!
  只要您住进新旅馆"客恋塔",您就能享受这一切!
- Hi-Fi, Hi-Fun, Hi-Fashion, only from Sony.
  高保真,高乐趣,高时尚,只来自索尼。
- It changed our well water to wonderful water.
  变井水为纯净水。

**Comments**: The first example is an advertisement of a hotel in Spain. The initial letter of every word in this advertisement except for "*and*" in the first line is "*s*". We can only translate its meaning without reproducing the rhyme. The second is an advertisement of Sony Hi-Fi appliances. The repetition of "*Hi*" in the first three words forms alliteration. This effect can be recreated by the repetition of 高 in the Chinese version. Alliteration is also used in the last advertisement: "*well*", "*water*", "*wonderful*", "*water*". The Chinese version is also producing the effect.

### 7) Hyperbole

Hyperbole used in advertisements is to make an overstatement about a product or service to attract people's attention or for emphasis. We can translate an English hyperbole literally if it is acceptable and comprehensible to Chinese consumers.

- We've hidden a garden full of vegetables where you'd never expect. In a pie.
  在您意想不到的地方,我们珍藏了满园的蔬菜——就是在那一个小小的馅饼里。
- Coverage so invisible; it's time to rewrite history!
  我厂的化妆品用后不见痕迹,效果之妙是改写历史的时候了!

**Comments**: The first advertisement uses hyperbole to suggest that the pie be prepared with all sorts of vegetables and rich in nutrition. Since this hyperbole is also understandable and acceptable to Chinese readers, it is translated literally into Chinese. Example two is an advertisement of a brand of cosmetics. The message of this advertisement is that this product is so transparent that it is invisible when used on face and it can make face more beautiful. "*It's time to rewrite history*" is a hyperbole, which not only emphasizes this message, but also adds a sense of humor to the advertisement. Since this hyperbole is also understandable and acceptable to Chinese readers, it is translated literally into Chinese.

### 7.2.3.4 Translation methods of English advertisements 英文广告的翻译方法

#### 1) Transliteration

Transliteration is to write (a word, name, sentence, etc.) in the alphabets of a target language or writing system according to the pronunciation of the original expression. Transliteration is often adopted in the translation of brand names, the names of firms and so on.

Absolutely pure transliteration is very difficult. Moreover, consumers cannot learn the characteristics of a product from the transliteration of its brand which has no actual meaning but only reproduces a similar pronunciation as the original. Such a translation just uses a brand to represent a product. Generally speaking, most transliterated brand names are well-known popular ones to Chinese consumers.

❖ Kodak 柯达(胶卷)　　　Lincoln 林肯(轿车)
　Casio 卡西欧(电子琴)　　Rolex 劳力士(手表)
　Lipton 立顿(茶)　　　　Heinz 亨氏(米粉)
　Parker 派克(钢笔)　　　Motorola 摩托罗拉(手机)

Sometimes we can use partial transliteration plus interpretation to render a brand so that the consumer can know its original name while understanding its meaning in the SL language. For example, "Back Saver" is the band of a bolstered seat which is specially designed for people with a chronic back pain. Its Chinese rendering is 背舒尔 which accounts for both its original pronunciation and meaning. Therefore Chinese consumers can have an idea of the function of this product at the sight of this brand name.

#### 2) Literal translation

Literal translation is to translate the source text literally into Chinese and keep the same sentence structure and word order as the original. Literal translation is often used in the translation of titles, slogans and texts of advertisements. Let's first have a look at the English advertisements of Philips (飞利浦电器) and Discovery Channel (探索频道).

❖ Let's make things better. (Philips)
　让我们做得更好。
❖ Explore your world. (Discovery Channel)
　探索您的世界。

**Comments** We can see that their translations are equivalent to the originals in terms of meaning, word orders or sentence structures. The translations keep intact the original information and are also smooth and natural in Chinese.

However, coincidences like these are not familiar sights. A lot of English advertisements use English idioms, proverbs and other peculiar expressions that defy literal translation.

❖ Don't just get onto it, get into it. (Intel P Ⅲ Personal Computer)
   不仅仅是登陆互联网,而且真正畅游其中。

**Comments** The ingenuity of this advertisement consists in using two phrases: "*get onto*" and "*get into*". "Get onto" means "to communicate with someone". "Get into" means "to influence or take control of (someone) so as to make them act strangely". They seem to have a subtle difference in meaning but their presence in the advertisement hints at the virtue of Intel P Ⅲ—high speed. The translation of this advertisement means "You can not only be on line but do whatever you want to on the Internet". Although such a translation is clear enough but it seems flat and insipid. The next translation method—free translation—may compensate for its defect.

❖ Good teeth, good health.
   牙齿好,身体就好。

**Comments**: This is the advertisement of Colgate(高露洁)toothpaste. Its Chinese version is produced by a literal translation of the original. But the translation keeps intact the message, the terseness, the rhyme and the parallelism of the original.

**3) Free translation**

Sometimes it may be infeasible to translate English idioms word-for-word, because in some cases, literal translation cannot re-express the implied meanings of the original and therefore fails to achieve the advertisements' purposes. If a translated advertisement of a foreign product wants to draw Chinese consumers' attention and boost the product's image, it should be translated flexibly according to Chinese linguistic habits, i.e. free translation or liberal translation.

Chinese four-character structure and seven-character structure are commonly used in advertisements' translation. They are more concise and rhythmic than complete sentences. They are also smooth, elegant and impressive.

❖ AIA (友邦保险): Trust us for life.
   **财政稳健**,信守一生。

❖ Audi (奥迪汽车): Advancement through technology.
   突破科技,**启迪未来**。

❖ Patek Philippe (百达翡丽腕表): Begin your own tradition.
   **代代相传**,由您开始。

**Comments** In these examples of liberal/free translation, four-character structures 财政稳健,启迪未来 and 代代相传 are used to produce the Chinese versions. Chinese readers will feel these idiomatic expressions familiar, intimate and welcome.

❖ Toshiba（东芝电器）: In Touch with Tomorrow. 尽显明日<u>新</u>境界。
　Panasonic（松下电器）: What's new by Panasonic. 松下<u>总</u>有新点子。

**Comments**: In the translation of the above advertisements, the translator adopts Chinese seven-character structure which sounds rhythmic and original. In the seven-character structure, the use of 新 and 总 improves the rhythm of the phrases.

### 4) Adaptation

Adaptation or interpretation means that the translator expresses his own understanding of the original in a way that suits the need, interest of the intended TL readers. This method is often used for the translation of brand names and texts of advertisements which cannot be translated literally.

When the car market, for instance, underwent a worldwide competition, American Ford Company wanted to go into the market of Taiwan, so they opened "Ford-Liuhe" Car Manufactory jointly with Liuhe Car Manufactory of Taiwan and they produced a type of brand "Cortina". But after the car was produced, the first problem they met in advertising was how to translate this brand. They thought the target audience were young people, so they translated it creatively as 跑天下. As a result, the car "Cortina" was popular with young consumers just because of this original name. Although 跑天下 is not Cortina's literal translation, it brings benefit for the manufacturers. Another example is "My goodness! My Guiness!", which is translated into "此酒只应天上有！"（啤酒广告）It is more significant and more fluent than "我的天,我的 Guiness 酒！"

### 5) Borrowing

Translators can borrow familiar Chinese expressions to translate English advertisements. Such expressions may include idioms, proverbs, poems or some popular slogans used in Chinese. In a word, they must be intriguing and familiar to the Chinese consumers. Translating by borrowing familiar Chinese expressions should not be employed mechanically regardless of specific conditions. Translators should possess bilingual and bicultural competence and have an imaginative mind. Furthermore, they should still follow the principles of creativeness as is required by advertisements.

❖ Vandermint isn't good because it's imported; it's imported because it's good.
　好酒不在进口;进口必是好酒。

**Comments** "*Vandermint*" is the brand name of a wine. The copywriter uses just seven words in two sentences. "*It's*" is repeated twice, "*imported*", "*because*" and "*good*" are repeated once respectively. The advertisement emphasizes one message time and again: Vandermint is out of the ordinary! If we want to keep the original advertisement's rhetorical feature in translation, we will have to depend on our inspiration; otherwise it is impossible to translate it well. After analyzing the advertisement, the translator thinks that the original advertisement explains the relation between "wine" and "importation" and hits on a similar Chinese idiom in mind, that is, 山不在高,有仙则名;水不在深,有龙则灵.

❖ I'll do a lot for love, but I'm not ready to die for it.

情爱诚销魂,生命价更高。

**Comments** This is an advertisement of condoms. It is challenging for copywriters to write such advertisements which may be too vulgar to be accepted by the general public, or may be too implicit to be understood by common readers. The success of this advertisement is that it takes advantage of people's psychology of fearing AIDS and expresses this theme implicitly. It really appeals to both the more and the less cultured. When we translate this advertisement into Chinese, it is difficult to achieve the same effect as the original with conventional methods of translation, for example, it is so flat to translate it as 我愿为爱情付出许多,但我不准备为爱情而死. Therefore, we can borrow the famous poem by a Hungarian poet: 生命诚可贵,爱情价更高,若为自由故,两者皆可抛 and rewrite it as 风流诚销魂,生命价更高 in this translation. But considering China's culture, we can change 风流 into 情爱. As a result, the Chinese version is not only elegant but also drives home the key message euphemistically.

## 7.2.4 Compare and Analyze 比较与分析

An Advertisement of Ericsson

①" It's about communication between <u>people</u>. The rest is technology."

We expect to be able to communicate with anyone, at any time, anywhere.

We want to be liberated from the constraints of time and space. Distances are shrinking. Traditional boundaries are losing their significance.

We want technology to ② <u>work for</u> us as individuals. We expect it to meet our sophisticated communications needs, but still be easy to use.

We expect technology to provide us with ③<u>global freedom</u>, and at the same time respect our privacy as individuals. It should allow us to reach others, but ④ <u>make ourselves available on our terms</u>. Today's technology makes almost anything possible. It is you and I who set the limits.

Ericsson provides innovative, flexible solutions and services for all types of telecommunications networks that are helping our

一则爱立信公司广告

"①<u>首先</u>是人与人的沟通,余下的才是技术。"

我们期待着能够随时随地与任何人进行交流。

我们想摆脱时空的限制。距离在缩短。传统的界限正在失去意义。

我们期望技术能够②<u>服务于</u>我们个人。我们希望它既能满足我们复杂的通讯需求,又便于使用。

我们希望技术能够让我们③<u>自由地进行全球通讯</u>,同时尊重我们的个人隐私。它应当允许我们同他人联络,但同时④<u>又能根据我们的条件让别人和我联络</u>。当今的技术几乎使任何事情都成为可能,"限制"是你我设置的。

爱立信公司为各种型号的通讯网络提供新一代灵活变通的通讯技术,这些技术帮助我们的客

customers to open up new business opportunities and supply superior service to users. We develop and maintain technologies not only for today's needs, but for tomorrow and well into the future.

70,000 Ericsson employees are active in more than 100 countries. Their combined expertise in switching, radio and networking makes Ericsson a world leader in telecommunications.

户开展新的业务,并为用户提供优良的服务。我们开拓和保持技术不仅仅是为了今天的需要,也是为了明天,乃至未来。

7万多名爱立信员工活跃在100多个国家。他们在切换技术、无线电技术及通讯网络方面的综合技能使得爱立信成为世界通讯领域的佼佼者。

**Notes:**

① In the Chinese version, a connective 首先 is added to make this sentence coherent with the following sentence.

② Here "*work for*" had better be translated as 服务于 instead of 为我们工作.

③ Here "*global freedom*" is translated flexibly according to the nature of this advertisement——a publicity for a mobile phone company.

④ The same is also true of "*make ourselves available*" in the following context.

### 7.2.5 Exercises 练习

Ⅰ. **Sentence translation.**

1. Selected materials, fine workmanship, modern designs, reasonable price, various specifications. Orders welcome. ("航空牌"人造革箱包广告)

2. More sun and air for your son and heir.（地域广告）

3. Spoil yourself and not your figure.（食品广告）

4. A deal with us means a good deal to you.（公司宣传）

5. Coke refreshes you like no other can.（饮料广告）

6. Ask for more!（百事可乐广告）

7. Every time a good time.（麦当劳广告）

8. It's happens within your reach.（AT & T 电讯广告）

9. You shop we drop.（商场广告）

10. Anycall（三星手机广告）

Ⅱ. **Passage translation.**

If you don't take care of this small tooth,

The permanent one might not be so cute.

Somehow, a lot of people figure it doesn't really matter, if a "Baby tooth"

gets a cavity. After all, it's just a little temporary tooth.

But it really does matter. First, the tooth is so small, a cavity in it

can be a big problem. So, the tooth might have to be pulled.

Then the space left by pulled tooth can cause bad spacing of the permanent

teeth which can affect anything from your baby's bite to his appearance.

So it makes sense to take care of those first little teeth just like you would big teeth. With the right foods, regular checkups and brushing after every meal with a good toothpaste.

We hope the toothpaste will be Crest.

## 7.3 Multimedia Translation 多媒体翻译

### 7.3.1 A Brief Introduction 简要介绍

In this fast technologically developing world, multimedia, used for advertising, entertainment, public information, training and education, plays a vital role in bringing the world closer. The applications of multimedia are constantly growing. They are becoming more domestic and millions of people are going to be affected in the way they communicate with one another. Almost everybody by now has heard the word "multimedia". Everybody reads about it, talks about it and wants it. Unfortunately most people hardly define the term multimedia exactly. Actually, multimedia has a very simple definition. It involves any combination of two or more of the following elements: text, image, voice, speech, video, and computer programs. For instance, the combination of voice and speech are used on the radio, newspapers use a combination of text and images, and film and television combine all these elements and use it to relay a message to the viewer. These mediums are digitally controlled by a computer(s). In order to get an idea across, one can use multimedia to convey his or her message. Multimedia enhances the information for better communication and understanding.

Multimedia translation is one of the most important changes that have taken place in recent years in the realms of communication and entertainment due to new technology and globalization. Translation no longer restricts itself to purely linguistic elements because this would not reflect the true nature of many transfer processes. Multimedia translation has a broad coverage. Multimedia translation services are applied in subtitling, dubbing, DVD, CBT (Computer-Based Test) and e-learning, games, flash movies, interactive voice recognition, voice-overs, etc. Dubbing, subtitling, and film translation are mainly discussed in this section.

### 7.3.2 Subtitling 字幕翻译

One of the core multimedia translation forms is subtitling, which refers to translation of the films dialogue in text form usually shown at the bottom of the screen. The text is written in the target language so that people can understand the movie. According to *Routledge Encyclopedia of Translation Studies*, "Subtitles, sometimes referred to as captions, are transcriptions of film or TV dialogue, presented simultaneously on the screen. "Almost every form of video requires subtitling in multiple languages. International markets are of critical importance for the success of educational and entertainment video content, and as such, subtitling is an essential part of reaching these international markets. Subtitling involves much more than a simple translation. It involves a highly technical and precise process to ensure that the audience is able to understand every scene with spoken or written content. The text versions of the spoken word of a video or a film are the subtitle or the caption. Subtitling allows the content of audio and video to be accessible not only to those who cannot hear the audio but also to those who may not be fluent in the language in which the audio is presented.

Subtitling is a part of multimedia translation and plays an important role in helping clients reach diverse, global audience. Studios, broadcasters, government, web casters, film and TV producers and syndicators are all required to capture and reflect content with the highest degrees of accuracy. Linguistically, two types of subtitling can be distinguished, one is intralingual subtitling and the other is interlingual subtitling. Intralingual subtitling includes "subtitling of domestic programs for the deaf and hard of hearing, subtitling of foreign-language programs for language learners. Intralingual subtitling is vertical, in the sense that it involves taking speech down in writing, changing mode but not language. Interlingual subtitling is diagonal, in the sense that the subtitler crosses over from speech in one language to writing in another, thus changing mode and language." (Gottlieb, 1992)

In this section, Interlingual subtitling is mainly discussed. As a rule, subtitles are placed at the bottom of the picture and are either centered or left-aligned. All subtitling work follows rigorous quality guidelines like as follows:

Synchronized: The caption or the subtitle should appear at exactly the same time that audio would be available.

Equivalent: Content should be equivalent to that of the spoken word.

Accessible: Content should be easily available and accessible to those who need it.

Selection: Proper selection of the most appropriate translator is needed for the project.

Subtitling is a highly specialized craft and quite different from standard textual translation. The mission of the subtitling translator is to render speech into a reading format on a visual medium. The audience need to read and understand the flow of the story and match what they hear. It involves an audio-visual medium and literary medium simultaneously. Therefore various constraints exist in such mission. Generally speaking, subtitling are governed by the constraints as follows.

**1) Time constraint**: It is also called the constraint of reading speed (or duration). Subtitling is the written translation of the spoken language (source language) of a television program or film into the language of the viewing audience (the target language); the translated text usually appears in one or two lines at the foot of the screen simultaneously with the dialogue or narration in the source language. For printing materials, we can reread the part which we could not understand at first glance or which has been presented before. However, we cannot reread the subtitles which we did not understand, because subtitles disappear nearly immediately after the end of speeches. The appearance and disappearance of each subtitle should coincide roughly with the beginning and end of the corresponding speeches, therefore, a subtitle can be kept on the screen for only several seconds. Therefore, the subtitling translator should take into account of time or reading speed. In order to satisfy this need, the subtitler can modulate the sentence structures, changing from passive and negative sentences to active and affirmative sentences, from long sentences to short ones, and from complex sentences to simple ones.

❖ Cathy: Isabella, don't you see what he's been doing? He's been using you, to be near me, to smile at me behind your back, to try to rouse something in my heart that's dead! (from *Wuthering Heights*)

凯西:伊莎贝拉,你难道不懂他在玩什么花样吗? 他一直在利用你,利用你来接近我,他背着你冲我笑,试图从我心里唤起那种已经熄灭的感情!

**Comments** In the original speech, we can find there are three infinitive verb phrases and an attributive clause; they are "*to be near me*", "*to smile at me behind your back*" and "*to try to rouse something in my heart that's dead*". If we just follow the original structure, the version will be lengthy and complicated, in the result that the version does not synchronize the sound and images. This will probably influence the viewer's understanding and the effects of the film. So the subtitle translator skillfully changes the sentence structure to overcome the time constraint.

**2) Spatial constraint**: The physical size of the medium, a TV or cinema screen, can only fit a maximum of two lines of text of limited length in each subtitle without impinging unacceptably on the picture on the screen. Considering the viewer's reading speed, some subtitle translators suggest that there should be only one line of Chinese subtitle each time, and the number of Chinese characters should be no more that 13 or 14.

❖ Ashley: Well, isn't it enough that you gathered every other man's heart today? You always had mine. You cut your teeth on it. (from *Gone with the Wind*)

阿希礼:今天你取得那么多男人的心,还不够吗? 我的心总是你的。

**Comments** Generally speaking, some redundant words like "you know", "get it", "well", "you see", "as I say", "I mean", "ok", "yeah" and the kinds of the like can be omitted in subtitling. So we can find that this subtitle, on the one hand, leaves out the word "*well*" because of the limits of time and space. On the other hand, the subtitle translator employs the method of omission to leave out the sentence "*You cut your teeth on it*" because it has the same meaning as the sentence "*You always had mine.*" As a result, the space is saved and language is more vivid.

**3) Cultural constraint**: Subtitling is quite different from standard textual translation in which such methods as footnotes and endnotes can be used to provide explanations of concepts and ideas that don't exist in English. However some other strategies like adaptation and assimilation should be used in subtitling.

❖ Classmate A: You can lead a blonde to water, but you can't make her drink.
  同学甲：你得到她的人也不会得到她的心。

**Comments** The original sentence is an idiom, which means that someone tries to win a pretty girl's favor, however the opposite side dose not necessarily accept the chasing. The subtitle translator cannot literally translate the phrases "*lead a blonde to water*" and "*make her drink*". Therefore, the method of adaptation can be used here to present the implication in Chinese version 你得到她的人也不会得到她的心。

❖ Legend tales of legendary warrior whose Kung Fu skills with the stuff of legend. He traveled the land in search of worthy foes. (from *Kung Fu Panda*)
  传说中有个传奇侠客，他的武功出神入化，浪迹江湖，一路行侠仗义。

❖ Then he spoke, "Enough talk! Let's fight!" (from *Kung Fu Panda*)
  他语出惊人："少废话！拿命来！"

**Comment** The two subtitles come from Kung Fu Panda(功夫熊猫), in which in the first subtitle, there are some phrases like "*stuff of legend*" and "*in search of worthy foes*" which cannot be literally translated into 东西, 寻找 and 值得一战的敌人. Instead very Chinese phrases like 出神入化, 行侠仗义 are used to convey the Chinese Kung Fu. In the second subtitle, the scene tells that Panda Po is determined to do or die after eating. If the subtitle employs the original verbal meaning, it is neither to fit the situation of the speech nor to reflect Po's knight-errant bearing. Therefore the subtitle translator uses the appropriate Chinese phrases 少废话, 拿命来 for Chinese viewers.

Because of the above mentioned constraints, especially time and spatial constraints, the subtitle translator has to take into account of the reading speed and the physical size. Let us compare and analyze the two versions of each subtitle below and understand the principles of conciseness and immediate comprehensibility to translate English-Chinese film and TV subtitles.

❖ He's probably not there, but if I don't at least look, I'll always wonder about it. (from *Sleepless in Seattle*)
  Normal translation：他也许没来，但至少我应该去看看，否则我会老想着这件事。
  Subtitling：他也许没来，但我不看不死心。

- ❖ Yes, I would just like to know where I could get this man's address. (from *Sleepless in Seattle*)
  Normal translation：是的，我想知道如何才能得到这个人的地址。
  Subtitling：我想知道他的地址。
- ❖ And for a while I could not enter, for the way was barred to me. (from *Rebecca*)
  Normal translation：由于大门深锁，一时不得其门而入。
  Subtitling：由于大门紧锁，一时无法进入。

**Comments** When comparing the subtitles and the literal translations, it can be seen that the language used is quite different. While subtitles are less formal in language, the language used in literal version is more formal. This characteristic reflects the way languages can be used—which can be written or oral. Considering scenes where their is a lot of information to be processed by the translator—it is a fact that the language used for subtitling needs to be more compact—it occurs not only because of space limits but also due to time constraints. Subtitles must generally compact all the information in only one line of about 10 Chinese characters each and the time available for display depends mainly on the speed at which the material is spoken. In order to know what information is more relevant, the translator needs to take into account that the film viewers also receive non-verbal information from the images. That imformation can never be disregarded. Thus, speech redundancy can and must be extremely concise if we do not want the audience to spend the whole film only reading subtitles. In addition, subtitling is sometimes designed to give the impression that the actors whom the audience sees are actually speaking in the target language. Therefore, it favours more colloquial language, and tends to be more "natural" and spontaneous.

### 7.3.3 Dubbing 配音翻译

Another core multimedia translation service is dubbing. Dubbing, including the precise dubbing of spoken audio content in video productions, refers to the method in which a foreign dialogue is adjusted to the mouth and movements of the actor or actress in the film and thus makes it familiar to the target audience. Its basic purpose is making the audience feel as if they are listening to actors actually speaking the target language.

Dubbing is widely used in markets where subtitling doesn't fully accomplish the producers' objectives and is a more universal method of converting video productions for international markets. As it does not require reading, it is ideal for children and less educated markets. Many video production companies prefer dubbing as it more closely reflects the experience of the original production. Dubbing is also a highly technical multimedia translation service, as it requires specialized software to ensure that the lip-syncing is as close as possible to the original production.

Dubbing is used to describe the replacement of one sound track whether music, dialogue, sound effects, natural sound, etc. by another. The technique is used in the production of both audiovisual and audio media. Dubbing is usually the post-production activity which allows flexibility in "editing" the audio component of the video. Dubbing includes various activities like the addition of music, the addition of sound effects, the addition of dialogue, the omission of poorly recorded audio, the re-recording of the entire dialogue, narration and music.

Another major form of dubbing is "language transfer", that is, translation of audiovisual works. Dubbing here means the replacement of the dialog of the movie and narration of the foreign or source language into the language of the viewing audience. Dubbing is extensively used for translating other-language television programs or movies. Dubbing of films is linked with replacing the language of the "original" film with the dubbed language. This is closely related to translation. First, the language of the original film is removed. The soundtrack of another language is superimposed on the film, depending on lip synchronization.

In order to seem "natural", the translation of dubbing must match as closely as possible with the movements of the lips of the speaker on the screen. Moreover, there should be a strict equivalence of not only of voice but also of gender and age. Another requirement of successful dubbing is the compatibility of the dubber's voice with the facial and body expressions showed on the screen. Lip-synchronization is very essential in dubbing in. It is dufficult to find target language words that match the source language lip movements. This becomes more evident when speakers are shown in close-up. Rather than locating meaning in each sentence, if translation aims at conveying the general tone of each scene there will be more difficult to find appropriate words for lip-synchronization.

To put it simply, dubbing consists of replacing SL verbal elements on the soundtrack wiht TL ones. It is a multiplex process in which the foreign dialogue is adjusted to the mouth movements of the actor in the film. The viewers then repress all awareness of the possibility of an incorrect translation and in fact, they forget that there has been any translation at all. Unlike subtitling, dubbing is essentially teamwork, involving not only a dubbing translator but also a number of actors and technical personnel, which is why dubbing costs are considerably higher than those of subtitling.

According to Goris(1993), the disadvantages for dubbing include "the cost and time factor, loss of authenticity where the original voices are replaced by those of a limited number of actors, impossibility of maintaining the illusion of authenticity given the presence of visual remainders of the foreignness of the setting and characters and—most importantly—the necessity to lip synchronization, which places heavy demands on the translator and is a major constraint in terms of omitting incomprehensible or insignificant elements." Generally speaking, the translator should take into account of the following aspects in dubbing.

**1) Lip-synchronization.** One of the major constraints of dubbing is that of synchrony, or "the agreement between the articulatory movements seen and the sounds heard". While the audience, to some extent, expect movements and sounds to match, the constraint of synchrony varies according to the camera angle and is greater in close-ups. The demand of synchrony also varies across cultures.

❖ Mrs. Bennet: Ten thou-! Isn't it fortunate to have two eligible young men coming to the neighborhood? Perhaps one of them will fall on love with your Charlotte.
Charlotte Lucas: Oh! Not if he sees Jane or Lizzie first!
Mrs. Lucas: You may not have beauty, my lamb, but, you have character…)
(from *Pride and Prejudice*)
班奈特太太:一万……啊,来这么两个可挑选的年轻人做邻居真是好事。也许有一位会看中你的夏洛特!
夏洛特·卢卡斯:噢,我可没简和莉齐漂亮。
卢卡斯太太:也许你不算漂亮,孩子,可你有个性……

**Comments** In this dialogue, we can find that Charlotte's answer is an elliptical sentence, which could be translated into 噢,如果(他)先看到简和莉齐就不会(看中我)了 in textual translation. But when the context is taken into account, such translation is very natural and simple. Most importantly, lip synchronization is a very necessary factor. Therefore, it is not only easy for the subtitler to match the mouth movements, but also proper to accord with the actors' manner and features.

**2) Voice and image synchrony.** The synchronization for voices and images is another element that the translator should take into account. This is because films and TV are visual and animated media in which what the actor or actress speaks should synchronize what he or she does. In this case, the viewer will feel as if the voice and the image are accordant.

❖ Mr. Darcy: If the dragon returns, then, George will know how to deal with him.
(from *Pride and Prejudice*)
达西先生:那恶龙要再来,降龙将军自有办法。

**Comments** Here the word dragon refers to Mr. Collins whom everybody is fed up with, and George refers to what Mr. Darcy who tastily calls himself to indicate that he is able to help Liz (Elizabeth) deal with Collins. The two words are respectively translated into "恶龙" and "降龙将军" because the dragon has often been associated with evil in the western culture, instead of 龙 in Chinese culture, and George, instead of a ordinary name, is the hero in the west who was the slaying of a dragon, as in the story of St. George in medieval legend and saved the Libya King's daughter. Actually, it is impossible to convey the legend to the viewer for there is any note in film to explain it. Therefore, it is necessary to add the Chinese character 恶 before 龙 because Chinese readers will have an association when reading 龙, and thus "*dragon*" and "*George*" have the opposite relationship. In the dialogue, Mr. Darcy, when mentioning the word "George", put his both hands on the chest to show that he could help Liz. So the versions 恶龙 and 降龙将军 are very appropriate not only to convey the actual meaning, but also to satisfy the need of voice and image synchronization.

**3) Cultural constraints in dubbing.** "In a dubbed film we constantly aware through images and non-matching mouth movements of the presence of a foreign language and culture," (Fawcett, 1996) which suggests that "the treatment of culture-specific material, including dialect, will pose serious problems in this context, and that functional approaches may not always offer the right kind of solution." (Baker, 2004) Like subtitling, dubbing cannot use such methods as footnotes and endnotes to provide explanations of concepts and ideas.

❖ Master Wu Gui: I've had a vision Tai Lung will return. (from *Kung Fu Panda*)
乌龟大师:我预感到黑豹太郎将重出江湖。

**Comments** In the subtitle, the translator, on the one hand, skillfully uses Chinese words 黑豹 to show the associative meaning of evil in the film. On the other hand, the word "*return*" is translated into 重出江湖, which not only answers for the status of Wushu master, Wu Gui, but presents Chinese culture, that is, what a Wushu master should say in the action movie.

In short, subtitling is, together with dubbing, the main form of translation or "language transfer" in television and film, which is increasingly developing into a global medium in a world. When we want to study audiovisual translation (AVT), a term used here to cover subtitling and dubbing as well as the wide variety of translational activity they entail, which is undoubtedly one of the commonest forms of translation encountered in everyday life in contemporary societies, we should fully consider their constraints. Meanwhile, their advantages and disadvantages should be taken into account. Subtitling is not expensive, does not take a very long time, and the original soundtrack is preserved. Do not forget that it may have a role in language learning, and is better for the hard-of-hearing, the deaf, immigrants and tourists. Its disadvantages include the greater loss of information due to compression, and the attention of the audience is split between image, soundtrack, and subtitles. As for dubbing, it does not distract attention from image, and has less reduction of the original dialogue compared to subtitling. Also it is better for children and people with poor reading skills. Its disadvantages include high cost, more time taking, loss of the original soundtrack, and the voices of dubbing actors can become repetitive after a while.

**7.3.4 Film Translation in Brief 电影翻译简介**

Film translation started way back with silent movies. However, during the era of silent movies, translation was relatively easy. The so-called inter-titles interrupted the course of a film every few minutes, so the target language titles were easily translated and put in place of the original ones. The problem arose with the appearance of "talkies" in the late 1920s. Initially, the American film companies produced the same film in various language versions using the same set and scenario but different directors and actors. However, this was a very costly option. Moreover, the films did not win over the public and were of poor artistic quality. The problem was solved by France where studios were founded to produce dubbed versions of films instead.

When it comes to translating foreign films, there are many reasons that contributed to the fact that France decided to adopt dubbing. First, the people of France always felt that the country had a cultural mission within the film art form. The French were deeply concerned about the purity of their culture and they always wanted to protect it from every foreign influence. Second, French was historically a successful instrument of political and cultural centralization. Moreover many French speakers believe that their language is superior to any other language and hence film translation or dubbing is important.

With France came Hollywood in film translation and it occupied a major potion of the film translation market. Hollywood, in order to avoid any interruption in its dominance of the international film market, took up voice dubbing and subtitling.

The introduction of talkies exerted a far-reaching influence over both larger and smaller countries. As film production costs rose, it became increasingly difficult for smaller countries to export their productions. These countries were so limited to their small domestic markets that their home production decreased and led to a rise in film imports. With film imports, dubbing of films in regional languages increased. Larger countries tended to dub imported foreign productions, while smaller ones settled on subtitling.

While initially the American (Hollywood) rigned over the film market, the European countries like France, Italy, Germany and Spain in 1950s took protective measures to lessen the influence of American films in their territories. For instance, import quotas were imposed special taxes to protect domestic production. At the same time, domestic film production in regional languages in France, Italy, Germany and Spain was supported by the government through various subsidies and loans. By that time it was evident that film had become an extremely influential and profitable medium. Soon, countries like India, China, and other South Asian countries moved into film production and translation.

Film translation plays a vital role in making people realize the importance of culture and language and respect the culture of other countries. This is one of the easiest way to shrink the virtual world beyond one could imagine and break the barriers with the art of language. Whether domesticating or internationalizing in its approach, any form of audiovisual translation or the transmission of cultural values in film translation plays an important role in developing both national identities and national stereotypes.

## 7.3.5 Exercises 练习

**I. Compare the following different translation versions and make comments.**

| Film titles | Mainland Versions | Hong Kong Versions | Taiwan Versions |
|---|---|---|---|
| The English Patient | 英国病人 | 别问我是谁 | 英伦情人 |
| The Pianist | 钢琴师 | 钢琴战曲 | 战地琴人 |
| Brave Heart | 勇敢的心 | 惊世不了情 | 英雄本色 |
| American Beauty | 美国丽人 | 美丽有罪 | 美国心,玫瑰情 |
| Scent of a Woman | 闻香识女人 | 女人香 | 女人的芳香 |
| Legends of the Fall | 燃情岁月 | 燃情岁月/秋日传奇 | 真爱一世情 |
| Mr. Holland's Opus | 霍兰先生的乐章 | 生命因你而动听 | 春风化雨 |
| Dead Man Walking | 死囚上路 | 死囚168小时 | 越过死亡线 |
| Seven | 七宗罪 | 七宗罪 | 火线通缉令 |
| Good Will Hunting | 好人威尔·杭廷 | 骄阳似我 | 心灵捕手 |
| Shakespeare in Love | 恋爱中的莎士比亚 | 写我深情 | 莎翁情史 |
| Cinema Paradise | 天堂电影院 | 星光伴我心 | 新天堂乐园 |
| Pretty Woman | 漂亮女人 | 风月俏佳人 | 麻雀变凤凰 |
| A Beautiful Mind | 美丽心灵 | 有你终身美丽 | 美丽境界 |
| Meet the Parents | 拜见岳父岳母大人 | 非常外父拣女婿 | 门当父不对 |
| A Room with a View | 看得见风景的房间 | 翡冷翠之恋 | 窗外有蓝天 |
| Ghost | 幽灵 | 人鬼情未了 | 第六感生死恋 |
| Mission Impossible | 谍中谍 | 职业特工队 | 不可能完成的任务 |
| The Horse Whisperer | 马语者 | 情深说话未曾讲 | 轻声细语 |

**II. Passage translation.**

Multi-medial texts used by Reiss to refer to a subsidiary text-type which supplements Reiss' basic text typology (expressive texts, informative texts and operative texts). The multi-medial category consists of texts in which the verbal content is supplemented by elements in other media; however, all such texts will also simultaneously belong to one of the other, main text-types. Reiss argues that this text-type forms a superstructure over the other three, as the special requirements of this type take precedence over whatever basic text type a given text otherwise belongs to. Songs, comic strips, plays, and writing for radio or television are all examples of this type, and the translator of such texts will need to ensure that the translation is equally suited as the original for use in the relevant medium. (From *Dictionary of Translation Studies* by Shutteworth & Cowie)

# Chapter 8: Some Terms in Translation Studies and Their Understanding
# 一些翻译术语及其理解

## 8.1 Literal Translation and Free Translation 直译与意译

Speaking of translation methods, people naturally think about the two methods "literal translation" and "free translation" in translation history. The translators and scholars in the world are constantly exploiting them. You may ask what literal translation is, what free translation is and how we distinguish between them. Actually the discussion is going on in translation field. Some scholars think that all the translators should stick to the two methods when translating, some suppose that there are utterly no methods in translation, and different people have different understandings of the methods.

Actually, *literal translation* is "a notion which has for many centuries been at the heart of most translation controversies, where it has been either staunchly defended against or vigorously attacked in favor of its rival, *free translation*. However, there is a certain amount of variation in the way this term is applied, as literal translation is sometimes understood as including the related notion of *word-for-word translation*. A literal translation can be defined in linguistic terms as a translation 'made on a level lower than is sufficient to convey the content unchanged while observing TL norms'". (Shuttleworth & Cowie, 2004:95) Catford (1969:25) argues that literal translation takes word-for-word translation as its starting point, although because of the necessity of conforming to TL grammar, the final TT may also display group-group or clause-clause equivalence. The term *metaphrase* put foreword by Dryden (1680/1989), is commonly used in translation studies, which is closely related to literal translation. It is defined as the process of "turning an author word by word, and line by line, from one language into another."

*Free translation* is a type of translation in which more attention is paid to producing a naturally reading TT than to preserving the ST wording intact; also known as *sense-for-sense translation*. Linguistically it can be defined as a translation "made on a level higher than is necessary to convey the content unchanged while observing TL norms" (Barkhudarov, 1969:1). In other words, the unit of translation in a free translation might be anything up to a sentence (or more) even if the content of the ST in question could be reproduced satisfactorily by translating on the word or group level. Furthermore, according to Catford it is a prerequisite of free translations that they should also be unbounded as regards the rank (or level) on which they are performed. Free translations are thus generally more "TL-oriented" than literal translations. (Shuttleworth & Cowie, 2004:63) *Paraphrase* put foreword by Dryden (1680/1989) is one of three methods of translating: imitation, metaphrase and paraphrase. "While imitation and metaphrase are the procedures which represent the two extremes of free and literal translation, paraphrase is conceived as a middle way between them." Paraphrase is defined as "translation with latitude, where the author is kept in view by the translator, so as never to be lost, but his words are not so strictly followed as his sense." (Shuttleworth & Cowie, 2004:121)

In China, translators and scholars also have different opinions about literal translation and free translation. Zhu Guangqian (朱光潜) said,"所谓"直译"是指依原文的字面翻译,有一字一句就译一字一句,而且字句的次第不更动。"(The so-called literal translation is to translate something literally, that is, the translation version will be definitely determined word for word, phrase for phrase, and the sequence of words and phrases will not be changed.) Mao Dun (茅盾) once said,"我以为所谓'直译'者也,倒并非一定是'字对字',一个不多,一个也不少。'直译'的意义就是不要歪曲了原作的面目,要能表达原作的精神。"(I think that the so-called literal translation is by no means the word-for-word translation, exactly judging by the words and phrases of the original. It should mean to express the original spirit without distorting the original features.) At the same time, there is a point of view against the two above-mentioned opinions. In 1951, Ba Jin(巴金)said,"我觉得翻译的方法其实只有一种,并没有'直译'和'意译'的分别。好的翻译应该都是'直译',也都是'意译'。(《翻译通报》,1951)" (I feel that there exists only one translation method. There is no distinction between "literal translation" and "free translation". The good translation should include both." Therefore, some scholars try to distinguish between them by changing the term from "free translation" into "liberal translation).

We think that the methods are present and very useful in translation, if we correctly define the two terms and properly employ them in translating. In our opinion, literal translation refers to the translation that a translator tries to keep the original form and meaning, including meaning, structure, style, figure of speech, etc. But it is not the word-for-word translation. Let us look at some English sentences for literal translation.

❖ to kill two birds with one stone 一石二鸟
 to shed crocodile tears 掉鳄鱼眼泪
 chain reaction 连锁反应

armed to the teeth 武装到牙齿

These phrases are very vivid and figurative. They are good examples for literal translation. It seems that the version is the word-for-word translation. But we can say that this is a coincidence, exactly speaking, this is one of the similarities between two languages and cultures. Because all the people own the same globe and resources and have experienced similar developing procedures, it is understandable and reasonable that they have certain similarities in some aspects. All English sentences, however, cannot possibly be translated like this. So the method of literal translation is used in one way. Sometimes we should employ the other way to deal with the original.

- We saw an acrobat standing on his head.
  我们看见一个杂技演员正站在他的头上。(word-for-word translation)
  我们看见一个杂技演员正在倒立。(literal translation)

Speaking of free translation, we think we had better use the word "liberal" instead of "free" because the definition of "free" is moving about at will, that is, translating at will or in one's own inclinations. As a matter of fact, a translator roughly expresses the original meaning, keeping the target language smoothly. But it is not the random translation.

- Don't cross the bridge till you get to it.
  到了桥边才过桥。(literal translation)

**Comments** This translation is difficult for Chinese to understand. So we have to use liberal translation to cope with it. Either of both versions below is much better: 不必担心过早。／不必自寻烦恼。

In actual translation, it is impossible for us only to use one method translating the original. And also it is very difficult for us to decide which is better, or worse. Let us analyze a couple of sentences.

- Don't lock the stable door after the horse has been stolen.
  不要等马被盗后, 才去锁厩门。(literal translation)
  不要贼走关门。(liberal translation)

- Smashing a mirror is no way to make an ugly person beautiful, nor is it a way to make social problems evaporate.
  砸镜子不能使丑八怪变漂亮, 也不能使社会问题烟消云散。(literal translation)
  砸镜子并不能解决实际问题。(liberal translation)

**Comments** We have found that in sentence 1, liberal translation is better than literal translation, but in sentence 2, literal translation is much better than free translation. How do we decide when to use literal or liberal? We probably follow such a principle "Translate literally, if possible, or appeal to liberal translation." Sometimes we can use the two methods together.

In short, the fundamental task of methodology of translation is how to take the advantages of the receptor language to have the original implication mood fully expressed, and at the same time keep the translation readable, faithful to the original both in essence and in form. It is an issue involving content and form. Translation is actually to emphasize appropriately approaching the original content while considering the form. Translation is to pursue formal correspondence with the original and to strive to reach correspondence in essential content. Translation is to realize the artistic form of the original and transfer the spirit of the original. Whether a translation is faithful to the original in all the aspects depends on the possibility of finding the closest, the most natural equivalent and depends on, to a great extent, a good command of the transformation of the kernel sentence and the choice of surface structure by a translator. In order to have this goal fully won, both literal and liberal translation should be simultaneously used. Any single one of the two will fail to work unless the source language and the target language are equivalent to a great extent like the above-mentioned examples. Let us compare a couple of sentences to find the advantages of literal and liberal methods.

❖ And I do not mistrust the future; I do not fear ①*what is ahead*. For our problems are ②*large*, but our ③*heart* is ④*larger*. ⑤*Our challenges are* ⑥*great*, but our will is greater. And if our flaws are ⑦*endless*, God's love is truly⑧ *boundless*.
Literal version：而我不是不相信未来；我不害怕①<u>即将来临的事情</u>。因为我们的问题是②<u>大的</u>，但是我们的③<u>心</u>④<u>更大</u>。⑤<u>我们的挑战</u>是⑥<u>大的</u>，但是我们的决心更大。如果我们的缺点是⑦<u>没完没了的</u>，上帝的爱是真正的⑧<u>无穷无尽的</u>。
Liberal version：我并非不信任未来；我不害怕①<u>我们面临的问题</u>。我们的问题②<u>很多</u>，但是我们的③<u>心胸</u>④<u>更宽广</u>。⑤<u>我们面临的挑战</u>⑥<u>很严峻</u>，但是我们的决心更大。如果我们的弊病⑦<u>层出不穷的话</u>，那么上帝的爱是真正的⑧<u>广袤无边</u>。

**Comments**: By comparison, liberal method can be used to flexibly choose words and phrases. As a result, the liberal method is much better than literal method.

❖ The mantle of your high office has been placed on your shoulder at a time when the world at large and this Organization are going through an exceptionally critical phase.
Literal version：正当全世界和本组织处于一个异常危机的时期中，这个崇高职务的重担落在了你的肩上。
Liberal version：整个世界和本组织正经历着一个异常危机的时期。在这样一个时期中，这个崇高职务的重担落在了你的肩上。

(冯庆华，《实用翻译教程》，上海外语教育出版社，2002)

**Comments**: Through comparison and analysis between source and target languages, it is obvious that the literal version is much better because the literal version retains the vivid and clear abstract of the original context, and maintains the original structural form.

## 8.2 Domesticating Translation and Foreignizing Translation 归化与异化

Domesticating translation and foreignizing translation are two terms used by Venuti (1995). *Domesticating Translation* (or domestication) is the translation strategy in which transparent, fluent style is adopted in order to minimize the strageness of the foreign text for TL readers. It "leaves the reader in peace, as much as possible, and moves the author towards him." (Schleiermacher, 1838/1963; Venuti, 1995:19-20) However, for Venuti the term domestication has negative connotations as it is identified with a policy common in dominant cultures which are aggressively monolingual, unreceptive to the foreign. Venuti argues that domestication is the predominant translation strategy in Anglo-American culture, and that this is consistent with the asymmetrical literary relations which generally exist between this and other cultures.

*Foreignizing translation* (or minoritizing translation) is a term used to designate the type of translation in which a TT is produced which deliberately breaks target conventions by retaining something of the foreignness of the original. It stresses that the translator "leaves the author in peace, as much as possible, and moves the reader towards him." (Schleiermacher, 1838/1963; Venuti 1995:19) It is adopted as the preferred translation strategy because it would represent "a strategic cultural intervention in the current state of world affairs" (Venuti, 1995:20) and challenge the mentality of the dominant culture which sought to suppress the foreignness (or otherness) of translated texts.

Translators and scholars also use the terms dissimilation and assimilation for domesticating translation and foreignizing translation. In fact, *dissimilation* (alienation) and *assimilation*, evolving from literal and liberal, are also two methods in translating, which are different from literal and liberal methods. The main difference is that the focus of the literal and liberal methods is how to deal with the form and meaning in the linguistic structural forms of the original, but the contribution of dissimilation and assimilation breakthrough the restriction of language and consider such aspects as language, culture and aesthetics. Literal translation and liberal translation lie in the value of language aspects. Dissimilation and assimilation base themselves upon the value in the cultural context. In other words, a translator is required to approach the author in dissimilation method, and employ the expressions the author uses, to convey the original content. In assimilation method, a translator is asked to come towards the target language readers, and apply to the expressions that they are accustomed to and like, to express the original content. Here are a couple of examples to compare. "To kill two birds with one stone" can be put into 一石二鸟. This method is called dissimilation method. If its version is 一箭双雕 or 一举两得, it is, we can say, the assimilation method. The version of "All roads lead to Rome" may be 条条大道通罗马 or 殊途同归, which belong to the different translation methods.

Early in the 1920s and 1930s of the last century in China, Mr. Lu Xun（鲁迅）put forward the advocate of alienation not assimilation. He said,"翻译必须有异国情调,就是所谓洋气。其实世界上也不会有完全归化的译文,倘有,就是貌合神离,从严辨别起来,它算不得翻译。"(Translation has to cover the foreign appeal, that is, the foreign flavor or style. There is, in fact, no completely domesticating or assimilating translation all over the world. It is, if any, seemingly in harmony but actually at variance. Strictly distinguished, it does not refer to translation.) Unfortunately, his advocate did not evoke emphasis to a great extent in translation field. Assimilation took the advantages for a long time. Since the reform and opening policy, with the coming of the Western translation theory, Chinese translators and scholars have had a new cognition between dissimilation and assimilation. They recognize the importance of dissimilation. As a matter of fact, form serves content, and certain form expresses certain content. The application of the expressions of the original can often express the original meaning accurately and thoroughly. Now a couple of examples are mentioned.

- ❖ I supposed I should be condemned in Hareton Earnshaw's heart, if not by his mouth, to the lowest pit in the infernal regions ... ( E. Bronte: *Wuthering Heights*)

  我想,哈雷顿·厄恩肖即便嘴里不说,心里也要诅咒我下到十八层地狱里去……

**Comments** At first looking, the translation of this sentence is very smooth and accurate in form and meaning. But if the reader is familiar with some common knowledge about religion, he or she will find the mistake the translator made. 十八层地狱 is the term used in Buddhism. The speaker, however, in the novel *Wuthering Heights* believes in Christianity. So the speaker cannot say the term like that. According to the method of dissimilation, the version of this sentence should be 我想,哈雷顿·厄恩肖即便嘴里不说,心里也要诅咒我下到地狱的最底层…… Language is the reflection of culture. A translator only follows the author's thought and expressive style by means of dissimilation, and he or she can fully reflect the cultural features and completely express the authentic meaning of the original.

- ❖ This hopeful young person soared into so pleasing a Cupid as to constitute the chief delight of the maternal part of the spectators.

  这个很有希望的年轻人就扮成极其讨人喜欢的插着翅膀的爱神丘比特。

**Comments**: In the West, Cupid is a pretty boy with wings who holds the bow and arrow by hands. He stands for love. Although the translator gave the explanation of the image "丘比特", he still translated the name into "丘比特" by transliteration. It is quite sure that many people now know about Cupid. If we employ the domesticating method of assimilation and put it into 月老 or something like that, the translation will lose cultural features of the original and will cause the cultural misconception or malposition (文化错觉或文化错位) to the reader.

❖ Unless you've an ace up your sleeve, we are dished.
    除非你有锦囊妙计,否则我们是输定了。

**Comments** The phrase in the original sentence, "*an ace up your sleeve*", is translated into 锦囊妙计, which is usually used in class as a good example for students. But judging from the method of dissimilation, a problem really exists in the translation. This is because the phrase "*an ace up your sleeve*" in English refers to the King card hidden in one's sleeve in gambling game in the Western countries. 锦囊妙计, however, is the schemes, stratagems or instructions sealed in a silk bag for dealing with an emergency in ancient Chinese battles or court strife. There is a great difference in the cultural background and implications between them. This will cause the reader to have different associations if we translate it from English to Chinese or from Chinese to English. Therefore the version of this sentence should be 除非你袖中藏有王牌,否则我们是输定了 by means of dissimilation.

In the process of translating, we cannot use only one method to deal with the original. We usually come across some gaps in translation because of linguistic and cultural differences. In this case, we may employ the other method, assimilation, to bridge these gaps, including lexical gaps and semantic gaps.

❖ Miss Sedley was almost as flurried at the act of defiance as Miss Jemima had been; for, consider, it was but one minute that she had left school, and the *impressions* of six years are not got over in that space of time. (W. M. Thackeray: Vanity Fair)
    赛特笠小姐看见这样大胆的行为,差不多跟吉米玛小姐一样吃惊。你想,她刚刚跨出校门一分钟,六年来受的**教诲**,哪里能在这么短短的一刹那给忘掉呢?

**Comments** Chinese definition of the word "*impressions*" in a dictionary is 印象,影响. If we, according to this definition, put it into 六年来得到的印象 or 六年来所受的影响, Chinese readers may feel it is not smooth enough, or fluent and natural enough. But the translator did not follow the definition in dictionaries, and thoroughly achieved mastery through a comprehensive study of the original and expressed it as 教诲 according to Chinese practice. The translation is very understandable and readable for Chinese readers. It is also a very good example of assimilation.

❖ High buildings and large mansions are springing up *like mushrooms* in Nanjing.
    在南京,高楼大厦**犹如雨后春笋般地**涌现。

**Comments** 雨后春笋 is a term commonly used in China, expressing something that develops so fast that it is just like bamboo shoots after a spring rain. This is a Chinese practice. But the term "*like mushrooms*" embodies British natural features and practice. If the term is translated into 犹如蘑菇般, by means of dissimilation, we believe that the reader cannot accept it, or even not understand it. Therefore we should follow such a principle: A translator tries to convey the foreign flavor or style; meanwhile he or she has to make sure whether the reader accepts the translation or not.

As for the two methods, some scholars suggest the use of dissimilation, and some stick to the other. As we know, the main task of translation is to faithfully reproduce the style and thought of the original, which naturally has strong foreign flavor and style, so much that a translator has to employ the method of dissimilation to fulfill the hard task. Also we have to apply to assimilation to bridge the gaps between two cultures. But we cannot over-assimilate Chinese translation. Here is an example to show over-assimilation.

❖ "Of course it may," said Angel. "Was it not proved nineteen hundred years ago, if I may trespass upon your domain a little?"

(T. Hardy: *Tess of the d'Urbervilles*)

"当然可以,"安琪说道,"一千九百年以前,不是有人做到了吗? 我这是班门弄斧了,请原谅。"

**Comments** Translating is conducted as a tool of communication. One of its purposes is to introduce a foreign culture to Chinese readers. So a translator should try to retain its culture when translating without over assimilation. Upon reading the Chinese set phrase 班门弄斧, a reader may associate it with the Chinese story about this set phrase. It seems that he or she reads a Chinese novel, not a foreign novel. This causes cultural infidelity(文化失真), that is, it is not true to the original.

To be honest, dissimilation and assimilation are two contradictory elements in one thing. They are the principle aspect and secondary aspect of the contradictions. We think that dissimilation is the principle aspect because of the need of our main task in translation, and assimilation becomes the secondary aspect because it is the method to clear the barriers between languages. Although they find their own positions, they are both important in translating; we cannot attend to one thing and lose sight of another. Generally speaking, we should follow the principles.

First, use dissimilation as possible as we can in translating. Generally speaking, the translation of formal and spiritual similarities is often the result of the method of dissimilation. Therefore, as a translator, dissimilation will be firstly used in translating.

❖ Second, there is the New York of the commuter—the city that is devoured by locusts each day and spat out each night. (E. B. White: *The Three New Yorks*)

其次是家住郊区、乘公交车到市内上班的人们的纽约——这座城市每到白天就被如蝗虫的人群吞噬进去,每到晚上又给吐出来。

**Comments** This sentence vividly describes the situation that the commuter in New York goes to work and goes back home. The writer compares the "*commuter*" to "*locusts*", which devours New York each day and spits it out each night. The language is vivid and figurative. In order to keep the form and spirit harmonious in translation, the translator successfully uses the method of dissimilation.

Second, if dissimilation does not completely express the meaning of the original or make it smooth, the practice of Chinese expressions can be considered to be used in Chinese versions.

❖ Among so many well-dressed and cultured people, the country girl felt *like a fish out of water*.

跟这么多穿着体面而又有教养的人呆在一起,这位乡下姑娘感到**很不自在**。

Comments  The phrase "*like a fish out of water*" means uncomfortable because one is in a strange place among people who are very different from oneself. If we translate it into 像一条离开水的鱼, the reader may not understand what the phrase means, and the version brings about different understandings and strays from the original meaning. We can say it cannot really convey its true meaning to the reader. So we might as well employ the Chinese habit of expressing 很不自在 or 很不适应.

Third, if dissimilation cannot be applied any more in translating, we may abstain from the form, that is, the surface meaning, but convey the deep meaning of the original.

❖ With determination, with luck, and the help from lots of good people, I was able to *rise from the ashes*.

凭着我的决心,我的运气,还有许多善良人们的帮助,我终于**获得新生**。

Comments  "*Rise from the ashes*" is an English set phrase, which comes from an Egyptian tale. If we stand firm for one method and translate this phrase into 从灰烬中再生 by dissimilation, the reader will be at loss when reading. In this case, 获得新生, by accommodation, is much better.

❖ "Oh! Tell us about her, Auntie," cried Imogen, "I can just remember her. She's the *skeleton* in the family cupboard, isn't she?"

"She wasn't much of a *skeleton* as I remember her," murmured Euphemia, "extremely well covered." (J. Galsworthy: *In Chancery*)

"哦,给我们讲一讲她的事儿吧,好姑姑,"伊莫根嚷嚷道,"我几乎记不得她了,她是咱们家衣橱里的**骷髅**,丑得见不得人,是吗?"

"我记得她并不像**骷髅**,"尤菲米娅低声说,"肌肉挺丰满的。"

(选自周方珠,《翻译多元论》,中国对外翻译出版公司,2004)

Comments  In this example, the word "*skeleton*" appears twice. The first one is used in the English allusion "*the skeleton in the family cupboard*", whose version is 家丑. The second one is used to describe her specific appearance and image, meaning 骷髅. Here we can use neither dissimilation nor assimilation. This is because the reader will be at loss if the version of "*the skeleton in the family cupboard*" is 家丑, and it is very hard for him or her to understand it and the English allusion will lose its implications when it is translated into 衣橱里的骷髅. Therefore we try to accommodate it to circumstances and put the sentence "*She's the skeleton in the family cupboard*" into 她是咱们家衣橱里的骷髅,丑得见不得人. In this way both the rhetoric effect and allusion implication are kept. At the same time, the national flavor or style is retained in the version.

## 8.3 Exercises 练习

**Passage translation.**

### My Life in the Country

None of us will ever forget our first winter. We were buried under five feet of snow from December through March. While one storm after another blasted huge drifts up against the house and barn, we kept warm inside burning our own wood, eating out apples and loving every minute of it.

When spring came, it brought two floods. First the river overflowed, covering much of our land for weeks. Then the growing season began, swamping us under wave after wave of produce. Our freezer filled up with cherries, raspberries, strawberries, asparagus, peas, beans and corn. Then our canned goods shelves and cupboards began to grow with preserves, tomato juice, grape juice, plums, jams and jellies. Eventually, the basement floor disappeared under piles of potatoes, squash and pumpkins, and the barn began to be filled with apples and pears. It was amazing.

The next year we grew even more food and managed to get through the winter on firewood that was mostly from our own trees and only 100 gallons of heating oil. At that point I began thinking seriously about quitting my job and starting to freelance. The timing was terrible. By then, Shawn and Amy, our oldest girls were attending expensive Ivy League Schools and we had only a few thousand dollars in the bank. Yet we kept coming back to the same question: Will there ever be a better time? The answer, decidedly, was no, and no—with my employer's blessings and half a year's pay in accumulated benefits in my pocket—off I went.

(Jim Doherty, *Exploring Through Writing*, 2nd edition, Cambridge University Press, 1998)

## 8.4 Semantic Translation and Communicative Translation 语义翻译和交际翻译

Semantic translation and communicative translation are two modes of translation put foreword by Newmark (1981/1988:22). *Semantic translation* means that the translator attempts, within the bare syntactic and semantic constraints of the TL, to reproduce the precise contextual meaning of the author. A semantic translation consequently tends to strive to reproduce the form of the original as closely as TL norms will allow; furthermore, no effort is made to shift ST into a target cultural context. Greater attention is paid to rendering the author's original thought-processes in TL than to attempting to re-interpret ST in a way which the translator considers more appropriate for the target setting; a semantic translation will therefore treat the original words as sacred, even if this requires reproducing inconsistencies, ambiguities and errors. Semantic translation is usually appropriate for literary, technical and scientific texts, as well as other contexts where the language of ST is as important as the content. (Shuttleworth & Cowie, 2004:151)

Communicative translation means that the translator attempts to produce the same effect on the TL readers as was produced by the original on the SL readers. This means that in communicative translation the emphasis should be on conveying the message of the original in a form which conforms to the linguistic, culture and pragmatic conventions of TL rather than mirroring the actual words of ST as closely as is possible without infringing the TL norms. When producing a communicative translation, the translator is permitted greater freedom to interpret ST and will consequently smooth over irregularities of style, remove ambiguities and even correct the author's factual errors, and in doing so will limit the semantic potential of ST by seeking to make TT fulfill one specific communicative function which is determined by the type of TL reader envisaged. Communicative translation would be appropriate for journalistic writing, textbooks, public notices and indeed most non-literary genres. (Shuttleworth & Cowie, 2004:22)

❖ We shall fight him by land, we shall fight him by sea, we shall fight him in the air...

Version 1: 我们将在地面与他作战,我们将在海上与他作战,我们将在空中与他作战……

Version 2: 我们将在地面、海上、空中与他作战……

**Comments** It is obvious that version 1 is semantic translation and version 2 belongs to communicative translation. But the first is much better because the original came from Churchill's speech in June 22nd, 1941 and he used parallelism, which manifests majestic vigor of the original and conveys the same effect on the reader.

## 8.5 Formal Equivalence and Dynamic Equivalence 形式对等和动态对等

Formal equivalence and dynamic equivalence are put foreword by Nida (1964). *Formal equivalence* is the quality of a translation in which the features of the form of the source text have been mechanically reproduced in the receptor language. Nida proposed his categorization in the context of Bible translation, and in many respects it offers a more useful distinction than the traditional notions of free and literal translation. The aim of a translator who is striving for formal equivalence is to allow ST to speak in its own terms rather than attempting to adjust it to the circumstances of the target culture. The frequent result of such strategies is of course that, because of structural differences between SL and TL, a translation of this type distorts the grammatical and stylistic patterns of the receptor language, and distorts message. For this reason it is frequently necessary to include explanatory notes to help the target reader. Like its converse dynamic equivalence, formal equivalence represents a general orientation rather than an absolute technique, so that between the two opposite extremes there are any number of intervening grades, all of which represent acceptable methods of translation. However, a general tendency towards formal rather than dynamic equivalence is characterized by, for example, a concern for accuracy and a preference for retaining the original wording wherever possible. In spite of its apparent limitations, however, formal equivalence is sometimes the most appropriate strategy to follow. (Shuttleworth & Cowie, 2004:61)

*Dynamic equivalence* is the quality which characterizes a translation in which the message of the original text has been so transported into the receptor language that the response of the receptor is essentially like that of the original receptors (Nida & Taber, 1969/1982:200). In other words, a dynamically equivalent translation is one which has been produced in accordance with the threefold process of analysis(分析), transfer(转移) and restructuring(重组); formulating such a translation will entail such procedures as substituting TL items which are more culturally appropriate for obscure ST items, making linguistically implicit ST information explicit, and building in a certain amount of redundancy(冗余信息) to aid comprehension. In a translation of this kind one is therefore not so concerned with matching the receptor-language message with the source-language message; the aim is more to relate the receptor to modes of behavior relevant within the context of his own culture. (Shuttleworth & Cowie, 2004:47)

❖ In the country of the blind, the one-eyed man is king.
　　Version 1：蜀中无大将,廖化充先锋。
　　Version 2：盲人眼里,独眼为王。

**Comments** Version 1 belongs to dynamic equivalence, which is identified in terms of the degree to which the receptors of the message in the receptor language respond to it in substantially the same manner as the receptors in the source language. Version 2 is equivalent in form and sense. We can say that both versions can be used, but there exists a question that whether foreignizing or domesticating method is chosen. As far as the first version is concerned, the reader will probably think that the westerner also knows the characters in *Three Kingdoms* or *Romance of The Three Kingdoms*(《三国演义》) quite well and the message of the original is lost although it is a acceptable translation. About version 2, it is not only to convey the deep meaning of the original, but also is understandable. This example tells us that formal equivalence or dynamic equivalence has its own limits and we constantly consider the reader's reception and the original meaning in adopting translation methods.

## 8.6 Flexibility and Accuracy 灵活与准确

About the two terms, translators and scholars have various descriptions and opinions, but Mr. Jin Di(金堤)gives more wholly descriptions in 1989. He takes it what accuracy does not equal indiscriminate copy suggests there must be flexible treatment in translation. The chief difficulty lies just here: while one is to be flexible, he must completely transfer the original content and aptly represent the original thoughts and feelings as well. It is just because of this, too, that one is necessitated to exert himself to learn and research it.

Flexibility is a relative concept. It is rigidity in translation if one preaches the exact equivalent in lexical system between two languages and urges formulaic equivalence between different syntactic systems. Mechanical ways of translation cannot lead a correct transfer of the original content, so the translative flexibility is by no means an adornment that we may as well without it as with it but an indispensable means used to reach the aim of accuracy.

> ❖ Poverty is often *off the beaten track*. It always has been. The ordinary tourist never left the main *highway*, and today he rides *interstate turnpikes*. He does not go into the valleys of Pennsylvania where <u>the towns look like movie sets of Wales in the thirties</u>. He does not see the company houses in rows, the rutted roads (the poor always have bad roads whether they live in the city, in towns, or on farms), and everything is black and dirty. And even if he were to pass through such a place by accident, the tourist would not meet the unemployed men in the bar or the women coming home from a runaway sweatshop.
> 
> （注：选自《新编英语教程》，上海外语教育出版社，2003.46）
> 贫穷常常<u>无人问津</u>，但却永远存在。在过去一般游客决不会离开<u>主干道</u>，而如今只驱车<u>穿梭于州际之间</u>。他不会进入宾夕法尼亚谷地<u>去参观破旧不堪的村庄，它们看上去很像20世纪30年代威尔斯的电影布景</u>；不去参观那一排排公司雇员的住房、坎坷不平的土路（穷人不管居住在城镇还是农场，其道路总是很糟糕的）以及任何污黑肮脏的东西。即使碰巧走过这样的地方，游客也不会会晤在酒吧里喝酒的失业男人，也不会拜访从<u>榨取血汗的工厂</u>下班回家的妇女。

**Comments** We find it little difficult to understand the underlined parts in the original. If we render them exactly on the basis of literal meaning, though the Chinese version follows the principle of accuracy, the reader probably feels confused about them. The writer uses synonyms like "*track*", "*turnpikes*" and "*highway*" for the sake of figure of speech. We, however, translate literally. "*The towns look like movie sets of Wales in the thirties*" is not hard for us to understand superficially, but we should know that in the 1930s, there was disastrous unemployment in South Wales, and after World War I Wales was a depressed area with a third of the population on relief. Movie sets are the furniture, scenery, etc., used for making moving pictures. Here the author means that the towns in the valleys of Pennsylvania are shabby and dilapidated. Therefore we have to exert the translative flexibility in translation just like the version in order to reach the aim of accuracy.

From the above-mentioned example, it is easy for us to find that the principle of flexibility consists precisely in sensitively discerning minute changes and rendering this sort of linguistic transformation really agreeable with laws of language in the transformation between two languages, without following some rigid, simple formulas. While linguistic phenomena are ever changing, there must be laws that govern the changes since language is an instrument for social communication, only that they are very subtle and complicated, and not capable of being covered with several formulas. The reason that so far machine translation has been applicable only in a very limited area, and that the electronic brain has not been capable of fulfilling such tasks as literary translation lies exactly in the fact that it has not been able to know well the complex laws in linguistic transfer although it is capable of no less than 100 million calculations per second and of helping humans go up into the sky and down into the earth. It is the human brain that is able to reflect laws as truthfully as possible by giving full play to the flexible spirit in the practice of translation although it is not necessarily capable of giving a complete revelation of the concrete laws. The fundamental reason that translation is endowed with both scientificalness and artistry resides precisely here.

Not restricted by any ready translated expressions, one is to bring TL positive factors into full play so that he will be able to choose the words and expressions that can really express the original intention; this is the meaning of flexibility in translation. Only by doing this can one arrive at accuracy.

## 8.7 Fuzziness and Accuracy 模糊与精确

Linguistic fuzziness and accuracy in translation are contradictory but dialectically identical. Both exist and develop with each other, and push language itself forward. Fuzziness is a kind of property of a language and objective reality. Accuracy is the translators' aim. This kind of relationship between them should be analyzed, and should be better studied because they play a great part in translation theory and practice.

To begin with, we should know that some terms, such as ambiguity, polysemy and generality in language are different from linguistic fuzziness. It exists in all the aspects such as phonetics, words and phrases, sentences, and even texts. It greatly influences the quality of translation. All the differences of above-mentioned terms and various aspects in linguistic fuzziness should be fully considered in practice so as to make the translated version greatly apt and accurate. Meanwhile, the objectivity of fuzziness in language provokes us into thinking about some theoretical studies and practice in translation. The fuzziness in a text is often unnoticed. Our goal in translation is to decode the fuzzy points of a discourse, and its method is the context analysis.

❖ They soon became good friends.

❖ He gave me a ring.

**Comments** In the first sentence, the word "*they*" is entitled to generality because it generalizes a kind of people or things. But on the certain circumstance, it may possess the nature of specificity, which can refer to female or male, children or adults. And the words "*soon*" and "*good*" in sentence one have the property of fuzziness because we do not know how soon or how good they are. Both notions remain a matter of unclear or subtle meaning in extension.

In the second sentence, ambiguity exists because this sentence can be rendered into two versions, 他给了我一个戒指 or 他给我打了一个电话. But this kind of ambiguity can be easily interpreted or decoded in the certain context. We can say that such ambiguity results from polysemy. It is not a matter of fuzziness. Therefore, we translators and theorists ought to strictly distinguish between ambiguity, polysemy and generality in language, and figure out their meanings respectively, so much that we can better study the science of fuzziness as independent, and make it more important in translation theory.

Secondly, we ought to locate the exact and right position of accuracy in translation. No matter whom he is, a home or an overseas scholar, one advocates accuracy in translating. The accuracy a translator pursues is beyond reproach. It is a truth that we cannot give up accuracy in translation. Actually, a large number of scholars and experts at home and abroad have stuck to the principle. Yan Fu's famous criteria of translation "信、达、雅" (faithfulness, communicability and elegance), Lu Xun's "信" (faithfulness), and Dr. Eugene A. Nida's Equivalence of Response(同等效应), here we just mention a few, stress accuracy of translation. As a matter of fact, accuracy is our aim in translating and we never quit this principle. The key is that we should scientifically deal with the relationship between accuracy and fuzziness.

At the very beginning of this section, we've already mentioned that linguistic fuzziness and accuracy in translation are contradictory but dialectically identical. Both exist and develop with each other, and push language itself forward. Fuzziness is a kind of property of a language and objective reality. Both of them may often be transformed with each other. This is the relationship between them.

- ❖ In *1977*, the sum total of Chinese imports and exports was less than *$ 15 billion*, putting China's share of world trade at *0. 6 percent*.
  <u>1977 年</u>，中国进出口总额低于<u>**150 亿美元**</u>，占世界贸易额的<u>**0. 6％**</u>。
- ❖ In a few minutes the students began to come in *by twos and threes*.
  几分钟后，学生开始<u>三三两两</u>走了进来。
- ❖ *Hundreds of millions* of people gathered there to celebrate the event.
  <u>成千上万的</u>人聚集在那里庆祝这个事件。

**Comments** In the first sentence, such numbers as "1977", "$ 15 billion", and "0. 6 *percent*" are really exact and specific ones. But we cannot employ the same method to deal with the numbers "*by twos and threes*" and "*hundreds of millions*" in the next two sentences. As we know, both accuracy and fuzziness, on the special circumstances, can be transformed with each other. In this case, such numbers have the quality of fuzziness, rather than exact, accurate and specific numbers.

❖ The trees grow leaves *overnight*.

一夜之间,林木着装,绿叶瑟瑟。

**Comments** The meaning of the word "*overnight*" is 一夜, which is an accurate concept in Chinese, but in fact, trees impossibly grow leaves overnight. So in such a situation and context, it becomes a fuzzy concept, which really creates beauty in fuzziness.

In short, the concepts of accuracy and fuzziness cannot stand at their own position for good. They may change their positions on certain circumstances or in a particular context. Man's thinking ability, in his long history, not only develops accuracy, but also cultivates fuzziness. At the same time, linguistic accuracy and fuzziness develop and enrich each other so that they push human language to become prosperous and progressive.

## 8.8 Exercises 练习

**Passage translation.**

### My Friend, Albert Einstein

When his wife died he was deeply shaken, but insisted that now more than ever was the time to be working hard. I remember going to his house to work with him during that sad time. His face was haggard and grief-lined, but he put forth a great effort to concentrate. To help him, I steered the discussion away from routine matters into more difficult theoretical problems, and Einstein gradually became absorbed in the discussion. We kept at it for some two hours, and at the end his eyes were no longer sad. As I left, he thanked me with moving sincerity. "It was a fun," he said. He had had a moment of surcease from grief, and then groping words expressed a deep emotion.

Einstein was an accomplished amateur musician. We used to play duets, he on the violin, I at the piano. One day he surprised me by saying Mozart was the greatest composer of all. Beethoven "created" his music, but the music of Mozart was of such purity and beauty one felt he had merely "found" it—that it had always existed as part of the inner beauty of the Universe, waiting to be revealed.

## 8.9 Rhythm and Flavor 节奏与韵味

Generally speaking, rhythm lies in two aspects: thought-rhythm and sound-rhythm. It refers to the quality of happening of sounds and movements at regular periods of time in speech, dancing, music, etc. Actually, it also frequently appears in writing, especially in prose. English prose writers manage to use such a technique to show readers the aesthetic value of their writing when they portray scenery, objects and characters, because rhythm in writing, which is also an integral part of style, embodies articles imposing manner, flavor, strength, etc. A translator ought to accurately know the rhythm in the text, and properly convert it in the translated. This is the highest goal for any translator.

### 8.9.1 Thought-Rhythm 意义节奏

It is a kind of rhythm created by means of phrases, clauses, sentences and even paraphrases. For the sake of rhythm and expressing ideas, writers often take it for consideration of simple, compound and complex sentences, inverted, elliptical, short and long sentences to regulate the rhythm in their writing. This writing device provides us with the variety of English sentences. Therefore, some aspects should be considered when we translate them.

**1) Repetition and its rhythm**

Repetition can create rhythm and make the writing natural and good-reading.

❖ It's *like* a windfall, *like* a godsend, *like* an unexpected piece of luck.
  它**像**飞来鸿运,**像**天降洪福,**像**意外喜事。

❖ We *waited and waited*, but the players, it seems, never turned up.
  我们**等啊,等啊**,但好像运动员永远不来了似的。

❖ Then, a man with an *old, old* face came along, supported on a stick.
  然后,一个**很老很老**的老头,拄着拐杖走来了。

**Comments** In the first sentence, the "*like*" is repeatedly used three times, and Chinese character 像 is also repeated three times. In sentence 2, "*waited and waited*" is for 等啊,等啊; "*old, old*" for 很老很老 in the third. Needless to say, such repetitions will give force of the original and show emphasis and rhythm for both languages.

**2) Parallelism and its rhythm**

Parallelism is often used in a language. Its structure is well-balanced, its meaning is clear and its reading is sonorous, forceful and full of rhythm. It can be used in different elements of a language. Now let us look at an excerpt by D. H. Lawrence.

❖ The car ploughed uphill through the long squalid struggle of Tevershall, the blackened brick dwellings, black slate roots glistening their sharp edge, the mud black with coal-dust, the pavements wet and black. It was as if dismalness had soaked *through* and *through* everything. *The utter negation of* natural beauty, *the utter negation of* the gladness of life, *the utter absence of* the instinct for shapely beauty which every bird and beast had, *the utter death of* the human intuitive faculty was appalling. *The stacks of soap in the grocers-shop, the rhubarb and lemons in the green-grocers', the awful hats in the milliners'*, all went by *ugly, ugly, ugly*, followed by the plaster and gill horror of the cinema with its wet picture announcements, *A Woman's Love*, and the new big Primitive chapel, primitive enough in its stark brick and big panes of greenish and raspberry glass in the windows…

汽车吃力地爬上山坡,穿过那漫长肮脏、杂乱无序的特韦沙尔矿区。这里的砖屋已变成了黑色;黑色的石板瓦闪现出轮廓清晰的棱角;泥土混杂着黑色的煤灰;道路污黑潮湿。抑郁阴沉似乎<u>彻彻底底</u>笼罩了这里的一切。<u>完全没有了</u>自然的美色;<u>完全缺少了</u>生活的喜悦;<u>完全失去了</u>鸟兽原有的美丽;<u>完全毁灭了</u>人类的直觉,使人充满了惧怕。<u>杂货店里成堆的肥皂;蔬菜水果店里的大黄和柠檬;女帽店里的那些令人嫌恶的帽子</u>,所有这些已变得<u>非常非常丑陋</u>。电影院墙上的灰泥惨不忍睹,上面贴有电影《一个女人的爱》的潮湿的海报。那座新建的古式大教堂,因其毫无装饰的砖块显得过分粗糙,窗户上的巨大玻璃已变成了浅绿色和紫红色……

**Comments** Throughout reading this excerpt by Lawrence, we deeply feel that he strongly expressed his awful and horror impression on Tevershall. This piece is full of parallelism and repetition. "*Through*" is used twice; "*ugly*" is used three times. Meanwhile, in the third sentence, he uses parallelism structure "*The utter negation of…*", "*the utter negation of…*", "*the utter absence of…*", "*the utter death of…*" In sentence 4, he again uses parallelism structure "noun + in + noun". Such use of parallelism and repetition creates a deep touch and artistic appeal on readers. The language is smooth, forceful and rhythmical to read. And then we translators fully consider the effects that parallelism and repetition give birth to in translating.

### 3) Variety of short and long sentences and their rhythm

The rhetorical functions of short and long sentences are two: Short sentences are characterized by speed and strength. They are commonly employed in the tense and dramatic occasions. Long sentences are properly applied to the detailed description. They are usually used to unhurriedly go on with a narration, or an account for the argument or proposition in order to show sufficient details and make one's argument clear and complete. Therefore a good and experienced writer pays special attention to the sentence varieties when writing, or uses both kinds of sentences alternately in his essays in order to judge and regulate rhythm. In other words, he often uses one or two short sentence after a series of long sentences so as to regulate rhythm of a passage and tedious or invariable sentences.

❖ Leaves wiggle. ‖ Grass sways. ‖ A bird chirps, | pecks the ground. ‖
   树叶摇曳;‖草丛摆动;‖一只小鸟啁啾而鸣,|在地上觅食。‖

❖ I kept quiet, | with my ears cocked, | about fifteen minutes. ‖
   我一声不响,|竖起耳朵,|这样过了大概有十五分钟。‖

❖ The moment that the case of the criminal was thus decided, | doleful iron bells were clanged, | great wails went up from the hired mourners posted on the outer rim of the arena, | and the vast audience, | with bowed heads and downcast hearts, | wended slowly their homeward way, | mourning greatly that one so young and fair,

| or so old and respected, | should have merited so dire a fate. ‖

一旦被告的案情做出判决，| 铁钟就会发出悲哀的响声；| 坐在角斗场四周受雇而来的哀痛者爆发出沉痛的号啕声，| 为这位年轻有教养，| 或者年长受尊敬的人有如此悲惨的命运而悲痛不已，| 大批观众垂着脑袋，| 怀着悲伤的心情，| 步履缓慢地朝家走去。‖

**Comments**: Look carefully at the first 2 examples, and we find that they are very short. Especially the first example, in which there are three simple sentences, however, shows the reader a natural and beautiful picture. It is rhythmical and clear, so the Chinese version should follow such a flavor. Though is not long the second example, it is set off into three clauses. We also render it in the same way, instead of putting it into 我一声不响地竖着耳朵听了大概一刻钟. The last example is a long sentence which is deliberately employed to express the detailed description and narration. We think that he or she, as a translator, should manage to keep the original style in their translation.

### 8.9.2 Sound-Rhythm 声音节奏

Sound may remind us of speech, or verbal language. As a matter of fact, in writing, language masters also manage to use such means as stress, weak stress, tone or intonation, long sound or diphthong, etc. so as to make sentences rhythmical.

**1) Use of stress and weak sound and its rhythm**

❖ There's little *movement* after *sunset*, in the *streets* of this *quiet village*.
   太阳**落山**后，这个**宁静**的村庄的**街道**上就没有什么**动静**了。

❖ *Huge* evergreens towered over us. *Gradually* the peace and *silence* of the *place* began to *fill* my *mind*.
   （两旁）**巨大**的常青树**高耸入云**，我**渐渐**感到一种**安详**和**宁静**。

**Comments** Stress and weak sounds are used to form the rhythm in English. We may use Chinese double-characters to fit the rhythm.

**2) Onomatopoeia and its rhythm**

Onomatopoeia is a kind of rhetorical device which can create "sound effects" in a language. Its functions lie in direct hearing, description and vividness. The "sound effect" seems as if we will be personally on the scene.

❖ The door *banged* open.
   门**砰**的一声开了。

❖ The leaves *rustled* in the breeze.
   树叶在微风中**飒飒**作响。

❖ The small locomotive engine, Number 4, came *clanking*, *stumbling* down from Selston with seven full wagons.
   四号小火车拖着七节满载的车厢，**跟跟跄跄**从塞斯顿**轰轰隆隆**地开了过来。

**Comments** In the above-mentioned sentences, "*bang*", "*rustle*", "*clank*" and "*stumble*" are all onomatopoeia words, most of which are single syllables and figuratively depict the sounds that certain objects produce. Correct and corresponding conversion of onomatopoeia words will reflect the features of the original and show the rhythm in the source language.

## 8.10 Sentence and Text 句子与语篇

Let us begin with the unit of translation (翻译单位) before we discuss sentence and text. Speaking of the unit of translation, we have to refer to grammatical units because both are closely related to each other. J. C. Catford in his book *A Linguistic Theory of Translation* divided English grammar into five units, namely sentence, clause, group, word and morpheme. He thinks, according to this kind of division, that two languages can find their own equivalent in translation. What he said is as follows.

"Thus, if we find that two languages operate each with grammatical units at five ranks (an example might be English and French, both of which appear to have five ranks: sentence, clause, group, word, morpheme), we can reasonably say that there is formal correspondence between the two hierarchies of units; each has the same number of ranks, and as (taxonomic) hierarchies each has the same kind of relationship between units of the different ranks... We may talk of formal correspondence between SL and TL elements of structure operating at corresponding ranks." (A *Linguistic Theory of Translation*, Oxford University Press, 1978)

Different people look at a thing in different ways. In our country, some think that words should be taken as the unit of translation. Some take it that phrases or groups should be the unit. Some say that clauses or sentences are the unit because whatever language it is, a sentence with a full stop can express a whole meaning. As long as the sentences are translated one after another, the version will stand as a whole of a coherent and clear paragraph or text. Some hold that a paragraph should be the unit of translation because a paragraph lies in the place between sentences and a text. It has apparent signs of beginning and ending from its appearance. In terms of discourse, it functions as the link between other paragraphs. In terms of communicative function, a paragraph has the nature of topic unity and the integrity of meaning. And some take it that a text should be taken as the unit of translation.

It is worthwhile mentioning a very influential theory proposed by Peter Newmark. He pointed out that, in his book *A Textbook of Translation*, "I have tired to show that all lengths of language can, at different moments and also simultaneously, be used as units of translation in the course of the translation activity. Each length has a functional contribution to make, which can be summarized as lexical for the word and the collocation; grammatical (Vinay and Darbelnets's avengement) for the group and clause; notional for the sentence, the paragraph and the text (Vinay and Darbelnet's message). Further I have tried to show that, operatively, most translation is done at the level of the smaller units (word and clause), leaving the larger units to 'work' automatically, until a difficulty occurs and until revision starts; further that in an expressive or authoritative text, there is a certain extra stress on the word; in an informative text, on the collocation and the group; in the vocative or pragmatic section of a text (the part intended to make the readers react), on the sentence and the text as a unit. Finally, although much of this chapter is devoted to text as unit of translation, I think its importance has been recently exaggerated, in particular by writers such as Wilss, Holmes and Neubert who hardly discuss the practical applications of this concept, and also by Delisle who does. To me the unit of translation is a sliding scale, responding according to other varying factors, and (still) ultimately a little unsatisfactory." (*A Textbook of Translation*, Prentice Hall, 1988)

We can find that Peter Newmark has quite a different opinion from others. His proposal, in which the unit of translation is "the minimal stretch of language that has to be translated together, as one unit", is relatively scientific. A sentence is foundational in considering the whole passage. We hold that the unit of translation cannot be too long or too short. A sentence actually serves as such an effect. And we hold that while rendering sentences, the text should be considered as a whole because a text is the biggest unit in translating, and each sentence in the text is not isolated to exist and it is an organic part of the text. We have to consider and analyze the text to find the exact version for each sentence, instead of putting it as an isolated unit into Chinese, or understanding and interpreting literally.

❖ Then, too, beauty and myths are perennial *masks* of poverty. The traveler comes to the Appalachians in the lovely season. He sees the hills, the streams, the foliage—but not the poor. Or perhaps he looks at a run-down mountain house and, remembering *Rousseau* rather than seeing with his eyes, decides that "those people" are truly fortunate to be living the way they are and that they are lucky to be exempted from the strains and tensions of the middle class. The only problem is that "those people", the quaint inhabitants of those hills, are undereducated, underprivileged, lack medical care, and are in the process of being forced from the land into a life in the cities, where they are *misfits*.

（注：选自《新编英语教程》，上海外语教育出版社，2003.46）
另外，自然的美丽与虚幻的理念永久地**掩盖**了贫穷。在优美的季节游客来到

阿巴拉契亚山脉观光,会去欣赏山川、小溪、绿色,但决不会是穷人。或许他看到一所破旧的山村小屋时,不去亲眼目睹真实的情况,而是回忆一下**卢梭的"回归自然论"**,然后就做出判断:"那些人"真是很幸运,有着自己的生活方式,没有中产阶级的生活压力和焦虑。但问题的关键是"那些人"——山区里生存的另类——缺乏教育、没有特权、缺少医疗,还要被迫离开自己生存的土地,去适应他们**不习惯的城市生活**。

**Comments** Compare the two versions and we can find that the meaning of each underlined word in the original differs from the definition in dictionaries. This is because each of these words should be understood and decided in a certain text and context. "*Mask*" cannot be simply rendered as the covering for the face. "*Rousseau*" can not be converted into a person, who is considered the most important forerunners of romanticism. It refers to his ideal primitiveness here, attributing superior virtue to primitive civilization. A "*misfit*", literally, is a piece of clothing that does not fit. Figuratively, as it is used here, it refers to a person who is badly adjusted to his environment. Therefore, in the target version, the translator uses 掩盖,卢梭的"回归自然论" and 不习惯的城市生活 instead.

## 8.11 Exercises 练习

**Passage translation.**

### I Have a Dream

I say to you today, my friends, that in spite of the difficulties and frustrations of the moment I still have a dream. It is a dream deeply rooted in the American Dream.

I have a dream that one day this nation will rise up and live out the true meaning of its creed: "We hold these truths to be self-evident; that all men are created equal."

I have a dream that one day on the red hills of Georgia the sons of former slaves and the sons of former slave owners will be able to sit down together at the table of brotherhood.

I have a dream that one day even the state of Mississippi, a desert state sweltering with the heat of injustice and oppression, will be transformed into an oasis of freedom and justice.

I have a dream that my four little children will one day live in a nation where they will not be judged by the color of their skin but by the content of their character.

I have a dream today.

I have a dream that one day the state of Alabama, whose governor's lips are presently dripping with the words of interposition and nullification, will be transformed into a situation where little black boys and black girls will be able to join hands with little white boys and girls and walk together as sisters and brothers.

I have a dream today.

I have a dream that one day every valley shall be exalted, every hill and mountain shall be made low, the rough places will be made plains, and the crooked places will be made straight, and the glory of the Lord shall be revealed, and flesh shall see it together.

(By Martin Luther King, Jr.)

# Appendix 1　Bilingual Reading 对比阅读

## Passage 1

### Railroads Reveal the American Dream

#### From Coast To Coast

Before the days of the automobile, trains were the best way to travel. Roads were bad, and horses were slow. There were few rivers and riverboats. Trains were new, safe, and fast.

The story of the railroads is one of the great stories of American history. In 1866, two big railroad companies agreed to build a railroad all the way across America.

The Union Pacific started from the east, and the Central Pacific① started from the west. Ten thousand men worked on both sides. They built the railroad over rivers and valleys, across the prairie and across the Rocky Mountains②. After three years, the two sides met, and the first trains began to run from coast to coast.

The railroad prompted the building of many small towns in the Midwest③. They sprang up at railroad stopping places. The railroad was the most interesting thing in town. At that time, of course, there were no movies or television. In their free time, people just watched the trains go past.

When the highways came, the railroads were less important. In many places, trains stopped running. It was even worse when air travel began. You could fly from New York to San Francisco in a few hours. It took more than two days by train.

### 铁路展现了美国的美景

#### 东海岸到西海岸

汽车时代之前，火车是旅行的最佳工具。公路路况欠佳、马匹行走缓慢、河流船只不多，而火车崭新、安全、快捷。

铁路是美国历史上最伟大的事件之一。1866年，两家大的铁路公司达成协议，计划修建一条贯通美国的铁路。

太平洋联合公司从东部开始修建，中央太平洋公司①从西部着手建造。两边总计有10,000多工人施工。这条铁路跨越河川、穿过大草原、横贯落基山脉②。三年后，全线贯通，首批火车在西海岸与东海岸之间运行。

铁路加速了中西部③许多小城镇的建设，它们在铁路沿线各站崛起。铁路成了小镇最有趣的地方。当然，那时候没有电影，也没有电视，人们在空闲时就去观看火车通过。

高速公路出现后，铁路就变得不那么重要了，火车在许多地方停运。乘飞机旅行开始后，铁路的情况就更糟了。你可以在数小时内从纽约飞到旧金山，但乘火车得花两天多的时间。

现在，人们又开始选择乘火车旅行了。汽油价格昂贵，驾车枯燥之味；乘飞机得驱车出城赶往机场，还得等很长

Now, people are choosing to travel by train again. Gas is expensive, and driving is tiring. When you go by air, you have to drive out of town to an airport and wait a long time for your plane. But trains go from one city center to another.

American trains are very modern and comfortable. Some have restaurants and bars, some have bedrooms. Trains that go through beautiful parts of the country sometimes have glass roofs. You can look all around and enjoy the wonderful forests and mountains.

But there are problems too. Many trains are old. They break down or arrive late. Stations are not always clean and friendly places.

It's the same all over the world. If you pay to go on the best trains, you get the best. If you travel cheaply, you must expect the worst.

It's Cheaper by Bus

You don't find millionaires on buses. Or movie stars. Or rich lawyers. Or Wall Street bankers④. But you'll find Mr. and Ms. America⑤.

Good people, and bad people, happy people, sad people, and people with stories to tell⑥. They all go by bus. It's cheap, the cheapest ride in the US.

The buses go, night and day, right across America. On the longest trips, you have to change the time on your watch.

Don't forget, the United States is big. When it's midnight in New York, it's only 9 p.m. in San Francisco. When it's 2 a.m. in Denver, it's 3 a.m. in Kansas City.⑦

This means you have to read the bus times very, very carefully.

Bus stations are not always the nicest places. They are full of tired people, crying children, busy ticket sellers, and empty Coca-Cola cans.

But climb onto the buses and they're like airplanes. The windows are made of dark glass to keep you cool.

时间才能登机。然而火车可以从一个城市的中心开到另一个城市的中心。

美国的火车非常先进舒适。一些火车上设有餐馆和酒吧,有些还配有卧室。有些经过国家美丽地区的火车有时装有玻璃顶棚,你可以观光四周,欣赏秀丽的森林和山脉。

但是,也存在一些问题。许多火车陈旧,随时停车或者晚点时有发生;车站有时污浊肮脏,也会发生不友好的事情。

世界各地都是如此。如果你付钱乘坐最好的火车,就会得到最好的待遇;如果你花很少的钱旅行,你必须考虑会出现最糟糕的情况。

## 乘公共汽车更便宜

在公共汽车上你见不到百万富翁,见不到电影明星,见不到大腕律师,见不到华尔街的银行家④。你见到的只是普普通通的美国人⑤。

乘坐公共汽车的有好人、坏人、愉快的人、悲伤的人,还有健谈的人⑥。乘坐公共汽车的确便宜,它是美国最便宜的旅行方式了。

公共汽车昼夜行驶在美国各地。在最长的旅途中,你得调整时间以适应时差。

不要忘记美国很大,纽约是午夜时,旧金山还是晚上9点;丹佛城在凌晨2点钟,堪萨斯城已经是凌晨3点钟了。⑦

你必须很仔细地查看公共汽车的时刻表。

公共汽车站不总是令人愉快的地方。各个车站挤满了疲惫的人群;哭叫的孩子;忙碌的售票员,还有随处可见的可口可乐空罐。

Appendix 1 Bilingual Reading

There's a toilet. There are people who want to talk to you. And outside, there's America. Mile after mile of it.

Dry red and yellow deserts. Flat green wheat fields. High snowy mountains. Great busy cities, towns and farms. Sandy beaches and ocean waves.⑧

Some buses go 1,000 miles in one day. And at the end of the day, you can stay on the bus if you like, and sleep on it all through the night. You can sleep all day too. But don't go to sleep when you're crossing the Rockies.

The mountains, rivers, and valleys are too beautiful. And you probably won't go to sleep when you're crossing Death Valley, in California. It can be dangerous too. You can't live long in Death Valley without water. If cars or buses break down there, it's a big problem.

If you don't want to sleep on the bus, you can always find a motel. The most interesting ones are the small family ones. The world of the great highways is their life.

The motel owners give beds to tired travelers and worried people looking for work. They cook steaks for truckers, and hamburgers for tourists.

They smile at lovers⑨ and watch carefully for the man with the gun. Their doors are always open when the bus comes into town. (By Elizabeth Laird and Longman)

一旦踏上汽车，它们快得像飞机一样。车窗是黑色玻璃制作的，以保证凉爽，车上配有厕所；也有愿意和你交谈的乘客。窗外就是美国，汽车一英里一英里地向前行驶，飞驰在美国的土地上。

那里你可以看到红黄相间的干燥沙漠，平坦无垠的绿色麦田，高耸入云的雪山，庞大繁忙的城市、小城镇和大农场，还有沙滩和海浪。⑧

有些汽车可日行1,000英里。到了晚上，如果你乐意可以在车上，睡上一夜。你可以整天在车上睡觉，但汽车经过落基山脉可不要睡觉了。

因为山脉、河流和山谷太美了。汽车经过加利福尼亚死亡谷的时候，你可不能睡着，因为那里太危险了，如果没有水你在死亡谷呆不了多久。假如车辆抛锚，那问题可就大了。

如果不想在车上睡觉，你完全可以找一家汽车旅馆休息。最有趣的旅馆是那些家庭开的小旅馆。庞大众多的高速公路是它们赖以生存的地方。

旅馆老板会为疲惫的游客以及为寻找工作而忧心忡忡的人提供床位；为卡车司机烹调牛排；为游客制作汉堡。

他们含笑迎接情侣⑨，小心警惕持枪的男人。他们的大门总是敞开的，以迎接进城的车辆。　　　（何三宁　译）

**注释：**① The Union Pacific and the Central Pacific 是指上文提到的两家大的铁路公司。翻译时注意衔接。

② the Rocky Mountains 是北美洲较大的山脉。

③ the Midwest 指美国中西部。因为该文讲述的是美国的事情。

④ 这几个句子用 or 开头，且都没有主语，这在较正式的英语中是少见的。翻译时注意汉语的排列。

⑤ 这里不能字面直译为"美国先生和太太"，它意指普通美国人。

⑥ 这句话的翻译需要上下文的帮助，所以需要增补内容。这篇文章较为口语化，语言简朴，结构简单，省略部分也较多。但我们需要知道文字简单就未必容易翻译，处理这类文章仍需我们认真对待。

⑦ 这里列举的是美国东、西、南、北不同地区的城市，时差较大。

⑧ 这句如同注④一样，翻译时注意汉语句式的排列。

⑨ lover 是情侣或情人，并不是"爱人"，应理解该词真正的内涵。

# Passage 2

### Roses, Roses, All the Way①

It has now been five years since Margaret Thatcher resigned as Britain's Prime Minister②. In her heyday she strode the international headlines with such bravura that she seemed inevitable, a natural force. The world stage seemed just the right size for her, as she chaffed her conservative soul mate Ronald Reagan or flattered the "new man", Mikhail Gorbachev③.

Now the political world has begun to focus on the immensity of her achievement. How on earth did she manage to get there? She was elected to Parliament at 32 in 1958 (five years before *The Feminine Mystique* was published). She parried her way through the complacent, male-dominated councils of power—no woman had ever roiled those waters. Couldn't the old boys see her coming? After all, there was nothing subtle about her personality or her approach.④

As *The Path to Power* (Harper-Collins; 656 pages; $30), the second volume of her autobiography, makes clear, Thatcher was probably too simple and direct for the Tories, with their heavy baggage of class and compromise. She traveled light, proud of her roots as a grocer's daughter from the small town of Grantham but never tethered by working-class resentments or delusions of inferiority. Her parents taught her the verities they believed in: Methodism, hard work, thrift and the importance of the individual. She has never wavered from them, and they run through the book.⑤

"Nothing in our house was wasted." Or, "I had

### 铺满玫瑰的路①

玛格丽特·撒切尔辞去英国首相②职务已经五年了。在她（政治生涯）的鼎盛时期，她以光彩照人的风格而成为国际上的新闻人物，她好像必然如此，她是一股必然的力量。在她跟她的保守党精神伙伴罗纳德·里根打趣时，或是在奉承"新人"米哈伊尔·戈尔巴乔夫③时，这个世界看来恰好是适合她驰骋的舞台。

现在政界开始把注意力集中在她的辉煌的政绩上。她到底是如何进入政界的呢？1958年（《女性的奥秘》发表前五年）她32岁被选进议会。她左挡右闪进了那些由自满的男人控制的权力机构——过去不曾有任何女人到那里去搅乱。难道那些老家伙们看不见她的到来吗？其实她的性格和施政手段并没有什么微妙之处。④

正如她的第二本自传《通往权利之路》（哈珀—科林斯出版社；656页；30美元）所说，对于那些阶级意识很重并善于折中的英国保守党党员，也许撒切尔过于简单，过于直来直去。她没有负担。她以自己是格兰瑟姆小镇一个杂货商的女儿而感到自豪，但是她没有被劳动阶级因为地位低下而产生的怨恨或迷惑所束缚。她的父母教她懂得了他们所相信的真理：卫斯理教、勤勉、节俭，以及个人的重要性。对于这些信仰，她从未动摇过。这些内容贯穿着全书。⑤

"我们家从不浪费任何东西。"或者是，"我的闲暇时间比别的孩子都少。"这

less leisure time than other children." These are boasts of a childhood recalled in tranquility. Later they became a philosophy: "Being conservative is never merely a matter of income, but a whole way of life, a will to take responsibility for oneself."

From the start, she notes almost with bemusement, there was a contrast between her own "executive style" and her colleagues' "more consultive style." Thatcher laid down the law. In her 11-year leadership, she broke the crippling power of British unions, made many thousands of her countrymen homeowners, strengthened British ties with the U.S. and the Soviet Union and gave voice to Britain's reluctance about joining Europe, a reluctance that still plagues her successor, John Major. ⑥

*The Downing Street Years*, the first volume of her memoirs, covered her time in power. This one is more interesting and better fun, a formidable leader looking back on her early winning battles. She is known now as the Iron Lady, but as a pretty, naive, young pol who cut through cant, prevarication and some very real problems, she must have been exhilarating. Her rise, as she once described the star-is-born press coverage that greeted her maiden speech in Commons, was "roses, roses all the way."

In a final section on the '90s political scene, she calls for renewed dedication to her principles. The imperiled John Major ⑦ cannot take comfort in the timing of *The Path to Power*. Thatcher has relentlessly flogged the book in Britain and the U.S., giving TV interviews that scourge what she sees as the collapse of her country's leadership. The one thing she doesn't say is that as this old century draws to a close, there simply aren't that many leaders. Thatcher was one.

(By Martha Duffy)

是在生活平静下来以后回忆童年时颇具自豪的语言。后来这些信仰变成了她的哲学:"信仰保守绝不仅仅是收入问题,而完全是一种生活方式,一种为自己勇于承担责任的意志。"

一开始,她几乎是带着一种困惑注意到,她自己的"施政风格"和她的同僚的"更喜磋商的风格"形成鲜明的对照。撒切尔夫人说了算。在她长达十一年的执政期间,她削弱了英国工会的破坏力,使成千上万的同胞有了自己的房子,加强了英国与美国和苏联的关系,并且明确表示了英国不愿意加入欧洲,她的这个意向至今仍在纷扰着她的继承人约翰·梅杰。⑥

她的第一本回忆录《唐宁街的岁月》涵盖了她的执政阶段。而这一本更有意思,一个令人敬佩的领导人回顾她初登政坛时所打的一个一个的胜仗。她现在以铁娘子著称,可是作为一个漂亮、天真、年轻的政治家,在虚伪和含糊其辞的人们中间以及问题成堆的地方披荆斩棘,她一定是令人兴奋不已。新闻界在报道她第一次在下院发表演说并对其表示赞许时说她是一颗已经诞生的新星;撒切尔在描述这一报道时说,她是沿着一条"铺满玫瑰的路"冉冉升起的。

在最后一部分论述90年代世界政局时,她号召人们重新献身她的原则。《通往权利之路》在这个时候出版,身陷困境的约翰·梅杰⑦是不会感到舒服的。撒切尔毫不客气地在英国和美国抛售此书,同时接受电视台采访,起到了鞭挞在她看来正在摇摇欲坠的英国领导的作用。有一件事她没有说明,在本世纪即将结束的时候,根本就找不出几个领导人。而撒切尔是一个。

(选自刘士聪《汉英·英汉美文翻译与鉴赏》,译林出版社,2002)

注释：① 该文是 Martha Duffy 写的书评，勾画了撒切尔夫人政治生涯的轮廓，信息丰富，语言简练，具有新闻体（journalism）特点，是练习翻译的好时文。

② Prime Minister 是英国首相。这里需要注意不同政体的元首可能名称叫法不同，如美国叫"总统"，英文是 president。

③ 此句中出现了两个人名：Ronald Reagan 是前美国总统里根，Mikhail Gorbachev 是前苏联总统戈尔巴乔夫。翻译人名时，需要搞清楚他们的背景，这样有助于对原文的理解与表达。

④ 理解该段对整篇文章的理解很重要。这里说明政界开始关注她的政绩，她是如何进入政界的。作者指出三点：她 32 岁进议会；在男性控制的政权机构里周旋；豁朗的性格和毫无隐秘的施政方式。

⑤ 该段有两点需要注意：Tories 指英国保守党党员，翻译时应与英国历史上的"托利党党员"区分开。Methodism 是个基督教概念，可译为"卫斯理教"或"卫理公会教"。

⑥ 该段也包括下一段回顾了她执政早期所赢得的一系列胜利和"铁娘子"的称谓，她的政治生涯宛如"铺满玫瑰的路"。

⑦ John Major 是英国前首相，接任撒切尔政权。

# Passage 3

## The Imperial Palace①

Built in the early fifteenth century (1406—1420A. D.), it is also called the Palace Museum or the Old Palace. As you pass through Tian An Men Gate you will enter a walled courtyard. Although you cannot see them, on either side of this courtyard are many gardens and halls. Of particular interest if you have time might be the Imperial Ancestral Temple, which is to the right and the Sun Yat-Sen Park, on the left.

Covering an area of 175 acres (72ha.), the Palace is enclosed by walls over 35ft. (10.4m.) high and surrounded by a moat 57 yd. (52m.) wide. Today this moat is still full of water. Four watchtowers are placed, one at each corner. Used as the imperial palace by both the Ming and Qing Dynasties (1368—1911 A. D.), the Imperial Palace is the largest and most complete group of ancient buildings standing in China.②

The halls and palaces which comprise the Imperial Palace are all built of wood and brick. With a total of over nine thousand rooms, most of the Palace had undergone some reconstruction to repair damage caused by fire and other ravages of time during the long years of its history. Throughout you will

## 故 宫①

皇宫也叫故宫博物院或故宫，修建于 15 世纪初（公元 1406 年—1420 年）。从天安门往里走便是四面有围墙的大庭院，庭院两侧有许多花园殿堂，只是看不到而已。太庙位于故宫的右边，中山公园坐落在左边，它们都是闲暇之余的好去处。

故宫共占地 72 公顷（175 英亩），四周环绕有 10.4 米（35 英尺）高的城墙和 52 米（57 码）宽的护城河，如今护城河仍然蓄满着水。故宫四角各有一座角楼。此皇宫为我国现存最大最完整的古代宫殿建筑群，是明清两朝（公元 1368 年—1911 年）的皇宫。②

众多殿堂宫殿组成的皇宫为砖木结构。整个故宫共有 9,000 余房间，因火灾的损坏和岁月的

find typical masterpieces of ancient Chinese architecture. Two notable examples are the ingeniously constructed watchtowers and the magnificent Hall of Supreme Harmony.

To further insure the Imperial Palace would be given special protection, in 1961 the Chinese government decreed that the entire area be considered one of China's "most important historical sites".

The Palace Museum, with four gates, has its main entrance to the south, known as the Meridian Gate. This is the gate you will approach as you continue along the cobbled roadway from Tian An Men. The Imperial Palace is divided into two ceremonial areas: the Outer Palace and the Inner Court. Through the Meridian Gate and across the Golden Water Bridge, one comes to the Gate of Supreme Harmony, the main gate of the Outer Palace. The main buildings in the Outer Palace are the Hall of Supreme Harmony, the Hall of Complete Harmony, and the Hall of Preserving Harmony. ③

(From *The Official Guidebook of China*)

侵蚀,大部分房间都经过修缮。整个皇宫代表着独特的中国古代建筑风格。其中两个最为突出的建筑是玲珑奇巧的角楼和雄伟壮丽的太和殿。

为了对皇宫进一步保护,中国政府于1961年颁布法令,指定故宫为"国家重点保护遗迹"之一。

故宫博物院有四座城门,主城门位于南面,称为午门。穿过此门,沿着一条鹅卵石大道往里走,便进了故宫。皇宫可分为两个不同的礼仪区:外朝与内廷。走进午门,跨过金水桥,便到了外朝的大门太和门。外朝内的主要建筑有太和殿、中和殿和保和殿。③

(何三宁 译)

**注释**:① 故宫是一个熟悉的话题,理解是较为容易的,但古迹名胜中的专有名称并不好表达,需要了解其历史背景和相关知识,方可达意。另外,游记类文章的文体特点也比较鲜明:语言简朴,结构流畅。翻译时应注意这些。

② 1~2 段中需要注意两点:一是结构,像 built in…, covering an area of…等结构表达汉语"建于……","占地面积为……"等意义。同样,我们在翻译具有同样意义的结构时也可效仿,如"位于……"(located in/on…),"追溯到……"(dating back…),"据记载……"(recording/recorded…)等,但要注意过去分词和现在分词的使用。二是量度和年代,英语中用公制量度或英制量度,在涉及中国景点或名胜时,注意用国人便于理解的量度(括号注释或脚注)。朝代/年代要注明公元或公元前。

③ 最后一段中出现了许多故宫内的不同的礼仪区名称和建筑名称。我国大多数名胜这样的名称都有其背景意义,翻译时要特别注意,切不可望文生义。有些可能已有约定俗成的英文名称。

# Passage 4

## Why Nothing Works

According to a law attributed to the savant known only as Murphy, "if anything can go wrong, it will." Corollaries to Murphy's Law ① suggest themselves as clues to the shoddy goods problems: If anything can break down, it

## 为何什么都不起作用

根据大学者墨菲的法则,"凡是可能出差错的事终究出差错。"墨菲法则①在劣质产品问题中也能得到验证:凡是可能损坏的产品终将损

will; if anything can fall apart, it will; if anything can stop running, it will. While Murphy's Law can never be wholly defeated②, its effects can usually be postponed. Much of human existence consists of efforts aimed at making sure that things don't go wrong, fall apart, break down, or stop running until a decent interval has elapsed after their manufacture. Forestalling Murphy's Law as applied to products demands intelligence, skill, and commitment. If these human inputs are assisted by special quality-control instruments, machines, and scientific sampling procedures, so much the better. But gadgets and sampling alone will never do the trick since these items are also subject to Murphy's Law. Quality-control instruments need maintenance; gauges go out of order; X rays and beams need adjustments. No matter how advanced the technology, quality demands intelligent, motivated human thought and action.

  Some reflection about the material culture of prehistoric and preindustrial peoples may help to show what I mean. A single visit to a museum which displays artifacts used by simple preindustrial societies is sufficient to dispel the notion that quality is dependent on technology③. Artifacts may be of simple, even primitive design, and yet be built to serve their intended purpose in a reliable manner during a lifetime of use. We acknowledge this when we honor the label "handmade" and pay extra for the jewelry, sweaters, and handbags turned out by the dwindling breads of modern-day craftspeople.

  What is the source of quality that one finds, let us say, in a Pomo Indian basket so tightly woven that it was used to hold boiling water and never leaked a drop, or in an Eskimo skin boat with its matchless combination of lightness, strength, and seaworthiness? ④ Was it merely the fact that these items were handmade? I don't think so. In unskilled or uncaring hands a handmade basket or boat can fall apart as quickly as baskets or boats made by machines. I rather think that the reason we honor the label "handmade" is because it evokes not a technological relationship between producer and product but a social relationship between producer and consumer⑤. Throughout

坏;凡是可能破碎的东西终将破碎;凡是可能出故障的产品终将会出故障。然而,墨菲法则并非无懈可击②,它的效应通常可以延迟。人们耗费大量精力,其目的是保证产品在使用相当长一段时间后仍完好无损。要使墨菲法则在产品中站不住脚,就需要知识、技能、信誉。如果有了人类的这些努力,外加专用的质检工具、机器以及科学的取样程序,情况就会好得多。然而仅靠工具和抽样调查决不会有效,因为这些工具仍然受墨菲法则的影响。质检工具需要维修;检测仪器也会损坏;X光及激光也需要调整。不管技术多么先进,质量仍需要人类的智慧、创新的思想和行动。

  史前和工业化以前人类的物质文明有助于证实我的观点。只要去史前社会古器物博物馆参观一下,就足以驳倒质量依赖于技术的观点③。这些器物或许简单,甚至还是非常原始的设计,但是由于特殊的用途,其制作方法很可靠,以至于可以终身使用。我们应该承认这样一个事实:我们在推崇"手工制品",宁愿多花钱购买珠宝、毛衣、提包的同时,而生产这些制品的技艺传人却日渐减少。

  看一看下面的例子,我们便可明白质量的根源是什么。波摩印第安人编织的篮子很密实,可以用来盛装沸水而滴水不漏;爱斯基摩人的小皮艇轻巧便捷、坚固耐用、适于航海,无与伦比。从这些事例中能找出质量的根源吗?④这些物品只是因为手工制作的吗?我不这样看。如果这些手工船或篮子出自技艺不高、责任心不强的工匠之手,那么它们与机器制造的一样也会很快损坏。我认为,

Appendix 1  Bilingual Reading

prehistory it was the fact that producers and consumers were either one and the same individuals or close kin that guaranteed the highest degree of reliability and durability in manufactured items. Men made their own spears, bows and arrows, and projectile points; women wove their own baskets and carrying nets, fashioned their own clothing from animal skins, bark, or fiber. Later, as technology advanced and material culture grew more complex, different members of the band or village adopted craft specialties such as pottery-making, basket-weaving, or canoe-building. Although many items were obtained through barter and trade, the connection between producer and consumer still remained intimate, permanent, and caring.

A man is not likely to fashion a spear for himself whose point will fall off in mid-flight ⑥; nor is a woman who weaves her own basket likely to make it out of rotted straw. Similarly, if one is sewing a parka for a husband who is about to go hunting for the family with the temperature at sixty below, all stitches will be perfect. And when the men who make boats are the uncles and fathers of those who sail them, they will be as seaworthy as the state of the art permits.

In contrast, it is very hard for people to care about strangers or about products to be used by strangers. In our era of industrial mass production and mass marketing, quality is a constant problem because the intimate sentimental and personal bonds which once made us responsible to each other and to our products have withered away and been replaced by money relationships. Not only are the producers and consumers strangers but the women and men involved in various stages of production and distribution—management, the workers on the factory floor, the office help, the salespeople—are also strangers to each other. In larger companies there may be hundreds of thousands of people all working on the same product who can never meet face-to-face or learn one another's names. The larger the company and the more complex its division

我们推崇"手工制品"的标签是因为生产者与使用者之间有着一种社会关系,并不是生产者与产品之间的一种技术关系⑤。在整个史前时期,有这样一个事实,生产者与使用者同属个人或亲缘关系,这保证了产品的高度可靠性和耐用性。男人为自己制作矛枪、弓箭、射弹。妇女为自己编织篮子、网兜,用兽皮、树皮或植物根须为自己制作衣服。随着技术的进步和物质文明的发展,不同村庄部落的人群采用了诸如制陶、编篮、造船的专业技术。尽管许多产品是通过物物交换来交易,但生产者与使用者之间仍然保持着亲密、持久和负责的关系。

一个男人为自己制作的矛枪不可能在投掷中矛头就掉了⑥;一个女人也不可能用腐烂的稻草为自己编制篮子。同样,丈夫要在华氏零下60度的冰天雪地为家人打猎,妻子为其缝制的毛皮大衣,每一针一线都会很仔细。造船者是船只使用者的叔叔和父亲时,会尽其所能使船只适应航海。

相反,人们很难去关心素不相识的人或他们使用的东西。在我们这个工业化批量生产和向大众销售的时代,质量一直是个问题,因为曾经让我们对他人和产品负责的亲密的情感纽带和个人关系,如今已经消失殆尽,逐渐被金钱关系所取代。不仅生产者和消费者之间彼此陌生,就连工作在生产和分销各个环节的成员——管理人员、车间工人、办公室助理、销售人员——彼此之间也成了陌生人。一些大公司里,有成千上万的人为生产同一件产品而工作,但他们从未谋面,也不知道对方的名字。公司规模越大,

of labor, the greater the sum of uncaring relationships and hence the greater the effect of Murphy's Law. Growth adds layer on layer of executives, foremen, engineers, production workers, and sales specialists to the payroll ⑦. Since each new employee contributes a diminished share to the overall production process, alienation from the company and its product are likely to increase along with the neglect or even purposeful sabotage of quality standards.

(By Marvin Harris)

分工越细,彼此关系就越疏远,墨菲法则的效果就越明显。在薪水册上可以看到行政人员、领班、工程师、生产工人到销售专员的层层关系,而且这种关系有增无减⑦。由于每一个新雇员在整个生产过程的分工更细,责任减少,随着员工对质量标准的漠视甚至故意破坏,其与公司及产品之间的关系也可能更加疏远。 (何三宁 译)

**注释:** ① Murphy's Law 即墨菲法则。墨菲是美国著名的学者、医师和航空机械师。他有一种俏皮的论断:凡有可能出差错的事终将出差错。

② 这里要注意部分否定意义的转换。英语中,否定词加 always, wholly, entirely 等常表示部分否定概念。参见 Chapter 3.1.2

③ 翻译此句时需要注意句子结构的分析和译文的结构安排。该句的主语是 A single visit,其定语部分较长,主句动词是 is;notion 后又有一个定语,这些都要清楚。译文句子组织时要注意到 is 前后的条件关系,才能使句子通顺。

④ 较长的问句是较难翻译的,需要注意几点:一,搞明白是修辞疑问句还是真正的疑问句。二,可以采取长句的翻译方法,根据语义进行拆译和组织句子。三,发问部分放在句末。

⑤ 这句英文可能会有两种组织方式,一种是"我认为,我们推崇'手工制品'的标签不是因为生产者与产品之间的一种技术关系,而是生产者与使用者之间有着一种社会关系。"另一种安排是"我认为,我们推崇'手工制品'的标签是因为生产者与使用者之间有着一种社会关系,并不是生产者与产品之间的一种技术关系。"两种安排都可行,但我们应分析作者强调的部分,根据汉语的特点,强调部分应放在后面。

⑥ fall off in mid-flight 意为矛枪头在飞行中掉落。

⑦ 这句英文看似简单,但能翻译成流畅的译文并非易事。建议采用意译处理此句。

# Passage 5

## About Electricity①

While the exact nature of electricity is not known, a great deal is known about what it can do. By the mere closing of a switch, buildings are lighted, wheels are turned, ice is made, food is cooked, distant voices are heard, and countless other tasks—ordinary and extraordinary—are performed. Although a great number of uses for electricity have been discovered and applied, the

## 电的知识①

人们对于电的确切性质还不大清楚时,对电的作用却已了解得很多了。只需合上电闸,房屋便可照亮;机轮便可旋转;可以制冰;可以做饭;可以听见远处的声音;还有其他无数大大小小的工作得以进行。虽然人们已发现了电的大量用途并已付诸实施(践),但其应

field is by no means exhausted. Electric machines and devices that have been in use for many years are being improved and are now finding wider fields of application. Extensive research is constantly bringing forth and developing new devices. Much is still to be learned about electricity.

Electricity is a convenient form of energy②. It is well known that when fuels such as coal, oil, and gas are burned, energy is released. A waterfall, whether it is man-made, or natural, also possesses energy. Yet, to be of value, this energy must be made available at points where it can be used conveniently. Electricity furnished the most practicable and convenient means yet devised for doing this. The energy of burning fuel or falling water is changed to a more convenient form—electricity—by electric machines. It is transmitted to distant points over electric circuits. It is controlled by other electric machines. At points where it is to be used, it is converted into useful work by still other electric machines and devices.

Since electricity is a form of energy, the study of electricity is the study of energy, its conversions from one form to another. Electric machines are energy-transmission devices, and electric circuits are energy, transmission devices.

Although no one knows precisely what electricity is, it has been possible to develop theories about electricity through experiment and by observation of its behavior. As a result, it is now believed that all matter is essentially electrical in nature.

用领域远不止这些。已经应用多年的电机和设备还在不断改进，开辟更为广阔的应用领域。人们正在进行着广泛的研究，不断创造和开发各种新的电机设备。对于电，我们还有许多问题有待进一步探明。

电是一种便捷的能量形式②。众所周知，煤、油和天然气之类的燃料在燃烧时，会释放出能量。不管是人工的还是自然的瀑布都具有能量。但是，要想使这种能量具有价值，就必须在某些方面获取它们，并能便捷地应用它们。电为此提供了迄今为止所发现的最为方便可行的手段。燃料燃烧或水流下落所产生的能量，通过电机便可转换成更为方便的形式——电。电通过电路传输到远处，再通过别的电机来控制。在电的使用场所，再由其他电机和设备把电转化成有用功。

因为电是能量的一种形式，研究电就是研究能量，也就是研究能量从一种形式到另一种形式的转换。电机是能量转化的设备，电路是能量传输的设备。

尽管无人精确地知道电是什么，但人们却能通过实验和观察其变化情况，以建立起各种理论。因此，人们现在已认识到，一切物质从本质上讲都是带电的。

（译文有改动）

**注释：**① 该短文是一篇练习被动句翻译的上好材料，认真对比原文与译文定能获益。全文共有25处使用了被动句，翻译方法也各异，对比时细心体会。英语被动句的翻译方法很多，这里不再逐个解释，可参考 Chapter 3.2。

② 此文属于科普文章，科技文体的用词特点、词义的变化、句子结构等都是我们翻译时需要注意的地方。就选词而言，文中出现的 energy, transmission, conversion, useful work, device 等词的语义变化也需留意。

## Passage 6

### An Hour before Sunrise①

An hour before sunrise in the city there is an air of cold, solitary desolation about the noiseless street, which we are accustomed to seeing thronged at other times by a busy, eager crowd, and over the quiet, closely shut buildings which throughout the day are warming with life. The drunken, the dissipated, and the criminal have disappeared; the more sober and orderly part of the population have not yet awakened to the labors of the day, and the stillness of death is over the streets; its very hue seems to be imparted to them, cold and lifeless as they look in the gray, somber light of daybreak. A partially opened window here and there bespeaks the heat of the weather and the uneasy slumbers of its occupants; and the dim scanty of a light through the blinds of yonder windows denotes the chamber of watching and sickness. Save for ②that sad light, the streets present no signs of life, nor the houses of habitation.

### 黎明前①

太阳升起的一小时前,寂静的城市街道四周有一丝寒冷、孤寂、凄凉的气息,而在其他时间,我们在那里习惯看到人头攒动,繁忙热切的人群。整个白天生机勃勃的大楼被宁静所包围。酗酒成习、放荡不羁和惹是生非的人没有了;而循规蹈矩的人还没有起床去忙一天的工作,死一般的寂静笼罩着整个街道;寂静的样子似乎就属于这些街道,在昏暗阴沉的黎明之中,它们看上去冷酷无情,毫无生机。到处半开的窗户表明天气的炎热和城市居民不安的睡眠;远处窗帘透出的暗淡灯光意味着有人守夜或有人生病。除了②那点黯淡的灯光外,整个街道没有任何生命的迹象,也看不到住人的房屋。

(何三宁 译)

**注释**:① 该短文属于描述性文体,篇幅不长,只有 4 句话,但是透彻理解和流畅表达都很难。需要细心揣摩,理清关系,采用长句的翻译方法去操作。这里仅指导大家如何理解结构:第 1 句要搞清 which 的指代和与其他部分的关系。第 2 句有 3 个分句,建议分开去理解,然后再组织句子。第 3 句有两个分句,从语义上看,也可分开理解。

② Save for:这是个介词短语,意为"除了……之外,撇开"。

## Passage 7

### Abraham Lincoln's Gettysburg Address①

Four scores and seven years ago② our fathers brought forth on this continent, a new nation, conceived in Liberty, and dedicated to the proposition that all men are created equal.

Now we are engaged in a great civil war, testing whether that nation so conceived and so dedicated, can

### 林肯在葛底斯堡的演讲①

87 年前②,我们的先辈们在这个大陆上建立了一个以自由为理想、以人人平等为宗旨的新国家。

现在我们正从事一场伟大的内战,以考验这样一个孕育于自由并奉行上述宗旨的国家是否能够长久存在下去。我们

long endure. We are met on a great battlefield of that war. We have come to dedicate a portion of the field, as a final resting-place for those who here gave their lives that nation might live. It is altogether fitting and proper that we should do this.

But, in a larger sense, we can not dedicate—we cannot consecrate—we cannot hallow—this ground. The brave men, living and dead, who struggled here, have consecrated it, far above our poor power to add or detract. The world will little note, nor long remember what we say here, but it can never forget what they did here. It is for us the living, rather, to be dedicated here to the unfinished work which they who fought here have thus far so nobly advanced. It is rather for us to be here dedicated to the great task remaining before us—that from these honored dead we take increased devotion to that cause for which they gave the last full measure of devotion—that we here highly resolve that these dead shall not have died in vain—that this nation, under God ③, shall have a new birth of freedom—and that government of the people, by the people, for the people, shall not perish from the earth.
(By Abraham Lincoln)

在这场战争中的一个大战场上集会，来把战场的一角献给为国家生存而牺牲的烈士，作为他们永久安息之地，这是我们义不容辞、理所当然该做的事。

但是，从更深刻的意义来说，我们不能使这一角战场成为圣地，我们不能使它流芳百世，我们不能使它永垂青史。因为在这里战斗过的勇士们，活着的和死去的，已经使这一角战场神圣化了，我们微薄的力量远远不能使它增光或者使之减色。世人不太会注意、也不会长久记住我们在这里所说的话，但全世界永远不会忘记勇士们在这里所做的事。因此，我们活着的人更应该献身于他们为之战斗并且使之前进的未竟事业。我们更应该献身于我们面前的伟大任务，更应该不断向这些光荣牺牲的烈士学习，学习他们为事业鞠躬尽瘁、死而后已的献身精神，更应该在这里下定决心，一定不让这些烈士的鲜血白流；这个国家在上帝的保佑下③，一定要得到自由和新生，这个民有、民治、民享的政府一定不能从地球上消失。

（许渊冲　译）

注释：① 该短文属于演讲题材，用语流畅自然，句子结构简单。另外，演讲者多用第一人称，充分体现语言的亲和力。翻译时应注意这些文体风格。

② Four scores and seven years ago：这里需要注意数字的翻译。Score 意为20，译文"87 年前"就不难理解了。但是，如果没有基数词的限定，scores 一词常常具有模糊概念，如，Scores died in the bombing. 许多人在爆炸中丧生。I have been there scores of times. 我曾多次去过那里。

③ under God：可采用增补法翻译，不可直接翻译。涉及的是"God"，增补"保佑"或"庇佑"非常到位。另外 under the new government 可翻译为"在新的一届政府领导下"。

# Passage 8

## Cultivating a Hobby

A gifted American psychologist has said, "Worry is a spasm of the emotion; the mind catches hold of something and will not let it go." It is useless to argue with the mind

## 培养一种爱好

一位才华横溢的美国心理学家曾经说过："忧虑是一种感情的冲动，只要心里有了它，将很难摆脱。"在此

in this condition. The stronger the will, the more futile the task. One can only gently insinuate something else into its convulsive grasp. And if this something else is rightly chosen, if it is really attended by the illumination of another field of interest, gradually, and often quite swiftly, the old undue grip relaxes and the process of recuperation and repair, begins.①

The cultivation② of a hobby and new forms of interest is therefore a policy of first important to a public man. But this is not a business that can be undertaken in a day or swiftly improvised by a mere command of the will. The growth② of alternative mental interests is a long process. The seeds must be carefully chosen; they must fall on good ground; they must be sedulously tended, if the vivifying fruits are to be at hand when needed.

To be really happy and really safe, one ought to have at least two or three hobbies, and they must all be real. It is no use starting late in life to say, "I will take an interest in this or that." Such an attempt only aggravates the strain of mental effort. A man may acquire great knowledge of topics unconnected with his daily work, and yet hardly get any benefit or relief. It is no use doing what you like; you have got to like what you do. Broadly speaking, human beings may be divided into three classes: those who are toiled to death, those who are worried to death, and those who are bored to death③. It is no use offering the manual labourer, tired out with a hard week's sweat and effort, the chance of playing a game of football or baseball on Saturday afternoon. It is no use inviting the politician or the professional or businessman, who has been working or worrying about serious things for six days, to work or worry trifling things at the weekend.

As for the unfortunate people who can command everything they want, who can gratify every caprice and lay their hands on almost every object of desire—for them a new pleasure, a new excitement is only an additional satiation. In vain they rush frantically round from place to place, trying to escape from avenging boredom by mere

情况下,要消除它是很难奏效的。越是想摆脱它,难度就越大(越是无法如愿)。人们只能心平气和地利用别的东西替代这种烦恼。那么如果能正确选择爱好,并受其启发,真正与之相伴,渐渐地,而且常常很快地,这种常见而烦人的情感方可变得松弛下来,恢复情绪的过程将随之开始。①

因此,对一个公务员来说,培养②一种爱好和新颖的兴趣是首要考虑的事情。然而,这绝非一朝一夕之事,也并非随心所欲,一蹴而就。培育②可供取舍的精神食粮需要一个漫长的过程,这就如同种植作物一样,首先种子要精挑细选,再把它们植入肥沃的土壤,并经过精心地呵护,这样才能收获到所需的丰硕果实。

一个人要想真正地生活快乐和泰然安宁,应该至少有两三种爱好,而且都必须是真正的爱好。一个人直到晚年才说"我将对这个或那个感兴趣",这已经没有任何意义了。这种努力只会加重精神负担。他只能得到不少与日常生活毫无联系的知识,却很难从中获益或减轻生活压力。努力去做你喜欢的事情已经没有什么意义了,你只好去喜欢你所做的事情。广义而言,人可分为三类:劳作而死的人;焦虑而终的人;无聊一生的人③。对于经过了一周的辛勤劳作的体力劳动者来说,在周六午后让他们踢足球或打棒球,这些都是没有多大用处的。同样,让连续工作和为正事操劳六天的政客、专业人士或商人在周末为鸡毛蒜皮的小事去烦恼伤身,也是无甚意义的。

clatter and motion. For them discipline in one form or another is the most hopeful path.

It may also be said that rational, industrious, useful human beings are divided into two classes: first, those whose work is work and whose pleasure is pleasure; and secondly, those whose work and pleasure are one. Of these the former are the majority. They have their compensations. The long hours in the office or the factory bring with them as their reward, not only the means of sustenance, but a keen appetite for pleasure even in its simplest and most modest forms. But Fortune's favoured children④ belong to the second class. Their life is a natural harmony. For them the working hours are never long enough. Each day is a holiday, and ordinary holidays when they come are grudged as enforced interruptions in an absorbing vacation. Yet to both classes the need of an alternative outlook, of a change of atmosphere, of a diversion of effort, is essential. Indeed, it may well be that those whose work is their pleasure are those who most need the means of banishing it at intervals from their minds.

(By Winston Churchill)

对于那些呼风唤雨、随心所欲、无所不能的人而言，一个新的喜悦，一个新的兴奋只能是一个额外的烦恼，他们都是些不幸的人。他们徒劳无获地匆忙奔波于各地，就是想摆脱喧哗和忙碌带来的烦恼。对他们来说，各种有规律的生活方式才是改变生活最有希望的途径。

或许有人认为，理智、勤奋和有用的人也可分为两类：第一类是把工作与娱乐泾渭分明的人；第二类是把工作与娱乐合二为一的人。其中前者占绝大多数。他们有自己的弥补方式。在办公室或工厂长时间的辛劳，都会给他们带来报酬，不仅能得到维持生计的薪水，而且还能使他们有着追寻最简单最朴素的快乐的强烈欲望。但命运之神的宠幸之子④却是第二类人。他们的生活自然和谐，工作时间对他们来说永远都不够长。每天都是他们的假日，反而当法定假日来临时，他们还会抱怨不已，认为这是强行打断了他们专心致志的度假。然而，这两类人还是需要调剂一下未来生活；需要改变一下生活环境；需要尝试一下放松消遣，这些都是必要的。实际上，那些以工作为乐的人偶尔也需要考虑摒弃一些自己所谓的快乐，这样或许会好一些。

(何三宁　译)

**注释：**① 第1段的翻译需要注意相同指代的不同表达。Worry 在此段中的不同表达有 a spasm of the emotion, something, convulsive grasp, the old undue grip 等，请认真比较译文中的不同翻译。

② the cultivation 和 the growth：注意词性转换的翻译技巧。这两个词都是名词，在译文中转换成了动词。

③ those who 引导的3个从句都是被动形式，译文应为主动概念。英语多用被动，汉语少用被动，这是英汉语言结构的特点之一。

④ Fortune's favoured children：应注意常用词首字母大写时必有特定意义，这在英语中屡见不鲜。Fortune 意为"命运之神"。

## Passage 9

### Termites

When① buying a house, you must be sure to have it checked for termites. A termite is much like an ant in its communal habits, although physically the two insects are distinct.

Like those of ants, termite colonies consist of different classes, each with its own particular job. The most perfectly formed termites, both male and female, make up the reproductive class. They have eyes, hard body walls and fully developed wings②. A pair of reproductive termites found the colony③. When new reproductive termites develop, they leave to form another colony. They use their wings only this one time and then break them off.

The worker termites are small, blind, and wingless, with soft bodies. They make up the majority of the colony and do all the work. Soldiers are also wingless and blind but are larger than the workers and have hard heads and strong jaws and legs. They defend the colony and are cared for by the workers.

The male and female of the reproductive class remain inside a closed-in cell where the female lays thousands of eggs④. The workers place the eggs in cells and care for them.

### 白　蚁

①购买房子时,你务必要检查一下有无白蚁。白蚁与蚂蚁在形体上是两种不同的昆虫,但在群居的习性上与蚂蚁非常相似。

白蚁群和蚂蚁群一样也是由不同的阶层组成的,各阶层有其各自的特定工作。蚁后和雄蚁的体态发育最为成熟充分,构成了白蚁的繁殖阶层。它们有眼睛、坚硬的躯壳和发育完全的翅膀②。一对能繁殖的白蚁便可建立自己的白蚁群体③。在新的一对能繁殖的白蚁发育后,它们便离开家园去构建新的白蚁群。它们的翅膀只用这一次,然后便脱落了。

工蚁体小,没有视觉,没有翅膀,躯体柔软。它们占据了白蚁群体的绝大多数,担负着蚁群的全部工作。兵蚁同样没有翅膀,没有视觉,但身体比工蚁要大,头部坚硬,上下颚和腿结实。它们的职责是保卫蚁群,但由工蚁养活。

蚁后和雄蚁的职责就是繁殖,它们呆在封闭的巢穴里,蚁后在那里产下成千上万个卵④。工蚁把卵放在一个个蚁巢(室)里并加以照料。

(何三宁　译)

**注释:**① when:英语连词在翻译中不必刻意译出,避免"翻译腔"(translationese)。

② hard body walls and fully developed wings:wall 用于昆虫指"躯壳",developed 用于动物指"发育"。不同题材中的正确选词和词义衍变的能力是每个译者应具有的素质。

③ colony:用于蚂蚁或蜜蜂,意为"群体"。

④ eggs:用于昆虫,意为"卵",而不是"蛋"。

# Passage 10

## Tempest①

Today I have read *The Tempest*...Among the many reasons which make me glad to have been born in England, one of the first is that I read Shakespeare in my mother tongue. If I try to imagine myself as one who cannot know him face to face, who hears him only speaking from afar, and that in accents which only through the labouring intelligence can touch the living soul, there comes upon me a sense of chill discouragement, of dreary deprivation. I am wont to think that I can read Homer②, and, assuredly, if any man enjoys him, it is I; but can I for a moment dream that Homer yields me all his music, that his word is to me as to him who walked by the Hellenic shore when Hellas lived? I know that there reaches me across the vast of time no more than a faint and broken echo; I know that it would be fainter still, but for its blending with those memories of youth which are a glimmer of the world's primeval glory. Let every land have joy of its poet; for the poet is the land itself, all its greatness and its sweetness, all that incommunicable heritage for which men live and die. As I close the book, love and reverence possess me. Whether does my full heart turn to the great Enchanter, or to the Island upon which he has laid his spell? I know not. I cannot think of them apart. In the love and reverence awakened by that voice of voices, Shakespeare and England are but one. ③

(By George Gissing)

## 读《暴风雨》①

今天我拜读了《暴风雨》……庆幸我能降生在英国的众多原因中,首要的原因是我能够以母语阅读莎士比亚。假如设想自己既不能与他当面相识,又不能聆听其诗篇,并且所用的言语还需经过辛苦的思考才能触及心灵,那么,我会有心灰意冷,意气消沉之感觉。我一向自以为能读懂荷马②,且深信不疑,如果说谁能欣赏荷马,那就是我。然而我几曾梦想荷马使我拥有了他全部和谐悦耳的诗篇;几曾梦想他的言辞对我而言与曾在希腊时期漫步小海滨的他竟如此的一致? 我深知经过漫长岁月打动我的仅仅是那微弱破碎的回声;我也深知这个回声会变得更加微弱,倘若回声没有与世界昌盛之光的青春回忆融为一体的话。愿每个国家因拥有诗人而拥有喜悦,因为诗人意味着国家本身;意味着国家的伟大和芳馨;意味着人们与之共生死的无法言表的传统。在我合上此书的那一刻,爱慕与崇敬之情便油然而生。全身心地崇敬这位伟大的诗人,还是爱恋他赋予了魅力的大不列颠呢? 我不得而知。我无法把他们分开。在那绝伦无比的声音唤起的爱慕与崇敬之中,莎士比亚与大不列颠同在。③

(选自何三宁《天中学刊》,2000年第三期)

**注释**:① 该文属散文文体,具有描述细腻,句子结构复杂,长短句结合等特点,翻译时应充分给予考虑。

② I can read Homer:按常规 read 只能跟文字类的东西,但文学作品中也用它表述"读懂","理解"或"欣赏"等概念。汉语中也有"吃不透某人","理解某人","看透某人"等表达。

③ 文章的后半部分长短句的使用非常典型,是我们练习翻译英语句子结构特点的上佳范例。长短句的结合使用,使得语言铿锵有力,悦耳动听,节奏感强,产生了语言的节奏美。翻译此类文章应充分考虑这些。

# Appendix 2　Common Titles 常用头衔

## I. Titles in research 研究系列
1. Full/research professor — 研究员
2. Associate professor; associate professor of… — 副研究员
3. Research associate — 助理研究员
4. Research assistant — 研究实习员

## II. The titles in colleges or universities 大学系列
1. Professor; professor of… — 教授
2. Associate professor; associate professor of… — 副教授
3. Lecturer — 讲师
4. Assistant — 助教

## III. The titles in secondary and elementary schools 中小学系列
1. Senior teacher (secondary school) — 中学高级教师
2. First-grade teacher (secondary school) — 中学一级教师
3. Second-grade teacher (secondary school) — 中学二级教师
4. Third-grade teacher (secondary school) — 中学三级教师
5. Senior lecturer — 高级讲师
6. Lecturer — 讲师
7. Assistant lecturer — 助理讲师
8. Senior teacher (primary school) — 小学高级教师
9. First-grade teacher (primary school) — 小学一级教师
10. Second-grade teacher (primary school) — 小学二级教师
11. Third-grade teacher (primary school) — 小学三级教师

## IV. The titles in medicine 医疗卫生系列
1. Professor; professor of… — 主任医师
2. Associate professor; associate professor of… — 副主任医师
3. Doctor-in-charge; …-in-charge — 主治医师
   - e.g. oculist-in-charge — 眼科主治医师
   - pediatrician-in-charge — 儿科主治医师
4. Doctor; doctor + … — 医师
   - e.g. doctor gynecologist — 妇科医师
5. Assistant doctor — 医士
6. Professor of pharmacy — 主任药师
7. Associate professor of pharmacy — 副主任药师
8. Pharmacist-in-charge — 主管药师

Appendix 2  Common Titles

9. Pharmacist — 药师
10. Assistant pharmacist — 药士
11. Professor of nursing — 主任护师
12. Associate professor of nursing — 副主任护师
13. Nurse-in-charge — 主管护师
14. Nurse practitioner — 护师
15. Nurse; nurse's aide — 护士
16. Full senior technologist — 主任技师
17. Associate senior technologist — 副主任技师
18. Technologist-in-charge — 主管技师
19. Technologist — 技师
20. Technician — 技士

Ⅴ. **The titles in library and archives science** 图书档案系列

1. Professor of library science — 研究馆员
2. Associate professor of library science — 副研究馆员
3. Librarian — 馆员
4. Library assistant — 助理馆员
5. Clerk — 管理员
6. Professor of archives science — 研究馆员
7. Associate professor of archives science — 副研究馆员
8. Archivist — 馆员
9. Assistant archivist — 助理馆员
10. File clerk — 管理员

Ⅵ. **The titles in news** 新闻系列

1. Full senior editor — 高级编辑
2. Associate senior editor — 主任编辑
3. Editor — 编辑
4. Assistant editor — 助理编辑
5. Full senior reporter — 高级记者
6. Associate senior reporter — 主任记者
7. Reporter — 记者
8. Assistant reporter — 助理记者

Ⅶ. **The titles in publication** 出版系列

1. Professor of editorship — 编审
2. Associate professor of editorship — 副编审
3. Editor — 编辑
4. Assistant editor — 助理编辑
5. Assistant technical editor — 助理技术编辑
6. Technical designer — 技术设计员

    7. First-grade proofreader      一级校对

    8. Second-grade proofreader      二级校对

    9. Third-grade proofreader      三级校对

**Ⅷ. The titles in translation 翻译系列**

    1. Professor of translation      译审

    2. Associate professor of translation      副译审

    3. Translator      翻译

    4. Assistant translator      助理翻译

**Ⅸ. The titles in ships 船舶技术系列**

    1. Senior captain      高级船长

    2. Captain      船长

    3. First mate; mate      大副

    4. Second mate      二副

    5. Third mate      三副

    6. Senior engineer; senior chief engineer      高级轮机长

    7. Chief engineer      轮机长

    8. First engineman      大管轮

    9. Second engineman      二管轮

    10. Third engineman      三管轮

    11. Senior electrician      高级电机员

    12. General electrician      通用电机员

    13. First electrician      一等电机员

    14. Second electrician      二等电机员

    15. Senior radioman      高级报务员

    16. General radioman      通用报务员

    17. First radioman      一等报务员

    18. Second radioman      二等报务员

    19. Special radioman      限用报务员

**Ⅹ. The titles in economics 经济系列**

    1. Senior economist      高级经济师

    2. Economist      经济师

    3. Assistant economist      助理经济师

    4. Economic clerk      经济员

    5. Senior accountant      高级会计师

    6. Accountant      会计师

    7. Assistant accountant      助理会计师

    8. Treasurer      会计员

**Note**: You may translate other titles by referring to the above-mentioned.

## XI. The titles in academic degree 学术系列

1. B. A. /Bachelor of Arts          文学士
2. B. S. /Bachelor of Science       理学士
3. M. A. /Master of Arts            文学硕士
4. M. S. /Master of Science         理学硕士
5. Ph. D. /Doctor of Philosophy     哲学博士
6. Litt. D. /Doctor of Literature   文学博士
7. Post-doctor                      博士后
8. Scholar/visiting scholar         学者/访问学者
9. Guest/visiting professor         客座教授

# Appendix 3   Common Expressions for Signs
# 常用公示语

I . **Some practical modes of the English translation of signs**
常用公示语的翻译模式
1. **Noun phrases**
**A. Nouns**

| | |
|---|---|
| Inquiries / Information / Help Point ( Desk ) | 问询处 |
| Baggage Check-in | 行李托管处 |
| Left-luggage Office | 行李寄存处 |
| Baggage Claim | 行李提取处 |
| Departure Lounge | 候机室 |
| Night Bell | 夜间有事,请按此铃 |
| Service Station | 加油站 |
| VIP Car Park | 贵宾停车场 |
| Entrance | 入口 |
| Exit | 太平门/出口 |
| Ticket Office/Booking Office | 售票处 |
| Reception | 旅客登记处 |
| Complaint-box | 意见箱 |
| Explosives | 易爆物品 |
| Pigeonholes | 取信处 |
| Lost And Found | 失物招领处 |
| Office Hours | 办公时间 |

**B. Noun + modifiers ( adj. / adv. )**

| | |
|---|---|
| Way In/Out | 由此进入/外出 |
| Seat By Number | 对号入座 |
| Compensation For Damage | 损坏赔偿 |
| Dangerous Substance / Hazardous Goods | 危险品 |
| Prohibited Zone | 禁区 |
| Consecutive Curves | 连续转弯 |
| Admission Free | 免费入场 |
| Admission By Invitation Only | 非请莫入 |
| Admission By Ticket Only | 凭票入场 |
| Workmen Ahead | 前方施工,禁止通行 |

Wet Paint                                            油漆未干
**2. Phrases beginning with "No"**
**A. "No" + noun / prep. phrases**
No Thoroughfare                                      禁止通行
No U Turns                                           禁止掉头
No Access To Vehicles/No Entry For Vehicles          车辆禁止入内
No To Drugs Yes To Life                              珍爱生命,拒绝毒品
No Admittance Except On Business                     非公莫入
No Garbage Here                                      此处禁倒垃圾
No Photographs/Photos                                禁止拍照
**B. "No" + "-ing"**
No Plucking The Flowers                              不准攀折花木
No Parking Except For Loading                        除装货外,禁止停车
No Overtaking                                        不准超车
No Trespassing                                       私家区域,不准入内
No Spitting                                          不准随地吐痰
No Smoking                                           禁止吸烟
No Tooting                                           禁止鸣笛
No Fishing                                           禁止垂钓
No Parking Here                                      禁止停车
No Dumping                                           禁倒垃圾
No Swimming                                          禁止游泳
No Littering                                         勿扔果皮纸屑
**3. Passive sentences**
Bathing And Fishing Prohibited                       禁止游泳和钓鱼
Visitors Declined                                    谢绝参观
Passes Must Be Shown                                 请出示证件
Felling Trees Is Forbidden, Violation Liable To Heavy Fines   禁止伐木,违者重罚
No Persons Allowed Beyond This Point                 任何人不许越过此处
Not To Be Taken Away                                 不准带出室外
Visitors Not Admitted                                游客止步
Road Ahead Closed                                    前方施工,不准通行
Children Not Allowed                                 禁止儿童入内
Cameras Forbidden                                    禁止拍照
Shooting Prohibited                                  禁止打猎
All Reserved                                         包场
**4. Imperative**
**A. Affirmative imperative**
Keep Off The Grass/Lawn                              请勿践踏草地

| | |
|---|---|
| Keep To The Right | 靠右行驶 |
| Keep Cool/Dry/Flat/Upright/Clean | 冷藏/防潮/平放/切勿倒置/保持清洁 |
| Keep Your Belongings With You At All Times | 随时照看好您的物品 |
| Shut The Door After You | 随手关门 |
| Ring | 请按电铃 |
| Look Out | 小心 |
| Beware Sharks | 提防鲨鱼 |
| Mind Your Head | 当心碰头 |
| Mind Your Steps | 留心脚下 |
| Handle With Care | 小心轻放 |
| Queue Up For The Bus | 请排队上车 |
| Help Us To Keep The Tube Litter Free | 请协助我们,保持地铁清洁卫生 |
| Please Use Yours With Consideration For Others | 请在您使用时,也为他人着想 |
| Open This End | 此端开启 |
| Cash Please | 请付现金 |
| Lift Under Repairs, Please Take The Stairs | 电梯维修,请走楼梯 |

### B. Negative imperative

| | |
|---|---|
| Post No Bills | 禁止张贴 |
| Please Do Not Lean On These Barriers | 请不要靠防护栏 |
| We Do Not Buy At This Door | 谢绝推销 |
| Do Not Feed Or Frighten Animals | 禁止投喂恐吓动物 |
| Don't Touch The Exhibits/Objects | 请勿触摸展品/物品 |
| Do Not Disturb | 请勿打扰 |
| Don't Scribble | 请勿乱涂 |

### 5. Formal styles

| | |
|---|---|
| The Law Requires You Wear A Seatbelt | 法规要求系安全带 |
| We Can Supply All Your Foreign Currency | 我们提供各国货币 |
| This Coach Is For Holders Of Full Fare | 本长途汽车专为持全程票者乘坐 |
| This Lift Is Only For Construction Personal | 此电梯仅供施工人员使用 |
| This Offer Is Available For All Stays To 31 October 2003 | 对截至2003年10月31日的住宿实行优惠 |
| These Seats Are Meant For Elderly And Handicapped Persons & Women With Child | 老人,残疾人及抱小孩的妇女专座 |
| How Can We Disturb It When The Grass Is Sleeping | 小草在睡觉,怎能吵醒它 |
| Better Late Than The Late | 宁晚三分,不抢一秒 |

### 6. Others

| | |
|---|---|
| Full | 客满 |
| Now Speaking | 发言席 |

Appendix 3  Common Expressions for Signs

| | |
|---|---|
| To Let / For Rent | 招租 |
| Road Ends | 此路不通 |
| Slow, School | 前方学校请慢行 |
| Luggage Pick Up | 取行李 |
| Out of Bounds | 游客止步 |
| Admission Free | 免费入场 |

**Note**: The modes mentioned above are more popular and available in the public, but they are not all for us to be handy. Yet you may create others from them when you come across some signs you will be required to translate.

Ⅱ. **Some English signs for traveling** 交通旅行公示语的翻译

**1. Transportation**

A. Road and traffic

| | |
|---|---|
| Approaching End Of Motorway | 即将驶出高速 |
| Dangerous Bend | 弯道危险 |
| Diverted Traffic | 交叉路口 |
| Left Junction | 左交叉口 |
| Low Bridge Ahead | 前方桥低 |
| No Trade Or Business Vehicle Unless Authorized | 未经允许货车禁止通行 |
| Speed Limit Of 48km/h | 限速每小时 48 公里 |
| Maximum Speed: 48km/h | 最高时速:48 公里/小时 |

B. Car and parking

| | |
|---|---|
| Cars Parked Here Without Permission Will Be Clamped | 未经允许在此停车将被拖走 |
| Guest's Car Park | 来客停车场 |
| Limited Parking | 停车位有限 |
| No Parking Constantly In Use | 此处经常使用,禁止停车 |
| Parking Permitted | 允许停车 |
| This Is A Pay And Display Car Park | 此停车场自动缴费并张贴票据 |

C. Bus and coach

| | |
|---|---|
| Bus Information | 公共汽车问讯处 |
| Bus Lane | 公共汽车道 |
| Bus Stand | 公共汽车停车 |
| When The Bus Is Moving, Do Not Speak To The Driver | 汽车行使中,严禁与司机交谈 |
| With Permission, But At Owner's Risk | 允许存放,但后果自负 |

D. Tube and train

| | |
|---|---|
| Luggage Must Not Be Put In The Gateway | 行李不准放到过道上 |
| Mind The Gap | 小心台阶间跨度 |
| Not Valid On Certain Trains | 车票对某些列车无效 |
| Please Retain Your Ticket For Inspection | 请保留车票待检 |
| Single Or Return Tickets Only | 单程或往返程票 |

| | |
|---|---|
| Ticket Valid Until 30 June 2003 | 车票有效期到2003年6月30日 |
| Toilet Engaged | 厕所有人 |

**E. Airport**

| | |
|---|---|
| Customers Lounges | 旅客休息室 |
| Departure Time | 离港时间 |
| Departure Times On Reverse | 返航时间 |
| Missing People Help Line | 走失求救热线 |
| No Smoking Except In Designated Area | 除指定区域外,禁止吸烟 |
| Nothing (Something) To Declare | 无(有)报关 |
| Passport Control | 入境检验 |

**2. Purchases and sales**

| | |
|---|---|
| Accessories & Spares Delivered To Your Door | 配件送货上门 |
| As Many Repairs As You Need, Free Of Charge | 随时免费维修 |
| Ask At The Counter For Details | 详情请问柜台 |
| Buy One And Get Anyone Free | 买一赠一 |
| Closing Sale | 关门大甩卖 |
| On Sale | 待售 |
| For Sale | 廉价出售/上市 |
| Fill In Your Selection Here And Take To A Pay Point | 在此选购商品填单,然后到收款台付款 |
| Hours Of Opening/Opening Times (Hours) | 营业时间 |
| Open For Business/Services As Usual | 照常营业 |
| Opening Soon | 即将开业 |
| Price Crash | 削价 |
| Save Your Money | 贱卖 |
| Special Offer | 特价 |
| Thank You For Your Custom | 感谢光临 |

**3. Office**

| | |
|---|---|
| Air Quality Improvement Area | 空气质量净化区 |
| Demonstration Available | 可以进行演示 |
| Electrically Operated Gate | 电动门 |
| Lift Out Of Order | 电梯发生故障 |
| Meeting In Progress, Quiet Please | 正在开会,请保持安静 |
| Please Close The Door On Leaving | 离开时请关门 |
| Please Do Not Help Yourself To Books From This Shelf | 请不要随便从架子上取书 |
| Please Wait Here For Enquiries | 请在此等候咨询 |

**4. Restaurant and pub**

| | |
|---|---|
| Air Conditioned | 空调开放 |
| Daily Specials | 每日特色菜 |
| Drinks Purchased Are For Taken Away Only | 饮料仅供外卖 |

Appendix 3  Common Expressions for Signs

| | |
|---|---|
| Eat In Or Take Away | 堂食或外卖 |
| Please Ask To Taste | 欢迎品尝 |
| Take Away Service Available | 提供外卖 |
| Today's Special / Today's Specialties | 今日特色菜 |

### 5. Construction site

| | |
|---|---|
| Danger, Building Site, Keep Out | 工地危险,禁止入内 |
| Danger, Evacuation | 危险,请走开 |
| Safety Footwear | 穿安全靴 |
| Safety Helmets Must Be Worn On This Site | 此工地必须戴安全帽 |
| Slow, Site Entrance | 工地入口请慢行 |
| We Apologize For Any Inconvenience Caused | 对施工期间引起的不便表示歉意 |
| Working Over This Works | 上面在施工 |

### 6. Banks and insurance

| | |
|---|---|
| 24-Hour Credit Card Bookings | 24 小时信用卡预约 |
| Bring Proof Of Identity To Open Your Account | 开户需带证件 |
| Bureau Exchange/Currency Exchange | 兑换外汇 |
| Foreign Exchange (Services) | 外币兑换 |
| Look Out Our Lowest Rate Loans On Personal | 提供个人低息贷款 |
| This Till Position Is Closed | 此取款机停止使用 |
| Travelers Cheque Commission | 旅行支票收手续费 |
| You Open An Account With At Least £ 10 | 开户至少 10 镑 |

### 7. Post office and communications

| | |
|---|---|
| Abroad | 国外信件 |
| All Prices Include Postage And Packing | 全部价格包括邮资和包装 |
| Calls Charged At The National Rate | 电话按国内长途收费 |
| Counter Service | 服务柜台 |
| Country Letters | 国内信件 |
| Please Post All Your Mail Here, Thank You | 请在此邮寄,谢谢合作 |
| Post Your Comments Here | 请留下您的意见 |
| Price Paid Including Fees And Vat | 所付价格包括服务费和增值税 |
| Stamp Vending Machine | 邮票销售机 |

### 8. Theatre and cinema

| | |
|---|---|
| 24 Hour Ticket Line | 24 小时售票电话 |
| All Prices Quoted Include Any Service Charges Applicable | 票价包括一定的服务费 |
| Booking By Post, Phone, Fax Or E-Mail Or In Person | 可通过邮寄,打电话,发传真,发电子邮件或亲自定票 |
| No Booking Fee | 不收订票费 |
| Performance Times | 演出时间 |
| Previews | 预演 |

| | |
|---|---|
| Regular Price | 普通票价 |
| Special Reductions Are Available To Groups 12 + At All Performances | 所有演出对12人以上的团体给予特别优惠 |
| This Ticket Will Not Be Exchanged Nor The Purchase Price Refunded | 此票不可交换，也不能按购买价退票 |
| Tickets Are Subject To Availability | 票在销售，售完为止 |

### 9. Tour and sightseeing

| | |
|---|---|
| 15% Off With This Flyer | 持本广告85折优惠 |
| Access All Day | 全天开放 |
| Admission Is Free | 不收门票 |
| All Tours Require Advance Booking | 旅游需要提前订票 |
| All-Inclusive Ticket | 票价包括所有费用 |
| Cafeteria Available | 提供自助餐 |
| Child Reductions | 儿童优惠 |
| Children Under 12 Half Price Throughout Season | 全季12岁以下的儿童半价 |
| Concessions | （票价）优惠 |
| Day Trip To… | ……一日游 |
| Discounts Available For Pre-Booked Groups | 团体提前预订优惠 |
| For More Detailed Information Please Call | 欲知详情，请打电话 |
| Pick Up Points And Times | 接站地点和接站时间 |
| Reservations | 预订 |
| Reserved Seating | 预订座位 |
| Self-Catering | 可自己做饭 |
| Shopping Offers | 提供购物机会 |
| Tours Take Up To Two Hours | 游程两个小时 |

### 10. Exhibition and museum

| | |
|---|---|
| … Are Now Free To Everyone… | 现免费向公众开放 |
| … Will Again Be Open To The Public… | 再次向公众开放 |
| Exhibition Opening Times | 开馆时间 |
| Extended Opening Hours During August | 八月延长开放时间 |
| Flash Photograph Is Not Permitted | 不准用闪光灯拍照 |
| Forthcoming Exhibitions | 即将展出 |
| Open 10:30 a.m. – 6:00 p.m. Every Day Throughout The Year | 全年每天上午10:30至下午6:00开放 |
| Open 7 Days A Week | 每周7天开放 |
| Photography And Video Are Not Permitted Inside The Building | 楼内不许拍照录像 |
| Ticket Office | 售票处 |
| Unemployed, Disabled, Students And Children Free | 失业者，残疾人，学生和儿童免费 |

With Access All Day　　　　　　　　　全天开放
**11. Others**
Bicycle / Cycle Hire　　　　　　　　　出租自行车
Call... To Book　　　　　　　　　　　打电话预订
Contact Us At E-mail...　　　　　　　同我们联系请发电子邮件……
Details See Over　　　　　　　　　　详情见背页
Direct Dial Telephones　　　　　　　 直拨电话
For Free Information Contact:...　　　索取免费信息,请联系:……
For Full Details Of..., Please See The Web Site:...
了解……详情,请访问网站:……
For Further Details, Please Contact Us On...
详情请打电话……和我们联系
For Further Information On... Please Call...
了解……详情,请打电话……
For More Information On The Full Range Of Products, Call... Or Visit The Web:...
更多了解各种产品的情况,拨打电话…… 或访问网站……
For More Information, Call..., Our Staff Will Be Pleased To Answer Your Questions
了解详情请打电话…… 我们的职员会给你满意的回答
For The Latest Information On Availability, Check Out Our Website:...
获取最新信息,查询我们的网站:……
Please Ring Our 24-Hour Information Line
请拨打我们24 小时咨询服务热线
Please Write Clearly In Blue Or Black Ink
请用蓝黑墨水填写清楚

# Appendix 4　Topics for Consideration in Theses on Translation
# 论文参考题目

1. On Varieties Of Translation Criteria　翻译标准的多元化
2. Relationship Between Stylistic And Translation　文体与翻译的关系
3. A Survey Of Cultural Factors In Translation　翻译中的文化因素
4. A Survey Of Non-Cultural Factors In Translation　翻译中的非文化因素
5. Distinctions Between Chinese And English Structures　汉语与英文在结构上的区分
6. Features In The Translation Of English For Science And Technology　科技翻译有哪些特点
7. A Survey Of The Translation In Practical English　应用性文体的翻译注意的方面
8. On Functions Of Contexts In Translating　语境在翻译中的作用
9. How To Embody Re-Creativeness In Translation　翻译的再创造性如何体现
10. Advantages And Disadvantages Of Translationese　如何看待翻译症
11. Relationship Between The Author's Style And Translator's Style　原作者风格与译者风格的关系
12. Function And Effect On Criticism In Translation　翻译批评的功能及作用
13. Relationship Between Fuzziness And Accuracy　翻译中模糊与精确的关系
14. Translation And English Rhetoric　翻译与英语修辞
15. On The Makings Of A Good Translator　论优秀译者的素质
16. Translation And Reading　翻译与阅读的关系
17. A Comparative Study Of Principles Set By Nida And Yan Fu　奈达与严复翻译原则的对比研究
18. Aspects Of Translation As An Art　翻译艺术论种种
19. Creativity In The Translation Of English Advertisements　英语广告翻译中的创造性
20. Cultural Context And Literary Translation　文化语境与文学翻译
21. Cultural Differences And Their Impact Upon Translation　文化差异及其对翻译的影响
22. Culturally Loaded English Words And Their Translation　富含文化内涵的英语词汇及其翻译
23. English Idioms And Their Translation—With Special Reference To The Chinese　英语习语及其翻译——兼论汉语特点
24. Equivalence　论对等
25. Journalistic English And Journalistic Translation　新闻英语及新闻翻译
26. On Word Order And Translation　语序与翻译
27. Translative Rhetoric And Psychology　翻译修辞与心理
28. On Translation Criteria In The Light Of Transcultural Communication　从跨文化交际看翻译标准
29. Science Of Translation　翻译学

30. A Brief Remark On The Objectivity And Subjectivity In Translation  简论翻译的主体性与客体性
31. The Fuzziness Of Language And Translation  模糊语言与翻译
32. An Analysis Of Cognitive Errors In Textual Translation  篇章翻译中的认识错误分析
33. On The Significance Of Textual Translation  论语篇翻译的意义
34. Translator's Creativeness In Literary Translation  谈文学翻译的创造意识
35. On Transliteration  音译杂谈
36. How To Make Correct Choices Of Words In Translation  如何在翻译中准确选词
37. A Brief Survey Of Linguistic Rhythm And Flavor In Translation  试论语言的节奏与韵味
38. How To Reveal The Distinctions Between Hypotaxis And Parataxis In Translation  如何在翻译中体现英汉形合与意合的差异
39. Translation Is A Process Of Pursuing Aesthetic Values  翻译是一个追求审美价值的过程
40. Translation And Word Frequency  翻译与词语使用频率
41. Influence of Text Typology on Translation  文本类型学对翻译的影响
42. Text Types and Their Functions  文本类型及其功能
43. On Sign Translation  公示语的翻译
44. On Literary Translation  文学翻译
45. Attentions on Multimedia and Audio/Visual Translation  媒体翻译需注意的方面
46. How to Deal with the Cultural Elements in Tourist Texts  如何处理旅游文本中的文化因素
47. On the Features of Scientific Texts  科学文本的特点
48. Functional Approach in Translation  翻译中的功能途径研究
49. The Trends of Translation Criticism  翻译批评研究的趋势
50. The Position of TQA in Translation  翻译质量评估研究在译学中的定位

# Appendix 5　Recommended Reading List
# 阅读书目

1　Newmark, Peter. A Textbook of Translation. London: Prentice Hall, 1988
2　Nida, E. A. & Taber, C. R. The Theory and Practice of Translation. Leiden: E. J. Brill, 1969
3　Reyburn, William. Meaning across cultures. American Society of Missiology Series, 1981, (4)
4　Pinkham, Joan. Translator's Guide to Chinglish（中式英语之鉴）. 北京：外语教学与研究出版社，2000
5　Baker, Mona. In Other Words: A Coursebook on Translation. London & NY: Routledge, 1992
6　Gentzler, Edwin. Contemporary Translation Theories. London & NY: Routledge, 1993
7　Nida, E. A. Language, Culture, and Translating. 上海：上海外语教育出版社，1993
8　Shuttleworth, Mark & Cowie, Moira. Dictionary of Translation Studies. Manchester, UK: St. Jerome Publishing, 1997
9　Wilss, Wolfram. Knowledge and Skills in Translator Behavior. Amsterdam & Philadelphia: John Benjamins, 1996
10　Bell, Roger T. Translation and Translating: Theory and Practice. 北京：外语教学与研究出版社，2001
11　王佐良. A Sense of Beginning: Studies in Literature and Translation（论新开端）. 北京：外语教学与研究出版社，1991
12　谭载喜.新编奈达论翻译. 北京：中国对外翻译出版公司，1999
13　王佐良.翻译：思考与试笔. 北京：外语教学与研究出版社，1989
14　庄绎传.英汉翻译教程. 北京：外语教学与研究出版社，1999
15　周方珠.英汉翻译原理. 合肥:安徽大学出版社,2002
16　许建平.英汉互译实践与技巧. 北京:清华大学出版社,2000
17　何自然.语用学与英语学习. 上海:上海外语教育出版社,1997
18　李运兴.英汉语篇翻译. 北京:清华大学出版社,1998
19　叶子南.高级翻译理论与实践. 北京:清华大学出版社,2001
20　刘宓庆.翻译教学:务实与理论. 北京:中国对外翻译出版公司,2003
21　刘宓庆.当代翻译理论. 北京:中国对外翻译出版公司,1999
22　刘士聪.汉英英汉美文翻译与鉴赏. 南京:译林出版社,2002
23　包惠南.文化语境与语言翻译. 北京:中国对外翻译出版公司,2001
24　陈宏薇.汉英翻译基础. 上海:上海外语教育出版社, 1998
25　谭载喜.西方翻译简史. 北京：商务印书馆,1991
26　喻云根.英美名著翻译比较. 汉口:湖北教育出版社,1996
27　邹振环.影响中国近代社会的一百种译作. 北京：中国对外翻译出版公司,1996

28  许均.译事探索与译学思考.北京:外语教学与研究出版社,2002
29  冯庆华.实用翻译教程.上海:上海外语教育出版社,2002
30  孙迎春.汉英双向翻译学语林.济南:山东大学出版社,2001
31  申雨平.西方翻译理论精选.北京:外语教学与研究出版社,2002
32  孙致礼.新编英汉翻译教程.上海:上海外语教育出版社,2003
33  各期《中国翻译》及相关外语杂志

# Bibliography
# 参考文献

[1] Baker, M. Routledge Encyclopedia of Translation Studies. 上海：上海外语教育出版社，2004.

[2] Bell, Roger T. Translation and Translating: Theory and Practice. 北京：外语教学与研究出版社，2001.

[3] Chesterman, A. Readings in Translation Theory. Helsinki: Finn Lectura, 1989.

[4] Gove, P. Babcook et al, Webster's Third New International Dictionary of the English Language. Springfield: Merrian-Webster INC. Publishers, 2002.

[5] Hamit, B. Communication across Cultures: translation theory and contrastive text linguistics. Exeter: University of Exeter Press, 1997.

[6] Hanks, P. Collins Dictionary of the English Language. London & Glasgow: William Collins Sons & Co. Ltd, 1979.

[7] Jin Di, Nida. On Translation. 北京：中国对外翻译出版公司，1984.

[8] Lefevere, A. Translation, Rewriting and the Manipulation of Literary Fame. London & New York: Routledge, 1992.

[9] Munday, J. Introducing Translation Studies, Theories and Applications. London & New York: Routledge, 2001.

[10] Newmark, P. (1988). A Textbook of Translation. 上海：上海外语教育出版社，2001.

[11] Newmark, P. About Translation. Clevedon: Multilingual Matters Ltd. 1991.

[12] Newmark, P. Approaches to Translation. Oxford: Pergamon Press, 1981.

[13] Nida, E. A. & Taber, C. R. The Theory and Practice of Translation. Leiden: E. J. Brill, 1969.

[14] Nida, E. A. & Waard, J.. From One Language to Another: Functional Equivalence in Bible Translating. Nashville: Thomas Nelson Publishers, 1986.

[15] Nida, E. A. Language, Culture, and Translating. 上海：上海外语教育出版社，1993.

[16] Nida, E. A. Toward a Science of Translating. Leiden: E. J. Brill, 1964.

[17] Nord, C. (1997). Translating As a Purposeful Activity, Functionalist Approaches Explained. 上海：上海外语教育出版社，2001.

[18] Schleimacher, F. (1838/1963). On the Different Methods of Translating // Translating Literature: The German Tradition from Luther to Rosenzweig. Assen & Amsterdam: Van Gorcum, 1977.

[19] Shuttleworth, Mark & Cowie, Moira. Dictionary of Translation Studies. 上海：上海外语教育出版社，2004.

[20] Venuti, L. (1995). The Translator's Invisibility, A History of Translation. London & New York: Routledge.

[21] 包惠南. 文化语境与语言翻译. 北京:中国对外翻译出版公司,2001.
[22] 陈 新. 英汉文体翻译教程. 北京:北京大学出版社, 1999.
[23] 陈安定. 英汉比较与翻译. 香港：商务印书馆, 1985.
[24] 陈福康. 中国译学理论史稿. 上海:上海外语教育出版社,2000.
[25] 陈宏薇. 汉英翻译基础. 上海:上海外语教育出版社,1998.
[26] 冯庆华. 实用翻译教程. 上海：上海外语教育出版社, 2002.
[27] 郭建中. 关于路名标识的拼写问题. 中国翻译,2003(9).
[28] 韩其顺等. 英汉科技翻译教程. 上海:上海外语教育出版社, 1990.
[29] 何三宁,唐国跃. 模糊语言的客观性对翻译的影响. 广东教育学院学报,2004(4).
[30] 何三宁,张春梅. 英文散文的节奏与翻译. 天中学刊,2002(3).
[31] 何三宁. 浅谈"模糊"与"精确". 青海师专学报,2002(4).
[32] 何三宁. 试论英语中的节奏及其对应翻译. 西北师大学报(社会科学版),2002.
[33] 何自然. 浅论语用含糊. 外语界,1990(3).
[34] 何自然. 语用学与英语学习. 上海:上海外语教育出版社,1997.
[35] 黄 湘. 科技英语汉译的词义引申. 中国科技翻译, 2001 (2).
[36] 贾文波. 应用翻译功能论.北京:中国对外翻译出版公司,2005.
[37] 金惠康. 广东旅游翻译探讨. 上海科技翻译,2003(2).
[38] 柯 平. 英汉与汉英翻译教程. 北京：北京大学出版社, 1993.
[39] 李贵升. 论商标的翻译. 中国科技翻译, 1996(2).
[40] 李剑波. 论法律英语的词汇特征. 中国科技翻译, 2003 (2).
[41] 李文阳. 浅论法律英语的语言特点及翻译. 中国翻译, 1994(6).
[42] 李学金. 高级技术职务名称英译初谈. 中国翻译,1991(4).
[43] 李运兴. 英汉语篇翻译. 北京:清华大学出版社,1998.
[44] 栗长江. 公安标示语和警示语的英译. 中国翻译,2003(5).
[45] 刘季春. 实用翻译教程.广东:中山大学出版社,1996.
[46] 刘宓庆. 当代翻译理论. 北京:中国对外翻译出版公司,1999.
[47] 刘宓庆. 翻译教学：务实与理论. 北京:中国对外翻译出版公司,2003.
[48] 刘士聪. 汉英英汉美文翻译与鉴赏. 南京:译林出版社,2002.
[49] 刘增羽,张晓莉. 试论中国专业技术职称的英译. 中国翻译,1993(4).
[50] 马 光. 英语翻译技巧百问百练. 北京：中国书籍出版社, 2000.
[51] 毛荣贵, 范武邱. 英汉翻译技巧示例. 上海:上海交通大学出版社,2002.
[52] 三 友. 广告翻译中的文化形象转换. 中国科技翻译, 2003(3).
[53] 邵启祥. 科技英语翻译中的陷阱、误区及其他. 北京：国防工业出版社, 1991.
[54] 申雨平. 西方翻译理论精选. 北京:外语教学与研究出版社,2002.
[55] 孙迎春,张谷若. 翻译艺术研究.北京:中国对外翻译出版公司,2004.
[56] 孙迎春. 汉英双向翻译学语林. 济南:山东大学出版社,2001.
[57] 孙致礼. 新编英汉翻译教程. 上海:上海外语教育出版社,2003.
[58] 王逢鑫. 英语模糊语法. 北京:外语出版社,2001.
[59] 王宏印. 文学翻译批评论稿. 上海:上海外语教育出版社, 2006

[60] 王秋生. 旅游景点翻译亟待规范. 中国翻译,2004(3).
[61] 王泉水. 科技英语翻译技巧. 天津:天津科学技术出版社,1991.
[62] 王振玉. 语言与文化. 北京:高等教育出版社,1999.
[63] 王治奎等. 大学英汉翻译教程. 济南:山东大学出版社,1999.
[64] 修月祯. 旅游英语选读. 北京:高等教育出版社,1999.
[65] 许建平. 英汉互译实践与技巧. 北京:清华大学出版社,2000.
[66] 叶 苗. 旅游资料的语用翻译. 上海翻译,2005(2).
[67] 叶子南. 高级翻译理论与实践. 北京:清华大学出版社,2001.
[68] 张培基. 英汉翻译教程. 上海:上海外语教育出版社,1980.
[69] 周方珠. 科技翻译的词义选择. 中国科技翻译,1996(1).
[70] 周方珠. 英汉翻译原理. 合肥:安徽大学出版社,2002.